CALVIN
and the
REFORMED
TRADITION

On the Work of Christ
and the Order of Salvation

Richard A. Muller

Baker Academic

a division of Baker Publishing Group
Grand Rapids, Michigan

© 2012 by Richard A. Muller

Published by Baker Academic
a division of Baker Publishing Group
P.O. Box 6287, Grand Rapids, MI 49516–6287
www.bakeracademic.com

Printed in the United States of America

Library of Congress Cataloging-in-Publication Data
Muller, Richard A. (Richard Alfred), 1948–
    Calvin and the Reformed Tradition : on the work of Christ and the order of salvation / Richard A. Muller
        p.   cm.
    Includes bibliographical references and index.
    ISBN 978-0-8010-4870-8 (pbk.)
    1. Reformed Church—Doctrines—History. 2. Jesus Christ—History of doctrines. 3. Jesus Christ—Person and offices. 4. Salvation—Christianity—History of doctrines. 5. Calvin, Jean, 1509–1564. 6. Calvinism. 7. Protestant Scholasticism. I. Title.
BX9422.3.M845 2012
232—dc23   2012028060

To
David C. Steinmetz
Teacher, Mentor, Colleague, Friend
with Gratitude

Contents

Preface

The essays in the present volume belong to the work of several decades and represent a series of related studies in the development of the Reformed tradition from the time of Calvin into the era of orthodoxy. At its most general level and approach, the book continues the basic argument posed in my other studies of the era, albeit in relation to different topics—namely, that the Reformed tradition is a diverse and variegated movement not suitably described as founded solely on the thought of John Calvin or as either a derivation or a deviation from Calvin (as if his theology were the norm for the whole tradition). The present essays press the methodological point further by raising foundational issues concerning the nature of a tradition and the problems inherent in the nineteenth- and twentieth-century master-narratives concerning the changes that took place in the early modern era.

As is also the case with my previous studies of Reformation and orthodox-era Reformed thought, this work is an exercise in intellectual history that engages in an examination of trajectories of Reformed thought, not a work of dogmatics engaged in the formulation of Reformed doctrines for the present day. Its method assumes that a writer cannot simultaneously wear two hats or serve two masters and that engagement in contemporary dogmatizing in the midst of the analysis of a historical document only results in the muddying of historical waters and the loss of genuine engagement with the thought of past centuries, a problem unfortunately characteristic of much of what still passes for studies of Calvin and Calvinism. Not that theologians should avoid reading and meditating on historical sources! Rather, there is a need for historians and theologians to exercise methodological care—so that the historian does not import foreign and anachronistic notions to the task of presenting an older theology to a modern readership and that the theologian does not distort the meaning of a document for the sake of contemporary re-presentation or retrieval.[1]

On a more specific level, the essays in the book pose the argument that developing Reformed approaches to the work of Christ and the order of salvation do

---

1. Superb examples of address to contemporary issues in and through the examination of the past can be found in John L. Thompson, *Reading the Bible with the Dead: What You Can Learn from the History of Exegesis That You Can't Learn from Exegesis Alone* (Grand Rapids: Eerdmans, 2007); Robert Kolb and Charles P. Arand, *The Genius of Luther's Theology: A Wittenberg Way of Thinking for the Contemporary Church* (Grand Rapids: Baker, 2008); and Robert Kolb, *Luther and the Stories of God: Biblical Narratives as a Foundation for Christian Living* (Grand Rapids: Baker, 2012).

not fit easily into a set of standard and sadly current caricatures and misrepresentations both of Calvin and of later Reformed thought on such issues as limited atonement, hypothetical universalism, union with Christ, and the order of salvation. The more closely one examines the documents, the older largely dogmatic narratives found in twentieth-century discussion of the era are revealed as fundamentally mistaken and tendentious. Thus, the narrative of Calvin as the founder of a uniformly Calvinistic Reformed tradition, the alternative narrative of "Calvin against the Calvinists," the notions of central dogmas or of predestinarian versus christocentric or covenantal systems of theology, the more recent claim of Calvin as the lonely representative of a theology of union with Christ, and the purported connections between humanistic or scholastic methods and particular dogmatic results need to be discarded. What appears when the dogmatic dross is set aside is a variegated Reformed tradition that drew variously and eclectically on the patristic and medieval backgrounds, that does not rest on the theology of any single founder but was diverse from its beginnings, and that developed in dialogue and debate during the early modern era. When, moreover, Calvin's thought is placed into the context of this developing tradition, he appears as one of several major codifiers or systematizers of the second generation of the Reformation, whose thought was not always appropriated directly into the theologies of later generations of Reformed exegetes, theologians, and pastors.

There are also several places in the present volume where the differences between my early work in *Christ and the Decree* and my present understanding of the place of Calvin in the development of Reformed thought and in relation to later orthodoxy are evident—notably in the discussion of Christ's work and its limitation and the discussion of the practical syllogism. In both instances, I recognize that my earlier analysis allowed more cogency to the neo-orthodox line of argumentation about sixteenth- and seventeenth-century sources than was warranted. Specifically, I allowed aspects of the faulty nineteenth- and twentieth-century master narratives of early modernity and elements of the neo-orthodox macro-theological generalizations about the thought of the Reformers and their successors to deflect my attention from the original contexts and implications of Calvin's thought and of the thought of various later Reformed writers.

The chapters provide a fairly cohesive line of argument resting on two basic issues, one methodological, the other topical. On the methodological side, chapter 1 engages the issues of problematic master narratives of the theology of the Reformation and the early modern era, of the nature of a theological tradition, specifically the Reformed tradition, and of how developments in doctrine, the reception of earlier argumentation by later thinkers (e.g., Calvin by later "Calvinists"), and transmission of confessional models into later contexts ought to be understood. On the topical side, all of the essays relate to the work of Christ and its application to believers. I make no attempt, however, to offer a complete survey of the issues or thinkers involved in the Reformed development, but have sought only to present some of the diverse strands of the development of Reformed thought. Thus, on the issue of the extent of Christ's work, I have noted issues in the interpretation of Calvin in the context of his contemporaries and some of his antecedents, and I have offered some evidences not only of the relationship of Calvin's approach to later versions of hypothetical universalism but also of the significant varieties of hypothetical universalism itself—but I have not traced out the more particularistic lines of Reformed development apart from various comparative remarks and a brief comment on my sense of the wide variety of formulations. That development, at the hands of thinkers like William Perkins, John Owen, and Francis Turretin, is left for the time being for further study.

The gathering of essays found in this volume owes its origin to the efforts of Pastor Nam Joon Kim of Yullin Church in Anyang-City, Korea, and of several other of my Korean colleagues, Professors Won Taek Lim of Baekseok Seminary and University, Byunghoon Kim and Sang Hyuck Ahn of Hapdong Theological Seminary, Sungho Lee of Kosin Theological Seminary, and Byung Ho Moon of Chongshin Theological Seminary, to organize and host a series of lectures in the autumn of 2011, to the hospitality of the four seminaries and of the Korea Evangelical Theological Society and the Society for Reformed Life Theology for giving me the opportunity to deliver a plenary address at their annual meeting. These lectures form the core of the book. An earlier form of the second chapter, "Was Calvin a Calvinist?," was originally delivered as a lecture sponsored by the H. Henry Meeter Center. A shorter version of chapter 4, "A Tale of Two Wills?," was previously published as an article in *Calvin Theological Journal*. The other essays in the volume appear in print for the first time here. I am most grateful for the careful reading of my text by Raymond A. Blacketer, Todd Billings, and John V. Fesko, each of whom made helpful suggestions both in content and composition. A word of profound thanks is also due to the translator of my lectures in Korea, Byung Soo Han, whose linguistic skills and theological expertise not only made the lectures possible but also served to clarify passages in the English text of the essays.

Richard A. Muller
Lowell, Michigan

1

From Reformation to Orthodoxy:
The Reformed Tradition in the Early Modern Era

Approaching Reformation and Orthodoxy

Between the beginnings of the Reformation in the first three decades of the sixteenth century and the deconfessionalization that took place between the late seventeenth and early eighteenth centuries, there was a significant development of Protestant religion and theology, ecclesial and intellectual culture. From the perspective of confessionality and theological formulation, that development can be described as the rise of an institutional form of Protestantism, founded on the historical datum of the Reformation-era break with Rome and framed in its approach to religious and doctrinal identity by the confessional documents written largely by the first and second generations of Reformers: in short, the development of confessionally orthodox Protestantism or as it is typically called, Protestant Orthodoxy. From a methodological perspective, the description and analysis of that development is far more complex than the simple account of the theologies of various individuals and major confessional controversies, as is typically found in the older literature.[1]

The teachings of no single theologian, not even one as important as Calvin, can account for the development of the Reformed tradition, not even in his own time, much less over the course of nearly two centuries. Nor does analysis of such debates as those with Rome, or with the Lutherans, or over the teachings of Arminius give an adequate picture of the development, given the large number of debates that did not rise to the confessional level and the even larger number of doctrinal points that were developed with some diversity of formulation but did not become the subjects

---

1. As, e.g., in Otto Ritschl, *Dogmengeschichte des Protestantismus: Grundlagen und Grundzüge der theologischen Gedanken- und Lehrbildung in den protestantischen Kirchen*, 4 vols. (Leipzig: J. C. Hinrichs, 1908-1912; Göttingen: Vandenhoeck & Ruprecht, 1926-1927); Arthur Cushman McGiffert, *Protestant Thought before Kant* (London, 1911; repr. New York: Harper & Row, 1961); Hans Emil Weber, *Reformation, Orthodoxie und Rationalismus*, 2 vols. in 3 parts (Gütersloh, 1937-1951; repr., Darmstadt: Wissenschaftliche Buchgesellschaft, 1966).

of significant debate.[2] And, of course, neither the Reformation in general nor the Reformed tradition in particular arose *ex nihilo*: there was not only a broad late medieval background of the Reformation; within that broad religious and theological culture of the later Middle Ages, there were also diverse currents that carried over into the Reformation and into post-Reformation Protestantism, the reception of which varied from theologian to theologian.

Recent studies of this development have begun to emphasize its complexity and variety, setting aside the over-simplified narratives of much of the earlier scholarship. The Reformation itself, once described as an almost hermetically sealed theological box, is now understood in the context of broader cultural patterns extending back into the Middle Ages and forward into the early modern era. Individual Protestant theologians are now understood not as creators of an entirely new and radically biblical theology but as fairly conservative Reformers whose immediate theological roots are to be found in the theological milieu of the later Middle Ages and whose positive sources included the greater part of the older tradition of the church. Beyond this, a larger portion of the scholarly community has recognized that individual Reformers like Luther, Melanchthon, Zwingli, Bullinger, and Calvin cannot rightly be understood as creators of unique theologies abstracted from the thought of their teachers and immediate predecessors or from the theological formulations of their contemporaries.

The importance of this approach to the complexity and variety of Protestant theological development is particularly evident in the specific case of the Reformed tradition, often identified as "Calvinism." Given that a significant number of Reformers contributed to the development of this tradition in the generation prior to Calvin, including several who either individually or in accord with others produced the first layer of Reformed confessional documents, and given that Calvin's own theology developed both out of this prior context and in dialogue with other Reformers of his own generation, the rise of Reformed theology, indeed, the formation of a specifically Reformed tradition cannot be adequately analyzed or properly understood if individual thinkers are abstracted from this broader religious and theological context. The theological formulations of the individual writers, in other words, cannot be rightly understood either in isolation or in one-to-one comparisons. The problem was recognized by John T. McNeill, who commented at the beginning of his *History and Character of Calvinism* that there were already, at the beginnings of the development of the Reformed tradition, "not inconsiderable" differences between the theologies of Calvin and Zwingli, but that these differences were not ultimately "divisive" of the confessional tradition. McNeill concluded, "There is therefore no incongruity involved in making Zwinglianism a part of the

---

2. See the discussion in Richard A. Muller, "Diversity in the Reformed Tradition: A Historiographical Introduction," in *Drawn into Controversie: Reformed Theological Diversity and Debates within Seventeenth-Century British Puritanism*, ed. Michael G. A. Haykin and Mark Jones (Göttingen: Vandenhoeck & Ruprecht, 2011), pp. 17-30.

wider movement that, in the unavoidable shorthand of language, is here called Calvinism."[3] Of course, the shorthand is avoidable and one might use the more accurate term "Reformed" in place of "Calvinist."

Accordingly, attempts to drive intellectual wedges between, for example, Calvin and Bullinger, by way of claiming two Reformed traditions—or between Calvin and Beza, by way of claiming differences in nuance between Calvin's theology and Beza's as "deviations" from Calvin—operate on a fallacious ground.[4] Such attempts fail to allow for individual diversity within a theological tradition. They fail to allow for differing antecedents, sources, and contexts for the formulations of individual theologians. They also fail to observe the rise and development of a confessional tradition at the hands of a rather diverse group of formulators, they fail to consider the tradition as itself represented by a series of documents arising from different contexts, and they fail to identify the patterns of relationship and difference belonging to the tradition itself. And from a methodological perspective, they also fail to observe how the more specific characteristics of one major theologian's formulations are rather differently received by other thinkers within the confessional tradition.

The issue addressed, therefore, in reassessing and reconstructing the historical development of Reformed orthodoxy as an exercise not in modern dogmatics but in intellectual history, is the tracing of patterns and trajectories of argumentation within the early modern Reformed confessional tradition, with a view to the historical context of the debates and developments productive of the rather diverse movement toward confessionalization and institutionalization in the Reformed churches. It is important to recognize, moreover, that the periodization of Reformation, early, high, and late orthodoxy, extending from circa 1517 to circa 1780, provides an imprecise framework: specifically, identifying the Reformation as an era from 1517 to 1565 and early orthodoxy as an era from 1565 to 1640 or thereabouts does not propose either a completed Reformation as of 1565, a fully developed early confessional orthodoxy as of 1565, or a uniformly identifiable high orthodoxy in 1640, any more than it claims a defined Reformation-era Protestantism in 1517. The rise of early orthodoxy in particular was a gradual development that had its beginnings in the confessional writings of the mid-sixteenth century and its

---

3. John T. McNeill, *The History and Character of Calvinism* (New York: Oxford University Press, 1954), p. viii.

4. Thus, J. Wayne Baker, *Heinrich Bullinger and the Covenant: The Other Reformed Tradition* (Athens, Ohio: Ohio University Press, 1980); idem, "Heinrich Bullinger, the Covenant, and the Reformed Tradition in Retrospect," *Sixteenth Century Journal*, 29/2 (1998), pp. 359-376; Basil Hall, "Calvin against the Calvinists," in *John Calvin: A Collection of Distinguished Essays*, ed. Gervase Duffield (Grand Rapids: Eerdmans, 1966), pp. 19-37; Brian G. Armstrong, *Calvinism and the Amyraut Heresy: Protestant Scholasticism and Humanism in Seventeenth-Century France* (Madison: University of Wisconsin Press, 1969); Alan C. Clifford, *Atonement and Justification: English Evangelical Theology, 1640-1790* (Oxford: Oxford University Press, 1990); and idem, *Calvinus: Authentic Calvinism, a Clarification* (Norwich: Charenton Reformed Publishing, 1996).

major systematic expression only in a series of rather different, albeit confessionally circumscribed, theologies written between 1590 and the decades after the Synod of Dort. Similar comments can be made concerning the high orthodox development and the waning of orthodoxy or late orthodoxy in the eighteenth century.

Deconstructing the Master Narratives

Reappraisal of the nature and character of the Reformation and of the developments that followed in the Protestant churches of the later sixteenth and seventeenth centuries has been a central concern of the theological historiography of the early modern era during the last fifty years and has resulted in a massive recasting of our understanding of early modern Protestantism. From the perspective of intellectual history, part of the reappraisal was grounded in the reception by historians of the Reformation of a significant body of scholarship on the scholasticism and humanism of the centuries preceding the Reformation that, when drawn into an analysis of the confessional, ecclesial, academic, and dogmatically formulative development of Protestantism, altered considerably our understandings both of the Reformation and of the orthodoxy that followed it.[5] This scholarship on scholasticism and humanism has never been fully assimilated by proponents of the older interpretations of the development from Reformation to orthodoxy. With these altered understandings of scholasticism and humanism in view, the new scholarship has also engaged in reading a rather vast array of documents that had been largely ignored by the previous scholarship—and, indeed, that continue to be ignored by proponents of the several older interpretations of the development of Protestant thought.

The work of reassessing and reappraising the early modern development of Reformed thought has typically framed its analysis in terms of continuities, discontinuities, and diversity in the Reformed tradition. These approaches to reassessment and reappraisal have also included discussion of the nature and character of the Reformed tradition itself and examination of the Reformed reception and use of older theological materials, whether patristic or medieval, both in the earlier strata of the Reformed tradition itself and in the subsequent generational layers of Reformed thought in what can be identified as the early and high orthodox eras. Given, moreover, the enormous broadening of the early modern bibliography of Reformed Protestantism, these various elements of the reassessment

---

5. Note the literature referenced in Richard A. Muller, *After Calvin: Studies in the Development of a Theological Tradition* (New York: Oxford University Press, 2003), pp. 27-33, 74-80, 199-200, 212-215; and idem, *Post-Reformation Reformed Dogmatics: The Rise and Development of Reformed Orthodoxy, ca. 1520 to ca. 1725*, 4 vols. (Grand Rapids: Baker, 2003), I, pp. 34-37.

ought to be understood as the proposal of a complete alternative to the defective master narrative of the older scholarship.[6]

That older narrative has been characterized by broad theological generalizations resting largely on nineteenth- and twentieth-century dogmatic concerns and by a series of philosophical assumptions grounded on post-Kantian understandings of early modern intellectual history. Both the theological and the philosophical versions of the narrative are characterized by assumptions of a fairly radical discontinuity between the Middle Ages and the Reformation, often defined in terms of the conflict between scholasticism and humanism defined largely as opposing philosophies. Scholasticism, moreover, understood as a medieval philosophical system, is viewed by this narrative as being antithetical to the theology of the Reformation and as functionally terminated with the end of the Middle Ages, at least from the perspective of Protestant thought properly understood. What is more, the narrative has been developed in terms of a "great thinker" approach to history that has tended to elevate individuals and certain documents to the exclusion of interest in contemporary thinkers or historical contexts.

In brief, most versions of the theological narrative have elevated Calvin out of his context and identified him as the founder either of the Reformed tradition or of "Calvinism" or have identified his *Institutes of the Christian Religion* not only as the fundamental source of his own thought but as the norm for understanding all subsequent developments in the Reformed tradition, breeding debates over the relationship, whether positive or negative, of Calvin to the Calvinists and mistaking the nature of a tradition. There are three variations on this basic approach—two from the nineteenth century relating to the doctrinal issues of predestination and covenant, and one from the twentieth century based on the notion of christocentricity associated with neo-orthodoxy. In the first of these approaches, associated primarily with the work of Alexander Schweizer but also drawing on the studies of Heinrich Heppe, predestination is understood to be the dogmatic center of Calvinism, with Calvin himself as the foremost early formulator of the position and as standing in continuity with the later development of Calvinism as a predestinarian system.[7] The second of these approaches, based on Heppe's distinction between a

---

6. The following essay uses the term "master narrative" rather than its near-synonyms, "grand narrative" and "metanarrative," given the association particularly of the latter term with an unspoken or untold narrative that unifies an entire cultural perspective or world-view—while master narrative can be identified somewhat less philosophically as an actual narrative designed to give sequence and cohesion to a series of lesser narratives concerned with more particularized contexts. The foundation of such master narratives will, typically, be an anachronistic assumption drawn from the philosophical and/or theological views of the writer rather than from the materials used to construct the historical narrative.

7. Alexander Schweizer, *Die Glaubenslehre der evangelisch-reformirten Kirche dargestellt und aus den Quellen belegt*, 2 vols. (Zürich, 1844-1847); idem, *Die protestantischen Centraldogmen in ihrer Entwicklung innerhalb der reformirten Kirche*, 2 vols. (Zürich, 1854-1856); Heinrich Heppe, "Der Charakter der deutsch-reformirten Kirche und das Verhältniss derselben zum Luthertum und zum

Calvinistic predestinarian trajectory and a Melanchthonian German Reformed theology, understood covenant as an alternative focus to the predestinarian approach of Calvin and the Calvinists.[8] The third approach, associated with various neo-orthodox writers, represents a reassessment of Calvin to conform his theology to the standards of neo-orthodoxy, specifically assimilating his thought to a christocentric model and creating a narrative that poses Calvin against the predestinarian Calvinists,[9] and more recently a Calvin focused on union with Christ against Calvinists intent on constructing a rigid *ordo salutis*.[10] All three of these approaches are highly reductionistic in that they superimpose large-scale dogmatic generalizations on a highly variegated historical development.

The problematic master narrative concerning the history of early modern philosophy, often read in tandem with these theological narratives, assumes the demise of scholasticism and of the Western Aristotelian or Peripatetic tradition with the dawn of the Reformation, regards its continuation into the seventeenth century as vestigial, and assumes that the rise of rationalism, whether of the deductive Cartesian or of the inductive Baconian variety, utterly replaced the older Aristotelianism with little competition from other variant philosophies—rendering incomprehensible either the lively continuation of the Peripatetic tradition or the ongoing use of scholastic method among seventeenth-century Protestants and yielding a detachment of Protestant orthodoxy from the thought of the Reformers.[11]

Calvinismus," *Theologische Studien und Kritiken*, Heft 3 (1850), pp. 669-706; idem, *Die Dogmatik der evangelisch-reformirten Kirche* (Elberfeld: R. L. Friedrichs, 1861).

8. George Park Fisher, *History of Christian Doctrine* (New York: Scribner's, 1901), pp. 347-348; more recently, Leonard Trinterud, "The Origins of Puritanism," *Church History*, 20 (1951), pp. 37-57; Jürgen Moltmann, *Gnadenbund und Gnadenwahl: Die Prädestinationslehre des Moyses Amyraut, dargestellt im Zusammenhang der heilsgeschichtlich-foederaltheologie Tradition der Akademie von Saumur* (Göttingen, 1951); Richard Greaves, "The Origins and Early Development of English Covenant Thought," *The Historian*, 31/1 (1968), pp. 21-35; and J. Wayne Baker, *Heinrich Bullinger and the Covenant: The Other Reformed Tradition* (Athens: Ohio University Press, 1980).

9. E.g., Hall, "Calvin Against the Calvinists"; Wilhelm Niesel, *The Theology of Calvin*, trans. Harold Knight (London: Lutterworth, 1956); Armstrong, *Calvinism and the Amyraut Heresy*; Alister McGrath, *A Life of Calvin* (Oxford: Blackwell, 1990).

10. Julie Canlis, "Calvin, Osiander, and Participation in God," *International Journal of Systematic Theology*, 6/2 (2004), pp. 169-184; William B. Evans, *Imputation and Impartation: Union with Christ in American Reformed Theology* (Carlisle: Paternoster, 2008); Charles Partee, "Calvin's Central Dogma Again," *Sixteenth Century Journal*, 18/2 (1987), pp. 191-200; idem, *The Theology of John Calvin* (Louisville: Westminster/John Knox, 2008).

11. As found in standard manuals that were highly influential in the late nineteenth and early twentieth centuries, highly influential in framing the understanding of Protestant scholasticism in nineteenth- and twentieth-century theological discussion: e.g., Friedrich Ueberweg, *Grundriss der Geschichte der Philosophie von Thales bis auf die Gegenwart*, 2nd ed., 3 vols. (Berlin: E. S. Mittler & Sohn, 1865-1866); in translation, *A History of Philosophy, from Thales to the Present Time*, trans. from the 4th German ed. by George S. Morris, with additions, by Noah Porter, 2 vols. (New York: Scribner, 1872-1874); and Johann Eduard Erdmann, *Grundriss der Geschichte der Philosophie*, 2 vols. (Berlin:

Indeed, in many histories of early modern philosophy, the only thinkers mentioned are Descartes, Spinoza, Malebranche, Leibniz, Locke, sometimes with the addition of Bacon and, more rarely, of Gassendi—and all treated as part of a massive break with the past and as founders of modernity. Associated with this broader philosophical narrative, there are two primary alternative approaches to Protestant thought. One of these approaches, perhaps by way of an older view of the Renaissance as beginning to strip away the superstitions of the Middle Ages and replacing them with a focus on humanity, identifies the Reformation as the wellspring of theological and philosophical freethought and the ancestor of rationalism, whether for good or for ill.[12] When this understanding is followed, the master narrative interprets Protestant Orthodoxy and its scholastic tendencies as a form of dogmatism contrary to the Reformation and so obscurantistic in its views that rationalism, the true heir of the Renaissance and Reformation, ultimately triumphed.[13] The alternative approach interprets the Reformation's emphasis on Scripture as a form of fideism, and reads the era of orthodoxy and Protestant scholasticism as a turn toward rationalism that opened the doorway to the Enlightenment.[14] In either case, the traditional Aristotelianism and scholasticism of seventeenth-century Reformed thought are understood as preliminary to the rise of rationalism, with the dominant line of argument identifying Protestant orthodoxy as a form of rationalism or proto-rationalism.[15] And, of course, when medieval scholasticism is improperly identified as a form of rationalism and the phenomenon of scholastic method not understood as itself developing and changing over the course of centuries, the purported rationalism of the Protestant scholastics becomes not only the predecessor of later but also a recrudescence of earlier rationalisms.

Nearly all of these theological and philosophical master narratives are indebted to the grand modern master narrative of the end of the Middle Ages in the Renaissance and Reformation as signaled by the rise of humanism and the downfall of scholasticism, the most famous version of which appeared in Jacob Burckhardt's *Civilization of the Renaissance in Italy*:

W. Hertz, 1869); in translation, *A History of Philosophy*, ed. Williston S. Hough, 2nd ed., 3 vols. (London: S. Sonnenschein; New York: Macmillan, 1890-1892).

12. Thus, Amand Saintes, *Histoire critique du rationalisme en Allemagne depuis son origine jusqu'à nos jours* (Paris: Jules Renouard, 1844); John M. Robertson, *A History of Freethought, Ancient and Modern*, 2nd ed., 2 vols. (London: Watts, 1906).

13. Cf. Friedrich August Tholuck, *Vorgeschichte des Rationalismus*, 4 vols. (Halle: E. Anton, 1853-1862); also note John Dillenberger, *Protestant Thought and Natural Science: A Historical Interpretation* (Nashville: Abingdon, 1960).

14. Evident in Armstrong, *Calvinism and the Amyraut Heresy*, pp. 32-42, 129; Jack B. Rogers and Donald K. McKim, *The Authority and Interpretation of the Bible: An Historical Approach* (San Francisco: Harper & Row, 1979), pp. 47, 75-76, 149-150, 160-169,175, 185-188, 221-223, etc.

15. Thus, Hans Emil Weber, *Reformation, Orthodoxie und Rationalismus*, 2 vols. in 3 parts (Gütersloh, 1937-1951; repr. Darmstadt: Wissenschaftliche Buchgesellschaft, 1966); and Ernst Bizer, *Frühorthodoxie und Rationalismus* (Zürich: EVZ Verlag, 1963).

In the Middle Ages both sides of the human consciousness—that which was turned within as that which was turned without—lay dreaming or half awake beneath a common veil. The veil was woven of faith, illusion, and childish prepossession, through which the world and history were seen clad in strange hues. ... In Italy this veil first melted into air; an *objective* treatment and consideration of the state and of all things of this world became possible. The subjective side at the same time asserted itself with corresponding emphasis; man became a spiritual *individual*, and recognized himself as such.[16]

According to Burckhardt, humanism stood utterly opposed to medieval culture:

as competitor with the whole culture of the Middle Ages, which was essentially clerical and was fostered by the Church, there appeared a new civilization, founding itself on that which lay on the other side of the Middle Ages. Its active representatives became influential because they knew what the ancients knew ... because they began to think, and soon to see, as the ancients thought and felt.[17]

The underlying problem with all of these narratives is that they are largely of nineteenth-century origin and do not at all reflect the currents of thought that were actually present in the sixteenth and seventeenth centuries. Reassessments of medieval thought and culture have clearly indicated that humanism was not only a product of the intellectual culture of the Middle Ages, but also that it arose, not as a successor to scholasticism, but as a parallel development in the university faculties of the thirteenth century.[18] Those reassessments have also pointed to both humanism and scholasticism as primarily descriptors of method—specifically of patterns or models of argument that were applied to the various subject areas of the medieval university curriculum, both of which carried over into the early modern era. Indeed, the most recent studies of scholastic method have indicated that, in a series of developments and modifications, including an accommodation to humanistic interests, it carried over from the Middle Ages as far as the first half of the eighteenth century.

Recent examinations of the writings of the Reformers have begun to detail medieval backgrounds, sometimes to be associated with the orders or academic backgrounds of individual thinkers, sometimes to be associated with diverse patterns of reception of late medieval materials. Thus, Martin Luther has been studied in terms of antecedents in late medieval nominalism and in the varied currents of thought within the Order of Augustinian Eremites and in terms of his reception of various threads of medieval thought in and through his studies at Erfurt and his

---

16. Jacob Burckhardt, *The Civilization of the Renaissance in Italy*, trans. S. C. G. Middlemore (London: S. Sonnenschein; New York: Macmillan, 1904), p. 129.

17. Burckhardt, *Civilization of the Renaissance in Italy*, p. 203

18. Perhaps most notably, Paul Oskar Kristeller, *Renaissance Thought: The Classic, Scholastic, and Humanist Strains* (New York: Harper & Row, 1961).

reading of Gabriel Biel's theology.[19] Peter Martyr Vermigli's thought has been analyzed in terms of its backgrounds in the Thomist and Augustinian trajectories of medieval theology.[20] John Calvin's work has been shown to evidence the impact of various lines of medieval thought extending from Bernard of Clairvaux to late medieval Scotism and Augustinianism, albeit without any definitive identification of his patterns of reception or his specific backgrounds other than from the sources actually cited by him.[21]

Similarly, recent scholarship has identified, both by way of the Reformers' academic study and by way of their diverse reception of materials both medieval and contemporary, a rather varied intermixture of humanistic and scholastic elements in their thought in addition to their often rather different patterns of appropriation and rejection of aspects of scholastic and humanistic approaches to the materials of theology. Appraisal of Luther's and Calvin's well-known polemics against scholastic theology and philosophy has been tempered and nuanced by recognition of the levels of continuity between their thought and the teachings of various late medieval thinkers and, in addition, by examination of the elements of scholastic method and vocabulary found throughout their writings.[22] So too has it been recognized that the very real debates of the Renaissance and early modern eras between advocates of scholastic and humanistic methods did not carry over into theology as neatly defined oppositions—and it marks a fundamental misapprehension of the materials to identify the Reformers as humanists and the Reformation as a humanistic

---

19. See, e.g., David C. Steinmetz, Luther and Staupitz: An Essay in the Intellectual Origins of the Protestant Reformation (Durham: Duke University Press, 1980); Dennis Janz, Luther and Late Medieval Thomism: A Study in Theological Anthropology (Waterloo: Wilfrid Laurier University Press, 1983); and John Farthing, Thomas Aquinas and Gabriel Biel: Interpretations of St. Thomas Aquinas on the Eve of the Reformation (Durham: Duke University Press, 1988).

20. Cf. John Patrick Donnelly, Calvinism and Scholasticism in Vermigli's Doctrine of Man and Grace (Leiden: Brill, 1975); idem, "Calvinist Thomism," Viator, 7 (1976), pp. 441-455; and idem, "Italian Influences on the Development of Calvinist Scholasticism," Sixteenth Century Journal, 7/1 (1976), pp. 81-101; with Frank A. James III, Peter Martyr Vermigli and Predestination: The Augustinian Inheritance of an Italian Reformer (Oxford: Clarendon Press; New York: Oxford University Press, 1998); and idem, De iustificatione: the Evolution of Peter Martyr Vermigli's Doctrine of Justification (Ph.D. diss. Westminster Theological Seminary, 2000).

21. Thus, e.g., Karl Reuter, Das Grundverständnis der Theologie Calvins (Neukirchen: Neukirchner Verlag, 1963); idem, Vom Scholaren bis zum jungen Reformator (Neukirchen: Neukirchner Verlag, 1981); A. N. S. Lane, John Calvin: Student of the Church Fathers (Grand Rapids: Baker, 1999), pp. 15-66, 87-150; and Dennis Tamburello, Union with Christ: John Calvin and the Mysticism of St. Bernard (Louisville: Westminster/John Knox, 1994). Also note Arvin Vos, Aquinas, Calvin, and Contemporary Protestant Thought: A Critique of Protestant Views of the Thought of Thomas Aquinas (Grand Rapids: Eerdmans, 1985).

22. See, e.g., David Bagchi, "Sic et Non: Luther and Scholasticism" in Protestant Scholasticism: Essays in Reassessment, ed. Carl Trueman and R. Scott Clark (Carlisle: Paternoster Press, 1999), pp. 3-15; David C. Steinmetz, "The Scholastic Calvin," in ibid., pp. 16-30; and Richard A. Muller, The Unaccommodated Calvin: Studies in the Formation of a Theological Tradition (New York: Oxford University Press, 2000), pp. 39-61.

phenomenon.[23] Not only does the thought of a humanistically-trained Reformer like Calvin evidence scholastic aspects, but Calvin's appropriation of humanism was itself tempered by polemic against philosophical developments brought on by humanistic study of the ancients—as is evident in Calvin's polemics against Epicureans, Stoics, and, in some cases, Sophists.[24]

Further, as examination of the extensive correspondence of the Reformers indicates, they consulted one another, discussed and debated doctrinal issues, and did not offer any indication that the formulations of one theologian had preeminence over another. Specifically, we have no indication from Calvin's correspondence that his theology was viewed as the primary expression of Reformed thought in his generation. A few examples should suffice. Bucer offered criticism to Calvin of several aspects of the *Consensus Tigurinus* of 1549, notably that the document had refrained from a clear language of union with or participation in Christ and that it had gone too far in indicating that Christ's body is located in heaven.[25] There is a correspondence among Calvin, Vermigli, and Laski from 1555 over various doctrinal issues in which Calvin noted, without any specifics, that there was a difference in the interpretation of predestination between himself and Laski and then, at some length, complained about Laski's emphasis on "participation" and "communion" with Christ in the Lord's Supper, when on most other points he and Laski were in fundamental agreement.[26] Laski, who was a decade older than Calvin and had discussed issues regarding the Lord's Supper with Bucer and Bullinger in the mid-1540s, did not alter his formulations on Calvin's account.[27] The extant letters between Calvin and Vermigli evidence a mutuality such that Vermigli (who was also a decade older than Calvin) might well be called the mentor of Calvin.[28] In the case of the doctrine of union with Christ, Vermigli's letters to Calvin and Beza indicate that he stands

Vermigli mentor of John Calvin.

---

23. Cf. Stephen Ozment, "Humanism, Scholasticism, and the Intellectual Origins of the Reformation," in *Continuity and Discontinuity in Church History*, ed. F. Forrester Church and T. George (Leiden: E. J. Brill, 1979), pp. 133-149; with Erika Rummel, *The Humanist-Scholastic Debate in the Renaissance and Reformation* (Cambridge: Harvard University Press, 1995), pp. 126-134.

24. Cf. Josef Bohatec, *Calvin et humanisme* (Paris: Revue Historique, 1939); and idem, *Budé und Calvin* (Graz: Herman Bölhaus, 1950), pp 121-147; with François Wendel, *Calvin et l'humanisme* (Paris: Presses Universitaires de France, 1976).

25. Bucer to Calvin, August 1549, in G. C. Gorham, *Gleanings of a few scattered ears, during the period of the Reformation in England and of the times immediately succeeding; A.D. 1533 to A.D. 1588* (London: Bell and Daldy, 1857), pp. 100-104.

26. Calvin to Vermigli (18 Jan. 1555), in *CO* 15, col. 388 (*Selected Works*, VI, p. 124).

27. Cf. Laski, *Catechismus ecclesiae Emdanae*, Q & R, 67, in *Opera*, ed. Kuyper, II, p. 530, with idem, *Catechismus ecclesiae Londini*, Q. 240, in ibid., II, p. 468; and note Laski to Bucer, 23 June 1545; Laski to Bullinger and Pellican, 23 March 1546, in Gorham, *Gleanings*, pp. 30-35.

28. Cf. Marvin W. Anderson, "Peter Martyr, Reformed Theologian (1542-1562): His Letters to Heinrich Bullinger and John Calvin," *Sixteenth Century Journal*, 4/1 (1973), pp. 41-64.

clearly with them as a primary formulator of the Reformed position and that he most probably added greater analytical clarity to the discussion.[29]

Beyond this, Reformed theologians of the seventeenth century typically took umbrage at being called "Calvinists" and viewed Calvin as one of a group of significant forebears—not, indeed, emphatically not, as the founder and norm of their confessional tradition.[30] Their patterns of doctrinal formulation also echo their comments about Calvinism: they formulated their doctrines in the context of then-contemporary debates and conversations, following out trajectories of biblical interpretation that typically can be traced through one or another of the major Reformers into the medieval and even patristic past. The specific patterns of definition found in their writings often indicate the influence of one or another of the Reformers, looking sometimes to Calvin but also, sometimes, to Bullinger, Musculus, or Vermigli—or, indeed, some other teacher of the era of the Reformation.

The methodological question that rather naturally arises at this point concerns the use of master narratives and, given the rejection of the older master narratives concerning the history of early modern Reformed thought, how, precisely, a new master narrative ought to be constructed. The simple answer is that a new master narrative ought not to be constructed. Any such narrative that would rest, as do the narratives just rejected, on philosophical or theological constructs would also be found lacking foundation in the historical sources. Nor is the issue to take up one or another of the postmodernist challenges to reject master narratives and metahistory by the creation of "local narratives" that recognize a "multiplicity of theoretical standpoints."[31] The problem of all such narratives, master, meta, or local, is precisely that they rest on so-called theoretical standpoints. The issue is to examine the sources and from the sources themselves construct a narrative that imposes as few of the historian's present philosophical and theological assumptions or prejudices as is methodologically possible.[32] In what follows, I propose to examine in more detail specific aspects of the older master narratives and of the work of reassessing early

---

29. Peter Martyr Vermigli, *Loci communes*, 2nd ed. (London: Thomas Vautrollerius, 1583), p. 1095 (letter to Calvin); p. 1109 (letter to Beza); in translation, *The Common Places of Peter Martyr*, trans. Anthony Marten (London: Henrie Denham et al., 1583), part 5, pp. 96-99, 105-106.

30. See the documentation in Richard A. Muller, "Reception and Response: Referencing and Understanding Calvin in Post-Reformation Calvinism," in *Calvin and His Influence, 1509-2009*, ed. Irena Backus and Philip Benedict (New York: Oxford University Press, 2011), pp. 182-201.

31. The latter phrase is taken from Michael A. Peters, *Poststructuralism, Marxism, and Neoliberalism: Between Theory and Politics* (Lanham: Rowan and Littlefield, 2001), p. 7.

32. See the magisterial essay by Perez Zagorin, "Rejoinder to a Postmodernist," *History and Theory*, 39/2 (2000), pp. 201-209; responding to Keith Jenkins, "A Postmodern Reply to Perez Zagorin," *History and Theory*, 39/2 (2000), pp. 181-200; and Zagorin's earlier essay, "History the Referent, and the Narrative: Reflections on Postmodernism Now," *History and Theory*, 38/1 (1999), pp. 1-24. Also note Thomas L. Haskell, "Objectivity is Not Neutrality: Rhetoric vs. Practice in Peter Novick's *That Noble Dream*," *History and Theory*, 29/2 (1990), pp. 129-157.

modern Reformed thought—as both furthering the critique of the older narratives and clarifying the premises of the newer approach.

Method and Content—Once Again

One of the issues central to the reappraisal of early modern Reformed thought and to the demolition of the problematic older master narratives is the proper identification of scholasticism and humanism as phenomena belonging to the intellectual history and, specifically, to the academic culture of the Middle Ages and early modern eras rather than as a particular theologies or philosophies. A distinction needs to be made between the methods employed in formulating and presenting theology in the early modern era and the conclusions drawn by the theologians, on the basis of exegetical, confessional, traditionary, philosophical, and contextual concerns—yielding what can properly be called the doctrinal content of their theologies. This point needs to be made with regard both to scholasticism and humanism and to their impact on the work of the Reformers and of the later Protestant writers. The point is not, of course, to declare that method and content can be utterly separated. Nor does the point constitute a denial of interrelationship between method and content. Rather, the point is that method (whether scholastic or humanistic) does not yield a specific doctrinal content, as, for example, an Augustinian or a Semi-Pelagian doctrine of grace or, for that matter, a metaphysically controlled so-called predestinarian system.[33]

The point is simple enough—indeed, it ought to have been self-evident and in need of no comment had it not been for the major confusion caused by older definitions of Protestant scholasticism, definitions that still remain in vogue in particular among the proponents of the "Calvin against the Calvinists" methodology. Several recent works, including one embodying this defective methodology, have further confused the point by misrepresenting the distinction, as if it were a denial that method has any effect on content.[34] It therefore bears further attention here, particularly in view of the confusion of scholasticism with predestinarianism and determinism and of scholasticism with Aristotelianism, so evident in the "Calvin against the Calvinists" literature.

As a preliminary issue, it needs to be emphasized that the definitions of scholasticism as primarily a matter of method, specifically, of academic method, rather than a reference to content and particular conclusions whether philosophical

---

33. Cf. the various definitional statements in Richard A. Muller, *Christ and the Decree: Christology and Predestination in Reformed Theology from Calvin to Perkins*, reissued, with a new preface (Grand Rapids: Baker, 2008), pp. ix-x, 11-12; idem, *After Calvin: Studies in the Development of a Theological Tradition* (New York: Oxford University Press, 2003), pp. 27-33, 74-78; idem, PRRD, I, pp. 189-204.

34. Thus, Partee, *Theology of John Calvin*, p. 22; cf. Myk Habets, Review of *Christ and the Decree*, *American Theological Inquiry*, 3/2 (2010), p. 107; and note my response, "Reassessing the Relation of Reformation and Orthodoxy—A Methodological Rejoinder," *American Theological Inquiry*, 4/1 (2011), pp. 3-12.

or theological—very much like the definitions of humanism as a matter of method, specifically, of philological method, rather than a reference to content and particular conclusions—were not definitions devised by a revisionist scholarship for the sake of refuting the "Calvinist against the Calvinists" understanding of Protestant scholasticism. Rather, they are definitions held in common by several generations of medieval and Renaissance historians,[35] definitions well in place prior to the dogmatic recasting of the notion of scholasticism by the "Calvin against the Calvinists" school of thought, definitions characteristically ignored by that school in its presentations of the thought of Calvin and later Reformed theologians. In other words, identification of scholasticism as primarily referencing method places the reappraisal of Protestant scholasticism and orthodoxy firmly in an established trajectory of intellectual history, while the content-laden definitions of the "Calvin against the Calvinists" school have been formulated in a historical vacuum filled with the doctrinal agendas of contemporary theologians. This problem is particularly evident in the more recent versions of the "Calvin against the Calvinists" claim, inasmuch as they cite the revisionist literature on the issue of Protestant scholasticism rather selectively and fail to engage the significant body of scholarship on the issue of nature scholasticism, indeed, of the nature of humanism as well, as has been consistently referenced as an element in the formulation of a revised perspective on early modern Protestant thought, and in addition, fail to engage the sources that have been analyzed in the process of reappraising the scholasticism of early modern Protestantism.

In brief, the "Calvin against the Calvinists" definition assumed that the intrusion of scholasticism into Protestant theology brought with it forms of "deductive ratiocination … invariably based upon an Aristotelian philosophic commitment" and implying "a pronounced interest in metaphysical matters, in abstract speculative thought, particularly with reference to the doctrine of God," with the "distinctive Protestant position" being "made to rest on a speculative formulation of the will of God."[36] This line of argument also offers a false dichotomy, grounded in notions of theological content, between scholasticism and humanism. The scholastic line is Aristotelian, predestinarian, and *a priori*, even utterly syllogistic in its argumentation—the humanistic line is anti-Aristotelian, perhaps Platonic,

---

35. See, e.g., the definitions in G. Fritz and A. Michel, "Scholastique," in *Dictionnaire de Théologie Catholique*, ed. A. Vacant et al., 23 vols. (Paris: Librairie Letouzey et Ane, 1923-1950), XIV/2, col. 1691; Kristeller, *Renaissance Thought*, pp. 92-119; David Knowles, *The Evolution of Medieval Thought* (New York: Vintage Books, 1962), p. 87; Armand Maurer, *Medieval Philosophy* (New York: Random House, 1962), p. 90; J. A. Weisheipl, "Scholastic Method," in *New Catholic Encyclopedia* (New York: Catholic University of America, 1967), XII, pp. 1145-1146; Calvin G. Normore, s.v., "Scholasticism," in *The Cambridge Dictionary of Philosophy*, ed. R. Audi (Cambridge: Cambridge University Press, 1995), pp. 716-717; and Ulrich G. Leinsle, *Einführung in die scholastische Theologie* (Paderborn: Schöningh, 1995), pp. 5-15.

36. Armstrong, *Calvinism and the Amyraut Heresy*, p. 32; cf. ibid, pp. 120-121.

covenantal, and *a posteriori* in its argumentation.[37] It is scholasticism that generates "limited atonement," rigid predestinarianism, and arid dogmatic theology while humanism presses toward "universal atonement," covenantal or salvation-historical thinking, and biblical theology.[38] Humanism, as the driving force in Calvin's thought, produced a "balanced" theology rather than a system inasmuch as Calvin scorned what was passed off as "systematic theology" in his time—scholasticism destroyed the balance of Calvin's thought.[39] These claims are not only characterized by neat and unsupportable dichotomies of predestinarianism versus christocentrism, predestinarianism versus covenantalism, a priorism versus a posteriorism, limited atonement versus universal atonement, and so forth, all artificially constructed around a basic scholasticism versus humanism dichotomy, as if history could be written as a neat series of pigeonholes.[40] They also rest on the rather bizarre assumption that Calvin can be placed in one of the pigeonholes and then used as a convenient index for the assessment of the development of a whole tradition, the assessment itself typically being based an a highly anachronistic approach to Calvin's theology pronounced by its modern dogmatic advocates to be "complete and sufficient subject" in and of itself for examination and, by implication, for the assessment of a whole tradition.[41]

There are at least two historical issues at play here: first, there is the issue of the relationship between humanism and scholasticism, and, second, there is the issue of the relationship of method to content. On the first of these issues, scholarship on the history of humanism and scholasticism in the later Middle Ages and the early modern era has indicated that humanism ought to be understood not as a successor movement to scholasticism but as a movement in the study of arts and language that began at about the same time as the rise of scholasticism in the thirteenth century and that developed alongside scholasticism. The same scholarship has indicated that both humanism and scholasticism ought to be understood primarily as methods.[42]

37. Cf. Armstrong, *Calvinism and the Amyraut Heresy*, pp. 120-121; with Jürgen Moltmann, "Zur Bedeutung des Petrus Ramus für Philosophie und Theologie im Calvinismus," *Zeitschrift für Kirchengeschichte*, 68 (1956-1957), pp. 295-318.

38. Armstrong, *Calvinism and the Amyraut Heresy*, pp. 140-141, 151; cf. Hall, "Calvin against the Calvinists," pp. 25-28; Kendall, *Calvin and English Calvinism*, pp. 29-31.

39. Cf. Armstrong, *Calvinism and the Amyraut Heresy*, pp. 38, 129, 136-139; idem, *"Duplex cognitio Dei,* Or? The Problem and Relation of Structure, Form, and Purpose in Calvin's Theology," in *Probing the Reformed Tradition: Historical Essays in Honor of Edward A. Dowey, Jr.*, ed. Elsie Anne McKee and Brian G. Armstrong (Louisville: Westminster/John Knox, 1989), p. 136; with Hall, "Calvin against the Calvinists," pp. 19-20, 25-26, 28; William J. Bouwsma, *John Calvin: A Sixteenth-Century Portrait* (New York: Oxford University Press, 1988), pp. 5, 238, note 24; and idem, "The Spirituality of John Calvin," in *Christian Spirituality: High Middle Ages and Reformation*, ed. Jill Raitt (New York: Crossroad, 1987), pp. 318-319.

40. Thus, Armstrong, *Calvinism and the Amyraut Heresy*, pp. 120-121, 123, 127-129, etc.

41. Thus, Partee, *Theology of John Calvin*, pp. 3, 4, 25, 27.

42. Cf. Kristeller, *Renaissance Thought*, pp. pp. 92-119.

This redefinition of the history and primary intellectual and curricular implications of scholasticism and humanism does not, however, lessen the impact or diminish the intensity of the debates between humanists and scholastics that took place during the late fifteenth and early sixteenth centuries. Rather, it refines and focuses our sense of the nature of the debates.[43] Whereas the "Calvin against the Calvinists" literature, as typified by Armstrong's account of the backgrounds and conduct of the Amyraldian controversy, tends to assume that the divergence between humanist and scholastic had vast implications for the content of theology, it also assumes that the early conflict between humanism and scholasticism that can be identified in the era of the Reuchlin controversy carried over into the second and third generation of Reformers and into the early seventeenth century without particular modification of the interrelationships between humanism and scholasticism.[44] In other words, it offers a rather static understanding of humanism and scholasticism and of their relationship.

Scholarship has shown, however, that this is not at all the case. There are, arguably, fairly distinct stages and a host of contextual nuances in the relationship between humanism and scholasticism,[45] some of which are conditioned by the subject areas and training of the thinkers and some of which are conditioned, at least from the perspective of what precisely is being criticized, by alterations in the application of the term "scholastic." (We remind ourselves that no one in the early modern era was using the term "humanist.") The early humanist-scholastic debates of the pre-Reformation era were over the clash of methods and approaches to documents that took place largely among members of university faculties and had

---

43. Cf. the rather different evaluations of the debates in John F. D'Amico, "Humanism and Pre-Reformation Theology," in *Renaissance Humanism: Foundations, Forms, and Legacy*, 3 vols. (Philadelphia: University of Pennsylvania Press, 1988), pp. 349-379; and Lewis W. Spitz, "Humanism and the Protestant Reformation," in ibid., pp. 380-411; Charles G. Nauert, "The Clash of Humanists and Scholastics: An Approach to Pre-Reformation Controversies," in *Sixteenth Century Journal*, 4 (1973), pp.1-18; idem, "Humanism as Method: Roots of Conflict with the Scholastics," *Sixteenth Century Journal*, 29/2 (1998), pp. 427-438; and Erika Rummel, "Et cum theologo bella poeta gerit: The Conflict between Humanists and Scholastics Revisited," in *Sixteenth Century Journal*, 23/4 (1992), pp. 713-726. Much of the difference between these accounts—recognized certainly by Nauert—arises because of the rather different contexts of humanism being examined, notably Spitz examining the Reformation-era theological context and Rummel looking primarily to disputes in the arts. The authors do, however, all agree with Kristeller that both scholasticism and humanism ought to be referred to method.

44. Thus, Armstrong, *Calvin and the Amyraut Heresy*, pp. 14-16, 38-41, et passim; Hall, "Calvin against the Calvinists," pp. 25-26.

45. Cf. Nauert, "Clash of Humanists and Scholastics," pp. 3-4, 13-14; with Erika Rummel, "Et cum theologo bella poeta gerit: The Conflict between Humanists and Scholastics Revisited," pp. 715, 725-726, who argues the intensity of the early sixteenth-century conflict but indicates the importance of recognizing "regional," "chronological," and "thematic variations."

little directly to do with theology.[46] In the era of the Reformation, the issue was complicated by the use of humanistic methods in debate with scholastic theologians and philosophers whose appeal to traditionary authorities could be critiqued from the perspective of an analysis of ancient sources, including the original language texts of Scripture. The humanist critics did not, of course, uniformly align with the Reformation. These early Reformation debates were in turn succeeded by debates in which theologians, some trained initially as humanists, others in a more traditional scholastic fashion, began to alter the context and blur the lines of debate—and these, in turn, gave way to debates over scholasticism, specifically over kinds and eras of nominally scholastic theology and philosophy in which the debaters typically had either dual training in both humanistic and scholastic approaches or at least evidence either scholastic characteristics in their more humanistic methods or strongly humanistic aspects to their scholastic methods. To make the point in another way, there is a significant difference between the character and conduct of the pre-Reformation humanist-scholastic debates and the developing Reformation and post-Reformation relationships between scholastic and humanistic methods in the fields of theology and philosophy.

Thus, for example, Calvin clearly evidences the humanist training but also elements of scholastic method and its distinctions in his theological argumentation.[47] Beza, despite the claims of some modern scholars, was arguably more the humanist than the scholastic, focusing on language and philology and evidencing only some of the characteristics of scholastic argumentation.[48] By the time of the Amyraut controversy, nearly all of the major Reformed writers were trained in a humanistic approach to language, as evidenced, among other things, by their delivery of academic orations in Ciceronian style, but they also were well-practiced in scholastic method as evidenced by their disputations and by their large-scale academic theological works. Quite specifically, at least in these theological circles, the early battles between humanistic and scholastic approaches were over, and the two methods had come to subsist together as aspects of the academic preparation of theologians. Attacks on the scholastics, from the time of Calvin down into the seventeenth century, were typically highly focused attacks on certain trajectories and doctrinal results in academic theology that distinguished between an older, acceptable scholastic theology and a more recent problematic late medieval or

---

46. Note the comments in D'Amico, "Humanism and Pre-Reformation Theology," pp. 349-350, 353-355, 366-373; and Spitz, "Humanism and the Protestant Reformation," pp. 393-395.

47. Cf., e.g., Steinmetz, "Scholastic Calvin," pp. 16-30.

48. Scott Manetsch, "Psalms before Sonnets: Theodore Beza and the *Studia humanitatis*," in *Continuity and Change: The Harvest of Late Medieval and Reformation History. Essays Presented to Heiko A. Oberman on His 70th Birthday*, ed. Andrew C. Gow and Robert J. Bast (Leiden: E. J. Brill, 2000), pp. 400-416; on the limitation of Beza's scholasticism, see Jeffrey Mallinson, *Faith, Reason, and Revelation in Theodore Beza (1519-1605)* (Oxford: Oxford University Press, 2003), pp. 67-70.

Roman Catholic theological trajectory, often with the proviso that the "scholastic" approaches of Protestants were not subject to the same criticism.[49]

As to the question of the relationship of method and content in scholasticism: any observant reader of the recent revisionist studies of Reformed orthodoxy would have noticed several points at which the issue of the relationship of scholastic method to doctrinal content has been raised, the point made that the two are not mutually exclusive, and some space devoted to indicating specifically either what kind of content and conclusions are not generated by the method as such or what kind of content specifically relates to the adoption of the method. It ought to be fairly evident even from a cursory survey of the scholastic method or methods employed by theologians from the thirteenth through the seventeenth century that scholasticism did not dictate specific doctrinal conclusions, certainly not such conclusions as indicated in the arguments offered by the "Calvin against the Calvinists" school of thought. The same can be said of humanism. Adoption of a scholastic approach did not lead either to predestinarianism or to synergism. Use of the Aristotelian fourfold causality, likewise, did not bring about a metaphysical interest, much less metaphysical determinism. Humanism did not lead to covenantal emphases in theology. How odd and ahistorical would it be to bifurcate Calvin and link his doctrine of predestination to a scholastic bent and his understanding of covenant to his humanistic training! How odd and ahistorical it is to bifurcate the Reformed tradition into scholastic predestinarians teaching limited atonement and kinder, gentler humanists teaching hypothetical universalism! (Perhaps we need to remind ourselves of those two humanists, Pietro Pomponazzi and Lorenzo Valla, who argued philosophical determinism—or of scholastics like Gabriel Biel, Luiz Molina, and Jacob Arminius, who argued forms of synergistic theology.) The presence of elements of scholastic or of humanistic method does not account either for the specific doctrines of predestination or covenant held by the writers of the sixteenth and seventeenth centuries or for the kinds of doctrinal nuances included in the formulations, as, for example, whether a given thinker held a supra- or an infralapsarian doctrine of the decrees.

For what kind of content, then, does method account? Given the academic nature and context of works that follow a scholastic method, a scholastic theology written in the early modern era would assume a grasp and deployment of a wide variety of sources and skills. Among the sources, the scholastic tradition assumed a demonstrable grasp of the text of Scripture; of the materials of the church's tradition, notably the works of the major church fathers; of major works of ancient philosophy; of trajectories of argument belonging to the medieval tradition; of the works of predecessors in the specific confessional tradition of the author; of writings of various opponents whether theological or philosophical; and so forth. Among the skills assumed by early modern scholastic writers were abilities in classical languages

---

49. See Muller, *Post-Reformation Reformed Dogmatics*, I, pp. 189-204.

typically associated with Renaissance learning and grasp of models of argumentation gleaned from training in logic and rhetoric. The content of a scholastic treatise, then, drew on the method in terms of the grasp and breadth of materials employed in argumentation, including assumptions concerning the relative authority of various sources, materials, and tools. Thus, in a scholastic theological work, content would include referencing and use not only of Scripture but also of various church fathers, various medieval theologians, and various philosophers whether ancient or more recent—and the content of these sources would influence the work. Once that has been said, however, the argumentative content and the theological conclusions reached have more to do with the choice of materials and the theological and philosophical proclivities of the individual author than with the method itself.

This scholastic methodological demand of broad grasp, positive and negative, formulative and polemical, of a wide range of sources, some of which had a relative authoritative status, leads to consideration of two related aspects of early modern scholastic method, both of which had roots in the medieval academic tradition and one of which, in particular, evidenced the impact of Renaissance dialectic or logic—namely, the disputation and the *locus*. The disputation was largely an academic exercise, related to the *locus* inasmuch as it was designed to argue a specific topic. A series of topical disputations, moreover, could be arranged into a basic, often thetical or propositional body of Christian doctrine, in which what had originally been a series of academic exercises had become the basis for a set of theological *loci*. The topics or *loci* were generated, as were the disputations, by a topical reading of the source materials, whether Scripture, the fathers, other traditionary sources, philosophical issues, or contemporary debates. Thus, clearly, the method did affect the content but, again, not in terms of the specific topic chosen, the sources emphasized, or the doctrinal conclusions drawn.

As argued elsewhere, one of the effects of this topical or *locus* method was an emphasis on the integrity or integral formulation of a topic and a deemphasis on, even a barrier to, the development of overarching dogmatic models such as used in the deductive, systematic, central dogma approaches characteristic of nineteenth-century theology.[50] This barrier to the rise of deductive approaches to the whole of theology was reinforced by the clear distinction (absent from those nineteenth-century works) between causal and logical necessity: an early modern Reformed theologian could, in other words, argue on biblical grounds the causal interconnection of such doctrinal topics as predestination, calling, faith, union with Christ, justification, sanctification, and glorification, and at the same time recognize that no one of these topics could be deduced logically from another. It is a misreading, therefore, of the method and the materials of early modern theology to conclude that the *locus* method stood in the way of identifying and developing those doctrinal interrelationships that had been indicated or implied in the sources

---

50. See the discussion in Muller, *Post-Reformation Reformed Dogmatics*, I, pp. 187-188.

themselves, just as it is a mistake to assume that theologians like Calvin and Bullinger who did not identify their more systematic works as *loci communes* were exempt from or somehow transcended the method. The method did stand in the way of a logical deduction of one *locus* from another (as would have been the case in a theology that deduced other doctrines from predestination or Christology or some other topic). This methodological issue, moreover, is not one that divided the Reformers from the later Reformed orthodox writers or that stood in the way of differences over the identification of the thematic contents of topics or over the ways in which the topics themselves were related. As illustrated by the early modern development of the concepts of a "chain" or causal structure of the work of salvation and of union with Christ in relation to this causal structure, there was significant common ground between Calvin and various of his contemporaries and later formulations, as well as a fairly wide variety in the deployment and interrelations of the various topics and subtopics.[51]

Also at the most general level of argumentation, method relates to content in terms of the genre of the work and its intended audience. Given that the writers of the era consistently distinguished between scholastic (or academic) method and popular, catechetical, or exegetical methods—as also between synthetic and analytic methods—method accounts for the content of the documents with regard to levels of detail, format, kinds of argument employed, topics to be included or excluded, and the order and arrangement of topics. This understanding of "scholastic" primarily as an identifier of method and, therefore, as related to the genre of a document is, moreover, embedded in the usages of later Middle Ages and early modern era. Reformed writers of the sixteenth and seventeenth centuries regularly distinguished between works of a scholastic, catechetical, and exegetical character, identifying as scholastic those works deriving from the academic setting.[52] They also did not assume, in identifying some as scholastic and others as catechetical, that the former would define basic doctrinal points differently than the latter—only that levels of detail, placement, and treatment of doctrines would differ.

Certain topics and subtopics appear in scholastic theological works, given that they are directed toward an academic audience, that do not appear, for example, in catechetical works. Similarly, catechetical works follow different patterns of order and organization than scholastic exercises or polemical treatments. Thus, for example, a fairly central element of the "Calvin against the Calvinists" theory, namely, the relatively *a posteriori* or analytic placement of predestination in Calvin's *Institutes*, as contrasted with the more or less *a priori* or synthetic placement of predestination in many of the theological systems of the seventeenth century, can be shown to have nothing to do either with differences in definition or with the

---

51. Contra Evans, *Imputation and Impartation*, pp. 46, 52-53. On Calvin and the *locus* method, see Muller, *Unaccommodated Calvin*, pp. 29-30, 101-117, 119-130.

52. Cf. Muller, *Post-Reformation Reformed Dogmatics*, I, pp. 189-204.

development of a predestinarian system; rather it has everything to do with differing orders of argument related to the various methods of organizing and teaching theology. The writers of the day understood the uses of scholastic, catechetical, and creedal orderings, the implications of following a more causal ordering in scholastic models or of a more analytical "Pauline" ordering in catechesis. Without changing his views on the theological content or implication of a doctrine, an author could, on grounds of method, alter placement, reduce the scope and detail of the topic, or remove the topic entirely.[53]

Even so, a more scholastic exposition will be clearly thetical; move to establish clear, often propositional definitions or conclusions, argue logically; pose and resolve questions—without the method determining either the questions raised or the conclusions reached. A more humanistically modeled exposition will be more discursive, moving toward a rhetoric or persuasion as distinct from a logic of demonstration—again, without the method ultimately determining either the topics identified or the content of the argumentation. Method does determine content when the work, given its genre and understood in terms of its detail, includes certain distinctions related to the particular topic: thus, the topic and genre determine the distinctions employed, and the distinctions guide the development of the argument. Still, given the flexible character or what could be called the neutrality of scholastic method and of its distinctions,[54] the distinctions themselves do not dictate the final direction or the conclusions of the argument.

Thus, a further illustration of the ways in which scholastic method influences content but does not prejudice conclusions can be drawn from the nature and use of distinctions in scholastic theology and philosophy. For example, the distinction between a hidden will of God (voluntas arcana) and the revealed will (voluntas revelata) adds to the content of the doctrine of the divine will the notion that some aspects of the divine willing are unknowable, other aspects knowable—but it does not specify what cannot be known and what is revealed. It can be used equally by theologians who argue a correlation between the ad intra divine standards of justice and righteousness and the ad extra revelation of the law and by those who argue that God's will is ex lex. Employment of causal language, distinguishing between efficient, formal, material, and final causality does, of course, add by way of content assumptions concerning the basic causes or, more precisely the reasons, that something exists or that a particular result obtains, but the distinction of causes does not lead to the specific identification of causes, so that causal language could be used to argue either monergistic or synergistic soteriologies, various understandings of the nature and character of Scripture, and so forth. There is, in short, an impact of method on content but not a determination of topic or doctrinal conclusion.

---

53. See Richard A. Muller, "The Placement of Predestination in Reformed Theology: Issue or Non-Issue?," in Calvin Theological Journal, 40/2 (2005), pp. 184-210.

54. This is the approach of L. M. de Rijk, Middeleeuwse Wijsbegeerte: Traditie en Vernieuwing (Assen: Van Gorcum, 1977); in translation, La philosophie au Moyen Age (Leiden: Brill, 1985).

So also, the distinction between an antecedent and a consequent divine will (*voluntas antecedens* and *voluntas consequens*) could be and was used to explain the Arminian doctrine of predestination and the non-Arminian doctrine of the decrees developed by the Reformed hypothetical universalist Moïse Amyraut—and it could be used, with qualification by more particularistic Reformed orthodox thinkers. Thus, contrary to what was claimed in the old "Calvin against the Calvinists" theory concerning such distinctions, they do not imply a "speculative" theology. Some of their uses are quite anti-antispeculative. Similarly, the standard distinction between the sufficiency and efficiency of Christ's satisfaction, like the alternative distinction between the accomplishment (*impetratio*) and the application (*applicatio*) of Christ's satisfaction, could be used to argue either an Arminian or a Reformed position, in each case with a different content and implication of the terms of the distinction. The distinction between a necessity of the consequent thing and a necessity of the consequence, namely, between an absolute necessity and a contingency, could be used to illustrate an argument either for or against free choice.

Once the issue of the nature and use of scholastic method in post-Reformation Reformed theology has been identified, it is also important that the impact of scholastic method on Reformed theology not be overestimated. The older scholarship, following out the implications of Armstrong's problematic definitions, tended not only to confuse the method with content and result but also to characterize Reformed orthodoxy in general as "scholastic" without properly recognizing the limitation of the method to specific genres of theological works and without acknowledging the deep impact of humanistic methods on all genres of writing, including the scholastic. Whereas there certainly was an increasing reliance on scholastic approaches in (as one would expect) academic settings, principally those dedicated to the positive and polemical elaboration of theological *loci*, there were other disciplines, like exegesis, and other settings, like the ecclesial, in which other methods were employed. Scholastic method had little impact on catechesis and the basic patterns of catechetical instruction carried over from Reformation into orthodoxy. Similarly, basic models of exegesis such as the philological annotation and theological commentary also carried over from Reformation into the era of orthodoxy. And not only did these methods carry over, but it is also possible to trace out trajectories of interpretation, argumentation, and formulation that run through the Reformation into the era of orthodoxy. There are, in other words, significant interrelationships between the theological content of the commentaries, catechisms, and sermons of the era and the more scholastic dogmatic works, clearly identifiable both in terms of basic doctrinal assumptions and in terms of the constructive relationship of the exegetical works to specific *loci theologici* that carried over into the systematic treatises. In other words, the rise of Protestant scholasticism hardly accounts for the entirety of the development of later Protestant thought.

Toward a Contextualized Intellectual History of Reformed Protestantism

A word needs to added here about the "Muller Thesis" as referenced in some of the more recent debates over the issue of Calvin and Calvinism. The term is not mine and, apart from this set of comments, is found nowhere in my own writing.[55] It is highly problematic, in my view, to reduce the arguments concerning reinterpretation and reassessment of developments in early modern Reformed theology to a single thesis, particularly when that thesis is described simply as an argument for continuity between the Reformers and the Reformed orthodox or, indeed, when the reassessment is reduced to a discussion of "continuities and discontinuities" or to a search for what might be called dogmatic equivalencies in the thought of Calvin and later Reformed thinkers.

To the extent that those who either appeal to the "thesis" on behalf of a particular dogmatic claim concerning the identity of Calvin's teaching with the formulations of a particular theologian in the later Reformed tradition, or declaim against it for the sake of highlighting differences in formulation, they are often inhabiting a rather narrow world of reductionistic argumentation. Neither side of this debate contributes anything significant to the historical discussion. To the extent, moreover, that these appeals to the thesis are actually to a reductionist portrayal of continuities or discontinuities between Calvin and purported "Calvinists," evidence presented in its favor does not support the work of analyzing the development of post-Reformation Reformed orthodoxy, and evidence presented against it has little relevance to arguing either for or against the actual proposals belonging to the work of reappraising the early modern development of the Reformed confessional tradition and its theology. In short, reappraisal of the relationship between the Reformation and the era of orthodoxy (at least as far as my own approach is concerned) does not claim a continuity unaccompanied by change and development between the time Calvin and his contemporaries and later phases of the Reformed tradition, does not assume a uniform pattern of reception of Calvin's thought or the thought of other early Reformers on the part of later Reformed theologians, and does not deny discontinuities.

The approach of the reappraisal or reassessment has been to emphasize the breadth and diversity of the early modern Reformed tradition as it formulated both its confessional documents and its more detailed expositions of theology, typically with acknowledgment of the confessional boundaries. This approach refrains from making Calvin or any other single Reformer the normative voice in the tradition; allows for multiple sources, backgrounds, and contexts of formulation; and assesses

55. See Martin I. Klauber, "Continuity and Discontinuity in Post-Reformation Reformed Theology: An Evaluation of the Muller Thesis," *Journal of the Evangelical Theological Society*, 33 (1990), pp. 467-475, for what is probably the first instance of a summary statement of the "thesis"; more recently, Thomas L. Wenger, "The New Perspective on Calvin: Responding to Recent Calvin Interpretations," *Journal of the Evangelical Theological Society*, 50/2 (2007), pp. 311-328; also note Habets, Review of *Christ and the Decree*, pp. 105-106, 107.

the question of orthodoxy in terms of the early modern standards themselves—recognizing that many of the controversies in which the Reformed engaged were internecine and involved neither determinations of heresy nor the framing of new confessional documents.[56] This approach also assumes change and development in the Reformed tradition, with differences in formulation arising both in the debates and in the positive formulations and reformulations that occurred in various national and geographical contexts and, as the tradition developed, among the various confessional subgroups. In addition, any examination of Reformed theology that attempts to span the entire early modern scene from Reformation through the era of orthodoxy will recognize significant change with regard to questions of the nature of religion, the authority of Scripture, and the formulation of specific doctrines that increasingly took place in the late seventeenth and the eighteenth centuries. Indeed, by the mid-eighteenth century, when the term "Calvinism" was generally received by the more predestinarian Protestants as a positive descriptor, the effects of deconfessionalization together with differences in doctrinal formulation, in the understanding of religion, and in the use of reason in theology had become significant enough that the theological heritage of both Reformation and orthodoxy was often highly attenuated and sometimes entirely lost. Arguably, this alteration of Reformed thought, splintering of the confessional tradition, and rise of increasingly rationalistic patterns of doctrine and piety belongs not to the era of orthodoxy, scholasticism, and modified Peripatetic philosophy in the Reformed tradition but to demise of orthodoxy, the withering away of scholastic method, and the loss of traditional, broadly Christian Aristotelian philosophical understandings that occurred toward the beginning of the eighteenth century.[57]

There is no single all-encompassing thesis to be applied across the board to the interpretation of post-Reformation Reformed theology, certainly not a simple theory of doctrinal continuity or discontinuity. Rather, there is a series of premises or understandings, reflecting positively, negatively, or in a somewhat mixed way on both the early modern materials and the history of scholarly discussion, some of which are more or less my own conclusions, some of which are the conclusions of older lines of scholarship, with which I have been in dialogue during the course of research.[58] There is also a series of subtheses that pertain to arguments concerning individual topics and issues in early modern Reformed theology. A primary example of a positively received thesis found in a major line of twentieth-century scholarship is the identification of scholasticism and humanism as primarily matters of method that, although they can influence content in fairly subtle ways, do not directly determine either the content itself or the conclusions that are drawn. Despite what

---

56. Cf. Muller, "Diversity in the Reformed Tradition," pp. 17-18.

57. See the comments in Muller, *Post-Reformation Reformed Dogmatics*, I, pp. 82-84, 309-310, 398; II, pp. 140-148; III, pp. 138-150.

58. As, e.g, the eleven premises presented in my essays on "Calvin and the 'Calvinists'" in *After Calvin*, pp. 63-102.

seems to be the assumption of many who appeal to the "Muller Thesis," I can hardly claim this as my idea—and my citations have consistently indicated the large body of scholarship on medieval and Renaissance learning that has argued and substantiated this understanding over many decades.[59] The only credit I can take on this point lies in my attempt (only partially successful) to induce modern writers on the subject of Calvinism to expand their understanding of the backgrounds to the work of Calvin and of other Reformed theologians, whether of the sixteenth or of the seventeenth century, and to expand their reading list not only into the works of highly criticized but largely unread Reformed writers of the late sixteenth and seventeenth centuries but also into a significant body of scholarship on the nature of scholasticism and humanism that they have typically ignored.

Similarly, identification of Calvin as one of a group of major second-generation codifiers of the Reformation, who influenced the development of the Reformed tradition and who was perceived by the theologians of the era of orthodoxy neither as their sole normative predecessor nor as the founding formulator of the Reformed faith is hardly a new thought.[60] Reinhold Seeberg long ago commented that

> it is of the first importance, for a proper appreciation of Calvin, to remember that he is a man of the second generation of this great period. He received his ideas and program of action by tradition, in an essentially complete form. It was his task, in the church as in theology, to complete and organize.[61]

George Park Fisher and John T. McNeill similarly identified Calvin as belonging to a second phase of the Reformation and as serving as a codifier and systematizer,[62] as did Williston Walker:

> Calvin belongs to the second generation of the reformers. His place chronologically, and, to a large extent, theologically, is among the heirs rather than with the initiators of the Reformation.[63]

---

59. Thus, e.g., Armand Maurer, *Medieval Philosophy* (New York: Random House, 1962), p. 90; David Knowles, *The Evolution of Medieval Thought* (New York: Vintage Books, 1962), p. 87; J. A. Weisheipl, "Scholastic Method," in *NCE*, 12, p. 1145; Fritz and Michel, "Scholastique," col. 1691; Kristeller, *Renaissance Thought*, pp. 92-119, with idem, "Humanism," in *The Cambridge History of Renaissance Philosophy*, pp. 113-114, and with Charles B. Schmitt, *Aristotle and the Renaissance* (Cambridge, MA: Harvard University Press, 1983), pp. 24-25; Stephen Ozment, *The Age of Reform, 1250-1550: An Intellectual and Religious History of Late Medieval and Reformation Europe* (New Haven: Yale University Press, 1980), pp. 304-309.

60. As it seems to be viewed in Partee, *Theology of John Calvin*, pp. 3-4, et passim.

61. Reinhold Seeberg, *Text-book of the History of Doctrines*, trans. Charles E. Hay, 2 vols. (Grand Rapids: Baker, 1977), II, p. 394.

62. George Park Fisher, *History of the Christian Church* (New York: Scribner's, 1894), p. 318; McNeill, *History and Character of Calvinism*, pp. 3-4.

63. Williston Walker, *John Calvin: The Organizer of Reformed Protestantism (1509-1564)*, repr., with a bibliographical essay by John T. McNeill (New York: Schocken, 1969), p. 1.

Nor did established scholarship on Calvin and Calvinism ignore the point that the Reformed themselves in the seventeenth century set Calvin into this second-generation context and did not view his thought as a norm for the Reformed tradition: it was stated with great clarity in relation to New England Puritan theology by Perry Miller. The Puritans, he commented, "did not think of [Calvin] as the fountain head of their thought, nor of themselves as members of a faction of which he was the founder."[64]

The issue broached by an identification of Calvin as a second-generation codifier or systematizer of Reformed thought is, once again, the issue of historical context and of the significant distortion of Calvin's thought and of his contribution to the Reformed tradition that occurs when scholarship ignores the context. The methodological problem in setting aside Calvin's second-generation codifier status lies in the creation of a "great thinker" approach to history and of a mythology of a Golden Age somehow abstracted from the actual course of events. Such argumentation recedes from a coherent examination of texts, whether primary or secondary, into a dogmatic and often hagiographical mode, steps away from a contextual examination of Calvin's thought, and isolates his reflections on a series of important theological issues from the similar formulations of his contemporaries and of later Reformed theologians.[65]

There appears to be, moreover, a presentizing dogmatic motivation behind such decontextualized readings of the theology of Calvin or, for that matter, the theology of other Reformers, most notably Luther. When Calvin is properly placed in his historical context as a second-generation codifier of Reformed thought, his theology is seen as part of a larger ecclesial development and is placed within the broader doctrinal patterns of a catholic orthodoxy extending back into the Middle Ages and the early church, sharing a series of interpretive assumptions and exegetical conclusions and, in the specific case of the Reformed branch of the tradition, guided by confessional norms written either by various predecessors of Calvin in the Reformed tradition or by Calvin himself and his own contemporaries. He is also placed into a tradition that, obliged by the same confessional documents, extends for several centuries after him, with notable attention in the later sixteenth and seventeenth centuries to the confessional boundaries set by Calvin and his contemporaries. Isolation of Calvin from this ecclesial and confessional context, indeed, often from the meaning and implication of his own words, places his theology at the disposal of modern systematic projects and renders his theology a projection

---

64. Perry Miller, *The New England Mind: The Seventeenth Century* (New York: Macmillan, 1939; repr. Boston: Beacon Press, 1961), p. 93; and note Richard A. Muller, "Reception and Response," pp. 182-184.

65. See the more specific critique of several such works in Richard A. Muller, "Demoting Calvin? The Issue of Calvin and the Reformed Tradition," in *John Calvin: Myth and Reality: Images and Impact of Geneva's Reformer*, ed. Amy Burnett (Eugene: Wipf & Stock, 2011), pp. 3-5; and cf. Muller, *After Calvin*, p. 193.

of the modern systematic exercise. Calvin's thought is, in other words, projected through a dogmatic lens, and Calvin becomes the ally, even the justification, of a particular modern theological stance, while at the same time that the modern theological stance has managed to detach itself from any responsibility either to the broader Reformed tradition or to the confessional documents produced by the pens of the Reformers and the second-generation codifiers of Reformation theology, including Calvin himself.

Indeed, the decontextualized Calvin can be juxtaposed with the Reformed tradition and its confessional documents as if they had little or nothing to do with the central theological developments of the Reformation and had no relation to Calvin's thought. One telling example is the use of Calvin's declamations against speculation to set aside the enumerations of divine attributes found in most of the Reformed confessions—as if these enumerations were somehow speculative and as if Calvin himself would have disagreed with the confessional formulations concerning God. The decontextualized (and misinterpreted) Calvin becomes a basis for dismissing the confessions.[66] A similar and similarly problematic claim involves the dismissal of brief statements concerning natural revelation found in the Gallican and Belgic confessions either on the ground that Calvin's theology does not countenance any positive reference to God's revelation in nature or, most oddly and ahistorically, on the ground that these documents, published in 1559 and 1561 respectively, do not represent "the original witness of the Reformed confessions of the 16th century"![67]

As Billings has pointed out, this modern dogmatic approach to Calvin and other Reformers involves a "primitivist" assumption that identifies what moderns presume to be doctrinal problems in the tradition and then searches for the earlier, purer form of the doctrine in order to claim an alternative trajectory of development from the original form of the doctrine, skipping over the developments that have been declared problematic as inconsistent with the original purer form and ending in the formulations of the modern theologian, now argued as a contemporary representation of the primitive or original teaching.[68] Following this approach, one can read Calvin apart from his background and context as a proponent of some nineteenth- or twentieth- or twenty-first-century theological approach and, accordingly, sever his thought from the tradition of which he was a part, presumably for the sake of severing oneself from a part of that tradition (typically the "scholastic"

---

66. See the important essay by J. Todd Billings, "The Catholic Calvin," in *Pro Ecclesia*, 20/2 (2011), pp. 120-134, on this point, p. 128.

67. Thus, Arthur C. Cochrane, *Reformed Confessions of the 16th Century* (Philadelphia: Westminster, 1966), p. 139.

68. J. Todd Billings, "The Contemporary Reception of Luther and Calvin's Doctrine of Union with Christ: Mapping a Biblical, Catholic, and Reformational Motif," in *Calvin and Luther: The Unfinished Conversation* (Göttingen: Vandenhoeck & Ruprecht, forthcoming); and cf. my comments in *Unaccommodated Calvin*, pp. 4-11, 181-188.

or "orthodox" part) on the claim that Calvin wrote "good theology" and others distorted its "balance," all for the sake of severing Calvin either from the Reformed confessional tradition or from other Reformed thinkers whether in his own time or in the centuries immediately following and claiming to offer good, balanced, but highly anachronistic Calvinian models for theology in the present. The techniques used to argue this primitivist model have employed generalizations that, for example, identify Calvin as a theologian of grace who put grace prior to law and identify later Reformed writers as legalists who put law prior to grace.[69] Equally so, such techniques have been used to identify Calvin as the theologian *par excellence* of union with Christ and later Reformed writers as either virtually lacking the doctrine or as having distorted its original Calvinian formulation by associating it with the order of salvation or with the categories of federal theology.[70] But that is not historiography at all—and its Calvin has little to do with the Reformation or the Reformed tradition.

Yet another example of an element in the argumentation associated with the reassessment of orthodoxy that belongs to a fairly long line of older scholarship is the point that the understanding of the relationship of faith and reason, theology and philosophy found among the Reformed orthodox writers of the seventeenth century (contra writers like Bizer and Kickel) is neither a form of rationalism nor a step toward rationalism, given among other issues, the nature and character of rationalism in the early modern era.[71] I can hardly claim this point as my own thesis. Several of the older histories of rationalism had argued its rise in theological circles

---

69. A series of particularly striking examples of this highly tendentious and distortive historiography in the service of modern dogmatics can be found in the essays by James B. Torrance, "The Concept of Federal Theology—Was Calvin a Federal Theologian?," in *Calvinus Sacrae Scripturae Professor*, edited by Wilhelm H. Neuser (Grand Rapids: Eerdmans, 1994), pp. 15-40; idem, "Covenant or Contract? A Study of the Theological Background or Worship in Seventeenth-Century Scotland," in *Scottish Journal of Theology*, 23 (1970), pp. 51-76; idem, "The Incarnation and "Limited Atonement," *The Evangelical Quarterly*, 55 (1983), pp. 83-94; and Thomas F. Torrance, *Scottish Theology: From John Knox to John McLeod Campbell* (Edinburgh: T&T Clark, 1996). Note, for example the trenchant critique of the latter work by Donald Macleod, "Dr T. F. Torrance and Scottish Theology: A Review Article," in *Evangelical Quarterly*, 72/1 (2000), pp. 57-72. The Torrances' problematic readings of the Reformed tradition continue to carry over into the historiography, including some of the essays identified in this volume, notably, Evans, *Imputation and Impartation*; so also is the Torrances' argumentation uncritically absorbed via Rolston's work on the Westminster Confession by Partee, *Theology of John Calvin*, pp. 17-18; cf. Holmes Rolston III, *John Calvin versus the Westminster Confession* (Richmond: John Knox, 1972).
70. As in Partee, *Theology of John Calvin*, pp. 3, 4, 25, 27; Canlis, "Calvin, Osiander, and Participation in God," pp. 177-184; Evans, *Imputation and Impartation*, pp. 57-83, 258-267, et passim; and note Richard B. Gaffin, *The Centrality of the Resurrection: A Study in Pauline Soteriology* (Grand Rapids: Baker, 1978), pp. 137-141, in particular, p. 141 n11; idem, "A Response to John Fesko's Review," *Ordained Servant*, 18 (2009), pp. 105-106; and idem, "Biblical Theology and the Westminster Standards," *Westminster Theological Journal*, 65 (2003), pp. 173, 176-177.
71. See Muller, *After Calvin*, pp. 78-80; and *PRRD*, I, pp. 123-146, 388-405.

as part of a reaction against a waning Protestant scholasticism.[72] The Protestant scholastics evidence a view of the relationship of revelation and reason that consistently identified revelation as foundational and reason as a tool in discourse and argumentation.[73] There is, moreover, a significant older discussion of the various relationships between revelation and reason in the history of theology and philosophy that have made much the same point with respect to medieval scholasticism.[74] Furthermore, there is a consistent recognition of the differences between the traditional more or less Christian Aristotelian philosophies of the seventeenth century and the new rationalisms in major recent histories of philosophy,[75] and there are recent studies of Reformed orthodoxy that have also drawn the conclusion of a traditional balance of faith and reason rather than a form of rationalism in the work of thinkers like Beza and Owen.[76]

The approach to the problem of describing and analyzing post-Reformation Protestantism that emerges from application of these several theses or premises, moreover, respects both the variety of views that inhabit the developing Reformed tradition and the rather varied relationships that can be identified between Protestant thought in the era of the Reformation and Protestant thought in the era of orthodoxy, particularly as focus shifts from one theological issue to another and as contexts and debates alter from one era to another. In fact, the language of continuity and discontinuity or of continuity understood in terms of development, elaboration, and modification of approaches in the light of altered contexts appears here not so much as the primary focus of investigation as a counter to the rather simplistic game of radical discontinuity proposed not only by the "Calvin against the Calvinists" school of thought but by proponents of a radical discontinuity between medieval scholastic theology and the theology of the Reformers. Thus, the issue is not a simple matter of identifying or claiming continuity or discontinuity between the views of one thinker and the views of another—rather, it is a matter of identifying both the place of a particular thinker in his own context and in relation to various trajectories or traditions of thought.[77] These trajectories or traditions, moreover,

---

72. E.g., Amand Saintes, *A Critical History of Rationalism in Germany, from Its Origin to the Present Time* (London: Simpkin, Marshall, 1849), pp. 90-91; John Fletcher Hurst, *History of Rationalism*, rev. ed. (New York: Eaton & Mains, 1901), pp. 336, 339, 346-347, 349.

73. See Muller, *Post-Reformation Reformed Dogmatics*, I, pp. 388-405.

74. E.g., Etienne Gilson, *Reason and Revelation in the Middle Ages* (New York: Scribner, 1938).

75. E.g., Frederick Copleston, *A History of Philosophy*, 9 vols. (Westminster, Md.: Newman Press, 1946-1974; repr. Garden City: Image Books, 1985), IV, pp. 1-33; Michael Ayers, "Theories of Knowledge and Belief," in *The Cambridge History of Seventeenth-Century Philosophy*, ed. Daniel Garber and Michael Ayers, 2 vols. (Cambridge: Cambridge University Press, 1998), II, pp. 1003-1049.

76. Jeffrey Mallinson, *Faith, Reason, and Revelation in Theodore Beza, 1519-1605* (Oxford: Oxford University Press, 2003); and Sebastian Rehnman, *Divine Discourse: The Theological Methodology of John Owen* (Grand Rapids: Baker, 2002), pp. 109-128.

77. See Carl R. Trueman, "The Reception of Calvin: Historical Considerations," *Church History and Religious Culture*, 91/1-2 (2011), pp. 19-27.

embody complex patterns of reception and use involving exegesis, formulae, and arguments drawn out of patristic and medieval backgrounds, as well as arguments and formulations either mediated through or derived from the Reformation-era debates.

To make the point in another way, the identification of differences between Calvin's formulations of a doctrinal argument and the formulations offered by any number of later Reformed writers does not substantially alter the argument for reassessment any more than the discovery of citations of Calvin's definitions as authoritative for Reformed thought in the latter quarter of the seventeenth century would substantiate it. The language of "continuity and discontinuity" applies, as a kind of shorthand, to the description of broader trajectories of argumentation within what in its medieval manifestation can be loosely called the tradition of Augustinian soteriology and in its Reformation and post-Reformation manifestation can be identified as the developing Reformed tradition. Thus, in rejecting a "Calvin against the Calvinists" approach, the thesis does not attempt to replace that approach with an equally flawed "Calvin for the Calvinists" theory—because, in short, it neither identifies Calvin as the founder or sole codifier of the Reformed tradition nor concedes to the identification of the Reformed tradition as "Calvinist" in a restrictive sense of the term.

One of the historical premises of the reassessment of Reformed orthodoxy is that Calvin did not invent the Reformed tradition and was not its sole second-generation codifier. Specifically, Calvin's work ought to be understood as a development of a Reformed tradition that began with such Reformers as Zwingli, Bucer, and Oecolampadius and, as such, represents one contribution, albeit a significant one, among others made by thinkers of Calvin's generation (e.g., Bullinger, Vermigli, Viret, Musculus, Hyperius, à Lasco) toward the confessional and dogmatic codification of a tradition. This is, moreover, a historical conclusion resting on examinations of patterns and trajectories of Reformed thought, specifically on the reception of the thought of the Reformers of the first part of the sixteenth century by later generations of Reformed writers—as opposed to the dogmatic identification of Calvin as the founder and norm of the Reformed tradition.[78] It is a simple historical datum that Calvin was neither the founder nor the sole continuator of the Reformed tradition—the witness of Calvin's correspondence with other Reformers bears out this point, and there are numerous instances in the development of that tradition, whether in Calvin's own time or among the later writers, in which Calvin's contribution was far from definitive.[79]

One can ahistorically pose Calvin against the Calvinists, claiming for him a normative status that was not accorded him either in his own time or in the later

---

78. Contra, e.g., Partee, *Theology of John Calvin*, pp. 25-26.

79. See my comments in "Demoting Calvin? The Issue of Calvin and the Reformed Tradition," pp. 3-17.

sixteenth and the seventeenth centuries and setting aside the broad continuities of
basic doctrine within an identifiable confessional tradition—all for the sake of
establishing an alternative narrative that leads directly from Calvin to the twentieth
or twenty-first century—an approach quite clearly adopted by T. F. Torrance.[80] One
can similarly either discount or selectively reappropriate the scholastic background
of and scholastic elements in Calvin's thought, and likewise ignore both the presence
of numerous nonscholastic works of theology written by the Reformed of the
seventeenth century and the relevant point that although method does have an
impact on content it does not have either the kind of impact or force the kind of
conclusions that the were hypothesized by the Calvin against the Calvinists school
of thought. And having thus abridged and reconstituted the historical narrative, one
can rather rigidly and ahistorically pose Calvin's theology against the scholastic
models of the seventeenth century, and continue to claim without any significant
documentation that the distinction between scholastic method and the orthodox
doctrine is unsuitable and that, given their scholasticism, the doctrines and doctrinal
emphases of later Reformed writers must be substantially different from Calvin's—all
in the name of retrieving the purity or balance of Calvin's theology for present-day
use.

The reassessment of Calvin and the Reformed tradition has recognized that
differences in formulation that can be identified among Calvin and his
contemporaries play out into the later history of Reformed thought and that in each
set of issues characteristic of the developing Reformed tradition, particularly debated
issues such as infra- and supralapsarianism and hypothetical universalism, there are
not only differences among the theologians of the era but also differences, generated
by altered contexts and new debates, between the formulations of the era of the
Reformation and the various eras identifiable in the trajectory of later Reformed
thought.

Similarly, the reassessment has also argued that there is an identifiable Reformed
tradition that established relative confessional boundaries in the era of what can be
called the second-generation Reformers and then proceeded to debate those
boundaries, sometimes solidifying, sometimes leaving them more or less vague during
the eras of orthodoxy. Once the broader trajectories of argument and their various
representatives within the Reformed tradition have been identified, whether on
exegetical, doctrinal, polemical, or philosophical matters, there will be different
patterns of reception and development, different continuities and discontinuities, to
be observed on different topics and issues. The developments previously traced out

80. Thus, e.g., Thomas F. Torrance, "Knowledge of God and Speech about Him according to
John Calvin," in *Theology in Reconstruction* (Grand Rapids: Eerdmans, 1966), p. 76; idem, *The School
of Faith: The Catechisms of the Reformed Church* (New York: Harper, 1959), pp. lxx-lxxix; and idem,
"Karl Barth and the Latin Heresy," *Scottish Journal of Theology*, 39 (1986), pp. 461-482; and see my
critique of Torrance in "The Barth Legacy: New Athanasius or Origen Redivivus? A Response to T.
F. Torrance," *The Thomist*, 54/4 (October, 1990), pp. 673-704.

with reference to issues in the theological prolegomena, the interpretation and doctrinal understanding of Scripture, and the doctrines of divine essence, attributes, and Trinity, all evidence rather different trajectories—and all also evidence significant variety in formulation, with some aspects of their argumentation having affinities with Calvin's, some with Bullinger's, some with Vermigli's views, with other aspects of their argumentation reflecting receptions of lines of argumentation found in the older theological and philosophical tradition, some mediated through the thought of the Reformers, some not.

Reassessment, then, has never coalesced around a simple issue of continuity or discontinuity between Calvin and later "Calvinists." That, as a matter of fact, has been the underlying issue argued by the "Calvin against the Calvinists" school, usually on the grounds that Theodore Beza "distorted" the balance of Calvin's theology. Calvin supplies the norm for the whole tradition, Beza distorts "Calvin's theology," producing a predestinarian system or predestinarian metaphysic that was then inherited by all of the "Calvinists" who, unfortunately, reproduced Beza's theology and not Calvin's.[81] The villain can, of course, equally well be identified as Zanchi, much to the same result.[82] Indeed, the "Calvin against the Calvinists" theory is a radical discontinuity theory grounded in the assumption that sixteenth- and seventeenth-century theologies, like modern theological systems, coalesce or cohere around a central dogma or central motif, and that the later Reformed tradition failed to accept Calvin's own central dogma—whether understood as "christocentricity" or, more recently, "union with Christ."[83]

The argument for continuities within a developing and variegated Reformed tradition is not at all a simple reversal of this "Calvin against the Calvinists" theory. Over against its claims, the newer approach has argued against single central dogmas in favor of a *locus* method characterized by a series of relatively independent doctrinal topics comprising a "body" of theology or divinity, as it has also argued against application of anachronistic notions of "system" and the interpretation of Calvin's thought or the thought of any other early modern theologian through the

---

81. Thus, the emblematic essay of the school: Hall, "Calvin Against the Calvinists"; so too, Johannes Dantine, "Das christologische Problem in Rahmen der Prädestinationslehre von Theodor Beza," *Zeitschrift für Kirchengeschichte*, 77 (1966), pp. 81-96; and idem, "Les Tabelles sur la doctrine de la prédestination par Théodore de Bèze," *Revue de théologie et de philosophie*, 16 (1966), pp. 365-377; Walter Kickel, *Vernunft und Offenbarung bei Theodor Beza* (Neukirchen: Neukirchner Verlag, 1967); R. T. Kendall, *Calvin and English Calvinism to 1649* (New York: Oxford University Press, 1979); and cf. Armstrong, *Calvinism and the Amyraut Heresy*, pp. 129-132.

82. Otto Gründler, *Die Gotteslehre Girolami Zanchis und ihre Bedeutung für seine Lehre von der Prädestination* (Neukirchen: Neukirchner Verlag, 1965); also idem, "The Influence of Thomas Aquinas upon the Theology of Girolamo Zanchi," in *Studies in Medieval Culture*, ed. J. R. Sommerfeldt (Kalamazoo: Western Michigan University Press, 1964), pp. 102-117.

83. The latter being proposed in Partee, "Calvin's Central Dogma Again," pp. 191-200; and idem, *Theology of John Calvin*, pp. 3, 4, 25, 27, 40-41, et passim. On the significant presence of the doctrine of union with Christ in later Reformed theology, see below, chapter 7.

grid of a superimposed notion of coherence nowhere indicated in the documents. There was no shifting from one central dogma to another because there was no central dogma in the first place.

In addition, my own argumentation has consistently avoided use of the term "Calvinist," on the ground that the term itself biases the case: the later Reformed writers did not identify themselves as Calvinists or ever claim to be the followers of *Calvinus solus*. Indeed, they were wary of identifying any theologian as the founder, author, or primary leader of the Reformed faith.[84] The Reformed tradition of the later sixteenth and seventeenth centuries, in other words, never made the claim that it was bound to Calvin's theology as a dogmatic norm: it claimed to be a confessional movement grounded in the work of a substantial group of sixteenth-century Reformers of the first and second generations of the Reform and identified not according to the standards of a particular volume of theological instruction, whether Calvin's *Institutes* or Bullinger's *Decades*, or some other document of the era, but by a loosely related set of national and regional confessions and catechisms. That confessional understanding, moreover, given the very nature of confessions as broad statements of doctrine purposely lacking many of the niceties of detailed theological systems, assumed a variety of results in exegesis and a variety of formulations in dogmatic or doctrinal treatises. One of the fundamental elements of the argument, from the very beginning, was the traditionary context, the relative breadth of what must be identified as Reformed (rather than Calvinist), and the corresponding breadth as well as limit of the confessional boundaries that were identified by the Reformers (primarily those of the second generation) and further argued by later generations of Protestant thinkers.

The character and direction of the reassessment can also be illustrated with reference to the later Reformed developments of infra- and supralapsarianism, of finely nuanced discussion of free choice, and of hypothetical universalism. On the first of these issues, the question of infra- and supralapsarianism, given that the debates of the seventeenth century concerned the very specific identification of the objects of divine elective and reprobative willing and involved questions of the ordering of priorities in the eternal divine decree, there is very little in the way of precise precedent for the detail of the seventeenth-century formulations in the thought of the Reformers of the first and second generations, and not much more in the writings of the first group of major early orthodoxy writers like Ursinus, Olevianus, Beza, and Zanchi. Given, of course, the presence of a fairly consistent refrain concerning the election of some out of the "condemned mass" of humanity in the works of most earlier Reformed theologians, there is major precedent for the specifically infralapsarian formulae of the later writers, even though this usage was

---

84. Thus, e.g., Andreas Rivetus, *Catholicus Orthodoxus, oppositus catholico papistae* (Leiden: Abraham Commelin, 1630), p. 5; Pierre DuMoulin, *Esclaircissement des controverses salmuriennes* (Leiden: Jean Maire, 1648), pp. 231-232; Jean Claude, *Défense de la Reformation contre le livre intitulé Préjugez légitimes contre les calvinistes*, 4th ed. (Paris: L.-R. Delay, 1844), pp. 210-211.

not accompanied by questions concerning the ordering of the decree with reference to election and reprobation, the creation, or the fall. There is, perhaps, also some indication of later Reformed arguments in the disagreement between Calvin and Bullinger on the inclusion of the fall in the divine decree—albeit, again, without any indication of order.

On the second of these issues, a significant reassessment of early modern Reformed thought has quite clearly shown Calvin to have had relatively little impact on later formulation, given that his rather pointed argumentation was directed only toward the issue of human inability in sin and not to the larger question of human freedom.[85] The recent scholarship has demonstrated medieval roots, both Thomistic and Scotistic, to the Reformed scholastic discussion and has identified lines of development running through thinkers like Vermigli and Zanchi, to later Reformed thinkers such as Junius, Gomarus, Voetius, and Turretin—the first three being supralapsarians. What comes as a surprise to proponents of the "Calvin against the Calvinists" school of thought is that it is not Calvin but the later tradition, including the supralapsarian thinkers, that offers a way to argue a gracious predestination and salvation by grace alone and also, at the same time, avoid determinism and argue the case for human free choice and human responsibility, points that Calvin himself arguably affirmed but did not formulate with great clarity.

The issue of hypothetical universalism and limited atonement also offers a highly useful example of the direction of my own argumentation as distinct from either a "Calvin against the Calvinists" or a "Calvin for the Calvinists" perspective. A sizeable body of literature has interpreted Calvin as teaching "limited atonement" or "particular redemption" in accord with later "Calvinists" like William Perkins, Pierre DuMoulin, or Francis Turretin and has, as a result, argued continuity between Calvin and the "Calvinists." An equally sizeable body of literature has claimed the opposite, interpreting Calvin as teaching "unlimited atonement" or "universal redemption," thereby associating his theology (typically) with that of Moïse Amyraut, and as a consequence arguing a discontinuity between "Calvin and the Calvinists."[86] If the terms "limited" and "universal atonement" are rather problematic and unrepresentative of the issues involved in the debate, the term "hypothetical universalism" must also be qualified, albeit for different reasons. It does not, after all, represent a fundamental departure from the formulae of the Synod of Dort and therefore can be subsumed under what had typically been called the Reformed doctrine of limited atonement.[87] The term itself, *universalismus hypotheticus*, may well

85. Thus, Willem J. van Asselt, J. Martijn Bac, and Roelf T. te Velde, trans. and eds., *Reformed Thought on Freedom: The Concept of Free Choice in the History of Early-Modern Reformed Theology* (Grand Rapids: Baker, 2010).

86. See the extensive literature cited below, chapter 3.

87. Alexander Schweizer, "Moses Amyraldus: Versuch einer Synthese des Universalismus und des Partikularismus," *Theologische Jahrbücher*, 11 (1852), pp. 41-101, 155-207, argued that Amyraut had retained the orthodox doctrine of a particularistic redemption but had added a dimension of

be of somewhat later origin than the debates that extended from around the time of Dort into the mid-seventeenth century.[88] The seventeenth-century debate, moreover, was not over hypothetical universalism *per se* but over the issue of universal grace (*gratia universalis*) as advocated by some of the proponents of hypothetical universalism, notably followers of John Cameron and Moïse Amyraut. Unlike "limited atonement," the term "hypothetical universalism" does relatively accurately reference the question of the divine intention underlying the infinite merit of Christ's death, albeit covering a series of rather different definitions.[89]

Whereas the issue of a positive relationship between Calvin's doctrine of the work of Christ and Amyraut's hypothetical universalism is fundamental to much of the "Calvin against the Calvinists" thesis, just as significant discontinuity is intrinsic to the alternative "Calvin for the Calvinists" narrative, the reassessment of developing Reformed thought as a variegated tradition does not rest on either of these resolutions of the question.[90] As in the case of the question of infra- and supralapsarianism, there are elements of the theologies of Zwingli, Bucer, Calvin, Bullinger, Musculus, Vermigli, and others among the Reformers of the first and second generations that point toward the variety of formulations found in later Reformed theology just as they also fit within the boundaries of formulation that can be identified in the confessional and catechetical documents of the Reformation and that framed the debates of seventeenth-century Reformed orthodoxy. Given, moreover, the presence of various sixteenth- and seventeenth-century forms of hypothetical universalism *within* those confessional boundaries and the diversity of formulations among the Reformed orthodox themselves,[91] although there may be some merit in ascertaining in which direction on particular doctrinal issues Calvin's formulae point, it makes no difference to the basic contention of a continuity in the

---

"ideal" universalism (p. 50).

88. Cf. Schweizer, "Moses Amyraldus," p. 49; with Ernest Brette, *Du système de Moïse Amyraut désigné sou le nom d'universalisme hypothétique* (Montauban: Forestié Neveu et Ce., 1855), p. 15; and note the use of the term in Salomon Deyling, *Observationes miscellaneae, in quibus res varii argumenti ex theologia, historia et antiquitate sacra enodate tractantur* (Leipzig: Frid. Lancksius,1736), pp. 686-687;and Joachim Lange, *Gloria Christi et Christianismi apocalyptico-prophetica*, 2 vols. (Amsterdam: Romberg, 1740), II, *Appendix de gratia Dei universali*, p. 148, where the term appears as a descriptor of what Lange also calls *universalismus Amyraldiani*.

89. For the terminology of *gratia universalis*, see, e.g., Moïse Amyraut, *Specimen animadversionum in Exercitationes de gratia universali* (Saumur: Lesnier, 1648); and his opponent, Friedrich Spanheim, *Exercitationes de gratia universali. Accessere l. erotemata auctori proposita, & ab eodem decisa, cum mantissa c. anterotematum* (Leiden: J. Maire, 1646). Amyraut does write of *gratia universalis sub conditione*: see Amyrait, *Specimen animadversionum*, pp. 7-8

90. Note that the conclusions concerning this issue, drawn largely in terms of Christ's limited intercession, in Muller, *Christ and the Decree*, pp. 33-35 and p. 194, notes 130 and 137, do not include any judgment on the question of whether Calvin's view of Christ's sufficiency might conduce to the view that if all would believe, all would be saved, or whether it implies a prior hypothetically universal divine intention.

91. Cf. the argument presented in *PRRD*, I, pp. 73-81.

broader traditionary development whether his formulations point toward Amyraut or Turretin, Owen, Cocceius, or Voetius.

Just as it is fallacious to claim reductionistically that Amyraut's theology represents a uniquely Calvinian tradition, so also is it fallacious to argue (equally reductionistically) that theologians like Du Moulin, Owen, and Turretin followed out a uniquely Bezan trajectory—as if there were not both similarities and differences between the thought of each of these theologians, including Beza, and the thought of Calvin.[92] (Both Du Moulin and Turretin held infralapsarian definitions of predestination and Du Moulin held a form of hypothetical universalism.) If Calvin's own teaching is the sole index of "Calvinism," then all parties in the seventeenth-century controversy, whether Amyraldian or anti-Amyraldian, Cocceian or anti-Cocceian, represent a "modified Calvinism," given that none of these parties in the seventeenth-century debates stated precisely what Calvin had argued, that all debated their formulations in contexts rather different from Calvin's, and that virtually all were arguing points demanding a more finely grained definition than Calvin (or, for that matter, Beza) had ever offered.

An Overview of the Study

All of the essays that follow deal with the question of the nature and character of the early Reformed theological tradition and specifically with the position of Calvin in that tradition. The focus of the essays is on the work of Christ and what came to be called (after the era of orthodoxy) the *ordo salutis*. Calvin remains, in the context of various antecedent and contemporary voices, one of the primary bearers of the Reformed tradition and one of the more significant second-generation formulators or codifiers on such issues as the satisfaction of Christ and the limit of its efficacy, union with Christ, and the various elements of the subordinate causality or administration of salvation. His contribution, however, cannot be properly understood apart from the contributions of others of his generation, like Vermigli, Bullinger, Musculus, and Viret—nor can the reception of his formulations be fully appreciated apart from an assessment of its place in the patterns of reception of the thought of other Reformers of his generation in broader Reformed tradition. The following chapters each offer a contribution to that understanding at the same time that they offer a portrait of patterns of argumentation belonging to that broader tradition of which Calvin was but a part.

"Was Calvin a Calvinist?" develops the methodological issue of "Calvinism," identified here in chapter 1 into a concrete discussion of the ways in which the question of Calvin and Calvinism has been misinterpreted, with specific reference to two points in the traditional "TULIP," total depravity and so-called limited

---

92. As, e.g., Alan Clifford, *Amyraut Affirmed, or Owenism a Caricature of Calvinism: A Reply to Ian Hamilton's 'Amyraldianism—Is It Modified Calvinism'* (Norwich: Charenton Reformed Publishing, 2004), p. 6.

atonement. The anachronistic nature of the acronym and of these two specific "points" is identified, and in particular the highly problematic identification of the limitation of the efficacy or application of Christ's work to the elect as "limited atonement" is registered. Christ's work and the nature of salvation serve as a topical focus of this chapter and remain the focus of the subsequent chapters. The essay examines various understandings of "Calvinism" and offers avenues of interpretation that reassess the relationship between Calvin and later writers in the Reformed tradition. The essay concludes that the terms "Calvinist" and "Calvinism" have contributed to a series of historical and dogmatic problems and ought to be set aside in favor of "Reformed" and "Reformed tradition."

The next three essays move forward with the theme of the limitation of the efficacy or application of Christ's work. "Calvin on Christ's Satisfaction and Its Efficacy: The Issue of 'Limited Atonement'" reassesses Calvin's understanding of Christ's work, in particular by critiquing the language of "limited atonement" and calling for a return to the actual vocabulary used by Calvin and in subsequent doctrinal debate among the Reformed. The essay also argues, largely by way of comparative references in the notes, a variety of nuancings of the exegetical backgrounds of the doctrine but also a broad agreement among Calvin and his contemporaries, none of whom precisely adumbrates the language or detail of later debates. Commentaries by predecessors and contemporaries of Calvin are referenced comparatively. The essays "A Tale of Two Wills? Calvin, Amyraut, and Du Moulin on Ezekiel 18:23" and "Davenant and Du Moulin: Variant Approaches to Hypothetical Universalism" address the later reception of and debate over understandings of Christ's work by soteriological particularists and hypothetical universalists in the seventeenth century. These two essays also address the question of later Reformed reception of and relation to Calvin's formulations.

It is not, of course, the intention of these chapters to indicate who among the seventeenth-century Reformed might be the purest Calvinian: that would only serve to validate the wrongheaded methodology of several generations of dogmatizing historians. These chapters attempt to look carefully at the actual vocabulary and at the distinctions made by early modern writers rather than to assimilate them to any particular dogmatic program. Accordingly, these chapters also serve to indicate that the aversion to a mis-defined scholasticism and its distinctions, characteristic of the work of Armstrong, Hall, Kendall, Clifford, and others, has prevented them from developing an accurate understanding of the early modern debates, given that the debates were consistently nuanced in ways incapable of being suitably handled by their anachronistic use of the term "limited atonement" and their stress on the exceedingly vague usage "for whom Christ died."

With the work of Christ as the foundational point of departure for Reformed discussion and debate over the application of salvation or *ordo salutis*, the next three chapters take up the issues of the exegetical roots of developing Reformed understandings of the order of salvation as a "golden chain" and the question of the causality of salvation, the relationship of union with Christ to the order of salvation, and the problem of assurance as related to the so-called practical syllogism. These chapters are interrelated and, in effect, deal with different aspects of the same broader topic, working through the issues with (hopefully) as little repetition as possible. They also reference questions raised in the current debates over union with Christ and the *ordo salutis* and demonstrate that much of the current attempt to cut Calvin adrift from the later Reformed tradition is fundamentally problematic.

The essay "The 'Golden Chain' and the Causality of Salvation" addresses the beginnings of what came to be called the order of salvation, or *ordo salutis*, in Protestant theology. The essay argues a close interrelationship between the exegesis of Scripture, in this case the text of Romans 8:28-30, and the development of doctrinal topics or *loci* in post-Reformation Reformed theology. The specific case of Romans 8:28-30, known in the era as the "chain" or "golden chain" of salvation, illustrates the interrelationship of exegetical argumentation with the beginnings of Reformed formulations concerning the order of causes of salvation. Taken in connection with other texts, such as Ephesians 1:4-11, and with issues arising from early Reformed understandings of grace and predestination, often in conflict with Roman and Lutheran understandings, the question of the causality of salvation demanded resolution. Examination of a series of Reformed theologians from Calvin, Bullinger, Musculus, and Vermigli to such later thinkers as Rennecherus, Perkins, and Bucanus reveals a developing tradition of interpretation in which a series of issues and conclusions were held in common and no single thinker stands as the primary formulator. Examination of this issue of causality illustrates, moreover, the way in which the exegetically-grounded *locus* method yielded interrelationships of doctrinal topics and subtopics without tending in the direction of the nineteenth-century central-dogma approach. These formulations, moreover, relate directly to the ways in which Reformed theologians argued the efficacy or application of Christ's work of satisfaction (the chapters 3, 4, and 5) and to the ways in which the Reformed understood the relationship of the ordering of salvation to the believer's union with Christ and, in view of their union to the issue of assurance of salvation and the practical syllogism (chapters 7 and 8).

Thus, "Union with Christ and the *Ordo Salutis*: Reflections on Developments in Early Modern Reformed Thought" continues this line of argument, with specific reference to several strands of modern scholarship in which the relationship of Calvin's teaching to the later Reformed tradition has been discussed. The essay clarifies the relationship of union with Christ to the early Reformed understanding of Romans chapter 8, taken as a whole, and therefore also to the exegetical development of the doctrine of union with Christ in relation to other elements of the order or economy of salvation. These doctrinal points are seen to be significantly interrelated, not only in the thought of Calvin, but also in the work of various contemporaries like Vermigli and Musculus; and the work of this early group of Reformed writers is seen as the beginning of a process of formulation that resulted in a somewhat varied doctrinal understanding of the economy of salvation in early Reformed orthodoxy. The conventional and rather trite "Calvin against the Calvinists" model, as well as the assumption that Calvin was the foundation and norm for the Reformed tradition, is shown to be both problematic and quite inapplicable to the actual historical case.

Finally, the essay on "Calvin, Beza, and the later Reformed on Assurance of Salvation and the 'Practical Syllogism'" takes up the question of the *syllogismus practicus*, or practical syllogism, noting in particular how the work of Christ, union with Christ, and elements of the order of salvation like calling and sanctification are drawn into Reformed thought on the nature of assurance of salvation. Much of the extant scholarship on the practical syllogism has tended to examine the topic in isolation from union with Christ and the order of salvation and has, accordingly, often missed or misunderstood the fundamental rationale of the doctrine. Here I offer a partial reassessment of aspects of my own earlier work in *Christ and the Decree* and a further critique of the neo-orthodox reading of issues of assurance, christocentricity, and the so-called practical syllogism. The basic conclusion that Calvin did teach the outlines of the practical syllogism is now reinforced and shown to be related to the broader Reformed conversation and debate concerning the work of Christ and its application to believers in the economy of salvation.

2

Was Calvin a Calvinist?

Defining the Question: Varied Understandings of "Calvinism"

Answering the perennial question "Was Calvin a Calvinist?" is a rather complicated matter, given that the question itself is grounded in a series of modern misconceptions concerning the relationship of the Reformation to post-Reformation orthodoxy. I propose here to examine issues lurking behind the question and work through some ways of understanding the continuities, discontinuities, and developments that took place in Reformed thought on such topics as the divine decrees, predestination, and so-called limited atonement, with specific attention to the place of Calvin in the Reformed tradition of the sixteenth and seventeenth centuries.

Leaving aside for a moment the issue of the famous "TULIP," the basic question "Was Calvin a Calvinist?" taken as it stands, without further qualification, can be answered quite simply: Yes … No … Maybe … all depending on how one interprets the question. The answer must be mixed or indefinite because the question itself poses a significant series of problems. There are in fact several different understandings of the terms "Calvinist" and "Calvinism" that determine in part how one answers the question or, indeed, what one intends by asking the question in the first place. "Calvinist" has been used as a descriptor of Calvin's own position on a particular point, perhaps most typically of Calvin's doctrine of predestination. It has been used as a term for followers of Calvin—and it has been used as a term for the theology of the Reformed tradition in general. "Calvinism," similarly, has been used to indicate Calvin's own distinctive theological positions, sometimes the theology of Calvin's *Institutes*. It also is used to indicate the theology of Calvin's followers. More frequently, it has been used as a synonym for "Reformed" or for the "Reformed tradition."

"Calvinism" as Calvin's own position. If the first option is taken as the basis for the question, the answer is simply, "Yes, of course Calvin was a Calvinist"— "Calvinist" and "Calvinism" indicating the specific position of Calvin on various

51

theological, ecclesial, political, and even philosophical issues. This is perhaps the intention of the title of a work such as Henry Cole's translation of Calvin's various treatises on predestination, namely, *Calvin's Calvinism*. It is also the usage of writers like Peter Toon and Basil Hall, the latter going so far as to apply the term "Calvinism" restrictively to the purportedly perfectly "balanced" theology of Calvin's 1559 *Institutes*.[1] There are, however, a host of problems posed by this approach—not the least of which is that it (apparently intentionally) leaves Calvin as the only Calvinist.

Beyond that, this approach begs the question of what criterion has been applied to the *Institutes* of 1559 to arrive at the conclusion that it represents a perfectly balanced theology in contrast to the presumably less well-balanced theologies of Huldrych Zwingli, Johannes Oecolampadius, Martin Bucer, Heinrich Bullinger, Peter Martyr Vermigli, Wolfgang Musculus, Zacharias Ursinus, and a host of others usually identified, together with Calvin, as belonging to the Reformed tradition. Arguably, that criterion has been the personal theological preference of various proponents of the approach, and it has consisted in modern readings of the *Institutes*, out of its historical context, as if it were a prototype for some modern theological system—whether that of Friedrich Schleiermacher, Karl Barth, G. C. Berkouwer, or some other recent theologian. The purported balance, whether found in Calvin's understanding of predestination, or his so-called christocentrism, or his advocacy of the *unio mystica*, claims a coherent dogmatic center to Calvin's thought that cannot be found in the thought of his contemporaries—but which also (unfortunately for the proponents of this approach) is not actually found in Calvin's thought. The coherentist approach not only leaves Calvin the only Calvinist, it also portrays Calvin's Calvinism as proto-Schleiermacherianism, proto-Barthianism, or proto-Berkouwerianism (to coin a somewhat less than euphonic term).

Once the modern mythologies of coherence around neo-orthodox or other themes have been dissipated, a further problem emerges. The identification of Calvinism with Calvin's own distinctive doctrines encounters the extreme difficulty of actually finding distinctive doctrines in Calvin. This problem has been enhanced by the numerous books that present interpretations of such decontextualized constructs as "Calvin's doctrine of predestination," "Calvin's Christology," or "Calvin's doctrine of the Lord's Supper," as if Calvin actually proposed a highly unique doctrine. We need to remind ourselves that the one truly unique theologian who entered Geneva in the sixteenth century, Michael Servetus, did not exit Geneva alive. Unique or individualized doctrinal formulation was not Calvin's goal. If, for example, there is anything unique in his doctrine of predestination, it arose from the way in which he gathered elements from past thinkers in the tradition and blended

---

1. Peter Toon, *The Emergence of Hyper-Calvinism in English Nonconformity, 1689-1765* (London: The Olive Tree, 1967), p. 143; and Basil Hall, "Calvin against the Calvinists," in *John Calvin: A Collection of Distinguished Essays*, ed. Gervase Duffield (Grand Rapids: Eerdmans, 1966), pp. 19, 25-26.

them into his own formulation. But the fact is that his formulation is strikingly similar to those of Bucer, Viret, Musculus, and Vermigli. Even Bullinger's formulation, which differed on several distinct points, like the relation of Adam to the decree, has clear affinities with Calvin's teaching.[2] Likewise, there are some distinctive elements in Calvin's doctrine of the Lord's Supper—but much was drawn from Bucer and Melanchthon. If one were to strip out these commonalities and focus only on the truly distinctive elements, one would not have a theology remaining nor would one have a series of related motifs sufficient to the construction of a theology—and even if one attempted to do this, one would not have a theology of Calvin but rather a kind of dogmatic Julia Child concoction made from a pile of chopped-up ingredients, varying in taste from cook to cook. In other words, the identification of Calvinism with the unique theology of Calvin represents a fallacy.

There is a final, deeper problem with this approach as well. The question also assumes that the theological tradition in which both Calvin and the later thinkers who have been identified as Calvinists reside was rather exclusivistically founded on the theology of Calvin himself and that Calvin's theology—typically identified with Calvin's *Institutes* in the final edition of 1559—supplies the foundational index by which membership in that tradition ought to be assessed. This form of the question assumes that later Reformed theologians either intended to be or should have been precise followers of Calvin rather than also followers of Zwingli, Bucer, Oecolampadius, Bullinger, and others, and not merely followers of Calvin in general or Calvin of the tracts, treatises, commentaries, and sermons, nor the Calvin of the 1539, 1543, or 1550 *Institutes*, but the Calvin of the 1559 *Institutes*.[3] This form of the question is aided and abetted by the numerous books on Calvin's theology that are based solely or almost solely on the *Institutes* and that do not examine the thought of any of Calvin's predecessors or contemporaries: his thought becomes its own criterion for its assessment and, by extension, the sole guide to all that is Calvinistic.[4] The effect of this approach is so misguided and reductionisitc that it needs no extended rebuttal; it abstracts Calvin from himself by denying the importance of the larger portion of his work even as it abstracts him from his historical context and from the tradition in which he was a participant.

"Calvinism" as the approach of Calvin's "followers." If, however, by "Calvinist" one means a follower of Calvin and by "Calvinism," the theology of his followers, it should be clear that no one can be his own follower. Whereas the first option leaves Calvin as the only Calvinist, this option either prevents the identification of Calvin

---

2. Note the conclusions in Cornelis P. Venema, *Heinrich Bullinger and the Doctrine of Predestination: Author of "the Other Reformed Tradition"?* (Grand Rapids: Baker, 2002).

3. Hall, "Calvin Against the Calvinists," p. 19.

4. E.g., T. H. L. Parker, *Calvin: An Introduction to His Thought* (Louisville: Westminster/John Knox, 1995); Charles Partee, *The Theology of John Calvin* (Louisville: Westminster/John Knox, 2008).

as a Calvinist or, falling back on the kind of sentiments fueling the first option, judges the followers on the basis of a rather narrow norm constructed out of Calvin's theology. It should also be clear, inasmuch as those identified as followers were seldom, perhaps never, precise imitators, that by the very way in which the question has been posed, it is usually looking for a negative answer. To the extent that later so-called Calvinists were not intellectual clones, Calvin ought not to be identified with them—and to the extent that Calvin's thought ought to supply the norm for all later Reformed theology, those usually called Calvinists can be viewed as theologically problematic for not following him. Framed in this way, the question is, quite frankly, bogus. It decontextualizes both Calvin and the later Reformed writers, and it replaces historical analysis with dogmatic generalization, as will be seen when we examine a few specifics concerning trajectories of formulation of doctrines such as predestination and the satisfaction of Christ.

At a somewhat more complex level, the question assumes that "Calvinist" is an appellation that might have been happily accepted by Calvin himself and by pastors, theologians, and exegetes who belonged to the same theological trajectory or tradition as Calvin within, let us say, a hundred years after his death. That assumption is false on both counts. Calvin himself viewed the term "Calvinist" as an insult and thought of his own theology as an expression of catholic truth. It has been quite well documented that the terms "Calvinism" and "Calvinist" arose among the opponents of Calvin, notably among Lutheran critics of Calvin's work on the doctrine of the Lord's Supper, and the beginning of the usage marks not a distinct tradition flowing from Calvin but the identification of a rift among the Reformers, who had initially understood themselves as "evangelical" and only after the middle of the sixteenth century began consciously to separate themselves into distinct confessional groups, namely, Lutheran and Reformed.[5] Later theologians in the tradition of which Calvin was a part typically identified themselves as Reformed Catholics, members and teachers in the reformed and therefore true Catholic Church, as distinct from the un-reformed Roman branch of the catholic or universal church.[6] When the noted exegete and theologian Andreas Rivetus (1573-1654) defended elements of Calvin's exegesis against various detractors, he also took pains to indicate that Calvin was neither the *autor* or the *dux* of "our religion."[7] Such

---

5. Cf. John Calvin, *Clear explanation of sound doctrine concerning the true partaking of the flesh and blood of Christ in the holy supper, in order to dissipate the mists of Tileman Heshusius*, in *Selected Works of John Calvin: Tracts and Letters*, ed. Henry Beveridge and Jules Bonnet, 7 vols. (Grand Rapids: Baker, 1983), II, pp. 502, 510, 526, 563, with the comments in Brian Gerrish, *The Old Protestantism and the New: Essays on the Reformation Heritage* (Chicago: University of Chicago Press, 1982), pp. 27-48.

6. E.g., William Perkins, *A Reformed Catholike: or, A declaration shewing how neere we may come to the present Church of Rome in sundrie points of religion: and vvherein we must for euer depart from them*, in *The Whole Works of … Mr. William Perkins*, 3 vols. (London: John Legatt, 1631), vol. I.

7. Andreas Rivetus, *Catholicus Orthodoxus, oppositus catholico papistae* (Leiden: Abraham Commelin, 1630), p. 5.

comments, often connected with repudiation of the name "Calvinist," are common among seventeenth-century Reformed thinkers.[8] In 1595, when William Barrett attacked the teachings of Calvin, Vermigli, Beza, Zanchi, and Junius, he was rebuked, among other things, for calling these stalwarts of the faith by the "odious name" of "Calvinists."[9] Relative acceptance of the terms "Calvinist" and "Calvinism" among Reformed theologians is not characteristic of the rise of Reformed orthodoxy or of English Puritanism—rather it can be seen beginning in the later seventeenth century and becoming more or less characteristic in the decline of orthodoxy in the eighteenth century,[10] at a time when the Reformed tradition had undergone so many developments that identifying it as "Calvinist" rested less on its larger body of doctrine than on the affirmation of a few distinctive points, such as those ensconced in the famous TULIP, an acronym of questionable pedigree. In short, virtually none of the theologians whose thought is at issue in the question, "Was Calvin a Calvinist?" identified themselves in this way.

By extension, then, the question raises the issue of the identification of followers—and this, albeit perhaps a somewhat clearer way of posing the query, is a rather difficult issue to settle historically. Precisely what constitutes a follower? If to be a follower one must identify oneself as a follower, then there was probably only a single Calvinist in the century following Calvin's death, namely, Moïse Amyraut. In the debate over Amyraut's so-called hypothetical universalism, moreover, various of the theologians usually identified as "Calvinist" thought of Amyraut as departing significantly from the spirit of Calvin's theology, particularly at the point of his citing Calvin.[11] Of course, after the era of Reformed orthodoxy, in the eighteenth and nineteenth centuries, self-proclaimed "Calvinists" abound, typically so called because of their advocacy of one or another form of the doctrine of predestination, whether or not clearly rooted in Calvin's own formulations, and because of their opposition to so-called Arminians, so called because of their soteriological synergism, whether or not (usually not!) they actually followed Arminius' teachings.

---

8. E.g., Pierre Du Moulin, *Esclaircissement des controverses Salmuriennes* (Leiden: Jean Maire, 1648), pp. 231-232; Jean Claude, *Défense de la Reformation contre le livre intitulé Préjugez légitimes contre les calvinistes*, 4th ed. (Paris: L.-R. Delay, 1844), pp. 210-211; Pierre Jurieu, *Histoire du Calvinisme et celle du Papisme mises en parallèle: Ou apologie pour les Réformateurs, pour la Réformation, et pour les Réformés ... contre ... Maimbourg*, 3 vols., 2nd ed. based on the Rotterdam printing of 1683 (S.l.: s.n., 1823), I, pp. 417-418.

9. See John Strype, *The Life and Acts of John Whitgift, D.D.*, 3 vols. (Oxford: Clarendon Press, 1822), III, p. 318: "eos odioso nomine appellans Calvinistas."

10. See the discussion of this issue in Dewey D. Wallace, *Shapers of English Calvinism, 1660-1714* (New York: Oxford University Press, 2011), pp. 10-14; and note the insistence on retaining the term despite its problematic nature in Christoph Strohm, "Methodology in Discussion of Calvin and Calvinism," in *Calvinus Praeceptor Ecclesiae*, ed. Herman J. Selderhuis, Papers of the International Congress on Calvin Research, 2002 (Geneva: Librairie Droz, 2004), p. 68.

11. Cf. Du Moulin, *Esclaircissement*, IX.i (p. 232); and see below, chapter 4, on the differences between Calvin's meaning and Amyraut's presentation of Calvin.

As a matter of fact, the vast majority of sixteenth- and seventeenth-century thinkers we identify as Calvinists did not identify themselves as followers of Calvin. Of course, founders of the Reformed tradition like Zwingli, Bucer, Oecolampadius, and Farel, all of whom belonged to a generation prior to Calvin's, would hardly have thought of themselves as followers of one of their younger protegés, no matter how talented. Neither did other Reformed writers closer in age to Calvin—among them Wolfgang Musculus, Peter Martyr Vermigli, Heinrich Bullinger, and Johannes à Lasco—view themselves as his followers or, indeed, as playing second fiddle to the virtuoso. Nor can we find Reformed writers of the next several generations— Zacharias Ursinus, Caspar Olevianus, Jerome Zanchi, Amandus Polanus, or even Calvin's own successor, Theodore Beza—claiming to be followers of Calvin or, indeed, "Calvinists."

If the issue of self-identification is set aside, there remains the problem of identifying followers in the context of a fairly broad tradition the content and character of which was not founded on an intention to follow in the footsteps of a single person and that did not, until more than a century and a half had passed, accept the name "Calvinist" as a useful designation. Should a theologian almost a decade older than Calvin, trained in the Universities of Padua and Bologna, who subsequently taught in Strasbourg, Oxford, and Zürich, and who, for all his general agreement with Calvin, did not speak of a double decree of predestination but rather identified predestination with election, who drew more positively on medieval scholastics (notably Thomas Aquinas and Gregory of Rimini) than Calvin, who did not view himself as a follower of Calvin, and whose abilities in Hebrew extended far beyond Calvin's be called a Calvinist? The theologian in question is Peter Martyr Vermigli, whose work was quite influential in the development of post-Reformation Reformed theology—and who, despite his own identity, has often been called a Calvinist.[12] Or, further, should a theologian at Cambridge University in the 1590s, who specifically identified himself as "Reformed" (not as Calvinist), who upheld episcopacy, whose teaching occupies a good deal of common ground with Calvin's doctrinal formulations but which also has affinities for the thought of Vermigli, Zanchi, Beza, Ursinus, and Olevianus, and also evidences some characteristics of later Reformed thought not found in the work of these predecessors, like a distinction between the covenant of works and the covenant of grace—should he be called a Calvinist? The theologian is William Perkins, often identified in the literature as a Calvinist and then, given the differences between his thought and Calvin's, used as a prime example in the attempt to pit "Calvin against the Calvinists." The list could be extended indefinitely.

One might, then, rephrase the question a bit and ask, "Were the Calvinists really Calvinists?" or, more pointedly, "Did the Calvinists ever intend to be Calvinists?" If

---

12. On Vermigli, see Frank A. James III, *Peter Martyr Vermigli and Predestination: The Augustinian Inheritance of an Italian Reformer* (Oxford: Clarendon Press, 1998).

a "Calvinist" is taken to mean an intentional follower of Calvin or, indeed, an imitator or duplicator of Calvin's thought, the answer is simple. No, there were no Calvinists—unless, of course, we fall back into the first-noted pattern of definition and make Calvin the only one.

"Calvinism" as a name for the Reformed tradition. There is, of course, third, another usage of the terms "Calvinist" and "Calvinism"—namely, as references to thinkers and teachings associated with the Reformed tradition. This is the more common usage, as evidenced in the works of historians like Perry Miller, John T. McNeill, and more recently Philip Benedict.[13] Framed in this way, the questions become "Was Calvin Reformed?" and "Were other writers who belonged to the same confessional trajectory as Calvin, whether or not they count as his followers, also Reformed?" On might think that the answers to these alternative questions are quite simple: namely, "Yes." But these questions too are complicated by the way in which one identifies what is properly Reformed—specifically by the way in which Reformed, used as a synonym of "Calvinist," is defined as more or less in agreement with Calvin's theology, whether as understood in its full extent and diversity or as resident in the 1559 *Institutes*. If the question is now rephrased with better attention to historical contexts and documents, it might read, "What is the nature and, potentially the source, of the continuities and discontinuities, similarities and differences that exist between the thought of John Calvin and later thinkers who stand within the boundaries of Reformed confessionality?"—which brings us to a series of theological considerations.

Theological Considerations: Calvin in Relation to the Later Reformed

The question "Was Calvin a Calvinist?" has, of course, been debated largely in terms of a series of theological issues, perhaps most notably predestination and so-called limited atonement, two of the "points" associated with the famous TULIP, plus the issue of covenant. When posed in these forms, the question is typically answered in the negative and usually on highly questionable grounds. For example, Calvin's views on predestination have been contrasted with later Reformed understandings of the doctrine on several grounds: Calvin purportedly "moved" predestination out of relation to the doctrine of God to a kinder, gentler place in the *Institutes*—the Calvinists reverted to the practice of placing the doctrine in proximity to the doctrine of God and created thereby a system of theology resting on

---

13. Perry Miller, *The New England Mind: The Seventeenth Century* (New York: Macmillan, 1939; repr. Boston: Beacon Press, 1961), pp. 93-97; John T. McNeill, *The History and Character of Calvinism* (New York: Oxford University Press, 1954), pp. vii-viii, et passim; Philip Benedict, *Christ's Churches Purely Reformed: A Social History of Calvinism* (New Haven: Yale University Press, 2002), pp. xxii-xxiii.

predestination and metaphysics.[14] Further, Calvin's theology was not so much predestinarian as "christocentric"—and the later Calvinists lost this christocentricity.[15] Or, by way of confusing issues of method and content, Calvin was a humanist, indeed, a humanist imbued with a covenantal approach to theology—the later Calvinists were predestinarian and scholastic, having lost the humanistic inclinations of the founder of the movement.[16] Or, finally, given the christocentric orientation of Calvin's theology, his views on the work of Christ tended toward "unlimited atonement" in contrast to the "rigid" view of "limited atonement" that resulted from later Calvinist predestinarianism.[17] In sum, Calvin taught a finely balanced, christocentric theology, whereas the Calvinists focused their theology on the divine decrees and produced the rigid, scholastic system of "five points" summarized by the acrostic TULIP.

The problem of TULIP. By way of addressing these issues, we should note first and foremost the problem of TULIP itself—an acrostic that has caused much trouble for the Reformed tradition and has contributed greatly to the confusion about Calvin and Calvinism. It is really quite odd and ahistorical to associate a particular document written in the Netherlands in 1618-1619 with the whole of Calvinism and then to reduce its meaning to TULIP. The Canons of Dort, after all, were never intended as a summary statement of Reformed theology, nor were they understood as a new confession for the Reformed churches. Rather, they stood as an interpretive codicil to the primary confessional documents of the Dutch Reformed churches, namely, the Belgic Confession and the Heidelberg Catechism, refuting the five articles of the Remonstrants.

It is perhaps worth noting that the Dutch word is not "tulip" but "tulp." "Tulip" isn't Dutch—sometimes I wonder whether Arminius was just trying to correct someone's spelling when he was accused of omitting that "i" for irresistible grace. More seriously, there is no historical association between the acrostic TULIP and the Canons of Dort. As far as we know, both the acrostic and the associated usage of "five points of Calvinism" are of Anglo-American origin and do not date back before the nineteenth century.[18] It is remarkable how quickly bad ideas catch on. When,

---

14. Hall, "Calvin against the Calvinists," pp. 19-37.

15. E.g., Walter Kickel, *Vernunft und Offenbarung bei Theodor Beza* (Neukirchen: Neukirchner Verlag, 1967).

16. Thus, Brian G. Armstrong, *Calvinism and the Amyraut Heresy: Protestant Scholasticism and Humanism in Seventeenth-Century France* (Madison: University of Wisconsin Press, 1969).

17. As, e.g., in M. Charles Bell, "Was Calvin a Calvinist?," *Scottish Journal of Theology*, 36/4 (1983), pp. 535-540; idem, "Calvin and the Extent of Atonement," *Evangelical Quarterly*, 55 (April, 1983), pp. 115-123; James B. Torrance, "The Incarnation and Limited Atonement," *Scottish Bulletin of Evangelical Theology*, 2 (1984), pp. 32-40; Kevin Dixon Kennedy, *Union with Christ and the Extent of the Atonement* (New York: Peter Lang, 2002).

18. See Ken Stewart, "The Points of Calvinism: Retrospect and Prospect," *Scottish Bulletin of Evangelical Theology*, 26/2 (2008), pp. 187-203. There are, of course, many early references to the

therefore, the question of Calvin's relationship to Calvinism is reduced to this popular floral meditation—did Calvin teach TULIP?—any answer will be grounded on a misrepresentation. Calvin himself certainly never thought of this model, but neither did later so-called Calvinists. Or, to make the point in another way, Calvin and his fellow Reformers held to doctrines that stand in clear continuity with the Canons of Dort, but neither Calvin nor his fellow Reformers, nor the authors of the canons, would have reduced their confessional position to TULIP.

In fact, it is quite remarkable how little the acrostic has to do with Calvin or Calvinism, as is most evident in the cases of the "T" and the "L." Calvin's references to the utter deformity or depravity of the human will and human abilities were directed against forms of synergism or Semi-Pelagianism and refer to the pervasiveness of sin—reducing this language to the slogan "total depravity" endangers the argument.[19] Calvin certainly never spoke of "limited atonement." Neither of these terms appears in the Canons of Dort, nor is either one of these terms characteristic of the language of Reformed or Calvinistic orthodoxy in the seventeenth century. Like TULIP itself, the terms are Anglo-American creations of fairly recent vintage.

Whereas Calvin himself used phrases like "totally depraved" or "utterly perverse," such terminology does not appear in the Canons of Dort, which declare briefly that "all have sinned in Adam" and are therefore under the curse and destined for eternal death.[20] In other words, on the issue of the "T" in TULIP, the language of the Canons of Dort is more measured than that of Calvin. "Total depravity," at least as understood in colloquial English, is so utterly grizzly a concept as to apply only to the

---

"five points" or "five articles" in controversy between Reformed and Arminian: e.g., Peter Heylin, *Historia quinqu-articularis: or, A declaration of the judgement of the Western Churches, and more particularly of the Church of England, in the five controverted points, reproched in these last times by the name of Arminianism* (London: E.C. for Thomas Johnson, 1660); and Daniel Whitby, *A Discourse concerning I. The true Import of the Words Election and Reprobation ... II. The Extent of Christ's Redemption. III. The Grace of God ... IV. The Liberty of the Will ... V. The Perseverance or Defectibility of the Saints* (London, 1710; 2nd ed., corrected, London: Aaron Ward, 1735), often referenced as "Whitby on the Five Points" or "Five Arminian Points": note George Hill, *Heads of Lectures in Divinity* (St. Andrews: at the University Press, 1796), p. 78. Phrases like "five distinguishing points of Calvinism" also occur earlier, referencing the Canons of Dort without, however, specification of the points themselves: see, e.g. Daniel Neal, *The History of the Puritans and Non-conformists ... with an account of their principles* (London: for J. Buckland, et al., 1754), I, p. 502; Ferdinando Warner, *The Ecclesiastical History of England, to the Eighteenth Century*, 2 vols. (London: s.n., 1756-1757), II, p. 509; note also that the editor of Daniel Waterland's sermons identified justification by faith alone as one of the "five points of Calvinism": see Waterland, *Sermons on Several Important Subjects of Religion and Morality*, preface by Joseph Clarke, 2 vols. (London: for W. Innys, 1742), I, p. xviii.

19. Note the language in John Calvin, *The Necessity of Reforming the Church*, in *Selected Works of John Calvin: Tracts and Letters*, ed. Henry Beveridge and Jules Bonnet, 7 vols. (Grand Rapids: Baker, 1983), I, pp. 133-134; and, in ibid., III, pp. 108-109.

20. Canons of Dort, i.1, in Philip Schaff, *The Creeds of Christendom, with a History and Critical Notes*, 6th ed., 3 vols. (New York: Harper and Row, 1931), III, p. 551.

theology of the Lutheran, Matthias Flacius Illyricus, who had an almost dualistic understanding of human nature before and after the fall, arguing the utter replacement of the *imago Dei* with the *imago Satanae* and indicating that the very substance of fallen humanity was sin. Neither Calvin not later Reformed thinkers went in this direction, and to the credit of the Lutherans, they repudiated this kind of language in the Formula of Concord. What was actually at issue, obscured by the imposition of the term "total depravity" on the early modern sources, is not the utter absence of any sort of goodness but the inability to save oneself from sin. Calvin's usage of *pravitas* and like terms, indicating perversity, viciousness, crookedness, or depravity of character was, thus, not intended to deny human ability outwardly to obey the law, but rather to indicate a pervasive inward distortion of character tainting all human acts and rendering the person utterly unworthy before God. On this basic theological point there is, moreover, clear continuity between Calvin's theology and later Reformed thought. Arguably, the Canons of Dort and the Reformed orthodox theologians who followed and supported its formulae, offer a clearer, more nuanced and, indeed, more moderate understanding of fallen human nature than what can be found in Calvin's writings.

The question of the "L" in TULIP, of "limited" versus "universal atonement," also looms large in the debate over whether Calvin was a Calvinist. This question, too, arises out of a series of modern confusions, rooted, it seems to me, in the application of a highly vague and anachronistic language to a sixteenth- and seventeenth-century issue. Simply stated, neither Calvin, nor Beza, nor the Canons of Dort, nor any of the orthodox Reformed thinkers of the sixteenth and seventeenth centuries mention limited atonement—and insofar as they did not mention it, they hardly could have taught the doctrine. (Atonement, after all, is an English term, and nearly all of this older theology was written in Latin.) To make the point a bit less bluntly and with more attention to the historical materials, the question debated in the sixteenth and seventeenth centuries concerned the meaning of those biblical passages in which Christ is said to have paid a ransom for all or God is said to will the salvation of all or of the whole world, given the large number of biblical passages that indicate a limitation of salvation to some, namely, to the elect or believers. This is an old question, belonging to the patristic and medieval church as well as to the early modern Reformed and, since the time of Peter Lombard, had been discussed in terms of the sufficiency and efficiency of Christ's satisfaction in relation to the universality of the preaching of redemption.

The question at issue between Calvin and the later Reformed does not entail any debate over the value or merit of Christ's death: virtually all were agreed that it was sufficient to pay the price for the sins of the whole world. Neither was the question at issue whether all human beings would actually be saved: all (including Arminius) agreed that this was not to be the case. To make the point another way, if "atonement" is taken to mean the value or sufficiency of Christ's death, only a very few theologians involved in the early modern debates taught limited atonement—

and if atonement is taken to mean the actual salvation accomplished in particular persons, then no one involved in those debates taught unlimited atonement (except perhaps the much-reviled Samuel Huber).

Historically, framed in language understandable in the sixteenth and seventeenth centuries, there were two questions to be answered. First, the question posed by Arminius and answered at Dort: given the sufficiency of Christ's death to pay the price for all sin, how ought one to understand the limitation of its efficacy to some? In Arminius' view, the efficacy was limited by the choice of some persons to believe, others not to believe, and predestination was grounded in a divine foreknowledge of the choice. In the view of the Synod of Dort, the efficacy was limited according to the assumption of salvation by grace alone, to God's elect. Calvin was quite clear on the point: the application or efficacy of Christ's death was limited to the elect. And in this conclusion there was also accord among the later Reformed theologians.

Second, there was the question implied in variations of formulation among sixteenth-century Reformed writers and explicitly argued in a series of seventeenth-century debates following the Synod of Dort, namely, whether the value of Christ's death was hypothetically universal given the infinite value or sufficiency of Christ's satisfaction.[21] More simply put, was the value of Christ's death such that it would be sufficient for all sin if God had so intended—or was the value of Christ's death such that if all would believe all would be saved? On this very specific question Calvin is, arguably, silent. He did not often mention the traditional sufficiency-efficiency formula, and he did not address the issue, posed by Amyraut, of a hypothetical or conditional decree of salvation for all who would believe, prior to the absolute decree to save the elect. He did frequently state, without further modification, that Christ expiated the sins of the world and that this "favor" is extended "indiscriminately to the whole human race," just as he also assumed, as the Canons of Dort would later declare, that God had the specific intention of saving some particular persons.[22] Various of the later Reformed appealed to Calvin on all sides of the debate over hypothetical universalism. (Only a few writers of the seventeenth and eighteenth centuries argued that Christ's death was sufficient payment only for the sins of the elect—and their views are not evident in the Reformed confessions either of the Reformation or of the era of orthodoxy.[23]) Later Reformed theology, then, is more specific on this particular point than Calvin had been—and arguably, his somewhat

---

21. Note that if acceptance of the doctrine that Christ's satisfaction is efficient or efficacious only for the elect is identified as "limited atonement," then one ought to identify all of the forms of hypothetical universalism judged by synods of the Reformed churches in the seventeenth century to be in accord with the Canons of Dort as alternative forms of limited atonement. Amyraut, in other words, taught limited atonement.

22. On these issues, see further below, chapters 3, 4, and 5.

23. For a tentative enumeration of the various positions on the extent of Christ's satisfaction, see below, chapter 3, note 22.

vague formulations point (or could be pointed) in several directions, as in fact can the formulae from the Synod of Dort.

The problem of predestination, christocentrism, and central dogmas. The issue of predestination is somewhat different: no one denies that Calvin taught the doctrine, although some have claimed that the christocentric Calvin moved predestination to a more gentle place in his 1559 *Institutes* and that his successors moved the doctrine back into relation with the doctrine of God in such a way as to create a more "strict" understanding of the doctrine. In fact, Calvin did not move the doctrine of predestination around. He kept it basically where he first placed it, having followed what he took to be a Pauline order suitable to catechesis.[24] The idea that this is a kinder, gentler placement of the doctrine ignores the fact of Calvin's definitions of predestination, election, and reprobation; does little or nothing to blunt the force of the doctrine; and also coordinate quite precisely with the definitions of later Reformed writers, regardless of the placement of the doctrine in a work of theology. Add to this that the later Reformed were hardly unaware of the relationship of placement of the doctrine to the literary genre of the theological work and also placed their formulations accordingly, some echoing Calvin's placement, some placing the doctrine ecclesiologically, many, of course, following a traditional placement in relation to the doctrine of God, arguably on the basis of a genre distinction between catechetical and creedal placements and more academic or dogmatically argued placements, suited to detailed theologies developed for university study.[25]

Yet another issue here is the problem of so-called central dogmas. Much of the reason that the question of Calvin's relation to Calvinism is asked has to do with the fairly consistent identification, typical in the nineteenth and early twentieth centuries, of Calvin's theology as focused on the doctrine of predestination. This assumption, together with the tendency to view the whole later Reformed tradition as massively focused on and, indeed, constructed around, the doctrine of predestination, created a sense of continuity between Calvin and Calvinism. Trends in the study of Calvin's thought, however, have changed. As already noted, there was a tendency to identify Calvin as "christocentric" in much twentieth-century theology. In the absence of a "christocentric" reading of later Reformed thought, it became fashionable to pose Calvin against the Calvinists—and, usually, to place the blame for the shift from christocentrism to predestinarianism on the shoulders of Theodore Beza.[26] Not only was this a highly dogmatized approach that paid little

---

24. Richard A. Muller, *The Unaccommodated Calvin: Studies in the Formation of a Theological Tradition* (New York: Oxford University Press, 2000), pp. 118-139.

25. See Richard A. Muller, "The Placement of Predestination in Reformed Theology: Issue or Non-Issue?," in *Calvin Theological Journal*, 40/2 (2005), pp. 184-210.

26. See, e.g., Hall, "Calvin against the Calvinists," pp. 25-28; Johannes Dantine, "Les Tabelles

attention to the breadth of the Reformed tradition or to the altered historical contexts in which later Reformed theology developed; it also had the further deficit of creating dogmatic caricatures and posing one against the other, as if Calvin's thought could be reduced to an anticipation of neo-orthodox christocentrism and later Reformed writers were simply predestinarians. Unfortunately, we are moving not so much beyond such fallacious argumentation as into a new phase of the same: as the language of christocentrism has worn old, the new centrism has tried to impose a model of union with Christ on Calvin's theology and then to make the same sort of negative claim about later "Calvinists": now that Calvin can be seen to focus on union with Christ, his thought can be radically separated from the later Calvinists who purportedly never thought of the concept; as Partee comments (without referencing any of the later Reformed as evidence of his claim), "Calvin is not a Calvinist because union with Christ is at the heart of his theology—and not theirs."[27] We can speculate that when the union with Christ theme has run its course, there will be another false center identified for Calvin's thought that can then be juxtaposed with the purported centers or omissions of later Reformed theology.[28]

As to the issue of christocentrism or of a christological focus juxtaposed with a decretal focus, this is, historically speaking, a fictitious issue based not on sixteenth- or seventeenth-century concerns but on particular patterns of twentieth-century theology. If by "christocentric" one means having a soteriology centered on Christ, then later Reformed writers were no more and no less christocentric than Calvin. All understood Christ's sacrifice to be the sole ground of salvation, and all defined election as "in Christ." If by christocentric one means something else, as for example, taking the "Christ event" as the sole revelation of God and therefore the center of one's theology (which is the typical twentieth-century usage), then the term does not apply either to Calvin or to the later Reformed—indeed, it arguably does not apply to any theologian or to any theology written between the second century and the nineteenth. In any case, "christocentrism" is not a useful category by which to assess Calvin's relationship to other Reformed writers of the early modern era.[29]

---

sur la doctrine de la prédestination par Théodore de Bèze," *Revue de théologie et de philosophie*, 16 (1966), pp. 365-377; Kickel, *Vernunft und Offenbarung bei Theodor Beza*, pp. 136-146.

27. Partee, *Theology of John Calvin*, pp. 3, 4, 25, 27, 40-41; cf. Julie Canlis, "Calvin, Osiander, and Participation in God," *International Journal of Systematic Theology*, 6/2 (2004), pp. 169-184. We will take up this issue at some length below chapter 5.

28. Note that there is a significant literature on Calvin's doctrine of union with Christ that handles the topic with due historical consideration and that explicitly avoids the mistaken reading given the doctrine by Partee and Canlis, e.g., J. Todd Billings, *Calvin, Participation, and the Gift: The Activity of Believers in Union with Christ* (Oxford: Oxford University Press, 2007), p. 19; and Mark A. Garcia, *Life in Christ: Union with Christ and Twofold Grace in Calvin's Theology* (Milton Keynes: Paternoster, 2008), p. 18.

29. Cf. Richard A. Muller, "A Note on 'Christocentrism' and the Imprudent Use of Such Terminology," *Westminster Theological Journal*, 68 (2006), pp. 253-260.

On the related issue of claims of later Reformed writers producing a "decretal theology," a form of determinism, or a "predestinarian metaphysic" foreign to Calvin's thought, it is perhaps important to note that these terms, like TULIP, "limited atonement," and "christocentrism," are not at all rooted in the sixteenth and seventeenth centuries: they are largely twentieth-century descriptors of an invented problem. Whereas there are, certainly, a series of nominally metaphysical assumptions shared by virtually all theologians of the older Christian tradition, such as the identification of God as absolute or necessary and the created order as relative or contingent, the older Reformed theology was hardly built on metaphysics, and in no way can it be classed as a form of determinism. Far more clearly than Calvin, later Reformed theologians identified God as utterly free and capable of willing otherwise, identified the world as contingent, and viewed rational creatures capable of acting freely according to their natures, having both freedom of contradiction and freedom of contrariety.[30] Here, one might claim a certain degree of discontinuity between Calvin and later Reformed writers, but it is such that a careful reading of his works and theirs will show him to be more susceptible to a deterministic reading, they less so. But the basic issue of the relationship between Calvin and later Reformed theology with regard to predestination is quite simple: Calvin and other Reformed thinkers, whether earlier or contemporaneous or later, all held to one or another form of the Augustinian understanding of predestination, as taught in Romans 9 and other biblical texts, namely, that salvation depends on the gracious will of eternal God, and therefore, it is intended by God from eternity that some be elected to salvation and others not. And since that is, historically, a long-held and widely argued pattern of formulation, it certainly cannot be the criterion by which either Calvin or anyone else ought to be identified as a "Calvinist."

The humanist-scholastic dichotomies. The humanist-scholastic dichotomy appears in several forms with regard to the relationship of Calvin to Calvinism. One form rather simplistically contrasts Calvin's humanism with the scholasticism of later Reformed theologians: in brief, Calvin was a humanist; later Calvinists were scholastic; Calvin was not a Calvinist. This approach is highly problematic inasmuch as it pits humanism and scholasticism against each other with reference to thinkers whose work embodied elements of both humanist and scholastic methods. As recent scholarship has quite definitively shown, Calvin, albeit trained philologically and rhetorically as a humanist, incorporated various elements of scholastic method, whether its topical and disputative models or its many distinctions, into his thought[31]—and the later Reformed, those benighted Calvinists, not only followed

30. As documented in Willem J. van Asselt, J. Martin Bac, and Roelf T. te Velde, trans. and eds., *Reformed Thought on Freedom: The Concept of Free Choice in the History of Early-Modern Reformed Theology* (Grand Rapids: Baker, 2010).

31. David C. Steinmetz, "The Scholastic Calvin," in *Protestant Scholasticism: Essays in Reassessment*, ed. Carl R. Trueman and R. Scott Clark (Carlisle: Paternoster Press, 1999), pp. 16-30;

scholastic method in their more finely grained academic and disputative efforts but also employed the fruits of humanist philological and linguistic training. Indeed, humanist philological training was typical of the era of scholastic orthodoxy.[32] What is more, various elements of so-called scholastic method, like the identification and ordering of standard topics or commonplaces (*loci communes*), are in fact of humanist origin.

Another form of the humanist-scholastic dichotomy attempts to overcome the obvious problem of claiming Calvin was entirely humanistic and later thinkers entirely scholastic, arguing a psychological bifurcation of Calvin into a thinker who had a broadly humanistic, gracious, and covenantal side to his personality and a rather dark, scholastic, predestinarian side.[33] When unleashed, this approach encourages a contrast between the humanistic Calvin and later Calvinists who, unfortunately, neglected Calvin the humanist and became the proponents of the scholastic predestinarian side of Calvin's legacy. This is a particularly problematic approach on several grounds. First, as is evident from Bouwsma's work, it rests on an unsubstantiated psychological argument that claims a bifurcated psyche in Calvin and then goes on quite arbitrarily to associate humanism with one side of the bifurcated psyche and scholasticism with the other.[34] Having drawn these conclusions, largely on the basis of one or another modern author's own preferences, this approach goes on to confuse the issue by associating humanistic and scholastic methods with particular contents, as if one could not be a humanistic predestinarian or a scholastic federalist. The conjunction of humanistic and scholastic elements in the thought of the Reformers was characteristic of the era.[35] There is absolutely no ground for associating humanism with covenantal thinking and predestinarianism or, indeed, determinism with scholastic thinking: one can easily point to humanists like Pietro Pomponazzi and Lorenzo Valla, who held deterministic philosophies, and to scholastic works written by covenantal theologians—just as one can point to so-

---

cf. Muller, *Unaccommodated Calvin*, pp. 36-61.

32. See Peter T. van Rooden, *Theology, Biblical Scholarship and Rabbinical Studies in the Seventeenth Century: Constantijn L'Empereur (1591-1648), Professor of Hebrew and Theology at Leiden*, trans. J. C. Grayson (Leiden: Brill, 1989); and Stephen G. Burnett, *From Christian Hebraism to Jewish Studies: Johannes Buxtorf (1564-1629) and Hebrew Learning in the Seventeenth Century* (Leiden: E. J. Brill, 1996).

33. William J. Bouwsma, *John Calvin: A Sixteenth-Century Portrait* (New York: Oxford University Press, 1988); and Philip C. Holtrop, *The Bolsec Controversy on Predestination, from 1551 to 1555*, 2 parts (Lewiston: Edwin Mellen, 1993).

34. See my critique of Bouwsma's reading of Calvin in *The Unaccommodated Calvin*, pp. 79-98.

35. See, e.g., Frank A. James III, "Peter Martyr Vermigli: At the Crossroads of Late Medieval Scholasticism, Christian Humanism and Resurgent Augustinianism," in Trueman and Clark, *Protestant Scholasticism*, pp. 62-78; and Scott Manetsch, "Psalms before Sonnets: Theodore Beza and the *Studia humanitatis*," in *Continuity and Change: The Harvest of Late Medieval and Reformation History. Essays Presented to Heiko A. Oberman on His 70th Birthday*, ed. Andrew C. Gow and Robert J. Bast (Leiden: E. J. Brill, 2000), pp. 400-416.

called covenant theologians, notably the archetypal covenant theologian Johannes Cocceius and his student Franz Burman, who held to typical Reformed doctrines of predestination and followed scholastic method,[36] or to Reformed theologians like Francis Turretin noted (perhaps unfairly) for their scholastic method and doctrine of predestination who also taught a fairly standard Reformed doctrine of the covenants.[37]

Calvin, Calvinism, and covenant theology. The relationship of Calvin's thought to later Reformed covenant theology has been a subject of much debate. Some have argued that Calvin was not at all a covenantal thinker, given his very brief and seemingly unilateral view of covenant in the *Institutes*, and that later Reformed writers were immersed in covenantal thinking and insistent on the bilateral character of covenant.[38] Others have claimed that Calvin was a strongly covenantal thinker whose emphasis on grace was lost to later Calvinistic thinkers, who descended into predestinarianism and legalism.[39] Of course, the historical case is more complex, far more complex, than either of these approaches indicates; but in its complexity it clarifies somewhat the question of the relationship of Calvin to so-called Calvinism. In the first place, there is the genuine oddity that the line of scholarship associated with a radically unilateral understanding of Calvin's covenantal thought has consistently dismissed the work of those scholars who have identified Calvin's rather careful distinction between the unilateral and the bilateral aspects of covenant at the same time that they have refused to examine Calvin's biblical commentaries in which this distinction resides. Arguably, the distinction is a commonplace of sixteenth- and seventeenth-century Reformed thought and is found not only in Calvin's work but also in the work of later Reformed writers.

There are also other significant relationships between Calvin's work and Reformed covenant theology. Calvin did, after all, state his definition of the covenant of grace as one in substance but differing in manner of administration or

36. See Willem J. van Asselt, "Cocceius Anti-Scholasticus?" in *Reformation and Scholasticism: An Ecumenical Enterprise*, ed. Willem J. van Asselt and and Eef Dekker (Grand Rapids: Baker, 2001), pp. 227-251.

37. See James Mark Beach, *Christ and the Covenant: Francis Turretin's Federal Theology as a Defense of Divine Grace* (Göttingen: Vandenhoeck & Ruprecht, 2007).

38. J. Wayne Baker, *Heinrich Bullinger and the Covenant: The Other Reformed Tradition* (Athens, Ohio: Ohio University Press, 1980); and idem, "Heinrich Bullinger, the Covenant, and the Reformed Tradition in Retrospect," *Sixteenth Century Journal*, 29/2 (1998), pp. 359-376.

39. E.g., James B. Torrance, "The Concept of Federal Theology—Was Calvin a Federal Theologian?," in *Calvinus Sacrae Scripturae Professor*, ed. Wilhelm H. Neuser (Grand Rapids: Eerdmans, 1994), pp. 15-40; idem, "Covenant or Contract? A Study of the Theological Background of Worship in Seventeenth-Century Scotland," *Scottish Journal of Theology*, 23 (1970), pp. 51-76; and idem, "The Incarnation and "Limited Atonement," *Evangelical Quarterly*, 55 (April, 1983), pp. 83-94.

dispensation from the Old to the New Testament,[40] a definition that carried over into the covenant theology of the seventeenth century. Yet Calvin was neither alone nor very original in this formulation: it is present almost identically in earlier works by Zwingli and Bullinger. The scholarship that has associated Bullinger with origins of covenant theology as distinct from a Calvinian predestinarianism has typically played down the significance of this parallel and has also typically failed to note that Calvin did not actually develop his covenantal thought in relation to this definition, which occurs in the *Institutes* in the initial chapter on the relationship of the testaments. There is not, in other words, apart from this definition, very much covenant theology to be dredged out of the *Institutes*—and, accordingly, the *Institutes* was not heavily cited by later Reformed covenant theologians. What they did cite and cite both frequently and at some length were Calvin's commentaries in which most of Calvin's thought on covenant is recorded, as can be easily documented from the work of a thinker like Herman Witsius.[41]

Conclusions

The term "Calvinism," like the acrostic TULIP, has been, in short, a cause of a series of problems concerning the identity of the Reformed tradition and of Calvin's relationship to the tradition. Both identifiers are anachronistic and reductionistic. Each of the several meanings of "Calvinism" results in mistaken understandings of the thought of John Calvin and its relation to the Reformed tradition of the sixteenth and seventeenth centuries. Use of the acrostic TULIP has resulted in a narrow, if not erroneous, reading of the Canons of Dort that has led to confused understandings of the Reformed tradition and of Calvin's theology.

The underlying issue that is posed by these terms and by examples noted above of the theological and intellectual relationship of Calvin's work to the later Reformed tradition concerns the nature of a tradition as well as the character and variety of continuities and developments within a tradition. As Carl Trueman has recently pointed out, the entire question of continuity and discontinuity requires considerable nuancing.[42] There is, in the first place, the fundamental continuity of the basic tradition of ecumenical and creedal catholicity, which, of course remained in place in the theologies of the Reformed and Lutheran branches of the Reformation as well as in the Roman church. Second, there are issues of the broad continuities belonging to a specific Reformation and post-Reformation era confessional tradition—in the

---

40. John Calvin, *Institutes of the Christian Religion*, trans John Allen, 7th ed., 2 vols. (Philadelphia: Presbyterian Board of Christian Education, 1936), II.x.2.

41. See the discussion of these citations in Richard A. Muller, "Reception and Response: Referencing and Understanding Calvin in Post-Reformation Calvinism," in *Calvin and His Influence, 1509-2009*, ed. Irena Backus and Philip Benedict (New York: Oxford University Press, 2011), pp. 182-201.

42. See Carl R. Trueman, "The Reception of Calvin: Historical Considerations," *Church History and Religious Culture*, 91/1-2 (2011), pp. 19-27.

case of the Reformed confessional tradition, there is a common theological ground enunciated in the major confessional works of the mid-sixteenth century, namely, the Gallican, Belgic, and Scots Confessions, the Heidelberg Catechism, and the Thirty-Nine Articles of the Church of England, all which were written in circles either in dialogue with or in one way or another indebted to Calvin and which, more importantly, represent the international community of Reformed belief to which Calvin belonged. In both of these cases, there is clear continuity between Calvin and his contemporaries as well as between Calvin and the later Reformed tradition, not, of course, because of the individuality of Calvin's thought but because of its catholicity.

There is also the issue of the relationship of Calvin's thought to a tradition of which he was a part and which developed and changed over the course of time in relation to a complex series of differing historical contexts. As often noted, Calvin stands in relation to the Reformed tradition as one second-generation codifier among others, arguably the most prominent of the group if not always the primary voice leading to a particular formulation or development of thought in that tradition. In Williston Walker's estimation, "Calvin's mind was formulative rather than creative."[43] He reflected on the work of predecessors like Zwingli, Bucer, Melanchthon, Farel, and Oecolampadius; he engaged in dialogue and debate with contemporaries like Bullinger, Vermigli, Musculus, Viret, and à Lasco; his work was received and defended in detail; and his formulations (perhaps most notably his exegetical formulations) were consulted, modified, and incorporated into a developing, changing, and variegated theological tradition. Calvin did not originate this tradition; he was not the sole voice in its early codification; and he did not serve as the norm for its development.[44]

As indicated from the beginning of this little survey of the relationship of Calvin to Calvinism, the issue is quite complicated—particularly if a proper understanding of "Calvinism" as loosely referencing the Reformed tradition is observed. The issue remains complicated, moreover, by the self-identification of various persons and groups as Calvinist or Calvinistic in the centuries after the decline of Reformed orthodoxy. These groups include Baptists, who, on grounds of their denial of baptism to infants, would have been unwelcome either in Calvin's Geneva or in any of the confessionally Reformed contexts of the era of orthodoxy. Also to be noted here are various modern theologians and philosophers who call themselves Calvinist on grounds of a strict metaphysical determinism or compatibilism, a view that also was less than welcome in Reformed circles of the sixteenth and seventeenth centuries.

---

43. Williston Walker, *A History of the Christian Church* (New York: Scribner, 1918), p. 392.

44. Cf. Williston Walker, *John Calvin: The Organizer of Reformed Protestantism (1509-1564)*, repr., with a bibliographical essay by John T. McNeill (New York: Schocken, 1969), p. 1; Reinhold Seeberg, *Text-book of the History of Doctrines*, trans. Charles E. Hay, 2 vols. (Grand Rapids: Baker, 1977), II, p. 394; George Park Fisher, *History of the Christian Church* (New York: Scribner's, 1894), p. 318; McNeill, *History and Character of Calvinism*, pp. 3-4; Perry Miller, *New England Mind*, p. 93.

There is, then, a high degree of irony as well as anachronism in these attempts to pit Calvin against a so-called rigid orthodoxy—largely on the basis of the failure of the orthodoxy rigidly to reproduce Calvin's theology and largely driven by doctrinal criteria and even doctrinal slogans originating in the nineteenth and twentieth centuries. Given that the picture of later Reformed thought that we have seen emerge from a more detailed study of the late sixteenth- and seventeenth-century documents is the picture of a rather diverse movement with numerous antecedents in the earlier traditions of the church and in the work of a sizeable group of Reformers, both predecessors and contemporaries of Calvin, the very diversity of the movement militates against the characterization of it as rigid. What is more, had later Reformed theology formulated itself in the way pronounced as ideal by those who raise the question "Was Calvin a Calvinist?" namely, duplicated Calvin's thought over and over again, not only would it have failed to survive as a confessional movement, it would also have attained a maximal rigidity. Quite to the contrary, the later Reformed tradition drew on and appealed to Calvin as one founding teacher among others, recognizing his abilities as a second-generation codifier of the Reformed faith, his limitations as a technical thinker, and his inability to address all of the issues that faced them in altered contexts and other times.

By way of conclusion, we return to the initial question, "Was Calvin a Calvinist?" The answer is certainly a negative. Calvin was not a "Calvinist"—but then again, neither were the "Calvinists." They were all contributors to the Reformed tradition. The moral of the story, perhaps, is to recognize the common ground on which Calvin, the various Reformed confessions, and the so-called Calvinists of the later sixteenth and seventeenth centuries stand, acknowledge the diversity of the tradition from the outset (within, of course, its confessional boundaries), and if you must, "gather ye rosebuds while ye may," but don't plant TULIP in your Reformed garden.

3

Calvin on Christ's Satisfaction and Its Efficacy:
The Issue of "Limited Atonement"

Calvin's doctrine of the work of Christ, particularly his treatment of Christ's death and its salvific import, have been the subject of a great number of inquiries, none of which have proved ultimately satisfactory. Various more or less traditional Reformed readings of Calvin's doctrine have argued the case for "limited atonement" or "limited redemption."[1] Among the contemporary monographic treatments of the problem, however, Van Buren, Hall, Armstrong, Anderson, Kendall, Daniel, Bell, Kennedy, and others have argued a concept of universal or perhaps hypothetically universal atonement in Calvin's thought, a view pointing away from the thought of Theodore Beza and more directly to the seventeenth-century theology of Moïse Amyraut than to the Canons of Dort or to the doctrines of the larger part of Reformed orthodox dogmaticians. In this view, the doctrine of limited atonement was the result of Beza's predestinarianism, not of Calvin's.[2] A mediating perspective

---

1. Cf. Archibald Alexander Hodge, *The Atonement* (1867; repr., Grand Rapids: Baker, 1974); idem, *Outlines of Theology* (1860; repr., Grand Rapids: Zondervan, 1976); Charles Hodge, *Systematic Theology*, 3 vols. (1871-1873; repr., Grand Rapids: Eerdmans, 1975); Robert L. Dabney, *Lectures in Systematic Theology* (1878; repr., Grand Rapids: Zondervan, 1972); Louis Berkhof, *Systematic Theology* (Grand Rapids: Eerdmans, 1939); idem, *Vicarious Atonement Through Christ* (Grand Rapids: Eerdmans, 1936).

2. Paul Van Buren, *Christ in Our Place: The Substitutionary Character of Calvin's Doctrine of Reconciliation* (Edinburgh, 1957); Basil Hall, "Calvin against the Calvinists," in *John Calvin*, ed. Gervase Duffield (Appleford: Sutton Courtnay Press, 1966), pp. 19-37; Brian G. Armstrong, *Calvinism and the Amyraut Heresy: Protestant Scholasticism and Humanism in Seventeenth-Century France* (Madison: University of Wisconsin Press, 1969), pp. 137-138; John S. Bray, *Theodore Beza's Doctrine of Predestination* (Nieuwkoop: De Graaf, 1975), p. 112; James William Anderson, "The Grace of God and the Non-elect in Calvin's Commentaries and Sermons (Th.D. diss., New Orleans Baptist Theological Seminary, 1976); R. T. Kendall, *Calvin and English Calvinism to 1649* (Oxford and New York: Oxford University Press, 1979); Curt D. Daniel, "Hyper-Calvinism and John Gill" (Ph.D. diss., University of Edinburgh, 1983); M. Charles Bell, "Was Calvin a Calvinist," *Scottish Journal of Theology*, 36/4 (1983), pp. 535-540; idem, "Calvin and the Extent of Atonement," *Evangelical Quarterly*, 55 (April, 1983), pp. 115-123; idem, *Calvin and Scottish Theology: The Doctrine of Assurance* (Edinburgh: Handsel, 1985); James B. Torrance, "The Incarnation and "Limited

is found in Peterson's study of Calvin's doctrine of the atonement, where it is argued that the later question of limited atonement cannot be pressed, anachronistically, against Calvin's text with any satisfactory result, while Rainbow rightly pointed out the problem of trying to define Calvin's doctrine with a term (namely, "atonement") that Calvin could not have used, and he recognized the Amyraldian *tendenz* of much of the scholarship on Calvin.[3] Letham has argued, similarly, that the debate was not Calvin's and that Calvin did "not commit himself on the question of the extent of the atonement," but certainly did not point in any way toward a doctrine of "unlimited atonement."[4] Strehle has raised the possibility that the historical debate itself was occasioned in part by the vagueness and inconclusiveness of earlier argument.[5] Nonetheless, as Wendel pointed out—without broaching the specific issue of a limitation of the efficacy of Christ's satisfaction to the salvation of the elect—in Calvin's view Christ's work "appears as a necessary consequence of the doctrine of election."[6] And there is no lack of more recent works that argue Calvin to have held a concept of "limited atonement," fully in accord with the Canons of Dort and the theology of the seventeenth-century Protestant orthodox.[7]

Atonement," *Scottish Bulletin of Evangelical Theology*, 2 (1984), pp. 32-40; Allan C. Clifford, *Atonement and Justification: English Evangelical Theology, 1640-1790* (Oxford: Oxford University Press, 1990); Kevin D. Kennedy, *Union with Christ and the Extent of the Atonement* (New York: Peter Lang, 2002); idem, "Hermeneutical Discontinuity between Calvin and later Calvinism," *Scottish Journal of Theology*, 64 (2011), pp. 299-312; Paul Hartog, *A Word for the World: Calvin on the Extent of Atonement* (Schaumburg: Regular Baptist Press, 2009); similar views are expressed in Otto Weber, *Foundations of Dogmatics*, trans. Darrell Guder, 2 vols. (Grand Rapids: Eerdmans, 1981-82), II, pp. 147, 475.

3. Robert A. Peterson, *Calvin's Doctrine of the Atonement* (Phillipsburg: Presbyterian and Reformed, 1983); Jonathan H. Rainbow, *The Will of God and the Cross: An Historical and Theological Study of John Calvin's Doctrine of Limited Redemption* (Allison Park, PA: Pickwick Publications, 1990), pp. 1, 4-8, noting that Armstrong's citations of Calvin were based on Amyraut's and Kendall's on Armstrong's (p. 153).

4. R. W. A. Letham, "Saving Faith and Assurance in Reformed Theology: Zwingli to the Synod of Dort," 2 vols. (Ph.D. diss., University of Aberdeen, 1979), I, p. 125; II, p. 67.

5. Stephen Strehle, "The Extent of the Atonement at the Synod of Dort," *Westminster Theological Journal*, 51/1 (Spring 1989), pp. 1-23; and idem, "Universal Grace and Amyraldianism," *Westminster Theological Journal*, 51/2 (Winter 1989), pp. 345-357; and see idem, "The Extent of the Atonement within the Theological Systems of the Sixteenth and Seventeenth Centuries" (Th.D. diss., Dallas Theological Seminary, 1980).

6. François Wendel, *Calvin: The Origins and Development of His Religious Thought*, trans. Philip Mairet (New York: Harper & Row, 1963), p. 231. Note that Wilhelm Niesel, *The Theology of Calvin*, trans. Harold Knight (London: Lutterworth, 1956; repr., Grand Rapids: Baker, 1980), p. 120 specifically omits discussion of Christ's work from his study. Neither does T. H. L. Parker, *Calvin: An Introduction to His Thought* (Louisville: Westminster/John Knox, 1995) deal with the issue.

7. William Cunningham, "Calvin and Beza," in *The Reformers and the Theology of the Reformation* (Edinburgh: T. & T. Clark, 1872), pp. 395-402; Roger Nicole, "Moyse Amyraut (1596-1664) and the Controversy on Universal Grace, First Phase (1634-1637)" (Ph.D. diss., Harvard University, 1966); idem, "John Calvin's View of the Extent of the Atonement," *Westminster Theological Journal*, 47 (1985), pp. 197-225 (including a significant analysis of the history of scholarship and debate);

Given these fairly wide differences of opinion in the literature, there is certainly room for yet another essay on the problem of Calvin's perspective on the divine intentionality in redemption and the extent or limitation of Christ's work. There is also need for an examination of the materials that takes into consideration both the difficulty of pressing them into the service of a particular predetermined dogmatic solution and the probable reasons for this inherent difficulty—whether in Calvin's own thought and method, or in the background and context of Calvin's work, or in the thought and method of the several generations of historians and theologians who have examined the question. Peterson was certainly correct in noting the problem of anachronism: the entire Reformed debate over "limited atonement" or, more precisely, over the ground of the limited efficacy of Christ's satisfaction, occurred after Calvin's death. Calvin did not speak directly to the issue. Once this point has been granted, however, we are confronted by the contextual problem of Calvin's own method of identifying in the course of his homiletical and exegetical labors, the *loci* or *topoi* and *disputationes* that needed to be addressed either in individual polemical treatises or as new sections and subsections added to the text of the *Institutes*.[8] What later Reformed theologians addressed as a specific topic in theology was not at all understood by Calvin or by various of his contemporaries—Bullinger, Vermigli, Musculus, and others—as a distinct *locus* or *topos*.

This problem of Calvin's method points in turn toward the historical background and context of his theological efforts. Rainbow has examined much of the dogmatic background in late patristic and medieval thought and Godfrey has presented the sixteenth-century context and development, also from a dogmatic perspective. Here, the positive and negative aspects of Calvin's relation to scholastic theology must also be brought into play—given that there is, in addition to the simple question of antecedents, also the question of the specific character of Calvin's appropriation of

---

William Robert Godfrey, "Tensions within International Calvinism: The Debate on the Atonement at the Synod of Dort, 1618-1619" (Ph.D. diss. Stanford University, 1974), idem, "Reformed Thought on the Extent of the Atonement to 1618," *Westminster Theological Journal*, 37/2 (Winter, 1975), pp. 133-171; John Murray, Review of Paul van Buren, *Christ in Our Place*, in *Westminster Theological Journal*, 22 (1959-60), pp. 55-60; idem, "Calvin on the Extent of the Atonement," *Banner of Truth*, 234 (March, 1983), pp. 20-22; Paul Helm, "Calvin, English Calvinism and the Logic of Doctrinal Development," *Scottish Journal of Theology*, 34/2 (1981), pp. 179-185; idem, "The Logic of Limited Atonement," *Scottish Bulletin of Evangelical Theology*, 3 (1985), pp. 47-54; and idem, *Calvin and the Calvinists* (Carlisle: Banner of Truth, 1982); Rainbow, *The Will of God and the Cross*; Frederick S. Leahy, "Calvin and the Extent of the Atonement," *Reformed Theological Journal*, 8 (November 1992), pp. 54-64; G. Michael Thomas, *The Extent of the Atonement: A Dilemma for Reformed Theology from Calvin to the Consensus (1536-1675)* (Carlisle: Paternoster Press, 1997); Henri Blocher, "The Atonement in John Calvin's Theology," in *The Glory of the Atonement: Biblical, Historical, and Practical Perspectives*, ed. Charles E. Hill and Frank James III (Downers Grove: InterVarsity, 2004), pp. 279-303.

8. Cf. Richard A. Muller, *The Unaccommodated Calvin: Studies in the Formation of a Theological Tradition* (New York: Oxford University Press, 2000), pp. 101-117, et passim.

the older materials, particularly in the case of the sufficiency-efficiency formula.[9] In addition, much of the scholarly discussion has ignored the basic terminological problem involved in examining the questions of limited "atonement" and "for whom Christ died," a problem recognized in the seventeenth century by such diverse thinkers as Jacob Arminius, Richard Baxter, and John Owen.[10] In short, fixation on the anachronistic term "limited atonement" and on the ancient but inherently vague language that "Christ died for all people" or, by contrast, "for the elect," has led to fallacious argumentation on all sides of the issue[11] and has transferred its confusion from Calvin to the examination of various later Reformed alternative formulations of the doctrine of Christ's sacrifice and its application to believers, whether in the case of the more particularistic understandings of the doctrine or in the case of the various forms of hypothetical universalism.

---

9. See Muller, *Unaccommodated Calvin*, pp. 39-58; and cf. Pieter L. Rouwendal, "Calvin's Forgotten Classical Position on the Extent of the Atonement: About Sufficiency, Efficiency, and Anachronism," *Westminster Theological Journal*, 70 (2008), pp. 317-335.

10. Cf. Jacob Arminius, *Apology against the Thirty-One Articles*, xii, in *The Works of James Arminius*, trans. James and William Nichols, with an intro. by Carl Bangs, 3 vols. (Grand Rapids: Baker Book House, 1986), II, pp. 9-10; Richard Baxter, *Universal Redemption of Mankind, by the Lord Jesus Christ: stated and cleared by the late learned Mr. Richard Baxter. Whereunto is added a short account of special redemption* (London: for John Salusbury, 1694), pp. 1-6; also note, against Baxter's own ambiguity with reference to "atonement," John Owen, *Of the Death of Christ, the Price He Paid, and the Purchase He Made; or, the Satisfaction and Merit of the Death of Christ Cleared; the Universality of Redemption thereby Oppugned; and the doctrine concerning these things, formerly delivered in a treatise against universal redemption, vindicated from the exceptions and objections of Mr. R. B.* (1650), in *The Works of John Owen*, ed. William H. Goold, 24 vols. (London: Johnstone and Hunter, 1850-1853), vol. 10, p. 383.

11. As, e.g., Kendall, *Calvin and English Calvinism*, p. 1, note 4, which defines "limited atonement" as "the belief that Christ died for the elect only"; Armstrong's approach is still more confused, *Calvinism and the Amyraut Heresy*, p. 42, note 122: "*Limited atonement* refers to the teaching that Jesus died for the elect only, and that his death was not intended to atone for the sins of all mankind"; cf. the similar terminology employed in Kennedy, *Union with Christ*, pp. 4-6. Note that the statement "Christ died for the elect only," if understood as referencing the efficacy of his satisfaction, could be confessed equally by Calvin, Beza, Amyraut, and Arminius, while the meaning of statement that his "death was not intended to atone for the sins of all mankind" depends entirely on whether atonement is understood in terms of its objective accomplishment (*expiatio, impetratio*) or its application (*applicatio*) and whether the "intention" references an effective divine willing or a revealed, preceptive divine willing. As stated, Kendall's, Armstrong's, and Kennedy's definitions are useless for understanding the early modern debates. Indeed, Armstrong's definition, depending on the referentiality of the divine intentionality, could either be applied equally to Du Moulin and Amyraut or be understood as inapplicable to either.

"Atonement" and "Limited Atonement": A Problem of Terminology

Peterson notes, with very incomplete insight into the historical problem, that "the extent of the atonement was not an issue in Calvin's time" inasmuch as "debate over limited or unlimited atonement belongs to the period of Reformed orthodoxy."[12] Calvin cannot be expected to oblige the categories of later debate—although this appears all too often to be the premise of inquiries into the question of "limited atonement." Of course, Calvin did know and, in an incidental fashion, use the older scholastic language of the sufficiency and efficiency of Christ's satisfaction, indicating that he recognized the terms of the traditional, scholastic approach to the limitation of Christ's work.[13] Much of the modern debate over Calvin's doctrine relates to a misunderstanding of this traditional language of satisfaction in relation to the so-called doctrine of the atonement. The distinction itself is not unclear, although, as Strehle also observes, the formula could be applied to argue "unlimited" as well as "limited atonement."[14] The problem is not in the formula but in the modern language of "atonement" as it has been retrojected onto early modern theological debates concerning the sufficiency, efficiency, intention, and extent of Christ's satisfaction.

There is not only an anachronism but also a linguistic problem present in virtually all of the discussions of the issue, including Peterson's and Strehle's. Simply stated, the term "limited atonement" would have been unintelligible to Calvin and, indeed, to the delegates to the Synod of Dort, who are typically credited with the confessional use of the formula in Reformed theology. "Atonement" is not only an English word; it is also an English word that, when associated with its actual Latin equivalents or examined in the English theological usage of the day, stands in what is at best an oblique relationship to the early modern debates over the limitation of

12. Peterson, *Calvin's Doctrine of the Atonement*, p. 90; similarly, Cunningham, "Calvin and Beza," pp. 395-398.

13. E.g., John Calvin, *Commentarius in Iohannis apostoli epistola* (1561), 2:2, in *Ioannis Calvini opera quae supersunt omnia*, 59 vols., ed. Guilielmus Baum, Eduardus Cunitz, and Eduardus Reuss (Brunswick: Schwetschke, 1863-1900), LV, col. 310: "sufficienter pro toto mundo passum esse Christum: sed pro electic tantum efficaciter"; hereinafter the *Calvini opera* are abbreviated CO; cf. idem, *Commentaries on the First Epistle of John*, p. 173, in *Commentaries of John Calvin*, 46 vols., translators various (Edinburgh: Calvin Translation Society, 1844-1855; repr., Grand Rapids: Baker, 1979), hereinafter abbreviated CTS, followed by the biblical book and volume of the commentary as necessary, e.g., CTS *Psalms*, II).

14. Cf. Strehle, "Extent of the Atonement and the Synod of Dort," p. 1, note 1, 16-17, 22-23, with the discussion of various forms of the distinction in Rainbow, *Will of God and the Cross*, pp. 36-38, 43. Rainbow does not recognize that the sufficiency/efficiency distinction was present in Lombard's *Sententiae* and therefore argued by virtually all medieval commentators in one form or another: see Peter Lombard *Sententiae in IV libris distinctae*, 3rd ed., 2 vols. (Grottaferrata: Collegium S. Bonaventurae ad Claras Aquas, 1971-1981), III, d. 20, c. 5.1: "Christus ergo est sacerdos idemque hostia et pretium nostrae reconciliationis, qui se in ara crucis non diabolo, sed Deo Trinitati obtulit, pro omnibus quantum ad pretii sufficientiam, sed pro electis tantum quantum ad efficaciam, quia praedestinatis salutem effecit."

Christ's work. Use of the terms "limited" and "unlimited atonement" has served only to obscure the issues in early modern debate and, frankly, to befuddle several generations of modern critics. The confusion is particularly evident in an essay by Kennedy, who attempts to argue that Calvin did not teach "limited atonement" but instead argued a limited "extent of salvation"—Kennedy fails to recognize that the whole point of what has typically been identified as limited atonement was not the limitation of the value or sufficiency of Christ's satisfaction but a limitation of the extent or efficacy of its application, precisely what he indicates that Calvin did actually argue.[15]

The English verb "to atone" can mean to "set at one," to expiate, to reconcile, or to make amends for an offense. Even so, the noun "atonement" can indicate a reparation made for an offense or an injury or, with specific reference to theological issues, either the redeeming effect of Christ's incarnation, sufferings, and death or the reconciliation between God and humanity effected in Christ. In the applications of the term to Christ's work in English theological works of the early modern era, it typically refers to Christ's objective sacrifice for sin universally considered, namely, according to its sufficiency,[16] or with reference to texts in the Epistle to the Hebrews, to the crucifixion understood as a "blood sacrifice" or "sin offering" after the manner of the Old Testament Levitical priesthood.[17] It is typically not the term used even in English-language theology of the early modern era to discuss the more technical questions concerning the death of Christ and the relationship of its merit to its application; the term typically used is "satisfaction."

15. Kennedy, "Hermeneutical Discontinuity," pp. 307-309.

16. See John Preston, *The Fulnesse of Christ for Us* (London: for John Stafford, 1639), p. 25; Benjamin Kennicott, *Two Dissertations: The first on the tree of life in paradise ... the second on the oblations of Cain and Abel* (Oxford: for the Author, 1647), p. 223; Samuel Rutherford, *The tryal & triumph of faith: or, An exposition of the history of Christs dispossessing of the daughter of the woman of Canaan. Delivered in sermons; in which are opened, the victory of faith; the condition of those that are tempted; the excellency of Jesus Christ and free-grace; and some speciall grounds and principles of libertinisme and antinomian errors* (London: John Field, 1645), p. 162; James Ussher, *A Body of Divinitie: or the summe and substance of Christian religion* (London: M.F. for Tho. Downes, 1645), p. 171; and John Scott, *The Christian Life*, 3 parts in 4 vols. (London: R.N. for Walter Kettilby, 1686-1696), I, p. 202; II/2, p. 714.

17. Cf. Richard Sibbes, *The Bruised Reed and Smoking Flax*, in *The Complete Works of Richard Sibbes, D.D.*. ed. Alexander Grosart, 7 vols. (Edinburgh: James Nichol, 1862-1864), I, pp. 246-247; David Dickson, *A Short Explanation of the Epistle of Paul to the Hebrews* (Dublin: Society of Stationers, 1637), Heb. 13:12 (p. 319); with Henry Ainsworth, *Annotations upon the Five Books of Moses* (1639), Lev. 16 (pp. 88-93); Jeremiah Burroughs, *An Exposition of the Prophesie of Hosea. Begun in divers lectures upon the first three chapters* (London: for R. Dawlman, 1643), pp. 449-450; David Pareus, *A Commentary upon the Divine Revelation* (Amsterdam: C.P., 1644), Rev. 9:13 (p. 187), where "atonement" translates *expiatio*; cf. idem, *In divinam apocalypsin s. apostoli et evangelistae Johannis commentarius* (Heidelberg: Jonas Rosa, 1618), col. 395; William Austin, *Devotionis Augustinianae flamma or, a certaine devout, godly, and learned meditations* (London: John Legat and Ralph Mab, 1635), p. 135.

In the English Bible, specifically, the Authorized Version, the words "atone" and "atonement" appear some forty-three times, for the most part in Exodus, Leviticus, and Numbers, in all cases rendering forms of *kippur* and *kaphar*. There is only a single occurrence in the New Testament, namely, Romans 5:11, where "atonement" renders *katallage*. When the translation of Scripture found in Calvin's commentaries is examined for renderings of *kippur*, *kaphar*, and *katallage*, one finds that the majority of passages in the Old Testament translation employ *expiatio* or *expiare*, with several places where *propitiare*, *oblatio*, and *emundatio* are used.[18] Calvin renders *katallage* as *reconciliatio* and in the text of his commentary uses *expiatio* as a synonym.[19] What is important to the present argument is that Calvin does not render any of these instances with *satisfactio* or *satisfacere*: there is, in other words, no correspondence in Calvin's usage between the various places in Scripture where atonement language is found and the Latin term at the heart of debates over so-called limited atonement, namely, *satisfactio*.

Calvin did, however, consistently use the term *satisfactio* or its verbal form, *satisfacere*, with reference to the death of Christ. Arguably, it is his primary doctrinal descriptor for the work of Christ on the cross—used some nineteen times in the christological section of the *Institutes*.[20] The term also appears in Calvin's commentaries with specific reference to Christ's sacrifice as payment for sin.[21]

The problem for the doctrine of "limited atonement," therefore, lies in the fact that the sixteenth- and early seventeenth-century debate concerned neither the objective sacrificial death of Christ considered as the atonement or *expiatio* offered to God for the price of sin, upon which all parties in the debate were agreed, or the unlimited value, worth, merit, power, or "sufficiency" of the *satisfactio*, upon which all parties were also agreed, nor precisely, indeed, the limited *efficacia* or *applicatio*, inasmuch as all parties to the debate denied universal salvation. The debates over hypothetical universalism also highlighted the question of the divine intention (*intentio*) in or behind the sufficiency of Christ's satisfaction. A relatively small group of Reformed theologians, for the most part in the late seventeenth and the

18. *Propitiare* is used in Exod. 32:30; *oblatio* in Lev. 4:35; 5:16, 18; 10:17; 14:19, 28; Num. 8:21; *mundatio/emundatio/emmundare*, in Lev.14:31, 53; 15:15; 16:10; following the text of *The Bible of John Calvin, Reconstructed from the Text of His Commentaries*, by Richard F. Wevers (Grand Rapids: Digamma, 1994), in loc.

19. John Calvin, *Commentarius in epistolam Pauli ad Romanos* (1540/1556), in CO 49, col. 94.

20. Cf. John Calvin, *Institutio christianae religionis* (Geneva: Robert Stephanus, 1559), II.xii.3 (twice), 4; xiii.4; xv.6 (twice); xvi.1, 2, 5 (twice), 6 (twice), 10, 19; xvii.3, 4 (twice), 5 (twice). I have also consulted the translation, *Institutes of the Christian Religion*, trans. John Allen, 3 vols. (Philadelphia: Philip Nicklin, 1816).

21. Cf., e.g., John Calvin, *Commentarii in Isaiam Prophetam* (1559), 53:10, in CO 37, col. 263 (CTS *Isaiah*, IV, p. 125); idem, *Commentarius in epistolam ad Galatas* (1548), 1:4; 2:20-21, in CO 50, col. 170, 200 (CTS *Galatians*, pp. 27, 76, 77), N.B., "atonement" in v. 20-21, translates *expiatio* and *expiando*); idem, *Commentarii in epistolam ad Hebraeos* (1549), 9:28, in CO 55, col. 120 (CTS *Hebrews*, p. 220); idem, *In Iohannis apostoli epistola*, 2:1, in CO 55, col. 309 (CTS *1 John*, p. 171).

eighteenth centuries, defined Christ's sufficiency or, more specifically, his accomplishment (*impetratio*) of salvation as limited—but this view was not present in Calvin's time, nor was it a prominent position at the time of the Synod of Dort. The actual issues relevant to the debate were (1) the divine intention concerning the sufficiency of Christ's satisfaction, specifically, the relationship between the hypothetical, "if all would believe," and the infinite value or merit of Christ's death, namely, its "sufficiency" for all sin; (2) the divine intention concerning the effective application of salvation to individuals, specifically, the grounds of limitation of the efficiency or efficacy of Christ's work; and (3) the relationship between the value or sufficiency and efficiency of Christ's satisfaction and the universal or, more precisely, indiscriminate proclamation and call of the gospel.[22] Debate over a hypothetical universal efficacy did not arise, given that an infinite potency or potentially universal efficacy, governed by the language of sufficiency, was generally assumed,[23] and that even advocates of hypothetical universalism, like Amyraut, assumed the efficacy or application of Christ's work to be governed by election.[24]

There are, then, several issues to be addressed, once the topic itself has been secured from the various modern confusions. Some clarity can be achieved simply

---

22. Arguably, once the language is suitably parsed, there are at least seven distinct patterns of formulation (not to mention variants within these basic patterns) among the early modern Reformed: (1) the unelaborated sufficiency-efficiency formula, e.g., Bastingius; (2) a simple statement of "ordained" or intentional sufficiency for all, a basic form of hypothetical universalism, e.g., Davenant; (3) a second form of hypothetical universalism that argues a prior, absolute decree to save the elect by grace and a subsequent universal promise or will to save all who believe, e.g., Twisse; (4) a third form of hypothetical universalism with its antecedent conditional decree to save all who believe and its subsequent absolute decree to save the elect only, e.g., Amyraut; (5) a particularism arguing "mere" or hypothetical sufficiency, e.g., Owen; (6) a more developed form of "mere sufficiency" stressing the impetration-application distinction, e.g., Lyford; and (7) a particularism arguing a limited sufficiency, usually by way of rejecting or modifying the sufficiency-efficiency formula, e.g., Piscator, Witsius. Further examination of the sources will be necessary in order to the full development of a paradigm.

23. See, e.g., Franciscus Gomarus, *An Christus pro omnibus et singulis hominiubs mortuus?*, in *Opera theologica omnia, maximam partem posthuma*, 2nd ed. (Amsterdam: Joannes Jansson, 1664), pt. I, p. 459; very similar to Calvin's statement in *De aeterna Dei praedestnatione*, in CO 8, col. 336 in translation, *Concerning the Eternal Predestination of God*, trans., with an intro. by J. K. S. Reid (London: James Clarke, 1961), pp. 148-149.

24. Cf. my comment in *Christ and the Decree: Christology and Predestination in Reformed Theology from Calvin to Perkins* (Grand Rapids: Baker, 2008), p. 35: the point (misunderstood in Clifford, *Calvinus*, p. 44; and Hartog, *Calvin on the Extent of Atonement*, p. 26) was not that it is superfluous to argue hypothetical dimension to the work of Christ, rather, specifically, that it is superfluous to argue a hypothetical dimension to its efficacy, as distinct from its sufficiency, given that the efficacy, as far as Calvin was concerned, was assumed to be governed by divine election and that the referent of the argument for the universality of Christ's satisfaction was its sufficiency. There is, however, a distinction between potential and actual efficacy found in Twisse that addressed the question of the extent of salvation if all would believe: see *Vindiciae gratiae, potestatis, ac providentiae Dei hoc est, ad examen libelli Perkinsiani de praedestinatione modo et ordine, institutum a J. Arminio, responsio scholastica.* (Amsterdam: Joannes Jansson, 1648), I.ii.21 (pp. 230-231).

by framing the question within the structure of the terms and distinctions used by early modern Reformed theologians—namely, the *satisfactio Christi*, distinguished in relation to its *sufficientia* and *efficientia*, or in relation to its *valor* or *virtus* and *efficacia*, or in relation to its *impetratio* and *applicatio*. The Reformed debates, including the debate at the Synod of Dort and during the Amyraldian controversy, were concerned with two issues: first, the reason or ground for the limitation of the efficacy of Christ's *satisfactio*; and, second, with the question of the nature of the ultimate divine intentionality in making a fully sufficient satisfaction for sin. With these actual issues in mind, Calvin's formulations can be examined, recognizing that his formulations, albeit seldom reliant on the language of the standard scholastic distinctions, nonetheless reflect their boundaries. Thus, given that Calvin did understand Christ's satisfaction as fully paying the price for sin, that is, as having an infinite or universal value or power, how did he frame the grounds of its limited application to or efficacy for believers? In addition, did Calvin offer an explanation of the divine intention underlying the sufficient satisfaction of Christ, specifically with regard to the question of whether God in some sense intended Christ's objective reconciliation for all sin to be such that if all believed all would be saved?

Universality of Offer and Limitation of Salvation: The Exegetical Issue

Calvin was one of the many Reformation-era inheritors of an Augustinian exegetical tradition within which those biblical passages that refer to an offer of salvation to the whole world or declare the saving power of Christ's death to all people are understood as coherent with the divine intention to save only the elect. Calvin's interpretation of these passages, notably John 1:29; 3:16; 6:33, 51; Romans 5:18; 1 Corinthians 15:22; 2 Corinthians 5:14, 19; 1 Timothy 2:4-6; Titus 2:11; Hebrews 2:9; 2 Peter 3:9; and 1 John 2:1-2, offers few unique insights and follows a pattern of understanding the divine offer to be universal or indiscriminate, given the abundant value or merit of Christ's death, but the effecting of salvation to be limited.[25] Given, moreover, Calvin's fundamental commitment to a view of salvation by grace alone, he also understood the limitation of salvation to be by divine intention rather than by human choice. With the exceptions of Calvin's exposition of 1 John 2:1-2, which contains a rather unique set of problems (and which will be discussed in a subsequent section), 2 Peter 3:9, where Calvin distinguishes between the hidden and the revealed will of God,[26] and Hebrews 2:9, where Calvin references only the objective accomplishment of Christ's work and does not address the issue of limitation,[27] the issue raised by the texts typically resolves into the meaning of such words or phrases as "world," "whole world," "all," and "all people."

---

25. Note the exhaustive listing of texts in Nicole, "Extent of the Atonement," pp. 199, 212-223.

26. John Calvin, *Commentarius in Petri apostoli epistolam posteriorem*, 2 Pet. 3:9, in CO 55, col. 475-476 (CTS 2 Peter, pp. 419-420).

27. Cf. Calvin, *In epistolam ad Hebraeos*, 2:9, in CO 55, col. 26-27 (CTS Hebrews, p. 61).

Calvin, like other exegetes in the Augustinian tradition, viewed these words and phrases as necessarily understood in the context of other declarations by the apostles, whether John or Paul, and, in their immediate context in particular biblical passages, as varied in meaning depending on the particular subject of the passage. Two factors are brought to bear on the understanding of "world," "whole world," "all," and "all people": how the word or phrase is used in a particular place and how the broader biblical expression of divine promise impinges on the understanding of a particular passage. Nor ought it to be viewed as an unfortunate complication that this interpretive issue appears in Calvin's writings—it not only belongs to a long tradition of interpretation of which Calvin was a part, it is also demanded by the text itself, given the patterns of interpretation found in pre-critical exegesis generally.[28]

Among those who argue a Calvinian doctrine of "universal atonement," Kendall in particular misreads the exegetical tradition and misunderstands the issue. He is egregiously insensitive to the patterns of Calvin's and of other interpreters' reading of texts, stating categorically that Calvin "generally leaves verses like these alone, but never does he explain ... that 'all' does not mean *all* or 'world' does not mean the *world*, as those after him tended to do."[29] Kendall is simply incorrect. The issue is not whether the interpretive restriction of "all" or of "world" to mean "all types and classes" of persons in the world appears consistently in every biblical passage containing a generalized reference to humanity as "all" or as the "world." Some of the references to "all" and to "world" are references to the human race or the created order in the most generalized terms; others indicate the extent of the promulgation of the gospel and the offer of salvation;[30] others denote the objective satisfaction,

---

28. Contra Bell, "Calvin and the Extent of the Atonement," pp. 116-117; also contra Kennedy, "Hermeneutical Discontinuity," p. 300, where the author confuses differences over specific exegetical results concerning the contextual understanding of the words "all" and "many" with "hermeneutical rules" that he proceeds to apply rather rigidly to Calvin in an attempt to contrast Calvin's exegetical results with the conclusions of later individual "Calvinists"—rather than looking at the broader exegetical tradition and recognizing that there are varied readings of these texts throughout the tradition, including varied readings among later so-called Calvinists. Kennedy also fails to examine these later Calvinists to sustain his conclusion.

29. Kendall, *Calvin and English Calvinism*, p. 13, note 2; a similar problem is found in Kennedy, "Hermeneutical Discontinuity," pp. 301-312, where the "atonement" issue is confused, and reference is made to later "Calvinists" differing substantively with Calvin and none are substantively cited: Kennedy mentions Owen but does not actually cite Owen's text, and all of the other references he makes to "Calvinists" are to twentieth-century proponents of "limited atonement," and not to early modern Reformed writers. The same problem is evident in Kennedy, *Union with Christ*, pp. 148-151, where he does not examine any later Reformed theologians but merely repeats the mantra that predestination became the "controlling" doctrine of their theologies, producing what Kennedy identifies as "limited atonement."

30. E.g., Calvin, *In epistolam Pauli ad Romanos*, 1:16, 11:32, in CO 49, col. 19, 229-230; idem, *In epistolam ad Ephesios*, 3:10, in CO 51, col. 182.

redemption, or reconciliation accomplished by Christ,[31] sometimes with a limiting qualification added;[32] others refer to the extent of sin;[33] and still others (in fact, very few) require consideration of the extent of the divine will to save human beings. Accordingly, the interpretation of biblical references to "all" as referring to "all types and classes" is in fact quite restricted and concerns only a few texts, namely, those belonging to the latter category. In such cases, moreover, contra Kendall and Kennedy, Calvin *does* typically follow the traditional Augustinian exegesis according to which "world" and "all" may be understood, in the specific contexts of 1 Timothy 2:4-6 and Titus 2:11, as indicating all believers, all of the elect, or all types and classes of people in the world.[34] The issue for Calvin, in other words, is the meaning of the universalizing phrases whether in their immediate textual context or in the broader context of Johannine or Pauline theology: Calvin does not, invariably, without attention to context, understand "world" or "all" with limitation—but he does so when an unlimited understanding of the terms clashes with what he understands to be the theological intention of the passage, given both its scope and the scope of the Johannine or Pauline theology in general. Of course, it must be remembered that this pattern is also characteristic of the traditional Augustinian exegesis, which did not invariably limit the implication of "world" or "all."[35] This understanding of Calvin's approach is born out by the examination of particular texts. It is also not the case, as Kendall and Kennedy claim, that later Reformed writers drastically altered this pattern of interpretation or lack variety in interpretation.[36]

Calvin's exegesis of the Johannine passages evidences a unity of theological perspective resting on Calvin's assumptions concerning the Fourth Gospel and its theology but also an attention to the specific scope and context of particular passages. In Calvin's reading of the texts, there is no tension or contradiction between the universalizing language of John 1:29, 3:16, and 6:33, 51 and the particularizing arguments of John 6:37, 39, 44; 17:9, 20, given the limit implicit in

---

31. E.g., Calvin, *Institutio* (1559), II.xiii.3; IV.xvii.5; idem, *In espitolam ad Galatas*, 3:13, in CO 50, col. 210; idem, *In epistolam Pauli ad Colossenses*, 1:14, in CO 52, col. 84.

32. E.g., Calvin, *In epistolam ad Hebraeos*, 9:28, in CO 55, col. 120.

33. E.g., Calvin, *Institutio* (1559), II.i.4, 6; vi.1; cf. the review and analysis of these and numerous other such passages in Rainbow, *Will of God and the Cross*, pp. 148-158.

34. John Calvin, *Commentarius in epistolam ad Timotheum I* (1548), 2:3-4, in CO 52, col. 268 (CTS 1 Timothy, p. 55); cf. Calvin, *Sermons sur la premiere epitre a Timothée* (1561), 2:11, in CO 53, col. 147-151; in translation, idem, *Sermons on the Epistles of Timothy and Titus* (London: G. Bishop, 1579), pp. 149-152; idem, *Commentarius in epistolam ad Titum* (1550), 2:11, in CO 52, col. 422-423 (CTS Titus, p. 317-318).

35. Contra Kennedy, "Hermeneutical Discontinuity," p. 300; see, e.g., Augustine, *Tractationes in Johannem*, cap. 110; idem, *Enchiridion*, cap. 61-62, 103; and see the extended treatment of Augustine's usage in Rainbow, *Will of God and the Cross*, pp. 9-22.

36. As will be seen in the various other Reformed readings of these texts referenced comparatively in the course of the following discussion.

the promises themselves. In his comments on 1:29, Calvin indicates that in this passage "world" does indeed mean all people. John 1:29, "The Lamb of God who taketh away the sin of the world," teaches "that every kind of unrighteousness that alienates human beings from God is taken away by Christ."[37] Since, moreover, the "whole world is involved in the same condemnation," the declaration of divine favor is also extended "indiscriminately [promiscue] to the whole human race." The point of the text, says Calvin, is that the Jews do not infer that Christ was sent for them only and that each and every human being should understand that "there is nothing to hinder him from obtaining reconciliation in Christ, provided that he comes to him by the guidance of faith."[38] Christ, thus, is shown to be the sole "refuge" of sinners and "the only propitiatory sacrifice, by which all our guilt is removed."[39] From Calvin's exegetical perspective, the point of the passage is not to raise the issue of the limitation of salvation, but rather to indicate, via its reference to the "world," that the problem of sin is universal, that the sole path to salvation is Christ, and that the promise of salvation has been made not only to the Jews but also to the Gentiles. There is an oblique reference to the limitation of salvation in Calvin's identification of faith as the means of receiving Christ's reconciling work. Given, moreover, that the passage, in Calvin's view, refers to the extension of the promise to both Jews and Gentiles, the scope of the passage itself excludes explicit discussion of the saving application of Christ's work to individuals.

When he comes to John 3:16, Calvin does not expand further on the meaning of "world"—he has already confirmed the universal sense of the word in his exegesis of the earlier passages. He does, however, indicate a divinely imposed limit on the effective application of Christ's work. In the passage, "life is promised generally [communiter] to all who believe in Christ"—indeed, but "faith is not common to all." Nor is faith an option for all people, "for Christ is made known [patet] and displayed [expositus] to all, but God opens the eyes of the elect alone, that they may seek him by faith." In addition, Calvin makes clear, in the same passage that faith is the means by which the benefit of Christ's death is effectively conferred: "since, therefore, faith embraces Christ, with the efficacy of his death and the fruit of his resurrection, we need not wonder if by it we obtain likewise the life of Christ."[40]

---

37. John Calvin, *Commentarius in Evangelium Joannis* (1553), 1:29, in CO 47, col. 26 (CTS *John*, I, p. 64); cf. Theodore Beza, *Jesu Christi Domini Nostri Novum Testamentum, sive Novum Foedus, cuius Graeco contextui respondent interpretationes duae ... Eiusdem Theod. Bezae Annotationes* (Cambridge: Roger Daniel, 1642), John 1:27 (p. 230), where Beza simply states that Christ's blood was the expiation from all sin (*ab omnibus peccatis*), without raising the issue of the meaning of "world."

38. Calvin, *In Evangelium Joannis*, 1:29, in CO 47, col. 26 (CTS *John*, I, p. 64); note that the CTS translation renders *promiscue* as "universally."

39. Calvin, *In Evangelium Joannis*, 1:29, in CO 47, col. 26-27 (CTS *John*, I, p. 65).

40. Calvin, *In Evangelium Joannis*, 3:16, in CO 47, col. 65 (CTS *John*, I, p. 125); Wolfgang Musculus, *Commentarii in Evangelium Ioannis in tres heptadas digesti* (Basel: Hervagius, 1554), pp. 87-88, like Calvin, identifies the "world" as indicating "the entire human race," but also cautions that the passage states that God "loved [*dilexit*]" not that God "chose [*diligit*]" the whole world. Musculus

The next references to "world" occur in John 6. In the first of these, verse 33, Calvin again understands "world" as a reference to all people, following out his earlier reading of the Johannine usage as referring to the universality of sin and the breadth of the promise: "this passage teaches that the whole world is dead to God, except to the extent that Christ enlivens it, because life will be found nowhere else but in him."[41] Calvin makes no significant comment on the extent of Christ's work with reference to John 6:51, the giving of Christ's flesh "for the life of the world."[42] But Calvin also indicates, in the same chapter, that the gift of Christ for the redemption of the universally sinful world belongs "to the counsel [consilium] of the Father"—from which one can gain the assurance "that the Gospel will always have power to gather the elect to salvation" and "that all who do not profit by the teaching of the Gospel are reprobate."[43] Or, again, in the same chapter, with reference to verse 44, "we ought not to wonder if many shrink back from the Gospel: for no one will be able to come to Christ unassisted [sponte] ... not all are drawn ... God bestows this grace on those whom he has elected."[44] In none of the contexts where he interprets "world" as indicating the universal human race, uniformly locked in sin and indiscriminately made aware of the promise of salvation, does Calvin indicate a divine intention to save all people or to send Christ to save all people—in fact, he consistently points toward the limit of salvation to the elect. Yet, as we have seen, Calvin also consistently points to Christ's death as full payment for the sins of the world, undergirding, as it were, the indiscriminate proclamation of the gospel.

Similarly, Calvin's interpretation of the various Pauline passages that have been applied to the question of the extent of Christ's work evidences less than significant interest either in developing detailed comment on the issue or in citing traditional dogmatic formulae, although he does, in a few places, indicate that the doctrinal issue belongs to the background of the interpretation of a text. Thus, at Romans 5:18, "Therefore, as by the offense of one judgment came upon all people to

---

also notes (p. 90) that this love for the whole world indicates the extension of calling but not of election to all: this passage, like Ezekiel 18, does not refer to the secret counsel of God but to those in the world who are converted to God and live. Beza, Annotationes, John 3:16 (pp. 236-237) does not raise the issue of "world."

41. Calvin, In Evangelium Joannis, 6:33, in CO 47, col. 143 (CTS John, I, p. 248); similarly, George Hutcheson, An exposition of the Gospel of Jesus Christ, according to John (London: for Ralph Smith, 1657), John 6:33 (p. 105), also noting the application of salvation not to Israel alone but to all the elect in all "nations and ranks."

42. Calvin, In Evangelium Joannis, 6:51, in CO 47, col. 153 (CTS John, I, p. 263); Beza, Annotationes, John 6:51 (p.252) here indicates briefly that "for the life of the world" in the context of v. 44, indicates those given to Christ by the Father as chosen from all nations of the earth; Hutcheson, Exposition, p. 115, indicates that world refers to the whole world as lost in sin and those throughout the whole world who are saved.

43. Calvin, In Evangelium Joannis, 6:39, in CO 47, col. 146 (CTS John, I, p. 253).

44. Calvin, In Evangelium Joannis, 6:44, in CO 47, col. 149 (CTS John, I, p. 257); similarly, Beza, Annotationes, John 6:44, not noting election but stating, "Non est enim volentis hominis, sed miserentis Dei."

condemnation; even so by the righteousness of one the free gift came upon all human beings to justification to life," Calvin comments, "He makes this favor [*gratiam*] common to all, because it is propounded [*exposita*] to all, and not because it is in reality extended to all. For though Christ suffered for the sins of the whole world, and is offered through God's benignity indifferently [*indifferenter*] to all, yet all do not receive him."[45] As in the case of Calvin's reading of Ezekiel 18:23, the universal or indiscriminate preaching of salvation belongs to a revealed or preceptive willing, here specifically identified as not effectively extending to all. In this particular text, Calvin leaves his readers with the problem that all do not receive, without providing a complete explanation in the manner of his *locus* in the *Institutes*, namely, that not all are elected.[46]

Two texts in the Corinthian correspondence (1 Cor. 15:22 and 2 Cor. 5:14, 19) do not raise for Calvin the issue of limited or unlimited application of Christ's satisfaction. On the former he merely comments on the corporate implications of the Adam-Christ parallel: "As, therefore, Adam did not die only for himself, but for us all: it follows, that Christ, who is the antitype, did not rise for himself alone. For he came, that he might restore everything that had been ruined in Adam."[47] On the latter text, "If one died for all," Calvin comments, "This design is to be carefully kept in view—that 'Christ died for us, that we might die to ourselves,'" without making reference to the issue of the limitation of Christ's death. Similarly, at verse 19, he writes, "*God was in Christ.* Some take this as meaning simply—*God reconciled the world to himself in Christ*; but the meaning is fuller and more comprehensive—*first*, that God was in Christ; and, *secondly*, that he reconciled the world to himself by his intercession," again, not raising the issue.[48]

The one Pauline text on which Calvin offers an extended discussion of the issue is 1 Timothy 2:4-6. The context of Calvin's interpretation of this apparently universalizing text is the Pauline command that Christians pray for all people,

---

45. Calvin, *In Epistolam Pauli ad Romanos*, 5:18, in CO 49, col. 101 (*CTS Romans*, p. 211); once again, Beza, *Annotationes*, Rom 5:18 (p. 400) does not take up the issue of limitation; Andrew Willet, *Hexapla: That is, a Six Fold Commentarie upon the Epistle to the Romans* (Cambridge: Cantrell Legge, 1620), p. 281, reads all as "the universall companie of the faithfull" on the ground that all human beings bear the sin of Adam and Christ, taking the place of Adam, will justify "all which beleeve in him"; similarly, David Pareus, *In divinam ad Romanos S. Pauli Apostoli Epistolam Commentarius* (Geneva: Paul Marcellus, 1617), pp. 369, 402.

46. Cf. Calvin, *Institutio* (1559), III.xxii.10; xxiv.1-3.

47. John Calvin, *Commentarius in epistolam priorem ad Corinthios* (1546), 15:21-22, in CO 49, col. 545 (*CTS 1 Corinthians*, p. 25).

48. John Calvin, *Commentarius in epistolam secundum ad Corinthios* (1546), 5:14, 19, in CO 50, col. 68, 71 (*CTS 2 Corinthians*, pp. 231, 236); note that Beza, *Annotationes*, 1 Cor. 15:22 (p. 506), does not argue that "all" means less than "all"; rather he indicates that all "universally and without exception" are subject to death in Adam and that the comparison with those in Christ refers only to those who "will be raised to glory." Beza offers no limiting comments at 2 Cor. 5:14, commenting only on the "infinite love" of God in Christ; at v. 19, he identifies "world" as "the elect from the entire world" and the Christian or catholic church (ibid., p. 527).

supported, Calvin indicates, by two arguments: first (v. 2), that such prayer conduces to a peaceful and godly life in society; and second (v. 3), that such prayer is "good and acceptable" in the sight of God. The fourth verse, "Who will have all people to be saved," Calvin writes, stands as "a confirmation of the second argument" in which the apostle indicates that "all our prayers should be subject to the decree of God."[49] Even more pointedly, the apostle further stated that God not only "will have all people to be saved" but also would have them "come to the acknowledgment of the truth." This divine intention, Calvin expands, is such that

> God has at heart the salvation of all, because he invites all to the acknowledgment
> of his truth. The argument is *a posteriori*. For, if the gospel is the power of God for
> salvation to all who believe, it is certain that all those to whom the gospel is
> addressed are invited to the hope of eternal life.[50]

Calvin is, in other words, quite intent on indicating a universal or indiscriminate aspect of the gospel: it has the power to impart salvation to all who believe. Calvin, however, immediately raises the issue of election, comments that "those who oppose this text [*locus*] to predestination hallucinate" and argues that the passage in no way indicates an indiscriminate willing on the part of God that each and every person be saved.[51] Bullinger does not raise the issue of predestination but nonetheless similarly notes that use of this text to argue salvation of all, including the wicked, would be blasphemous, inasmuch as those who believe will be saved and those who do not will be damned.[52] Calvin, as would various later Reformed writers including Owen, goes

---

49. Calvin, *In epistolam ad Timotheum I*, 2:3-4, in CO 52, col. 268: "ut huic Dei decreto vota nostra subserviant." (CTS *1 Timothy*, p. 54); Peter Martyr Vermigli, *Loci communes*, 2nd ed. (London: Thomas Vautrollerius, 1583), III.i.45 (p. 466), offers an almost identical approach to the text. Beza, *Annotationes*, 1 Tim. 2:4 (p. 628) argues differently, reading the "all human beings" as *quosvis homines*, human beings everywhere, but noting that *omnes homines* would be adequate if it were taken "not universally but collectively & indefinitely." Note that it was Johannes Piscator, *Analysis logica omnium epistolarum Pauli ... una cum scholiis & observationibus locorum doctrinae* (London: George Bishop, 1608), p. 606, who denied the sufficiency-efficiency formula at this point, arguing it to be self-contradictory unless it was taken to mean that Christ died both sufficiently and efficiently for the elect alone. The Canons of Dort should be understood as quietly rebutting Piscator as well as overtly condemning the Remonstrants. On the history of exegesis of the text as a background to Calvin, see Martin Foord, "God Wills All People to Be Saved—Or Does He? Calvin's Reading of 1 Timothy 2:4," in *Engaging with Calvin: Aspects of the Reformer's Legacy for Today*, ed. Mark D. Thompson (Nottingham: Apollos, 2009), pp. 179–203.
50. Calvin, *In epistolam ad Timotheum I*, 2:3-4, in CO 52, col. 268, citing Rom. 1:16 (CTS *1 Timothy*, p. 54); cf. Beza, *Annotationes*, 1 Tim. 2:4 (p. 628), also citing Rom. 1:16 and arguing that the text refers to the universal or indiscriminate proclamation and noting that the apostle does not mean that all human beings will be saved.
51. Calvin, *In epistolam ad Timotheum I*, 2:3-4, in CO 52, col. 268 (CTS *1 Timothy*, p. 54); note how Kennedy, *Union with Christ*, pp. 44-46, confuses a universal or indiscriminate offer with universal "atonement."
52. Heinrich Bullinger, *In D. Apostoli Pauli as Thessalonicenses, Timotheum, Titum, et Philemonem commentarii*, p. 567, bound in Bullinger, *In omnes apostolicas epistolas, divi videlicet Pauli XIII et VII*

on to state the basic Augustinian conclusion, that the "all" of the passage indicates that "no people [*populum*] and no rank [*ordinem*] in the world" is excluded from salvation, that therefore the gospel ought to "be proclaimed to all without exception" because "God invites all equally to partake of salvation," quite specifically in the sense that Paul's language indicated "classes of human beings [*hominum generibus*], and not to individual persons [*non singulis personis*]."[53]

Similarly, in his sermon on 1 Timothy 2:4, Calvin refers to those who interpret the passage as indicating a divine will or intention to save each and every human being as "beasts" who lack understanding of Scripture and who would "nullify" God's election.[54] Calvin continues,

> They might have had some basis for saying this, if Paul were speaking here about individual persons: but even then the issue would not have lacked a solution. For, although the will of God ought not to be judged from his secret decrees, when he reveals them to us by outward signs, it does not therefore follow that he has not determined with himself what he intends to do as to every individual person. But I say nothing on that subject, because it has nothing to do with this passage. For the Apostle simply means, that there is no people and no rank in the world that is excluded from salvation; because God wishes that the gospel should be proclaimed to all without exception.[55]

Both in his treatise *De aeterna Dei predestinatione* and in his sermon on 1 Timothy 2:4, Calvin presses the issue of the text one step further, arguing in a manner that would be echoed by Beza: if God does in fact will that all without distinction "come unto the knowledge of the truth," has his will changed since the beginning of creation? God's truth was never given to each and every human being: how then can God now will all to know his truth unless his will has changed? After all, the apostle

canonicas commntarii (Zürich: Froschauer, 1549), continuously paginated; and cf. the similar conclusion drawn in Foord, "God Wills All People to Be Saved," pp. 192-193.

53. Calvin, *In epistolam ad Timotheum I*, 2:3-4, in CO 52, col. 268 (CTS 1 Timothy, pp. 54-55); so also Owen, *Death of Death*, in *Works*, X, pp. 345, 381; cf. Nicole, "Extent of the Atonement," pp. 212-213.

54. Calvin, *Sermons sur la premiere epitre a Timothée*, 2:3-4, in CO 53, col. 149-150.

55. Calvin, *In epistolam ad Timotheum I*, 2:3-4, in CO 52, col. 268 (CTS 1 Timothy, p. 54); Thomas, *Extent of the Atonement*, p. 33, somewhat misleadingly views Calvin as shifting "back and forth between generic and unrestricted universality," arguably mistaking distinctions for divergences in formulation, and notably mistaking Calvin's distinction between the revealed and the secret will of God for a doctrine of double will. On the issue of a double will, see below, chapter 4. There is a similar misunderstanding in Foord's reading of these texts, where he claims that Calvin's reading of "all" can actually mean "*all* from all kinds." The problem appears to be that Foord misreads *tous peuples* as meaning, strictly, "all people" when the plural, *peuples*, clearly indicates nations, not individuals: cf. Foord, "God Wills All People to Be Saved," p. 198; with Calvin, *Sermons sur la premiere epitre a Timothée*, 2:3-4, in CO 53, col. 148. Thus, Foord's conclusion ("God Wills All People to Be Saved, pp. 201-202) that Calvin departs from the standard Augustinian reading of the text is mistaken.

puts two phrases together in the passage—"to be saved" and "to come unto the knowledge of the truth." Calvin answers the question with another question:

> For if he willed that his truth be known to all, why did he not proclaim his law also to the Gentiles? Why did he confine the light of life within the narrow limits of Judaea?[56]

Inasmuch as "no other will of God is understood, than that which appears in the external preaching of the gospel," Paul simply means by "all" that "God wills the salvation of all whom he mercifully invites to Christ."[57] This must be so, since not only is it the case that not all persons who could profit from the gospel are saved, but it is also true that the gospel has not been preached to vast masses of humanity in the past, namely all of the gentiles before the advent of Christ and large numbers of gentiles not reached by the gospel since the advent of Christ.[58] Calvin, in short, denied universal grace.[59]

As Calvin concludes in the commentary, drawing once again on the Augustinian "all types and classes" argument,

> the preaching of the gospel gives life; and hence [the apostle] justly concludes that God invites all equally to partake salvation. But the present discourse relates to classes of human beings, and not to individual persons; for his sole object is, to include in this number princes and foreign nations.[60]

More briefly, but in the same vein, at Titus 2:11 he writes,

> *Bringing salvation to all people.* That it is common to all is expressly testified by him on account of the slaves of whom he had spoken. Yet he does not mean individual people, but rather describes individual classes, or various ranks of life.[61]

---

56. John Calvin, *De aeterna Dei praedestinatione*, in CO 8, col. 302-303, 336; (*Eternal Predestination*, pp. 108, 148); cf. John Calvin, *Sermons sur la premiere Epitre a Timothée*, 2:3-4 (sermon 13), in CO 53, col. 151; and see Theodore Beza, *Quaestionum et responsionum christianarum libellus, in quo praecipua Christianae religionis capita kat' epitome proponuntur* (London: Henry Bynneman, 1571), pp. 122-124; idem, *Christian questions and answers* (1578), fol. 79v-80v.

57. Calvin, *De aeterna Dei praedestinatione*, in CO 8, col. 304: "Quod tamen non alia sit Dei voluntas intelligenda, quam quae patefit externa evangelii praedicatione ... Deum significat Paulus omnium velle salutem, quod benigne ad Christum invitat"; similarly, ibid., col. 308 (*Eternal Predestination*, pp. 109).

58. Calvin, *Sermons sur la premiere Epitre a Timothée*, 2:3-4 (sermon 13), in CO 53, col. 151.

59. Cf. Calvin, *In epistolam Pauli ad Romanos*, 5:8, in CO 49, col. 101; and see the conclusions in Cunningham, "Calvin and Beza," pp. 398-399; note also that Calvin is more consistent here than Hans Boersma, "Calvin and the Extent of the Atonement," *Evangelical Quarterly*, 64/4 (1992), p. 353, allows: it is not as if Calvin "wants to maintain a universal offer" while at the same time denying a universal extent of Christ's work—the offer is indiscriminate, not absolutely universal.

60. Calvin, *In epistolam ad Timotheum I*, 2:3-4, in CO 52, col. 268 (CTS 1 Timothy, p. 55).

61. Calvin, *In epistolam ad Titum*, 2:11, in CO 52, col. 422-423 (CTS Titus, pp. 317-318); similarly, Beza, *Annotationes*, Titus 2:11 (p. 650). Note that Owen, without indicating any restriction, refers the text to the preaching of the promises of the gospel: John Owen, *The Doctrine of the Saints*

Quite simply, "all" does not mean all individuals or each and every individual—and the universal proclamation of the gospel is understood as an indiscriminate offer, not as an offer that had been proclaimed or would be proclaimed to each and every human being.[62]

Nor is Calvin's Augustinian reading to these Johannine and Pauline passages to be set against or understood and modified by his reading of the places in Scripture where the text indicates a salvation or ransom for "many." A case in point is Calvin's reading of Matthew 20:28 and its parallel, Mark 10:45, "the Son of Man came … that he might give his life as a ransom for many," in connection with Romans 5. Calvin comments,

> Many is not put definitely for a certain number, but for a greater number; for he contrasts himself with all others. And in this sense it is used in Romans 5:15, where Paul does not speak of some part of humanity, but embraces all humankind.[63]

Kennedy is correct that Calvin does not take the "opportunity to limit this passage to apply only to the elect" but is quite mistaken in his next comment, that Calvin

---

Perseverance Explained and Conformed (1654), in *Works*, XI, p. 402. Concerning Owen's development on the issue of the necessity of Christ's work and the positive relation of his later thought on this particular point to Cameron and Amyraut, see Carl R. Trueman, "The Necessity of the Atonement," in *Drawn into Controversie: Reformed Theological Diversity and Debates Within Seventeenth-Century British Puritanism*, ed. Michael G. A. Haykin and Mark Jones (Göttingen: Vandenhoeck & Ruprecht, 2011), pp. 204-222.

62. Bullinger, like Calvin, sees the text as referring to the universality of preaching the gospel but understands "all" differently: the "all" does not refer to all nations and conditions (*non uni alicui genti aut aetati*) but genuinely to "all human beings" (*sed omnibus hominibus*): the preaching of the gospel excludes no one except those who are excluded by their own wickedness, given that it announces the fullness of truth and grace in Christ: In *D. Apostoli Pauli as Thessalonicenses, Timotheum, Titum, et Philemonem commentarii*, p. 628. Bullinger thus provides a clearer precedent than Calvin for later hypothetical universalism—as also does Musculus, who allows an Ockhamist solution indicating an antecedent divine willing that all human beings might be saved on the condition of their accetance of the gospel: see Musculus, *Loci communes theologiae sacrae* (Basel: Sebastianus Henricpetrus, 1599), xlv (p. 451). Vermigli, by contrast, offers a reading of the *voluntas beneplaciti/signi* distinction that disallows any conditional antecedent willing in the *voluntas beneplaciti* and therefore stands more clearly with Calvin than either Bullinger or Musculus: see Vermigli, *Loci communes* (1583), I.xiv.38; III.i.45 (pp. 114, 466); and cf. the comments in Foord, "God Wills All People to Be Saved," pp. 194-196.

63. Calvin, *Commentarius in harmoniam evangelicam*, Matt. 20:28 in CO 45, col. 559 (CTS Harmony, II, p. 427); Beza, *Annotationes*, Matt. 20:28 and Mark 10:45 (pp. 68, 132), does not deal with the issue limiting the "many"; nor does Bullinger, *In sacrosanctum Evangelium domini nostri Iesu Christi secundum Marcum commentariorum* (Zürich: Froschauer, 1545), lib. IV, fol. 27v; Bullinger does, however, raise the issue of Matt. 20:28 specifically in the context of Rom. 5:15, where he indicates, as in his comment onTitus 2:11, that "many" indicates "all" and specifically that the promise of "redemption for all" means redemption "for all the faithful," to the exclusion of the "unfaithful": see Heinrich Bullinger, *In … Pavli ad Romanos Epistolam, … Commentarius* (Zurich: Christoph Froschauer, 1533), pp. 78-79.

"universalizes it."[64] Calvin simply reads "many [multos]" as meaning "for a greater number," literally, "for more [pro pluribus]"—he does not take it to mean "all" in the sense of an extension of salvation to each and every human being, and he rather carefully selects plus, the comparative of multus, rather than plurimus, the superlative. Nor does Calvin's reference to "all humankind [totum humanum genus]" in the next sentence imply a different meaning. The actual issue lodged in Calvin's comment is made clear in his reading of the passage in Romans to which he refers. The whole passage, Romans 5:15-19, includes statements to the effect that the grace of God has "abounded to many" (v. 15), that "the free gift came upon all human beings [in omnes homines] for justification to life" (v. 18), and "by the obedience of one shall many be made righteous" (v. 19). There, Calvin does not see any need to explain the "many," but, as noted previously, he distinguished between the general or indiscriminate preaching of the gospel, grounded in the suffering of Christ for the sins of the whole world, and the limited extension of Christ's benefits to those who actually "receive him."[65] Calvin, in other words, disavowed a notion of universal grace in the sense of a proclamation of the gospel to each and every human being in all ages of the world: his typical language of universality referred to the indiscriminate, indifferent, or general preaching of the gospel and to the general or universal offer presented therein that those who hear and believe will be saved. We are left with a conclusion very much like the traditional sufficiency-efficiency distinction, with the efficiency understood as limited by God's will to the elect.

Calvin and the Traditional Scholastic Distinction: Infinite Sufficiency and Limited Efficiency

The specific terms used by Calvin reflect a certain degree of flexibility as determined by context. Thus, Calvin employs a series of terms that typically relate to the objective nature of Christ's work as a sacrifice (sacrificium), expiation (expiatio), offering (oblatio), price (pretium), or satisfaction (satisfactio); he also employs terms that can refer either to Christ's objective work or to its subjective apprehension or application, namely, reconciliation (reconciliatio), redemption

---

64. Kennedy, "Hermeneutical Discontinuity," p. 302; note, contra Kennedy, that John Owen did not argue that "many" ought consistently to be read as indicating a limit. Indeed, while identifying a limit in Matt. 20:28, Owen specifically indicated that "many is sometimes meant absolutely for all, as Rom.v.19": see Owen, Death of Death, in Works, X, p. 214.

65. Calvin, In epistolam Pauli ad Romanos, 5:18, in CO 49, col. 101 (CTS Romans, p. 211). Cf. Peter Martyr Vermigli, In epistolam s. Pauli apostoli ad Romanos . . . commentarii (Zürich: s.n., 1559), Rom. 5:16 (p. 268); Vermigli also saw no need to offer an extended discussion of how the "many" who perish in Adam indicates all humanity while the "many" who are saved in Christ indicates only some of the human race, pointing out that "we are all infected in Adam, but we are not all delivered in Christ" and that the apostle here "did not refer ... to the number of those who are damned or saved: but only to the effects that have come forth from Adam and Christ. ... Though all human beings are not brought to salvation, nonetheless the merit and grace of Christ was of itself sufficient [ex se satis] for all" but "not all are predestined to salvation."

(*redemptio*), and salvation (*salutus*); and he variously refers to the value or worth (*valor*), the power (*virtus*), and the limited efficacy (*efficacia*) of Christ's sacrifice. A survey of the various terms and their implications does little to define precisely how Calvin's understanding of the divine intentionality underlying fullness or universality or Christ's work related to the rather varied later formulations offered by Reformed hypothetical universalists and their opponents—nor, certainly, given the problems of terminology in the modern debates over his teaching, can the terms be wedged into the modern, rather vague language of either unlimited or limited atonement.[66]

As indicated above, Calvin did know and accept, with some qualification, the medieval distinction between the "sufficiency" of Christ's satisfaction for all sin and its "efficiency" for the elect alone. This is also a point that demands some exposition, given the attempts of several writers to sidestep the implication both of the formula and of Calvin's arguments concerning it. By way of example, Kendall indicates that Calvin "rejects" the formula but allows, in a limited sense, for its truth insofar as "only the elect savingly believe," while Bell rightly notes that "Calvin allows for the truth of the statement but rejects its use because the issue is not the power of Christ's death, but those for whom it was intended" while at the same time missing Calvin's underlying point.[67] Calvin did not, in fact, reject the formula. Kendall's argument rests on the mistaken assumption that the sufficiency-efficiency/efficacy distinction implies "limited atonement" and on the claim that election can be somehow segmented off from the issue of the extent of Christ's work, leaving an "unlimited atonement" intact—indicating both the confusion caused by use of the term "atonement" and a resultant confusion over the meaning of "efficacy."

---

66. Revising my overly optimistic comment on the terms in *Christ and the Decree*, p. 34; note also that, given the objective and subjective use if the terms *reconciliatio* and *redemptio*, neither can the modern debate be resolved by adopting language of "universal" and "particular redemption" as Rainbow, *Will of God and the Cross*, pp. 1-2, and throughout, attempted to do, given among other things that "particular redemption" can be (and was) used to refer not only to the limitation of the efficacy of Christ's death but also to the limitation of divine intention and even to the limitation of the sufficiency. There is some basis for speaking of "definite redemption," but even this requires further definition and qualification: note Canons of Dort, ii, rejection of errors 1: "Qui docent, 'Quod Deus Pater Filium suum in mortem crucis destinaverit, sine certo ac *definito* consilio quemquam nominatim salvandi, adeo ut impetrationi mortis Christi sua necessitas, utilitas, dignitas sarta tecta, et numeris suis perfecta, completa atque integra constare potuisset, etiamsi impetrata *redemptio* nulli individuo unquam actu ipso fuisset applicata.'" The very specific point made by the canons is that salvation has been obtained (*impetrata*) by a certain and definite counsel (*certo ac definito consilio*), so that the redemption obtained (*impetrata redemptio*) is perfectly accomplished, i.e., is absolutely coordinate with the purpose of saving some particular individuals. The intent of the canons here is to use the *impetratio/applicatio* against the Remonstrant claim that God antecedently and indefinitely wills to save the human race. This definition, moreover, coheres with Calvin's assumption that the promise of salvation to all who believe represents not an antecedent divine willing but rather a revealed will concerning the truth of the gospel as indiscriminately preached.

67. E.g., Kendall, *Calvin and English Calvinism*, p. 16, note 2; Bell, "Calvin and the Extent of Atonement," p. 117; cf. Kennedy, *Union with Christ*, pp. 38-40, 50-51.

"Calvin," he comments, "holds that the issue with regard to Christ's death is not the efficacy in itself but to whom Christ gives himself to be enjoyed."[68] "Efficacy in itself" makes no sense inasmuch as the efficacy of Christ's satisfaction lies, as the traditional distinction indicated, precisely in its application—what Kendall thinks of as "efficacy in itself" is actually the sufficiency.[69] Examination of the two passages in which Calvin references the distinction is in order.

In commenting on the text of 1 John 2:1-2, "And if any man sin, we have an advocate with the Father, Jesus Christ the righteous: And he is the propitiation for our sins; and not for ours only, but also for the sins of the whole world," Calvin argues that Christ is "the sole advocate" inasmuch as he alone is capable of undertaking the priestly "office" of providing God with a sacrifice for sin. Indeed, Calvin echoes the traditional Anselmic language when he notes, by way of further explanation of the point, "when God is offended, in order to pacify him, a satisfaction [*satisfactio*] is required."[70]

Calvin also recognizes that verse 2, "and not for ours only, but also for the sins of the whole world," raises the question of the universality of Christ's satisfaction. These phrases, he indicates, expand upon the first verse "in order that the faithful might be assured that the expiation made by Christ, extends to all who by faith embrace the gospel."[71] The implication of this universalizing statement, Calvin continues, is that application of Christ's work extends not merely to the faithful known to those addressed by the apostle but to all who "by faith who embrace the gospel," wherever and whenever that may be. Once this limitation is expressed, then the question again arises concerning the universalizing language of the text: what is the meaning of the word "*all* or whole," or, as Calvin comments, "how have the sins of the whole world been expiated"? Calvin now turns to the "delirium of the fanatics" that "deserves no refutation"—specifically use of the text as a "pretense" to "extend salvation to all the reprobate, and therefore to Satan himself."[72] The text does not indicate universal salvation resting on the infinite value of the sacrifice. Thus, the application of Christ's work is limited to the faithful, but the objective propitiation or sacrifice has a universal dimension related specifically to the salvation of all who faithfully hear and receive the gospel.

The exegetical tradition, Calvin recognized, had here often introduced the time-honored scholastic distinction that "Christ suffered sufficiently for the whole world,

---

68. Kendall, *Calvin and English Calvinism*, p. 32; cf. ibid., p. 16.

69. Note that Kendall's citation of Calvin's *Eternal Predestination* is from the Reid translation, "For our present question is not how great the power of Christ is or what efficacy it has in itself, but to whom He gives Himself to be enjoyed" (p. 148)—but Calvin's Latin does not contain the phrase "what efficacy it has in itself." Rather it reads, "quid per se valeat," i.e., "what it is worth of itself": CO 8, col. 336.

70. Calvin, *In Iohannis apostoli epistola*, 2:1, in CO 55, col. 309 (*CTS 1 John*, p. 171).

71. Calvin, *In Iohannis apostoli epistola*, 2:2, in CO 55, col. 310 (*CTS 1 John*, p. 173).

72. Calvin, *In Iohannis apostoli epistola*, 2:2, in CO 55, col. 310 (*CTS 1 John*, p. 173).

but efficiently only for the elect" in order "to avoid this absurdity." "This solution," Calvin adds, "has commonly prevailed in the schools."[73] Having stated the distinction—presumably because he recognized it to be the standard solution to the problem of the text as found in the older tradition, notably in the works of such late medieval exegetes as Nicholas of Lyra and Dionysius the Carthusian, and therefore assumed that he ought to mention it at this point,[74] despite his usual restraint in reserving the substance of "dogmatic disputations" or *loci communes* for his *Institutes*,[75]—Calvin proceeds to indicate that it does not apply to this particular text, while at the same time indicating the theological correctness of the distinction: "Though then I allow that what has been said is true, yet I deny that it is suitable to this passage. The design of John was no other than to make this benefit common to the whole church."[76] Calvin thus accepts the standard scholastic distinction, but appears to indicate that the text itself did not intend to speak either in general theological terms of the sufficiency of Christ's sacrifice for all sin or of the restriction of that sufficient payment by efficient application to the elect only; rather, the text intended to speak directly to the question of the application of Christ's propitiatory work to the church. Significantly, Bullinger refrained from use of the sufficiency-efficiency distinction as an explanation of the text.[77]

The problem here—both for the interpretation of the text and for the interpretation of Calvin—is the strict reading of the message in its declaration of salvation to Christians, in the specific context of the apostle's hope that those he addresses will not sin or, as Calvin says, will "abstain from sins." The apostle's primary intention in his message "was to keep human beings from sinning"—while at the same time to assure his readers that, since they cannot be "perfectly righteous," Christ is still our advocate before God.[78] What Calvin does not do here is raise the later question of hypothetical universalism, namely, whether the sufficiency of Christ's satisfaction, beyond undergirding the universal proclamation of the gospel, also represents a hypothetical salvation of all if all would believe,

---

73. Calvin, *In Iohannis apostoli epistola*, 2:2, in CO 55, col. 310 (CTS 1 John, p. 173).

74. Cf. Nicholas of Lyra, *Postilla super totam bibliam* (Venice: Octavianus Scotus, 1488), 1 John 2, fol. E2 verso: "*pro totius mundi.* scilicet quantum ad sufficientiam, sed per electis tum quantum ad efficaciam"; so also Dionysius Carthusianus, *In epistolas omnes canonicas, in Acta apostolorum, & in Apocalypsin, piae ac eruditae enarrationes* (Cologne: Petrus Quentell, 1533), 1 John 2, fol. Kiii verso.

75. Calvin, *Institutes* (1539/59), Joannis Calvinus lectori; cf. Muller, *Unaccommodated Calvin*, pp. 27-29.

76. Calvin, *In Iohannis apostoli epistola,*, 2:2, in CO 55, col. 310 (CTS 1 John, p. 173). Calvin was hardly alone in this reading: Pellican had argued in much the same way, indicating that the "whole world" was not meant to include those who hated Christ but "the whole church, namely, all those who come to him in true faith": see Conrad Pellican, *In omnes apostolicas epistolas ... commentarii* (Zürich: Froschauer, 1539), p. 758.

77. Heinrich Bullinger, *In epistolas apostolorum canonicas septem commentarii* (Zürich: Froschauer, 1549), pp. 80-81.

78. Calvin, *In Iohannis apostoli epistola*, 2:1, in CO 55, col. 308-309 (CTS 1 John, p. 170).

although his declamation against the extension of salvation to the reprobate militates against finding a tendency toward hypothetical universalism in Calvin's exegesis of this text. Bullinger, incidentally, much more clearly than Calvin directs the text toward the issue of the fullness of divine grace in Christ—but argues not a case for hypothetical universalism but rather a case against the "Pontifici" who would rest salvation on alternative satisfactions.[79]

Even so, the "conditional particle, *if,*" Calvin argues, ought to be understood as "causal": "if any man sin, we have an advocate." Sin is ultimately unavoidable in our fallen condition, even after the work of redemption has begun. The apostle indicates, therefore, that the gospel both calls us from sin and then, when sin continues to ensnare believers, offers a further message of redemption:

> In short, John means, that we are not only called away from sin by the gospel, because God invites us to himself, and offers to us the Spirit of regeneration: but also that a provision is made for miserable sinners, that they may have God always propitious to them, and that the sins by which they are entangled, do not prevent them from becoming just, because they have a Mediator to reconcile them to God.[80]

The apostle's intention, in other words, was to place the problem of the continuing sinfulness of believers into the context of the requirement of obedience and of the sacrifice of Christ, without diminishing the requirement but nonetheless without removing the promise of "remedy" and of "reconciliation" with God for all those sinners who belong to Christ through faith. Christ is, therefore, declared to be "the only true salvation of the world" with the understanding that "the word *all* or whole ... does not include the reprobate, but designates those who will believe as well as those who were then scattered through the various parts of the world."[81]

The context of the apostolic message, therefore, dictates the meaning of the text and excludes the use of the somewhat more formal theological construct distinguishing the sufficiency of Christ's satisfaction from its efficacy. Nonetheless, Calvin not only indicates his acceptance of the distinction, he also indicates that the "reprobate" are excluded from Christ's propitiation: if he was unwilling to declare, by using the traditional distinction, that John's text limited the efficacy of Christ's satisfaction to the elect, he was quite ready to state without any qualification that the apostle surely meant to exclude the reprobate. In this particular comment, therefore, Calvin both acknowledges the theological rectitude of the distinction later used in the Canons of Dort and asserts quite categorically that Christ's expiatory death was not intended by God to save the reprobate. There is no hint of an Amyraldian hypothetical universalism in Calvin's argument.[82]

79. Bullinger, *In epistolas apostolorum canonicas septem commentarii,* p. 81.
80. Calvin, *In Iohannis apostoli epistola,* 2:1, in CO 55, col. 308-309 (CTS 1 John, p. 171).
81. Calvin, *In Iohannis apostoli epistola,* 2:2, in CO 55, col. 310 (CTS 1 John, p. 173).
82. See my analysis of Amyraut's use of Calvin, below, chapter 4.

A further clue to Calvin's view of the traditional distinction between sufficiency and efficiency is found in his treatise on predestination against Pighius and Georgius. Here again, he notes the distinction as the "common solution" to the problem, but observes that the distinction "does not avail" against the "absurdity" of Georgius' claim that, if indeed as Scripture insists, Christ was the "propitiation for the sins of the whole world," then to exclude the reprobate from Christ's payment is to "place them outside the world."[83]

Nonetheless, in the treatise De aeterna Dei praedestinatione, as in the commentary on 1 John 2:1-2, Calvin does not deny the distinction between sufficiency and efficiency, but only denies its applicability or usefulness in settling a particular argument: the distinction, in fact, does identify Christ's propitiation as sufficient to pay for the sins of the whole world and then it does restrict efficacy to the elect. Given that the distinction refers sufficiency to the payment for sin and not to all persons, it cannot answer the question of referentiality of the universal payment to all persons, including the reprobate. That is Calvin's point, as is apparent from the subsequent argumentation: Christ died for the "expiation of the sins of the whole world" and the elect are scattered throughout the world, mixed together with the reprobate. Christ's expiation is extended to the faithful. Calvin then restates the issue in his own language, noting that the issue was not the power (virtus) of Christ's death or its objective worth (valor), but to whom Christ gives himself.[84] Christ's work was the "expiation of the sins of the whole world." Reconciliation is therefore "placed before all," but the benefit is "peculiar to the elect," because the potentially universal work of Christ is actually effective only for some.[85] The universal offer here extends to all, elect and reprobate alike, and it is a valid offer given the full expiation (in itself sufficient) made for all sin—but the particularity of the application is limited by divine election.[86] Calvin also here briefly references his other point,

---

83. Calvin, De aeterna Dei praedestinatione, in CO 8, col. 336 (Eternal Predestination, p. 148).

84. Cf. Calvin, De aeterna Dei praedestinatione, in CO 8, col. 336: "Nec vero qualis sit Christi virtus, vel quid per se valeat, nunc quaeritur: sed quibus se fruendum exhibeat" (Eternal Predestination, p. 149); with Calvin, In Ioannis apostoli epistola, 2:2, in CO 55, col. 310 (CTS 1 John, p. 171).

85. Calvin, De aeterna Dei praedestinatione, in CO 8, col. 336: "Unde colligimus quamvis per ipsum offeratur omnibus reconciliatio, peculiare tamen electis beneficium" (Eternal Predestination, p. 149). There has been debate among various dogmaticians over the translation of offero in this context—i.e., whether it should be rendered "offer," "place before," or "proffer." Without entering the modern debate over a "well-meant" or "free offer," it can be observed that Calvin's usage here parallels the use of exhibeo in his doctrine of the Lord's Supper, where the sense is clearly that Christ and his benefits are genuinely presented, and it is only sin that bars the way to reception. On Calvin's understanding of exhibeo, see Richard A. Muller, "From Zürich or from Wittenberg? An Examination of Calvin's Early Eucharistic Thought," Calvin Theological Journal, 45/2 (2010), pp. 243-255; and note idem, "Calvin on Sacramental Presence, in the Shadow of Marburg and Zürich," Lutheran Quarterly, 23 (2009), pp. 147-167.

86. Calvin, De aeterna Dei praedestinatione, in CO 8, col. 336: "Atqui ego sis universalem Dei gratiam esse fateor, ut in hoc tantum situm esse discrimen addam: quod non omnes secundum Dei

namely, that God cannot be viewed as willing to save each and every human being given the vast number of human beings left outside of the preaching of salvation since the beginning of the world.[87] We are back to the outlines of the sufficiency/efficiency distinction, now modified in terms of the problem of the universal or, more precisely, the indiscriminate preaching of salvation over against its particular application—and perhaps looking toward the alternative distinction between accomplishment (*impetratio*) and application (*applicatio*) preferred by some later Reformed writers after the debates with Arminius and the Remonstrants.[88] Georgius' argument has been answered in such a way as to prevent the illusion that inclusion of the sins of the reprobate within the sufficient payment made by Christ also somehow extends participation in Christ to the reprobate as individuals.

It was, presumably, Calvin's intention to exclude the reprobate from Christ's payment and, at the same time, to interpret "world" in such a way as to limit its meaning in this particular text—namely, generally and broadly rather than as absolutely universally. Even so, the phrases used by Calvin in his response echo strongly the terms used in his exposition from the following year (1553) of the Johannine passages, including his exposition of 1 John 2:1-2: when used salvifically, "world" or "whole world" indicates all of the faithful, the elect in all times and places, throughout the whole world; when used in its broadest possible meaning, "world" means all people, including the reprobate. The resemblance between the two discussions, moreover, is hardly accidental: we ought, certainly, to assume that, given the length of time requisite to the preparation of his Johannine commentaries, Calvin was writing on the Fourth Gospel at the same time that he was engaged in the refutation of Pighius and Georgius.[89]

Calvin did, moreover, in a few places, indicate the "sufficiency" of Christ's death for all, albeit without clear reference to the whole formula. Commenting on Isaiah's statement that the servant of the Lord bore the sins of "many," Calvin indicates that

---

propositum vocantur" (*Eternal Predestination*, p. 148); cf. Rainbow's critique of Kendall on the point in *Will of God and the Cross*, pp. 133-134.

87. Calvin, *De aeterna Dei praedestinatione*, in CO 8, col. 337 (*Eternal Predestination*, p. 149).

88. Cf., e.g., William Ames, *Medulla ss. theologiae, ex sacris literis, earumque interpretibus, extracta, & methodicè disposita* (London: Robert Allott, 1630), I.xx.18, 22; xxiv.1, 7-9; idem, *Coronis ad collationem hagiensem, qua argumenta pastorum Hollandiae adversus remonstrantium quinque articulos de divina praedestinatione, et captibus ei adnexis, producta, ab horum exceptionibus vindicantur*, 4th ed. (London: Felix Kingston, 1630), II.iii, vi (pp. 138-139, 161-163); Walter Balcanqual in John Hales, *Golden remains of the ever memorable Mr. John Hales of Eaton-Colledge, &c. With additions from the authors own copy, viz., sermons & miscellanies, also letters and expresses concerning the Synod of Dort. From an authentick hand*, 3rd ed. (London: T. B. for George Pawlet, 1688), pp. 507-508; Owen, *Death of Death*, III.i, in *Works*, X, pp. 232-236; John Flavel, *A Brief Account of the Rise and Growth of Antinomianism; the deduction of the principal errors of that sect, with modest and seasonable reflections upon them*, in *The Works of John Flavel*, 6 vols. (London: Baynes and Son, 1820), III, pp. 559-560; Salomon van Til, *Compendium theologiae revelatae* (Leiden: Jordan Luchtmans, 1704), II.vii (p. 151).

89. Cf. T. H. L. Parker, *Calvin's New Testament Commentaries*, 2nd ed. (Edinburgh: T. & T. Clark, 1993), pp. 28-29.

"many" and "all" often have the same meaning—so that the text does not stand in contradiction to other places that use "all" rather than "many." Jesus was "presented to the whole world" and "suffered for all of us," leaving unbelievers "inexcusable" and giving believers to know that no matter how many turn to him, Christ will nonetheless "suffice for each one of us [*suffice a chacun de nous*]"—Christ is "sufficient to save us all [*suffisant pour nous sauver tous*]."[90] Note that in the commentary Calvin references Romans 5:18 as another place where "many" references "all," but neither there nor in the commentary on Isaiah 53:12 does he argue either universal grace or identify Christ's satisfaction according to its efficacy or application.[91]

Nor does Calvin's refusal to raise the issue of the sufficiency and efficiency of Christ's propitiation in his *Antidote* to the Council of Trent constitute any counter evidence.[92] The third and fourth decrees of the sixth session of Trent teach, as preparatory theses to the discussion of justification, that Christ was sent by the Father as the propitiation for sins, "not only for ours, but also for the sins of the whole world," and that although Christ "died for all, all do not receive the benefit of his death." Calvin responded simply with the comment, "The third and fourth heads I do not touch."[93] The response does not indicate either total agreement with the two decrees or a partial disagreement—but only Calvin's formal unwillingness to offer a close exegesis of a doctrinal point not specifically at issue in the debate over justification. Of course, had Calvin held to a doctrine of the radical limitation of redemption, in which Christ's death was not an all-sufficient propitiation for sin, then some response might have been expected. Assuming, however, Calvin's basic acceptance of the sufficiency/efficiency distinction in the context of an Augustinian exegesis of the universalistic texts, no further comment was necessary. Several of the delegates at Trent, like Seripando, would certainly have taken a similar view.[94]

I differ also with Rainbow's understanding of Calvin's objection to the use of the distinction between infinite sufficiency and limited efficiency: the objection arose not, as Rainbow argues, because Calvin denied the infinite sufficiency of Christ's propitiation, but simply because the issue *in the particular text* of Scripture in question (1 John 2:1-2) is not the contrast between the infinite sufficiency of Christ's

90. Calvin, *Sermons sur la prophetie d'Esaïe*, Septième Sermon: Isa. 53:12, in CO 35, col. 679, 681; Calvin, *In Isaiam Prophetam*, 53:12, in CO 37, col. 267 (CTS *Isaiah*, IV, p. 131).

91. Cf. Calvin, *In Isaiam Prophetam*, 53:12, in CO 37, col. 267 (CTS *Isaiah*, IV, p. 131) with Calvin, *In Epistolam Pauli ad Romanos*, 5:18, in CO 49, col. 101 (CTS *Romans*, p. 211).

92. Contra Kendall, *Calvin and English Calvinism*, pp. 14-15; and Bray, *Theodore Beza's Doctrine of Predestination*, p. 60.

93. John Calvin, *Acta Synodi Tridentini cum Antidoto*, in CO 7, col. 430-431, 443; translation in *Selected Works of John Calvin: Tracts and Letters*, edited by Henry Beveridge and Jules Bonnet, 7 vols. (Grand Rapids: Baker, 1983), III, pp. 93, 109.

94. Cf. Hubert Jedin, *Papal Legate at the Council of Trent: Cardinal Seripando*, trans. Frederic C. Echoff (St. Louis: Herder, 1947), pp. 355-257, 366-370; with Paul Pas, "La doctrine de la double justice au Concile de Trente, *Ephemerides Theologiae Lovanienses*, 30 (1954), pp. 13-14, 27-30.

propitiation and its limited efficacy in application. Similarly, the issue addressed by Calvin's response to Georgius is not a problem with the notion of the infinite sufficiency of Christ's propitiation; rather the issue is that the term "whole world" cannot be used to extend salvation to the reprobate, since "whole world" in 1 John 2:1-2 indicates not "all people," but believers throughout the whole world. That Christ's satisfaction is sufficient for all sin is not at issue in the debate.[95]

We may hypothesize that Calvin's hesitance concerning the sufficiency-efficiency distinction lies in its failure to account for all of the issues at play in the question of the value and application of Christ's death—a point that Beza would make with considerable clarity in his qualified acceptance of the formula at Montbéliard.[96] For in between the categories of infinite sufficiency for the sins of the whole world and limited efficiency for the elect or believers there stands the category of the divine intentionality in Christ's death. The sacrifice stands as payment for sin and, as we have noted, that payment must be infinite given the nature of the problem of sin—but the sacrifice also stands as the ground of the salvation of the elect and in this category, unlike the category of sufficiency, the divine intention is not without limit.

Manducatio indignorum and the Limitation of Sacramental Efficacy

Calvin's debate with the Lutherans over the Lord's Supper also sheds light on the question of the limitation of Christ's redemptive work—and, indeed, it provides the context for what may well be Calvin's clearest statement of the doctrine that Christ did not die for the reprobate. The connection between the two doctrines—the eucharistic presence and the efficacy of Christ's satisfaction—ought to be clear given Calvin's assumption "that the body which he once offered to the Father in sacrifice he now offers as food to human beings" in such a way that it is received by the faithful but not by unbelievers.[97] For Calvin, the efficacy of Christ's propitiatory death was related directly and causally to the efficacy of the sacraments, inasmuch as believers not only receive Christ as the "substance" of the sacraments and as the "source and substance of all good," but they also receive in and through the sacrament "the fruit and efficacy of his death and passion."[98] This substance-efficacy

---

95. Cf. Rainbow, *Will of God and the Cross*, pp. 133-134.

96. Theodore Beza, *Ad Acta Colloquii Montisbelgardensis Tubingae edita Theodori Bezae responsio, Tubingae edita*, 2 vols. (Geneva: J. le Preuz, 1587–1588), II, pp. 215-221; and see the careful examination of Beza's argumentation in Raymond A. Blacketer, "Theodore Beza and the Development of Particular Redemption in the Reformed Tradition," in David Gibson and Jonathan Gibson, eds., *From Heaven He Came and Sought Her: Definite Atonement in Historical, Biblical, Theological & Pastoral Perspective* (Wheaton, IL: Crossway, forthcoming).

97. John Calvin, *Secunda defensio piae et orthodoxae de sacramentis fidei contra Ioachimi Westphali calumnias*, in CO 9, col. 48 (*Selected Works*, II, p. 249).

98. John Calvin *Petit traictéde la saincte cene*, in CO 5, col. 437-438 (*Selected Works*, II, pp. 169-170).

distinction echoes the distinction between the sufficiency and efficacy of Christ's satisfaction. Calvin could therefore argue against Heshusius,

> the first thing to be explained is, how Christ is present with unbelievers, as the spiritual food of souls, and the life and salvation of the world. And as he adheres so doggedly to the words, I should like to know how the wicked, for whom he was not crucified, can eat the flesh of Christ, and how they can drink the blood which was not shed to expiate their sins. ... Christ, as he is the living bread and the victim immolated on the cross, cannot enter any human body which is devoid of his Spirit.[99]

Bell's understanding of this passage as strictly eucharistic and not related to the doctrine of Christ's satisfaction and its extent is surely unsupportable, given Calvin's consistent linkage of these issues throughout his sacramental treatises and Calvin's assumption that union with Christ and sanctification were signs of true membership in the church and of the church's communion.[100] So too is Bell's contention, following Daniel, that the central retort is merely hyperbole and a rhetorical device that does not express Calvin's actual opinion: on the contrary, the text itself indicates the intimate relationship between Calvin's understanding of Christ's satisfaction for (or expiation of) sin and Calvin's understanding of the gracious presence of Christ in the Lord's Supper. What is more, an extremely hyperbolic reference to so important an issue in the midst of polemic would hardly have served Calvin's purpose of undermining his opponent's position.[101]

Of course, as Bell has pointed out, Calvin's remark to Heshusius can be juxtaposed with his statement in a sermon on 2 Timothy 2:19 that "it is not a little thing, that souls perish that have been purchased by the blood of Jesus Christ."[102] If nothing else, the two statements illustrate the vagueness and difficulty in using such phrases as "for whom Christ died" or "for whom Christ shed his blood." In both places, of course, Calvin quite clearly indicates that not all are saved, and in the sermon he adds, "nonetheless, one must be content that God will protect what he has chosen for himself."[103] Calvin's full approach to the text, moreover, began with a reflection on the phrase "the foundation remains firm," inasmuch as the number

---

99. John Calvin, *Dilucida explicatio sanae doctrinae de vera participatione carnis et sanguinis Christi*, in CO 9, col. 484-485 (*Selected Works*, II, p. 527); early on noted by Cunningham, "Calvin and Beza," p. 396.

100. Cf. Calvin, *In priorem epistolam Pauli ad Corinthios*, 1:2, in CO, 49, col. 308 (*CTS 1 Corinthians*, I, p. 52).

101. Cf. Bell, "Calvin and the Extent of the Atonement," pp. 119-120; idem, *Calvin and Scottish Theology*, pp. 16-17; cf. Daniel, "Hyper-Calvinism and John Gill," pp. 817-819; similarly, Clifford, *Atonement and Justification*, p. 87; and, against Bell, see Rainbow, *Will of God and the Cross*, pp. 118-120; and note Nicole, "Extent of the Atonement," pp. 200, 223.

102. John Calvin, *Sermons sur la seconde epitre a Timothée* (1561), 2:19, in CO 54, col. 165; cf. Bell, *Calvin and Scottish Theology*, p. 14; and Boersma, "Calvin and the Extent of the Atonement," pp. 333-334.

103. Calvin, *Sermons sur la seconde epitre a Timothée*, 2:19, in CO 54, col. 165.

of God's chosen children was established "before the creation of the world," and then turned to the issue of maintaining a zeal for the increase of the gospel and a concern for fellow Christians despite the fact that many fall away from the faith.[104]

The difficulty of these texts for understanding Calvin's views on the extent of Christ's satisfaction lies in a different place than either Daniel or Bell or, for that matter, their opponents, have argued.[105] Given the sacramental context of Calvin's remarks to Heshusius, the issue being addressed, as in other places where Calvin asserts his views on Christ's presence over against the Lutherans is, as the last sentence cited indicates, that Christ "cannot enter any human body which is devoid of his Spirit" or, as Calvin more frequently indicates, whereas Christ is offered to all in the Lord's Supper, he cannot be received except by faith, and the unfaithful, therefore, cannot receive him.[106] Thus, in the context of Calvin's sacramental theology, the point of his argument against Heshusius is concerned not with the objective value or sufficiency of Christ's satisfaction but rather with its subjective apprehension or efficacy. Calvin's denial that Christ was crucified for the wicked and his statement that Christ's blood was not shed to expiate their sins references their failure to receive Christ's benefits—his point no more undermines the universal preaching of the gospel and the gospel's offer of salvation to all who have faith than it denies that in the sacrament Christ is truly offered to all.[107] What Calvin certainly affirms, in a eucharistic context, is the limitation of the efficacy or Christ's satisfaction. The passage from Calvin's sermons on 2 Timothy reflects an entirely different context, namely, the universal or indiscriminate preaching of the gospel for the expansion of the church, where the objective value of Christ's work must remain the focus, even though only some human beings are elect and many to whom Christ is genuinely presented will not be saved. Abstracted from their respective contexts, Calvin's statements stand in a high decree of tension with one another. Examined in context, however, the interpretive problem is considerably lessened: the comment against Heshusius in no way diminishes Calvin's sense of the fullness of Christ's payment for all sin; the statement in his sermon affirms the universality of the proclamation of Christ without universalizing either the ultimate intention of God or the extent of God's grace.

104. Calvin, *Sermons sur la seconde epitre a Timothée*, 2:19, in CO 54, col. 165; cf. the comments on this passage in Helm, *Calvin and the Calvinists*, p. 40.

105. Cf. Boersma, "Calvin and the Extent of the Atonement," pp. 352-353; with Nicole, "Extent of the Atonement," pp. 200, 223.

106. John Calvin, *Institutio* (1559), IV.xvii.33; cf. *Defensio sanae et orthodoxae doctrinae de sacramentis*, CO 9, col. 27 (*Selected Works*, II, p. 234); and idem, *Optima ineundae concordiae ratio*, in CO 9, col. 523-524(*Selected Works*, II, p. 579).

107. See Muller, "Calvin on Sacramental Presence," pp. 160-162.

Limited Salvific Intention, Limited Intercession, and Limited Union: Correlative Aspects of Christ's Priestly Office

Several writers, myself included, have recognized that Christ's high-priestly intercession, namely, the lengthy prayer found in John 17, provided Calvin with a biblical and exegetical foundation for discussing the limitation of Christ's saving work to the elect alone.[108] What is remarkable, however, is that this form of the limitation of Christ's work has been used to argue against the attribution of a doctrine of "limited atonement" to Calvin. Kendall even goes so far as to state that although, in Calvin's view, Christ intercedes for the elect alone, "what Calvin does *not* do is to link the scope of Christ's intercessory prayer to Christ's death, as those after him tended to do."[109]

Of course, Calvin argued precisely what Kendall denies: Kendall's attempt to sever the issue of Christ's intercession from the limitation of Christ's work fails in view of Calvin's own direct statements. Thus, for example,

> we see that we must begin from the death of Christ in order that the efficacy and benefit of his priesthood may reach us. It follows that he is an everlasting intercessor: through his pleading we obtain favor. ... in Christ there was a new and different order, in which the same one was to be both priest and sacrifice.[110]

Calvin's entire exposition here relates intercession and sacrificial death as aspects of a single priestly work. If this passage from the *Institutes* does not clearly enough link the "scope" of Christ's intercession to his death, the link is certainly made in various places in Calvin's commentaries. Calvin specifically declared a "necessary conjunction" between "the sacrifice of Christ's death, and perpetual intercession" inasmuch as these are the "two parts of Christ's priesthood."[111]

Similarly in his exegesis of Christ's intercessory prayer in John 17—Calvin comments that in the prayer of intercession Christ "offered [*obtulit*] us to the Father in some manner in his own person [*in sua persona quodammodo*], that we may be renewed to true holiness by his Spirit." He continues by noting that "though this sanctification [*sanctificatio*] extends to the whole life of Christ, the greatest

---

108. Cf. Muller, *Christ and the Decree*, pp. 33-35; Thomas, *Extent of the Atonement*, pp. 33-34; Kendall, *Calvin and English Calvinism*, pp. 13-14, 16-17.

109. Kendall, *Calvin and English Calvinism*, p. 14, note 1; Bell, "Calvin and the Extent of the Atonement," p. 121-123, disagrees, as does Helm, "Calvin, English Calvinism and the Logic of Doctrinal Development," pp. 181-182.

110. Calvin, *Institutio* (1559), II.xv.6: "Ita videmus a morte Christi incipiendum esse, ut ad nos perveniat sacerdoti eius efficacia et utilitas. Hinc sequitur aeternitas esse deprecatorem, cuius patrocinio favorem consequimur. ... diversa et nova in Christo fuit ratio, ut idem esset hostia qui sacerdos"

111. Calvin, *In epistolam ad Timotheum I*, 2:6, in CO 52, co. 272; note the comments in Thomas, *Extent of the Atonement*, pp. 33-34.

illustration of it was given in the sacrifice [*in sacrificio*] of his death."[112] The intercession hardly removes or replaces the elective purpose of God as the limiting factor in the application of Christ's work—rather, in Calvin's view, Christ's intercession, like the effectual calling of the Word, belongs to the discussion of how the divine will or decree is executed in the temporal order: "Both repentance and forgiveness of sins ... are conferred on us by Christ, and both are attained by us through faith."[113] The limitation of the efficacy of Christ's work, albeit grounded in the eternal decree, is a limitation that pertains directly to the working out of salvation in the world, through the agency of Christ. Christ, after all, in Calvin's understanding is, with the Father, the *electionis author* who chooses those who are his.[114]

Beyond this, Christ's work on the cross is the temporal ratification or confirmation of the eternal decree, given that the decree was eternally constituted in him.[115] There is, in other words, a very clear connection in Calvin's thought between election and Christ's intercession, a connection that relates directly to the offer of Christ in the preaching of the gospel and to the foundational location of union with Christ in Calvin's ordering of the application of salvation. Kendall's argument to the contrary rests on a misinterpretation of Calvin's comment on Romans 10:16—where Calvin argues that the gospel's universal invitation of all people to salvation in no way implies the election of all. Kendall turns the text on its head, as if Calvin denied the connection between election and the efficacy of the death of Christ in order to affirm the universality of salvation.[116] By concentrating his comments on the vague language of "for whom Christ died," Kendall confuses efficacy with sufficiency, application with impetration, and fails to see that Calvin's consistent limitation of the efficacy or application of Christ's work to the elect neither impinges on the merit or value of Christ's death nor implies a limit to indiscriminate preaching of the gospel. In none of these places does Calvin raise the Amyraldian question of a conditional intention or will to save in relation to the

112. Calvin, *In evangelium Ioannis*, 17:19, in CO 47, col. 385 (*CTS John*, II, p. 181).

113. Calvin, *Institutio* (1559), III.iii.1; xxiv.3.

114. Contra Armstrong, *Calvinism and the Amyraut Heresy*, pp. 137-138; see Calvin, *Institutio* (1559), III.xxii.7; II.xvii.5; II.ii.35; xxii, i, 7, 10.

115. Cf. Calvin, *In epistolam Pauli ad Ephesios*, 3:11, in CO 51, col. 183: "fuisse aeternum semperque fixum decretum: sed quod debuerit in Christo sanciri, quia in ipso statutum erat"; with idem, *In evangelium Ioannis*, 6:38, in CO 47, col. 146: "Christus, se mundo exhibitum fuisse asserit, ut ratum faciat ipso effecto quod de salute nostra decrevit pater." Cf. Wendel, *Calvin*, pp. 231-232; and Rainbow, *Will of God and the Cross*, pp. 78-79.

116. Calvin, *In epistolam Pauli ad Romanos*, 10:16, in CO 49, col. 206: "Unde facile liquet quam stulte quidam ratiocinentur, promiscue electos esse omnes, quia universalis est salutis doctrina, et promiscue omnes ad se Deus invitat. Neque enim promissionum generalitas sola et per se communem omnibus salutem facit: quin potius eam ad electos restringit peculiaris ista revelatio" (*CTS Romans*, p. 401); cf. Kendall, *Calvin and English Calvinism*, p. 15.

value, sufficiency, or infinite merit of Christ's death. Calvin consistently denied any notion of two wills in God.[117]

We note in particular the connection between mediation and intercession, and Calvin's interpretation of the apostle's "all" as "all classes of men." If this constitutes a distortion of the text to fit the concept of a predestinating will of God, the distortion is not Calvin's but belongs to the traditional Augustinian exegesis of this and like passages.[118] On the matter of limited intercession, Calvin's commentary on John 17:9, "I pray not for the whole world, but for those whom thou hast given me," is definitive. In addition, Calvin notes in his commentary on 1 John 2:2 that he accepts the distinction of Lombard on Christ's suffering as sufficient for all sin but efficient only for the elect.[119] Calvin was, however, somewhat dissatisfied with the extant dogmatic formula, at least in its application to particular biblical passages, but he did not, for whatever reason, propose a new or revised formula.[120]

Satisfaction theory, after all, develops in relation to Christology and not primarily under the head of predestination, but we do encounter the interrelationship and interpenetration of the doctrines of atonement and election under the larger complex of soteriological formulations. The efficacy of Christ's satisfaction and election are parallel aspects of the economy of salvation.

This limitation of saving intention is not drawn out at length in Calvin's *Institutes*, but it does receive explicit attention in his commentaries on the Gospel and First Epistle of John. Several verses in particular indicate the limitation of the intercession: first, Jesus expressly states, "I have manifested my name to the men whom thou gavest me out of the world.... I am praying for them; I am not praying for the world but for those whom thou hast given me" (vv. 6, 9). Further, granting that these few for whom Jesus prays can be identified as the circle of disciples, he adds, "I do not pray for these only, but also for those who are to believe in me through their word" (v. 20): the broadening of the intercession is itself quite clearly limited. These verses, moreover, parallel the references in Jesus' earlier discourse in John 6 to the elective will of God and the limitation placed on the work of salvation by it: "All that the Father gives me will come to me; and him who comes to me I will not cast out" and, even more pointedly, "No one can come to me unless the Father who has sent me draws him" (John 6:37, 44). The issue here is one of relationship, not of absolute

117. See below, chapter 4.

118. Cf. Augustine, *Enchiridion*, cap. 103 (PL.40.280-281), and idem, *De correptione et gratia*, sec. 44 (PL.44.913) with Calvin's comments on John 17:9 in CO 47, col. 380.

119. Calvin, *In Iohannis apostoli epistola*, 2:2, in CO 55, col. 310 (CTS *1 John*, p. 173). The phrase "all classes of men" and the distinction between the sufficiency and efficiency of Christ's death are crucial in later Reformed discussions of limited or "definite" or "limited atonement," particularly in the debates at Dort: see William Robert Godfrey, "Tensions within International Calvinism: The Debate on the Atonement at the Synod of Dort, 1618-1619" (Ph.D. diss., Stanford University, 1974) for discussions of the problem of the universal implications of 1 Tim. 2:3-4, 1 John 2:2, and John 3:16.

120. Cf. A. A. Hodge, *Atonement*, pp. 387-391.

correspondence or abstract logical consistency: the issue is simply that Christ prays that "some," not all, be redeemed—and that those "some" would appear to be those individuals who are the objects of the work of salvation that would culminate in his death and resurrection. There is a coherence, in other words, between Calvin's language of a limited application of Christ's death and the limitation of Christ's intercession,[121] given that Christ is the one in whom the decree was constituted and who provides its temporal confirmation.

Kendall was, therefore, fundamentally mistaken to sever Calvin's teaching on Christ's satisfaction from Calvin's views on Christ's intercession—and to argue that Calvin taught "unlimited atonement" but "limited intercession."[122] Calvin certainly did teach a limited intercession of Christ—just as he also taught that union with Christ was limited to some persons. But Kendall's argument (and Daniel's as well) labors under the imprecision of its own terminology and fails, for several reasons, to understand what Calvin and others of his era intended. In the first place, the work of satisfaction and the act of intercession belong to the same official function of Christ, the priestly. What is more, Kendall's proposal of unlimited atonement and limited intercession as the proper Calvinian understanding of the problem points both toward Kendall's own misunderstanding of the issues in the older debate and to the problem of so describing a doctrine of "unlimited atonement"—in Kendall's terms, the "unlimited atonement" refers to the fullness or sufficiency of Christ's death for all sin, while "limited intercession" indicates the way in which Christ applies this all-sufficient sacrifice to some (given that not all are redeemed). But the juxtaposition of full accomplishment and unlimited value, power, or sufficiency with limited application is precisely what the whole Reformed tradition has argued, whether Calvin or the Canons of Dort—and what Kendall repudiates as "limited atonement."

In the second place, Kendall's argument—posed against Wendel—that "election is not rendered effectual by the death of Christ" and that Christ's death, therefore, need not correspond with the divine intention in election, is simply not to the point. The issue for Calvin, as for later Reformed theologians, was that Christ's death, infinite or utterly sufficient in its value, was rendered effectual or applicable to certain individuals by God's elective willing or, indeed, by Christ's intercession, understood as an aspect of the divine elective willing. For Calvin, as for the later Reformed, Christ's death is fundamental to the order of means to the end of salvation—specifically, in Calvin's terms, as the material cause.[123] Calvin's rather distinctive contribution to such formulations is that the electing will of God (which

---

121. Cf. Calvin, *In Iohannis apostoli epistola*, 2:2, in CO 55, col. 309: "Intercessio Christi continua est mortis eius applicatio in salutem nostram"; with Calvin, *Institutio* (1559), II.xvi.6; III.ii.34, 39; iii.9.

122. Kendall, *Calvin and English Calvinism*, pp. 13-17; cf. Nicole, "Extent of the Atonement," pp. 221-222.

123. See further below, chapter 7 on the "Causality of Salvation."

[handwritten marginal note, left margin:] Christ's Sufficient → Mt. 13:44, 45-46 – Hidden Treasure Sacrifice Titan to and Pearl of great price.

[handwritten note, bottom:] Calvin – "limited atonement" "limited intercession"

ought to be understood as a trinitarian work *ad extra*) is expressed in Christ's intercession for those whom the Father has given to him—and this element of Calvin's thought clearly passed over into the later Reformed tradition's approaches to the limitation of the efficacy of Christ's work.

Conclusions

It is certainly correct to note, as Peterson and several others have done, that Calvin had little interest in speaking to the issue of the limitation of Christ's satisfaction to the elect, and that it is somewhat anachronistic to press the question of later Reformed debate upon him for an answer. Nonetheless, as we have seen, Calvin did broach the topic in a few places, most usually in the context of *loci classici* in his commentaries. To comment of these passages that "Calvin's commentaries contain some passages that favor limited atonement, but ... the data is insubstantial"[124] is therefore, unsatisfactory—and for the very reason that Peterson offers for the scantiness of the discussion: granting that the historical debate over the problem occurred in the decades following his death, Calvin cannot be expected to offer lengthy comments on the problem. His method did not call for the development of a theological *locus* or of a doctrinal *disputatio* on every conceivable topic, but only on those topics that were viewed as significant for discussion or were currently under debate.[125]

Calvin, however, did do precisely what he could have been expected to do within his own historical context—to reflect on the limited application or efficacy of Christ's satisfaction in terms of the boundaries established by the centuries-old scholastic distinction and in terms of the traditional exegesis of certain biblical passages that he encountered in the course of his homiletical and exegetical work. He apparently preferred to say that the sacrifice of Christ was propounded to all indifferently or indiscriminately, but extended only to all of the elect, rather than use the traditional sufficiency/efficiency formula. Calvin did, moreover, offer a partial alternative to the formula, instead of "sufficiency" arguing the "power" and "value" or "worth" of Christ's sacrifice, while either retaining the usage of "efficacy" or referring to the application of Christ's benefits.

In addition, as in the debate with Heshusius or in his comments about Christ's intercession, he could note the doctrinal point in contexts when argument concerning other theological issues might be facilitated through examination of doctrinal interrelationships, namely, the benefits of the Lord's Supper in relation to the sacrifice of Christ, or the extension of Christ's satisfaction to the elect in relation to Christ's high priestly intercession. From this perspective, the "data" are not "insubstantial." Calvin did assume the limitation of the extension or efficacy of

---

124. Peterson, *Calvin's Doctrine of the Atonement*, pp. 90-91, citing 1 Tim. 2:5, Titus 2:11, and 1 John 2:2.

125. Cf. Muller, *Unaccommodated Calvin*, pp. 101-117.

Christ's propitiatory sacrifice to the elect, just as his understanding of the universal proclamation of the gospel did not assume that God had intended each and every person to hear the Word preached. Indeed, Calvin's language concerning the offer of salvation to all appears to be consistently related to the indiscriminate preaching of the gospel and therefore to a revealed or perceptive as distinct from an effectual willing of God. Bullinger, as noted in several places, more clearly and unreservedly argued the universal scope of the preaching of the gospel, but he also quite clearly denied that the passages indicating a divine will to save "all" meant the actual application of the gospel to all: Bullinger preferred to resolve the issue in terms of human wickedness and of the failure of the wicked to respond to the gospel.

Examination of commentaries by a variety of other early modern Reformed writers, including Beza, indicates, moreover, a similar result. Whereas there appears to have been no rush uniformly to render biblical references to "all" human beings, or to the salvation of "many," or to the salvation of the "world" in a manner any more restrictive than Calvin's exegesis had indicated, there was among these exegetes and theologians a fairly consistent reading of specific texts, like 1 Timothy 2:4, as referencing the indiscriminate preaching of the gospel to all types and classes of human beings or to all nations and ranks of people or as indicating the actual application of salvation to all types and classes, all nations and ranks.

As to the specific issues usually gathered together under the vague language of "limited atonement, the nature of the evidence, given the context and the method of Calvin's theology, precludes a neat dogmatic conclusion—and the patterns of relationship to specific aspects of Calvin's thought are rather diverse. Whereas there is an easily identifiable continuity of argument that runs from Calvin's thought through that of writers like Beza, Ursinus, and Zanchi to the Canons of Dort (indeed, from the patristic and medieval materials, through Calvin and others of his time, to the Canons of Dort), there is also a body of material, including statements made by Calvin, most notably in commentaries and sermons, that points toward several non-speculative forms of hypothetical universalism, notably as found in the thought of Davenant and DuMoulin, as argued within the bounds of the traditional formula, *sufficienter pro omnibus, efficienter pro electis*,[126] but that fails to point to the more speculative form of hypothetical universalism found in Amyraut's model of multiple divine decrees. In other words, Calvin most surely held, without qualification, the basic sense of the second clause of the formula, *efficienter pro electis*, whether interpreted in terms of his views on Christ's limited intercession, or his views on the intention of the preached Word, or his views on the limitation of the extent of the preaching of the gospel throughout the ages. He did not, however, labor to remove the ambiguity of the first clause, *sufficienter pro omnibus*, preferring to speak of the *valor* and *virtus* of Christ's work as extending to all sin or to the

---

126. See below, chapters 4 and 5.

redemption of the world, undergirding the indiscriminate preaching of the gospel and the promise that all who believe will be saved.

If we leave aside the rather slippery phrases "limited" and "unlimited atonement," we can draw some more accurate conclusions concerning Calvin's views on the extent and limitation of Christ's work in relation to other writers in the Reformed tradition. Calvin taught that the value, virtue, or merit of Christ's work served as sufficient payment for the sins of all human beings, and provided the basis for the divine promise that all who believe will be saved, assuming that believers are recipients of God's grace and that unbelievers are "left without excuse"—as also did, granting different nuancings of the relation of divine intentionality to the value or sufficiency of Christ's death, Theodore Beza, the Canons of Dort, John Davenant, Pierre Du Moulin, Moïse Amyraut, Francis Turretin, and a host of other often forgotten and sometimes maligned Reformed writers of the next two centuries, among them both particularists and hypothetical universalists. On the other hand, Calvin assumed that Christ's work, albeit sufficient payment for the sins of the world and for securing the salvation of all human beings in even a thousand worlds, is by divine intention effective for the elect only, as did Beza, Gomarus, Du Moulin, Davenant, Turretin, and, in his own way, Amyraut as well. He argued this limitation of efficacy in terms of the limited intercession of Christ, the divine intention and effective will to save only the elect, and the historical limitations of the preaching of the gospel as, he believed, intended by God—again assumptions shared by various particularists and non-Amyraldian hypothetical universalists alike.

There are, in other words, continuities between Calvin's teaching and various currents in later Reformed theology on this issue, just as there are differences typically brought about by altered contexts of debate and formulation. These continuities, however, as well as the discontinuities or differences, are not matters of simple one-to-one correspondences, as assumed in the standard literature on limited and unlimited atonement. Rather, they are more precisely described as complex patterns of reception, adoption, and adaptation of exegetical traditions and traditionary vocabulary and formulae, and of nuances given to them in debates and conversations that were often mediated to the later Reformed through the writings of the Reformers, with various Reformers, notably Calvin, but also often with equal influence, other formulators of his generation, serving as significant points of inception for the specifically Reformed argumentation.

In the case of the doctrine of Christ's satisfaction for sin, since Christ paid the price of all sin and accomplished a redemption capable of saving the whole world, his benefits are clearly placed before, proffered, or offered to all who hear: what Calvin does not indicate is any sort of universalizing intentionality flowing from the sufficiency into the actual efficacy of this offering. Calvin's approach to the value, merit, or sufficiency of Christ's work assumed that it was unlimited and could therefore undergird the universality of the promise and the indiscriminate preaching of the gospel, but, equally so, his approach to the eternal divine will and intention to save in Christ, to the efficacy or application of Christ's work, and to Christ's own high-priestly intercession assumed its limitation to the elect. The conditional or hypothetical dimension of Calvin's doctrine, therefore, belongs to the revealed will of God in the promise of salvation to all who believe and not, clearly not, to an ultimate willing of God to save all on condition of belief.

What cannot be documented from Calvin is a notion of two wills in God, one hypothetical, the other absolute, as characteristic of Amyraut's approach.[127] Nor does Calvin allow an unfulfilled or somehow thwarted divine intention to apply the sufficient satisfaction of Christ effectively or efficiently to all people: the divine intention in the indiscriminate preaching of the gospel is to save the elect wherever they may be. Very much against the direction taken by Amyraut, Calvin denied universal grace—and, thus, on this central issue of the seventeenth-century controversy, was rightly cited by Amyraut's opponents. Insofar as Calvin's sense of the indiscriminate proclamation and offer is linked to a divine willing akin to what had been traditionally called the preceptive will of God, his formulation has affinity with Davenant's concept of an "ordained sufficiency," albeit not an exact correspondence. Calvin clearly held to the promise of the gospel that all who believe would be saved—he did not argue that God conditionally willed to save each and every human being on the hypothesis that all might believe, nor did he argue the collateral assumption that God willed for the gospel to be offered to each and every human being.

Carefully parsed, there are, therefore, both universalizing and limiting dimensions to Calvin's doctrine of Christ's work, dimensions that carry over variously into the later Reformed tradition—but not in such a way as to enable a set of utterly clear distinctions to be made among the parties of the later debates and certainly not in such a way as to give credence to those who divide the orthodox writers into "Bezan" and "Amyraldian" categories. Those debates, as identified here and more fully shown in the next two chapters, took place typically within the general boundaries of the language of the Synod of Dort and did not concern the universal sufficiency of Christ's sacrifice, the limitation of its efficacy or application to the elect, or the universal or indiscriminate proclamation of salvation for all who believe. The debates, quite specifically, were concerned with the divine intentionality underlying the sufficiency or infinite value of Christ's death and its relation to the universal or indiscriminate preaching of the gospel. The muddled nature of the historiography has been caused in large part by continued recourse to terms, namely, "unlimited atonement" and "limited atonement," that were not used in the sixteenth and seventeenth centuries and that do not properly reflect the issues in debate. Like that other slippery anachronism, "christocentric," "limited" and "unlimited atonement" are terms that ought to be avoided, indeed, removed from the historical discussion.

---

127. On this point, see also below, chapters 4 and 5.

4

A Tale of Two Wills?
Calvin, Amyraut, and Du Moulin on Ezekiel 18:23

Amyraut, Calvin, and Exegesis: The Issue of Ezekiel 18:23

Much of the modern scholarship on the hypothetical universalism of Moïse Amyraut has focused on his consistent and detailed citation of Calvin as evidence of Amyraut's allegiance to aspects of Calvin's theology neglected or even rejected by the majority of those who have come to be identified as orthodox "Calvinists" in the seventeenth century.[1] On the broader question of whether Calvin held to a doctrine of "universal atonement" or "limited atonement," the scholarship had been very mixed. A significant group of writers has argued for a doctrine of universal atonement in Calvin.[2] An equally significant group has argued the opposite, namely,

---

1. Thus, Lawrence Proctor, "The Theology of Moyse Amyraut Considered as a Reaction against Seventeenth-Century Calvinism" (Ph.D. diss., University of Leeds, 1952), pp. 233, 240-241; François Laplanche, *Orthodoxie et prédication: l'oeuvre d'Amyraut et la querelle de la grâce universelle* (Paris: Presses Universitaires de France, 1965), pp. 273-289; Brian G. Armstrong, *Calvinism and the Amyraut Heresy: Protestant Scholasticism and Humanism in Seventeenth-Century France* (Madison: University of Wisconsin Press, 1969), pp. 38-42, 173-174, et passim; Frans Pieter van Stam, *The Controversy over the Theology of Saumur, 1635-1650* (Amsterdam: APA-Holland University Press, 1988), pp. 53-56, 167-170, 432; Alan C. Clifford, *Calvinus: Authentic Calvinism, a Clarification*, 2nd ed. (Norwich: Charenton Reformed Publishing, 2004); idem, *Amyraut Affirmed, or Owenism a Caricature of Calvinism: A Reply to Ian Hamilton's 'Amyraldianism—Is It Modified Calvinism'* (Norwich: Charenton Reformed Publishing, 2004).

2. Paul Van Buren, *Christ in Our Place: The Substitutionary Character of Calvin's Doctrine of Reconciliation* (Edinburgh: Oliver and Boyd, 1957); Basil Hall, "Calvin Against the Calvinists," in *John Calvin*, ed. Gervase Duffield (Appleford: Sutton Courtnay Press, 1966), pp. 19-37; Armstrong, *Calvinism and the Amyraut Heresy*; James William Anderson, "The Grace of God and the Non-elect in Calvin's Commentaries and Sermons (Th.D. diss., New Orleans Baptist Theological Seminary, 1976); R. T. Kendall, *Calvin and English Calvinism to 1649* (Oxford: Oxford University Press, 1979); M. Charles Bell, "Was Calvin a Calvinist," *Scottish Journal of Theology*, 36/4 (1983), pp. 535-540; idem, "Calvin and the Extent of Atonement," *Evangelical Quarterly*, 55 (1983), pp. 115-123; James B. Torrance, "The Incarnation and Limited Atonement," *Scottish Bulletin of Evangelical Theology*, 2

that Calvin taught limited atonement.[3] There is also a smaller group of scholars who have found Calvin's teaching indeterminate.[4] (In what follows, I refrain from using the term "atonement" whether limited or unlimited on the ground that it is highly anachronistic and has only contributed to the confusion present in much of the modern scholarship.)

One of the many places in Calvin's works cited by Amyraut in support of his own version of hypothetical universalism is the comment on Ezekiel 18:23,[5] which Amyraut cited *in extenso* as a foundation for his interpretation in his own sermon on the text.[6] In the view of at least one line of modern scholarship, moreover, the

---

(1984), pp. 32-40; Alan C. Clifford, *Atonement and Justification: English Evangelical Theology, 1640-1790* (Oxford: Oxford University Press, 1990); idem, *Calvinus* and *Amyraut Affirmed*; Kevin Dixon Kennedy, *Union with Christ and the Extent of the Atonement* (New York: Peter Lang, 2002).

3. Archibald Alexander Hodge, *The Atonement* (1867; repr., Grand Rapids: Baker, 1974), pp. 387-391; William Cunningham, "Calvin and Beza," in Cunningham, *The Reformers and the Theology of the Reformation* (Edinburgh: T. & T. Clark, 1872), pp. 345-412; François Wendel, *Calvin: The Origins and Development of His Religious Thought*, trans. Philip Mairet (New York: Harper & Row, 1963), p. 231; Roger Nicole, "Moyse Amyraut (1596-1664) and the Controversy on Universal Grace, First Phase (1634-1637)" (Ph.D. diss., Harvard University, 1966); idem, "John Calvin's View of the Extent of the Atonement," *Westminster Theological Journal*, 47 (1985), pp. 197-225; John Murray, "Calvin on the Extent of the Atonement," *Banner of Truth*, 234 (1983), pp. 20-22; Paul Helm, "Calvin, English Calvinism and the Logic of Doctrinal Development," *Scottish Journal of Theology*, 34/2 (1981), pp. 179-185; idem, "The Logic of Limited Atonement," *Scottish Bulletin of Evangelical Theology*, 3 (1985), pp. 47-54; and idem, *Calvin and the Calvinists* (Carlisle: Banner of Truth, 1982); Jonathan H. Rainbow, *The Will of God and the Cross: An Historical and Theological Study of John Calvin's Doctrine of Limited Redemption* (Allison Park: Pickwick, 1990); Frederick S. Leahy, "Calvin and the Extent of the Atonement," *Reformed Theological Journal*, 8 (November 1992), pp. 54-64; G. Michael Thomas, *The Extent of the Atonement: A Dilemma for Reformed Theology from Calvin to the Consensus (1536-1675)* (Carlisle: Paternoster Press, 1997), notably, pp. 213-214, arguing significant differences between Calvin and Amyraut.

4. Robert A. Peterson, *Calvin's Doctrine of the Atonement* (Phillipsburg: Presbyterian and Reformed Publishing Co., 1983); R. W. A. Letham, "Saving Faith and Assurance in Reformed Theology: Zwingli to the Synod of Dort," 2 vols. (Ph.D. diss., University of Aberdeen, 1979), I, p. 125; II, p. 67; A. N. S. Lane, "The Quest for the Historical Calvin," *Evangelical Quarterly*, 55 (1983), pp. 95-113; Hans Boersma, "Calvin and the Extent of the Atonement," *Evangelical Quarterly*, 64 (1992), pp. 333-355; A. T. B. McGowan, *The Federal Theology of Thomas Boston* (Carlisle: Paternoster, 1997), pp. 48-53; Pieter L. Rouwendal, "Calvin's Forgotten Classical Position on the Extent of the Atonement: About Sufficiency, Efficiency, and Anachronism," *Westminster Theological Journal*, 70 (2008), pp. 317-335.

5. *Ioannis Calvini in viginti prima Ezechielis prophetae capita praelectiones ... cum praefatione Theodori Bezae* (Geneva: Franciscus Perrinus, 1565), also in *Ioannis Calvini opera quae supersunt omnia*, 59 vols., ed. Guilielmus Baum, Eduardus Cunitz, and Eduardus Reuss (Brunswick: Schwetschke, 1863-1900), vol. 40, hereinafter abbreviated as CO; in English, John Calvin, *Commentaries on the First Twenty Chapters of the Book of the Prophet Ezekiel*, trans. Thomas Myers, 2 vols. (Edinburgh: Calvin Translation Society, 1849-1850), hereinafter abbreviated as *CTS Ezekiel*. I have used the Myers translation, emending it as necessary from the text in CO.

6. Moïse Amyraut, *Sermon sur les paroles du Prophete Ezechiel, Chap. 18. v. 23*, in idem, *Sermons*

exegesis of this passage is crucial to the understanding of Amyraut's relationship to Calvin and proves rather conclusively that Amyraut correctly understood Calvin's theology—specifically as teaching a "dual divine intention."[7] Indeed, it is the interpretation of such passages that marks out the difference between a "true disciple" of Calvin, like Amyraut and those later Reformed writers who are actually disciples of Beza.[8] Examination of Amyraut's and Calvin's reading of the passage in Ezekiel is, certainly, significant to the understanding of the relationship of the two thinkers inasmuch as this is one of the few passages cited by Amyraut from Calvin that is also accompanied by a significant exposition on Amyraut's part.

Although an examination of the exegesis of a single text cannot resolve the larger issue of Calvin's relationship to later understandings of the divine intention to save and the extent of salvation, the centrality of the exegesis of Ezekiel 18:23 to Amyraut's own claims renders a close comparative reading of Calvin's and Amyraut's interpretations potentially useful to the evaluation of the relationship of their theologies and to resolution of the question of Calvin's relationship to the variant doctrines of redemption that appeared in Reformed circles in the late sixteenth and early seventeenth centuries. Specifically, Calvin's comments on Ezekiel 18:23 bear on the debate over the direction of his doctrine inasmuch as this text is one of the few places in his writings that not only represents the universal offer of salvation but also discusses it in relation to the eternal counsel or decree of God and moves to resolve the relationship of universal promise and particular election with reference to distinctions concerning the divine will. In support of his own teaching, Amyraut cited Calvin's lecture on Ezekiel 18:23, arguing that Calvin's interpretation of the text supported a view of two mercies and two wills in God.[9] In the view of Amyraut's indefatigable opponent, Pierre Du Moulin, Calvin never hypothesized two divine wills and certainly not "conseils de Dieu frustratoires."[10] Du Moulin also objected to the practice of citing Calvin from the pulpit—a human author, referenced as an authority was, in itself a serious deviation from Reformed practice.[11]

---

sur divers textes de la sainte ecriture, 2nd ed. (Saumur: Isaac Desbordes, 1653), pp. 37-73, citing Calvin's commentary at length, pp. 48-52.

7. Clifford, *Amyraut Affirmed*, pp. 28-29; cf. idem, *Calvinus*, pp. 16, 27-28; cf. Armstrong, *Calvinism and the Amyraut Heresy*, pp. 188-189, 198-205.

8. Clifford, *Amyraut Affirmed*, p. 8; cf. Armstrong, *Calvinism and the Amyraut Heresy*, pp. 38-42, 136-138, 158-160.

9. Amyraut, *Sermon sur les paroles du Prophete Ezechiel*, pp. 61-66; cf. Clifford, *Amyraut Affirmed*, pp. 9-10; Armstrong, *Calvinism and the Amyraut Heresy*, pp. 188-190, assuming Amyraut's agreement with Calvin.

10. Pierre DuMoulin, *Esclaircissement des controverses salmuriennes* (Leiden: Jean Maire, 1648), p. 233; cf. Rainbow, *Will of God and the Cross*, pp. 150-151, arguing Amyraut's misreading of Calvin.

11. DuMoulin, *Esclaircissement*, pp. 231-241.

Reading Calvin's Exegesis: Amyraut on the Interpretation of Ezekiel 18:23

That "excellent servant of God," Amyraut comments, has "provided us with two memorable points" to consider in the text of Ezekiel 18:23. First, Calvin evidences a "beautiful modesty" that ought to be observed in considering the "incomprehensible counsels of God."[12] Specifically, when God reveals something concerning the economy of his willing concerning the human race, it is not our place to speculate about what relates or does not relate to his ultimate nature, or whether differing revelations evidence two opposing wills in God, inasmuch as the divine nature is a depth that neither human beings nor angels can penetrate.[13] The second point offered by "this great personage," Calvin, is "an excellent solution to the difficulty" of the seeming contradictions in the divine willing—namely, that "the word of God ... presents his mercy to be considered in two ways."[14] According to the first of these modes of divine mercy, the human reception of eternal salvation, as evidenced in the remission of sins and the gift of new life, would require "a certain precedent quality" in human beings, "without which their pardon would be impossible."[15] According to the other mode of divine mercy, however, this precedent quality is not required or presupposed in human beings but rather created in them by God.[16] There are, therefore, two "degrees" or "kinds" of mercy indicated in Scripture, the latter of which alone is "simply and absolutely free."[17]

Much as he had argued an absolute divine right over creation against Arminius,[18] Amyraut here indicates that there can be no necessity imposed on God, but that God works according to *sa proper necessité*: when his creatures are good and holy, God cannot but love them, not because he owes anything to the creature, but because he is infinitely good. Even so, when the creature is corrupt, God cannot but hate him because of the sin—not because God is answerable to a standard outside of himself, but because he is infinitely just. And so, finally, when the sinful creature has recourse to the mercy of God, God cannot but have compassion, not because he

---

12. Amyraut, *Sermon sur les paroles du Prophete Ezechiel*, p. 52.

13. Amyraut, *Sermon sur les paroles du Prophete Ezechiel*, p. 52.

14. Amyraut, *Sermon sur les paroles du Prophete Ezechiel*, pp. 55: "La parole de Dieu ... nous presente sa misericorde à considerer en deux manieres."

15. Amyraut, *Sermon sur les paroles du Prophete Ezechiel*, p. 56: "vne certaine qualité prealable, sans laquelle il est impossible qu'elle leur pardonne."

16. Amyraut, *Sermon sur les paroles du Prophete Ezechiel*, p. 57: "L'autre maniere en laquelle elle nous presente cette misericorde à considerer, est entant qu'elle ne requiert point cette qualité, mais qu'elle de deploye à la former dans les hommes."

17. Amyraut, *Sermon sur les paroles du Prophete Ezechiel*, p. 57: "la derniere est purement, & simplement, et absolument libre."

18. Cf. Moïse Amyraut, *De iure Dei in creaturas dissertatio*, in *Dissertationes theologicae quatuor* (Saumur: Isaac Desbordes, 1645), p. 102; on Arminius' understanding of the limitation of divine right, see Richard A. Muller, "God, Predestination, and the Integrity of the Created Order: A Note on Patterns in Arminius' Theology," in *Later Calvinism: International Perspectives*, ed. W. Fred Graham (Kirksville, MO: Sixteenth Century Journal Publishers, 1994), pp. 431-446.

is in any way obligated to the creature, but because he is infinitely merciful.[19] Accordingly, God has revealed two covenantal relationships with his fallen creatures, a covenant of nature or legal covenant (*alliance de la nature, alliance legale*) and an evangelical covenant or covenant of grace (*alliance Evangelique, alliance de la grace*)—the former requiring for salvation a condition of perfect holiness, in effect, presupposing a condition in human beings as the basis for salvation; the latter requiring for salvation the condition of faith but, rather than presupposing it as a condition for salvation, creating it in human beings as the basis for their salvation.[20] The evangelical covenant, therefore, "is an absolute promise, and nonetheless a conditional formula of covenant," because it is founded on a mercy "that demands the condition, 'if you believe, you will be saved.'"[21]

Amyraut continues, setting aside his own declaration that Calvin had shown the unsuitability of speculation over whether God might have two wills and declares, "We therefore now see, my brethren, how these observations serve to reconcile the two wills of God that had seemed repugnant each other, and in the same way [serve] to explain the solution provided by that great man [i.e., Calvin]."[22] There is "no contradiction between these two kinds or two degrees of mercy," namely, the two covenants,

> so also is there none at all between these two wills on which they depend. He wills that all human beings might be saved. This is true: and he wills this fondly [*avec affection*]: but this is according to that mercy which presupposes the condition, and not the other. If he does not find the condition in them, he does not so will. He wills that some of the human race might be saved. This is true: but it is according to this second kind of mercy which does not demand the condition, but creates it: which does not presuppose it, but creates it in human beings.[23]

Arguably, this distinction of two wills, one hypothetically universal given the conditionality of the promise, the other particular and resting on grace alone,

---

19. Amyraut, *Sermon sur les paroles du Prophete Ezechiel*, p. 59.

20. Amyraut, *Sermon sur les paroles du Prophete Ezechiel*, pp. 59-60.

21. Amyraut, *Sermon sur les paroles du Prophete Ezechiel*, p. 61: "c'est vne promesse absoluë, & non pas vne formule conditionelle d'alliance. L'Alliance Evangelique donc a son rapport à cette autre misericorde qui exige la condition, Si tu crois, tu seras sauué."

22. Amyraut, *Sermon sur les paroles du Prophete Ezechiel*, p. 61.

23. Amyraut, *Sermon sur les paroles du Prophete Ezechiel*, p. 61: "Certes comme il n'y a point de contradiction entre ces deux sortes ou ces deux degrez de misericorde, aussi n'y an a-t'il point entre les deux volontez qui en dependent. Il veut que tous les hommes soient sauuez. Il est vray: & il veut avec affection: mais c'est selon certe misericorde qui presuppose la condition, & non autrement. Si la condition ne se trouve pas en eux, il ne le veut pas. Il veut que peu d'entre les hommes sont sauuez. Il est vray: mais c'est selon sette seconde sorte de misericorde qui n'exige pas la condition, nais la crée: qui ne la presuppose pas, mais la fait en l'homme."

represents a form of scholastic argumentation.[24] The question is how Amyraut will root it in or link it to Calvin's exegesis.

Calvin states that "the prophet does not dispute subtly concerning the secret counsel of God." "Certainly," Amyraut continues, in his own rather subtle hypothesis concerning the eternal counsel,

> he does not wish to speak of the decree that depends on this second kind of mercy, the counsel of which is so free that one cannot plumb its reasons, and concerning which one cannot advance anything other than the divine good pleasure: the kind that, when one comes to examine why some believe, and others do not believe, why God has given faith to some and not to others, one must halt, as if at the edge of an abyss.[25]

Rather, the prophet speaks of the first kind of mercy and of the first kind of divine will, according to which God wills that all human beings be saved on grounds of belief, based on the preaching of the gospel.[26]

That, concludes Amyraut, is the solution to the great difficulty: these two kinds of mercy are taught throughout the Word of God and ministers of the gospel "announce one or the other as the occasion requires," recognizing that there is a significant difference between the two occasions—specifically whether it is a matter of drawing their hearers toward faith and repentance.[27] The minister will then not mention the two kinds of mercy and the will that arises from them, inasmuch as no minister will say "believe, because God has ordained that you believe," or "believe, because it is only God who can make you believe," or "believe because your are reprobated, and God will never give you faith."[28] Rather the minister will say, "believe, because if you believe you will be saved: believe, because if you do not believe, the wrath of God will rest on you: believe, because it is the only way to enter into life."[29]

24. Cf. the argument in Stephen Strehle, "Universal Grace and Amyraldianism," *Westminster Theological Journal*, 51 (1989), pp. 345-357.

25. Amyraut, *Sermon sur les paroles du Prophete Ezechiel*, pp. 63-64: "Certes qu'il ne veut parler du decret qui depend de cette seconde sorte de misericorde dont le conseil est si libre qu'on n'en peut sonder les raisons, & n'en peut-on alleguer aucune que son bon plaisir: de sorte que quand on vient à examiner pourquoy les vns croyent & les autres ne croyent pas, pourquoy Dieu a donné de croire à ceux-cy, & non à ceux-là, il se faut arrester là comme sur le bord d'vn abysme."

26. Amyraut, *Sermon sur les paroles du Prophete Ezechiel*, p. 64.

27. Amyraut, *Sermon sur les paroles du Prophete Ezechiel*, p. 64.

28. Amyraut, *Sermon sur les paroles du Prophete Ezechiel*, p. 65.

29. Amyraut, *Sermon sur les paroles du Prophete Ezechiel*, p. 65.

Calvin's Interpretation of Ezekiel 18:23

Calvin commented on Ezekiel 18:23 at least three times: a significant meditation on the passage in Calvin's *De aeterna Dei praedestinatione* (1552), the as yet unrecovered sermon on the passage (1552-1553), and the comment in Calvin's *In Ezechielis prophetae praelectiones*, delivered in 1563-1564 and published posthumously in 1565, the latter being the passage cited by Amyraut. Calvin also referenced Ezekiel 18:23 in the *Institutes* as an illustration of the mercy of God in the law and the prophets and the readiness of God to offer "mercy to a people covered with innumerable transgressions.[30]

In the *Praelectiones*, at the conclusion of his reading of Ezekiel 18:21-22, Calvin notes the two essential elements of conversion, a turning away from sin and a new obedience to God: the prophet teaches that those who are penitent "pass at once from death to life, since God blots out all their transgressions."[31] This comment leads Calvin, at verse 23, to offer one of his universalizing statements concerning the will of God in relation to the yearnings of the heathen to appease divine anger, the clearer declarations of the law and the prophets, and the full promise of pardon in the preaching of the gospel:

> He confirms the same sentiment in other words, that God desires nothing more earnestly than that those who were perishing and rushing to destruction should return into the way of safety. ... And this is the knowledge of salvation, to embrace his mercy which he offers us in Christ. It follows, then, that what the prophet now says is very true, that God wills not the death of a sinner, because he meets him of his own accord, and is not only prepared to receive all who fly to his pity, but he calls them towards him with a loud voice, when he sees how they are alienated from all hope of safety.[32]

The promise of salvation is universal but conditional: all people are equally called to repentance, and all who seriously repent will be saved.[33]

The passage in Ezekiel does not refer to the decree or to predestination, but, given its clear identification of a universal offer of salvation on condition of repentance and new obedience, Calvin expresses the concern that the prophet's words not be used to undermine the doctrine of election:

---

30. John Calvin, *Institutio christianae religionis*, IV.i.25: Latin text in *Ioannis Calvini opera quae supersunt omnia*, 59 vols., ed. Guilielmus Baum, Eduardus Cunitz, and Eduardus Reuss (Brunswick: Schwetschke, 1863-1900), vol 2; following the English of John Calvin, *Institutes of the Christian Religion*, trans. Henry Beveridge, 2 vols. (Edinburgh: Calvin Translation Scoiety, 1845), emended as necessary.

31. Calvin, *In Ezechielis prophetae*, 18:21-22, in loc. (CO 40, col. 445; CTS *Ezekiel*, II, p. 246).

32. Calvin, *In Ezechielis prophetae*, 18:23, in loc. (CO 40, col. 445; CTS *Ezekiel*, II, pp. 246-247).

33. Calvin, *In Ezechielis prophetae*, 18:23, in loc. (CO 40, col. 445; CTS *Ezekiel*, II, p. 247); similarly, Calvin, *Institutio*, IV.i.25.

If any one should object—then there is no election of God, by which he has predestinated a fixed number to salvation, the answer is at hand: the prophet does not here speak of God's secret counsel [hic prophetam verba non facere de arcano Dei consilio], but only recalls miserable men from despair, that they may apprehend the hope of pardon, and repent and embrace the offered salvation.[34]

Calvin has here begun to broach the issue of the simplicity and unity of the divine will: it is not as if the promise of salvation upon repentance and election point in different directions and indicate a *duplex* or equivocal willing in God. The prophet's words of universal promise do not refer to the eternal counsel of God, nor do they set the universal promise of the gospel against the eternal counsel as a different will. Rather God always wills the same thing, presumably, the salvation of the elect, albeit in different ways, namely, in his eternal counsel and through the preaching of the gospel:

If any one again objects—that in this way God acts in two ways [Deum hoc modo fieri duplicem], the answer is ready, that God always wishes the same thing [Deum semper idem velle], though by different ways [sed diversis modis], and in a manner inscrutable to us.[35]

There is a clear parallel in Amyraut's reading: God appears to act in two rather different ways—but, unlike Amyraut, Calvin is not referring to two revealed mercies. Indeed, Calvin specifically states that these two apparent ways of willing are actually ways in which God wills one and the same thing.

Where Amyraut has begun to move toward an argument concerning two divine mercies and two divine wills, Calvin insists on a single divine volition. Further, also in contrast to Amyraut's reading, Calvin nowhere raises the issue of different covenant relationships or of two different mercies of God, deployed, as Amyraut indicates, in relation to differing covenants. Amyraut's argument evidences a later stratum of Reformed thought in which the language of two covenants, one of nature or law and one of grace or the gospel had become a prominent feature of theological argument, with the covenant of nature or law standing after the fall as a subsidiary covenant alongside the covenant of grace.[36] Calvin did, of course, elsewhere refer to the Mosaic law as a "legal covenant" (*pactio legalis*) in contrast to the "evangelical

---

34. Calvin, In Ezechielis prophetae, 18:23, in loc. (CO 40, col. 445; CTS Ezekiel, II, p. 247); cf. Wolfgang Musculus, Commentarii in Evangelium Ioannis in tres heptadas digesti (Basel: Hervagius, 1554), p. 90, making much the same comment, that Ezekiel 18 refers not to the counsel or decree of God but to the preaching of the gospel.

35. Calvin, In Ezechielis prophetae, 18:23, in loc. (CO 40, col. 445; CTS Ezekiel, II, p. 247).

36. See the discussion of this development in Richard A. Muller, "Divine Covenants, Absolute and Conditional: John Cameron and the Early Orthodox Development of Reformed Covenant Theology," Mid-America Journal of Theology, 17 (2006), pp. 11-56.

covenant" (*pactio evangelica*), but he does not identify the legal covenant as reflecting an alternate will in God or a alternate mercy.[37]

What is not developed in Calvin's argument, however, is how Calvin understood this one will of God in relation to its different or diverse modes: Amyraut saw the diverse modes through the pattern of two distinct covenants, whereas Calvin did not specify. There is, for Calvin, one will indicated in the prophet's preaching—which is to save all those who repent. Calvin does not posit a *duplex* willing in the offer of salvation, but rather and only a *duplex* willing or diverse modes of willing when one compares the universal preaching of salvation that the prophet does mention to the secret counsel or decree that the prophet does not mention.

An almost identical explanation of this issue is offered in Calvin's *Harmony of the Gospels*:

> it may justly be said that he wills to gather all to himself. It is not, therefore, the secret purpose of God [*Non ergo hic nobis arcanum Dei consilium*], but his will [*sed voluntas*], which is manifested by the nature of the word, that is here described. For certainly, whoever he efficaciously wills to gather, he inwardly draws by his Spirit, and does not only invite by the outward voice of human beings. If it be objected, that it is absurd to suppose a double will in God [*absurde duplicem in Deo voluntatem fingi*], I reply, we believe nothing other than that his will is one and simple [*quam unicam et simplicem esse eius voluntatem*]; but since our minds do not penetrate the abyss of secret election, because of our weakness, the will of God is set forth to us in a double manner [*pro infirmitas nostrae modulo bifariam nobis Dei voluntatem proponi*].[38]

To very much the same effect, Calvin's sermon on 1 Timothy 2:4 looks at the Pauline phrase, that God "will have all men to be saved," and notes that Paul did not write concerning the eternal counsel of God or of eternal election but only referenced the expression of God's will in the world. "It is utterly true that God does not change," Calvin continues, "and that he does not have a double will: as also that there is absolutely no pretense in him, as if he willed one thing and it were not so."[39] Then why, Calvin asks, does Scripture "speak of his will in a double manner"—it is, he responds, "not at all because this will is double, but it is to accommodate itself to our weakness."[40] In all three places, Calvin denies that God has two wills—and, significantly, even when he comments on the double (*duplex*) manifestation of God's willing, he refers to the will in the singular. Amyraut's language, by contrast, consistently identifies two wills corresponding to two divine mercies.

---

37. John Calvin, *Commentarius in Epistolam ad Galatas*, CO 50, col. 238.

38. John Calvin, *Commentarius in harmoniam evangelicam*, Matt. 23:37, in CO 46, col. 643-644; cf. Calvin, *Commentary on a Harmony of the Evangelists*, trans. William Pringle, 3 vols. (Edinburgh: Calvin Translation Society, 1845-1846), III, p. 109.

39. John Calvin, *Sermons sur le premiere Epitre a Timothée*, 2:3-5 (sermon 13), in CO 53, col. 151.

40. Calvin, *Sermons sur le premiere Epitre a Timothée*, 2:3-5 (sermon 13), in CO 53, col. 151-152.

Calvin further defines his understanding of Ezekiel 18:23 by indicating that, although God's will is simple, there are nonetheless distinctions to be made concerning it: "Although, therefore, God's will is simple, yet variety is implied in it [*Quanquam itaque simplex est Dei voluntas, varietas quidem est illic implicita*], as far as our senses are concerned ... we cannot certainly judge how God wishes all to be saved, and yet has devoted all the reprobate to eternal destruction, and wishes them to perish."[41] These distinctions, however, given Calvin's previous comment, *Deum semper idem velle, sed diversis modis*, do not indicate either two actual wills or two different goals of God's single will. Rather, they indicate "diverse ways" of executing a single will—again in fairly clear contrast to Amyraut's conclusion of two wills in God.[42] Calvin's rather strenuous objections to a notion of two wills, specifically to a view that would place the universalizing promise of the gospel into some ultimate, secret, and unfulfilled divine will, may rest on his recognition that such an argument had been proposed in the late medieval scholastic tradition, perhaps as identified by his contemporary and colleague Wolfgang Musculus, although not in relation to the text of Ezekiel 18:23.[43]

Resolution of the issue—how the "diverse ways" of executing a single will are accomplished—lies in the nature of conversion itself as an act required of all who are to be saved but as not within human ability to accomplish:

> God is said *not to wish the death of a sinner*. How so? Since he wishes all to be converted. Now we must see how God wishes all to be converted; for repentance is surely his peculiar gift: as it is his office to create men, so it is his province to renew them, and restore his image within them. For this reason we are said to be his workmanship, that is, his fashioning (Eph. 2:10). Since, therefore, repentance is a kind of second creation, it follows that it is not in man's power; and if it is equally in God's power to convert men as well as to create them, it follows that the reprobate are not converted, because God does not wish their conversion; for if he wished it he could do it: and hence it appears that he does not wish it.[44]

We have here a positive parallel with Amyraut's reading: Amyraut very clearly points out that God supplies the power lacking in human beings to come to faith. Where he differs with Calvin is in his positing of two divine mercies, one which is set to respond to those who come to faith of themselves, the other that supplies the condition of faith in some human beings.

---

41. Calvin, In *Ezechielis prophetae*, 18:23, in loc. (CO 40, col. 445-446; CTS *Ezekiel*, II, p. 247).

42. Differing somewhat with the analysis in Thomas, *Extent of the Atonement*, pp. 214-215.

43. Wolfgang Musculus, *Loci communes theologiae sacrae* (Basel: Sebastianus Henricpetrus, 1599), xlv (p. 451), with reference to 1 Tim. 2:4; and cf. the discussion by Martin Foord, "God Wills All People to Be Saved—Or Does He? Calvin's Reading of 1 Timothy 2:4," in *Engaging with Calvin: Aspects of the Reformer's Legacy for Today*, ed. Mark D. Thompson (Nottingham: Apollos, 2009), pp. 194-195.

44. Calvin, In *Ezechielis prophetae*, 18:23, in loc. (CO 40, col. 446; CTS *Ezekiel*, II, p. 247).

Calvin acknowledges the double implication of the promise to all and the salvation of some only, but denies the possible contradiction, given only the consistent relationship between the gift of salvation and the fulfillment of the condition.

> But again they argue foolishly, since God does not wish all to be converted, he is himself deceptive, and nothing can be certainly stated concerning his paternal benevolence. But this knot is easily untied; for he does not leave us in suspense when he says, that he wishes all to be saved. Why so? for if no one repents without finding God propitious, then this sentence is filled up. But we must remark that God puts on a twofold character [Deum duplicem personam induere].[45]

Where Armstrong, accepting Amyraut's argument, sees Calvin as teaching not only a "twofold character" in God's revelation, but also a "twofold character of God's will; indeed ... of God himself,"[46] Calvin resolves the problem not by moving from the "twofold character" of the revelation to a twofold will but by making a strict distinction between the eternal counsel of God to save some and the universal call of the gospel:

> the prophet does not here dispute subtly about his incomprehensible counsel [propheta hic non disputat subtiliter de consilio eius incomprehensibili] ... all are called to repentance, and the hope of salvation is promised them when they repent. This is true, since God rejects no returning sinner: he pardons all without exception: meanwhile, this will of God which he sets forth in his word [haec Dei voluntas, quam in verbo suo proponit] does not prevent him from decreeing before the world was created what he would do with every individual [quin decreverit ante creatum mundum quid facturus esse de singluis hominibus]: and as I have now said, the prophet only shows here, that when we have been converted we need not doubt that God immediately meets us and shows himself propitious.[47]

Calvin also commented, much to the same effect, on the implications of Ezekiel 18:23 in his treatise on the Eternal Predestination of God. Calvin meditates on the issue of universal exhortation and, given the nature of exhortation, comments,

> since the prophet's word here exhorts to repentance, it is no wonder for him to declare that God wills all human beings to be saved. For the mutual relation between threats and promises shows that such forms of speaking are conditional [loquendi formas conditionales esse]. In this same manner God declared to the Ninevites, and to the kings of Gerar and Egypt, that he would do what he did not intend to do. Since their repentance averted the punishment he had threatened to inflict upon them, it is evident that the punishment was decreed only if they remained obstinate. Yet, the

---

45. Calvin, In Ezechielis prophetae, 18:23, in loc. (CO 40, col. 446; CTS Ezekiel, II, p. 247).

46. Armstrong, Calvinism and the Amyraut Heresy, p. 188.

47. Calvin, In Ezechielis prophetae praelectiones, 18:23, in loc. (CO 40, col. 446; CTS Ezekiel, II, pp. 247-248).

declaration was positive, as if the decree had not been revocable [*ac si revocabile non esset decretum*].[48]

Calvin here parallels one of the points we have seen in Amyraut, namely, that the language of the prophet, as a language of promise, does not refer to the decree, but merely indicates the promise of salvation on fulfillment of the condition, without also indicating how the condition is to be fulfilled. But he also, very unlike Amyraut, comments in his example of the Ninevites and the kings of Gerar and Egypt, that the conditional decree referred to something that God did not intend to do, thereby pressing away from a sense of universalistic intention on God's part, albeit not offering an argument for limiting the scope of the promise. Arguably, Calvin's language maintains the broad sense of the traditional sufficiency-efficiency distinction concerning Christ's work, a distinction held both by Amyraut and by his opponents.[49]

Armstrong's reading of the text also falls short at this point. Calvin certainly speaks of a conditional willing to save on grounds of repentance and belief, but Armstrong reads this language in an Amyraldian fashion as indicating a will or willing in God rather than as a revealed promise—in other words, as if it referred to an eternal divine willing, such as could be identified as a decree, counsel, or divine good pleasure.[50] Calvin, however, refers to a revealed willing in the form of promise or invitation, such as could be identified as the revelation itself or as a preceptive will, or *voluntas signi*, that is, not an eternal determination to save all on condition parallel to the unconditional determination to save the elect.[51]

There is a clear distinction to be made, therefore, between God's invitation to salvation and his counsel or decree:

> So it is with respect to the promises of God, which invite all men to salvation: they do not simply or precisely indicate what God has decreed in his secret counsel [*non simpliciter nec praecise quid in arcano suo consilio statuerit*], but only what God is ready to do to all those who are brought to faith and repentance.[52]

The declaration that God invites all human beings to be saved is conditional, akin to the threats and promises of the Old Testament. Although such declarations take

---

48. John Calvin, *De aeterna Dei praedestiontione*, in CO 8, col. 300; cf. the translation in *Calvin's Calvinism: Treatises on the Eternal Predestination of God and the Secret Providence of God*, trans. Henry Cole (London: Wertheim and Mackintosh, 1856), p. 99.

49. Cf. the analysis in Rouwendal, "Calvin's Forgotten Classical Position," pp. 323-326, 333-335.

50. Armstrong, *Calvinism and the Amyraut Heresy*, pp. 189-190.

51. Cf. Nicole, "Extent of the Atonement," p. 214.

52. Calvin, *De aeterna Dei praedestiontione*, in CO 8, col. 301; cf. the similar argument in William Perkins, *A Christian and Plaine Treatise of the Manner and Order and Order of Predestination, and of the Largenesse of Gods Grace*, in *The Whole Works of ... Mr. William Perkins*, 3 vols. (London: John Legatt, 1631), II, p. 608, col. 2-p. 609, col. 1.

the form of irrevocable decrees, they are not a direct indication of the divine intention as lodged in the eternal counsel:

> It is alleged that we hereby attribute to God a double will [*hoc modo duplex affingitur Deo voluntas*], who is not at all variable [*varius non est*], that no shadow of turning pertains to him, even in the most remote degree. ... God is said to will life, even as he wills repentance. This indeed he wills, because he invites all to it by his Word. This is not contrary to his secret and eternal counsel [*cum arcano ipsius consilio non pugnat*], by which he decreed to convert only his elect [*quo nonnisi suos electos convertere decrevit*]. Nor can he, on this account, be considered variable, because, as a lawgiver, he enlightens all men with the external doctrine of life [and] in this prior manner he calls all to eternal life: in the latter manner, he brings to life those whom he will, as an eternal Father, regenerating by his Spirit, his own children only.[53]

What is significant about distinction concerning the divine willing made here by Calvin is that it parallels other distinctions made by him concerning the divine will, specifically between the hidden will of God and the revealed will or between the ultimate will of the divine good pleasure and the revealed will in the divine commandments. These are the traditional distinctions between the *voluntas arcana* and *voluntas revelata* or the *voluntas beneplaciti* and *voluntas signi*—with the decree corresponding to the *voluntas arcana* or *beneplaciti* and the will of God set forth in the Word to the *voluntas revelata* or *signi*. Such distinctions indicate differences between the fullness of divine willing *ad intra* and the manner and extent of revelation *ad extra*, but they in no way imply two distinct wills *ad intra*. Or to make the point in another way, "will of God which he sets forth in his word" is neither a causal willing that brings about a particular effect nor an antecedent will, set prior to the decree to elect some and not others. Indeed, this revealed will, namely, the *voluntas signi* is not an effective or irresistible willing.[54]

Amyraut's use of the text, however, draws not on the *voluntas arcana/revelata* or the *voluntas beneplaciti/signi* distinctions but rather on a distinction between a *voluntas antecedens et hypothetica* and a *voluntas consequens et absoluta*. This latter distinction does, by contrast, indicate two wills *ad intra* and arguably reflects the scholastic background noted already in the earlier Reformed tradition by Musculus. In other words, Amyraut takes Calvin's reference to a "will of God which he sets forth in his word" as a reference to a hypothetical or conditional will in God antecedent to the decree—just as he reads Calvin's reference to the decree as a will

---

53. Calvin, *De aeterna Dei praedestiontione*, in CO 8, col. 301.

54. Note that Calvin here clearly echoes Augustine and, with less precision, Vermigli. Vermigli parsed the text of I Tim. 2:4 rather carefully with reference to the traditional distinctions in the *voluntas Dei*. Thus, he notes that some (as would Calvin) rightly identify the indifferent invitation of the gospel with an antecedent *voluntas signi* (i.e., antecedent in the sense that it precedes the human act) and not with a hidden and effective *voluntas consequens*: see Peter Martyr Vermigli, *Loci communes* (London: Thomas Vautrollerius, 1583), III.i.45 (p. 466). Foord, "God Wills All People to Be Saved," p. 196, misreads the "antecedent" as a reference to the *voluntas beneplaciti*.

in God consequent upon the "will of God which he sets forth in his word," now willed absolutely for the sake of the elect.

Response to Amyraut: Du Moulin on Citation of Calvin and the Interpretation of Ezekiel 18

Among Amyraut's opponents, Pierre du Moulin took particular umbrage at the Saumur theologian's citation and use of Calvin's works as justifications of his "innovations" concerning the divine decrees and other doctrinal issues in debate following the Synod of Dort. In Du Moulin's view, there were two fundamental problems with Amyraut's citation of Calvin, particularly in sermons. In the first place, while Du Moulin clearly acknowledged that "Calvin was an excellent individual, whose memory was, with good reason, a blessing to the Church of God," the religion of the Reformed was "in no way founded on human beings" and sermons ought to rest on no "authorities other than those of the Holy Scriptures."[55] Were the pastors of Geneva to preach Calvin in their sermons, Du Moulin comments, they would be in danger of being dismissed from the pulpit! What is more, such citations "give occasion to adversaries to say that they call us Calvinists with good reason," as if Calvin's writings were held forth as "oracles, and indubitable proofs" of doctrine.[56]

In the second place, Du Moulin continues, the passages from Calvin used by Amyraut do not actually support his views—indeed, "it is certain that the writings of Calvin powerfully overturn the teaching of the Innovators."[57] Specifically, examination of the statements of Calvin cited by Amyraut reveals that "some are utterly not to the point and others are contrary" to Amyraut's point: when Amyraut "discusses the Decrees of the counsel of God, he produces passages from Calvin that do not speak at all of the Decrees of God, but of God's commandments and exhortations."[58] Even so, Du Moulin indicates, Calvin never spoke of "general Predestination, or of a first and second mercy, or of frustrated counsels of God."[59]

As to the interpretation of Ezekiel 18, the text clearly indicates that God "desires not the death of a sinner," but Du Moulin notes that this in no way declares that God is regretful or reluctant or that there is any change in the divine decree. Indeed, "it is without regret, and with a full approval, that God wills that a sinner, if he repents and returns, he will live and not perish."[60] Those who continue in their sinful and impenitent state, however, will be punished, as the prophet Ezekiel himself

55. Pierre du Moulin, *Esclaircissement des controverses Salmuriennes, ou defense de la doctrine des eglises reformées sur l'immutabilité des decrets de Dieu, l'efficace de la mort de Christ, la grace universelle, l'impuissance à de se convertir et sur d'autres matières* (Leiden: J. Maire, 1648), IX.i (p. 231).

56. Du Moulin, *Esclaircissement*, IX.i (p. 232).

57. Du Moulin, *Esclaircissement*, IX.i (p. 232).

58. Du Moulin, *Esclaircissement*, IX.ii (p. 233).

59. Du Moulin, *Esclaircissement*, IX.ii (p. 233).

60. Du Moulin, *Esclaircissement*, III.vi (pp. 55-56).

declares in several places—"justice," Du Moulin declares, is also "a virtue of God: and God does not exercise any of his virtues with regret."[61] Beyond this, the citation of Ezekiel is simply not to the point: the passage is concerned not with the final salvation of human beings, but with the temporal punishments that have come on the Jews because of the sins of their ancestors, as clearly attested by the second verse of the chapter, "the fathers have eaten sour grapes, and the children's teeth are set on edge." Thus, when God subsequently states that if the wicked turn from their ways, they will live and not die, "he promises to protect them from the sword of their enemies and from death"—but he does not "regret that he has condemned the souls of the reprobate."[62] In short, Du Moulin concludes, Amyraut "has not at all understood the sense of this chapter."[63]

Du Moulin's interpretation, we note, embodies both agreement with and distance from Calvin's: like Calvin, and very much to the point of the debate with Amyraut, Du Moulin understood the text as requiring repentance as the sole path to reconciliation with God. In accord with Calvin's interpretation, Du Moulin also indicated that the required repentance did not reflect a hypothetical intention to save the reprobate or an alteration in the divine decree. Nonetheless, Du Moulin's reading of the text as referencing only the temporal punishment of Israel is not found in Calvin's commentary, and Du Moulin does not indicate a distinction between the *voluntas beneplaciti* and the *voluntas praecepti*, as was adumbrated by Calvin. Of course, following his own advice, Du Moulin does not cite Calvin in justification of his own interpretation of the chapter!

Conclusions

The question raised with regard to Calvin's exegesis of Ezekiel 18:23 (and, by extension, of Matthew 23:37) is whether his argumentation looks toward the Amyraldian form of hypothetical universalism or belongs to another strand of argumentation within the Reformed tradition—specifically whether, as Amyraut claimed and, in the recent scholarship, Armstrong and Clifford have maintained, Calvin's reading of the biblical passage anticipates Amyraut's understanding of two wills in God, one conditional and the other absolute. Examination of Calvin's text, Amyraut's reading of Calvin, and Du Moulin's counter to Amyraut do not, of course, resolve the larger questions of broad trajectories of doctrinal formulation in the Reformed tradition and of the relationship of Calvin's thought on the question of divine intentionality in Christ's death or in the offer of salvation to those trajectories. It does, however, address the issue raised by Armstrong and Clifford that Amyraut's citations of Calvin reveal him as the true follower of Calvin.

---

61. Du Moulin, *Esclaircissement*, III.vi (p. 56), citing Ezek. 5 and 13 as well as Isa. 1:24 and Deut. 28:63.

62. Du Moulin, *Esclaircissement*, III.vi (pp. 56-57).

63. Du Moulin, *Esclaircissement*, III.vi (p. 57).

Calvin does indicate *varietas* in manner of execution of the *simplex voluntas* of God, but he also denies that this means that *Deum hoc modo fieri duplicem*: there are not two wills or an equivocal willing in God, rather *Deum semper idem velle, sed diversis modis*—so that the universal conditional proclamation of the gospel serves the same will as the election of some to salvation. Then, after having said that the prophet's words concerning the call of all to salvation "do not dispute subtly concerning [God's] incomprehensible counsel," Calvin distinguishes between the decree and before the creation to determine the ends *de singulis hominibus* and the will of God, revealed in the Word, to preach the gospel to all types and classes of human beings throughout the world. The distinction that Calvin makes, therefore, parallels the traditional *voluntas beneplaciti/signi* distinction, not a *voluntas antecedens/consequens* distinction: the will to save all is a revealed will, not referencing the secret counsel. Nor is the conditional promise lodged in the revealed will of God ever associated by Calvin with an eternal will, counsel, or decree.[64]

Calvin might be taken to mean in his exegesis of Ezekiel 18:23 that, by a temporally revealed, preceptive divine intention, not claiming an actual divine willing of any sort to this effect, if all would believe all would be saved—assuming what John Davenant would call an ordained sufficiency[65]—but the case for such an implication is unclear and, in fact, highly doubtful, particularly inasmuch as Calvin does not here deal with the sufficiency or impetration of Christ's death and given that he understands both eternal election and temporal promise as serving the same divine will. Calvin certainly did assume that anyone who truly responded to the gospel would be saved. What Calvin in no way countenanced was a notion of a double will in God, one hypothetical to save all, the other absolute to save only the elect: there was, in Calvin's view, one divine will and one will only, and that, to save the elect. Calvin's use of the same passage in his *De aeterna Dei predestinatione*, moreover, tends in the opposite direction by offering an example of an expressed threat that God never intended to carry out in parallel with the language of universal conditional promise. In both cases, as in the sermon on 1 Timothy 2:4, Calvin's intention was to identify, on the one hand, the particularity of God's and, on the other, the universality not of a distinct will to save but of the preaching of salvation. In other words, it is possible that Calvin's understanding of the merit or value of Christ's death in this, as in various other passages, might undergird the universal proclamation of the gospel in such a way as to validate the promise that all who believe will be saved, as various later Reformed writers, including Davenant, would argue, without recourse to a structure of multiple wills or multiple decrees. There is no ground, however, for interpreting Calvin's exegesis as looking in the direction of Amyraut's doctrine of two wills or decrees, one hypothetical, the other absolute.

64. Cf. Rainbow, *Will of God and the Cross*, pp. 149-151.

65. John Davenant, *Dissertatio de morte Christi ... quibus subnectitue eiusdem D. Davenantii Sententia de Gallicana controversia: sc. De Gratiosa & Salutari Dei erga Homines peccatores voluntate* (Cambridge: Roger Daniels, 1683), iv (pp. 98-106).

As to Amyraut's reading of Calvin's exegesis, it stands quite clearly as a use of Calvin's text that observes its basic pattern of a promise of salvation or reconciliation on condition, the qualification that hovers in the background of the promise that the condition can only be met by a divine act of creating it in the individual, and the eternal decree or counsel to bring about this condition and, consequently, salvation in the elect alone. It matters little to the argument that the condition in Calvin's interpretation of Ezekiel is repentance and obedience and Amyraut's condition is faith—although this is an easily identifiable difference of interpretation. There are some points, then, on which Amyraut's reading does reflect Calvin's argument. Amyraut, however, uses common ground to argue an entirely different point. He builds on Calvin's argument and, indeed, claims to be interpreting and clarifying it by arguing two mercies and two wills in God where Calvin did not, in fact, where Calvin had specifically stated that the will of God is one and simple, albeit with distinctions that can be observed in its revelation. Where Calvin resolved the issue of the universal call and particular election by simply declaring a resolution in the fact that, as promised, the repentant are saved, Amyraut indicated a double divine intentionality. Du Moulin was quite correct in this particular criticism: neither the passage itself, nor Calvin's reading of it, had anything to do with two wills in God or with the ultimate salvation of all sinners. Calvin in fact stated that it was "absurd to suppose a double will in God," a passage that Amyraut, presumably, did not see fit to cite. Armstrong and Clifford, in other words, greatly exaggerated the proximity of Amyraut to Calvin.

In addition, there arises a fundamental irony in Armstrong's reading of Amyraut as a humanist, opposed to the scholastic tendencies of his various opponents, given Armstrong's own contention that "the distinctive scholastic Protestant position is made to rest on a speculative formulation of the will of God."[66] Where Calvin insisted that the will of God was one and single, Amyraut indulged in a rather speculative distinction of the divine will into a prior, hypothetically universal willing and a subsequent particular elective willing. In terms of Armstrong's own definition, Amyraut—contra Calvin!—exhibits the "distinctive" characteristic of scholastic Protestant teaching. Even when scholasticism is properly defined as primarily a matter of method, this resolution of a problem by making distinctions, here in the divine willing, is certainly a characteristic of scholastic, not humanistic, method.[67]

---

66. Armstrong, *Calvinism and the Amyraut Heresy*, p. 32.

67. On the problematic nature of Armstrong's definition, see Richard A. Muller, *After Calvin: Studies in the Development of a Theological Tradition* (New York: Oxford University Press, 2003), pp. 27-36, 67-68, 74-80, 94-98; also note Armstrong, *Calvin and the Amyraut Heresy*, pp. 135-136, where he hypothesizes an "attempt to bring scholasticism into the French Reformed Church," and notes Quick's rendering of the synodical description of academic approach, "une Maniere Scholastique," as "as becomes a Scholar": cf. John Quick, *Synodicon in Gallia Reformata: or, the Acts, Decisions, Decrees, and Canons of those famous National Councils of the Reformed Churches in France*, 2 vols. (London: T. Parkhurst and J. Robinson, 1692), II, p. 62, with Jean Aymon, *Tous les synodes nationaux des églises de France.* 2 vols. Den Haag, 1710), II, p. 210. Armstrong understands Quick's version as

Amyraut's distinction, moreover, between and antecedent hypothetical willing and a consequent absolute willing has distinct medieval roots and indicates, on this point at least, an affinity with Aquinas and other medieval thinkers that cannot be found either in Beza or in opponents of Amyraldianism like Du Moulin.[68]

Still, the way in which Amyraut develops the covenantal argument in his exegesis does stand in positive relation to Calvin's language of a legal and an evangelical covenant—of which it is not a duplication but a development. Even if Amyraut had added, as he would do at the Synod of Alençon, that his language of two decrees was by rational distinction and intended "without any succession of Thought, or Order of Priority and Posteriority" in God,[69] his exegesis still would differ from Calvin's in its postulation of two divine mercies and two intentions. The exegesis of this particular text, therefore, does not support those who appeal to it in order to interpret Amyraut as a precise follower of Calvin.

On the other hand, Calvin's exegesis of this particular text offers little useful ammunition to the other side of the modern debate. Calvin's reading of Ezekiel 18:23, like the similar comment on Matthew 23:37, offers neither a foundation for Amyraldian hypothetical universalism nor a definitively particularistic reading of the divine intention underlying the work. Where Calvin did not raise this issue, Amyraut offered his own conclusion, modifying and supplementing Calvin's argument with a concept of two wills in God—a scholastic distinction not found in Calvin's reading of the text and related probably to Amyraut's own training under John Cameron.[70] At least as far as his interpretation of Ezekiel 18:23 is concerned, Amyraut hardly fits the interpretation offered by Armstrong and Clifford: he is not the pure Calvinian responding to deviations from Calvin's exegesis. Amyraut, in fact, moves away from Calvin's exegesis to make a point that was rather far from Calvin's mind. Du Moulin, it should be noted, indicated that the passage was simply not to the point: he did not use it to argue a more particularistic reading of Christ's satisfaction, nor did he justify his exegesis by appeal to Calvin.

Nor, indeed, ought Du Moulin's opposition to Amyraut be understood as a broad antagonism to hypothetical universalism: his response dealt primarily with the issue of multiple decrees and the problem of a consequent willing in God and in fact shared with Amyraut a concern to indicate that Christ's death was sufficient for all in such a way as to save all who would believe. As in the case of other developments of Reformed thought in the era of scholastic argumentation and confessional

---

perhaps advocating a non-scholastic Salmurian model—whereas, in fact, unlike Armstrong, Quick has merely correctly understood the meaning of "scholasticism," namely, an educational method suitable to the school or academy.

68. Aquinas, *Summa theologiae*, Ia, q. 23, a. 4; as noted in Rainbow, *Will of God and the Cross*, p. 35.

69. Synod of Alençon, xv.21, in Quick, *Synodicon in Gallia Reformata*, II, p. 355.

70. Cf. Strehle, "Universal Grace and Amyraldianism," pp. 346-349; with Armstrong, *Calvinism and the Amyraut Heresy*, pp. 158, 192.

orthodoxy, Amyraut's reception of this aspect of Calvin's thought drew it into the context of debates to which Calvin did not provide a clear solution and projected his arguments toward a more specified conclusion than Calvin himself had proposed. Such development, of course, did not so much distinguish Amyraut's thought from that of other Reformed orthodox in his era as identify the shared character of the scholastic orthodoxy within which they debated, often bitterly, raising and attempting to resolve issues that had not been either raised or resolved in the writings of the Reformers. It was the direction of Amyraut's specification of the argument concerning hypothetical universalism, particularly with regard to his rather speculative understanding of the divine decrees, in the wake of Arminius' similar formulation and of the decisions of the Synod of Dort, that led to the debates over his teaching and to Du Moulin's polemic, not Amyraut's hypothetical universalism per se.

5

Davenant and Du Moulin:
Variant Approaches to Hypothetical Universalism

The early modern history of the doctrine of Christ's satisfaction for sin—loosely and, to my mind, somewhat problematically identified as the doctrine of the "atonement"—particularly as it developed among the Reformed churches, has been fraught with a series of difficulties, some arising from a failure to analyze a broad enough sampling of the sources in a suitable level of detail, some brought about by a failure to recognize the breadth and diversity of the Reformed tradition within its confessional boundaries, and others deriving from various modern dogmatic biases against certain lines of development and certain patterns of theological expression within the tradition. The diversity of the tradition on the specific question of the limitation of Christ's satisfaction was rather carefully broached in Godfrey's study of the delegations to the Synod of Dort.[1] Nonetheless, discussion of hypothetical universalism, most famously associated with the theologies of John Cameron and Moïse Amyraut, has typically focused on the issue of the relationship of Amyraldianism to Calvin's theology and has, accordingly, run aground on the reef of the Calvin-Calvinism question, either praising hypothetical universalism as "true" to Calvin or condemning it as a departure from Calvin's thought—thereby failing to observe the diversity of usages and avoiding the question of the relationship of these varied formulations to the Reformed tradition.[2] The present essay advances the

---

1. William Robert Godfrey, "Tensions within International Calvinism: The Debate on the Atonement at the Synod of Dort, 1618-1619" (Ph.D. diss., Stanford University, 1974), pp. 165-224; cf. the comments in Anthony Milton, ed., *The British Delegation and the Synod of Dort (1618-1619)* (Woodbridge: Boydell Press, 2005), pp. xlii-xlvii; and note Jonathan Moore, *English Hypothetical Universalism: John Preston and the Softening of Reformed Theology* (Grand Rapids: Eerdmans, 2007), in which some of the variety in Reformed approaches to hypothetical universalism is demonstrated.

2. As, e.g., Brian G. Armstrong, *Calvinism and the Amyraut Heresy: Protestant Scholasticism and Humanism in Seventeenth-Century France* (Madison: University of Wisconsin Press, 1969); Alan C. Clifford, *Atonement and Justification: English Evangelical Theology, 1640-1790* (Oxford: Oxford University Press, 1990); idem, *Calvinus: Authentic Calvinism, a Clarification*, 2nd ed. (Norwich: Charenton Reformed Publishing, 2004); idem, *Amyraut Affirmed, or Owenism a Caricature of*

argument that there were alternative versions of hypothetical universalist formulation developed among the Reformed of the early modern era and examines two of these versions of specifically non-Amyraldian hypothetical universalism, one (that of John Davenant) posed against the hypothetical universalism of Cameron, the other (that of Pierre du Moulin) against both the "categorical" universalism" of Arminius and the hypothetical universalism of Amyraut.[3]

John Davenant and the Gallican Controversy over Hypothetical Universalism

Davenant, Dort, and dating the debate. The theological work of John Davenant (1572-1641), Lady Margaret Professor of Divinity at Cambridge, a delegate to the Synod of Dort, and later bishop of Salisbury,[4] has recently been recognized as occupying a significant position in the development of a spectrum of Reformed orthodox views on the extent and limitation of Christ's work of satisfaction. Davenant has been identified as a forerunner of the hypothetical universalism of Moïse Amyraut,[5] as an Amyraldian before Amyraut or as virtually Amyraldian,[6] and

---

Calvinism: A Reply to Ian Hamilton's 'Amyraldianism—Is It Modified Calvinism' (Norwich: Charenton Reformed Publishing, 2004).

3. Clifford has commented, *Atonement and Justification*, p. 154, that the term hypothetical universalism ought to be applied to Arminius rather than to Amyraut; while several other writers, notably Benjamin B. Warfield, "Modern Theories of the Atonement," *Princeton Theological Review*, 1 (1903), p. 85; and Craig Troxel, "Amyraut 'at' the Assembly: The Westminster Confession of Faith and the Extent of the Atonement," *Presbyterion*, 22 (1996), pp. 46-47, have argued that both Amyraut and Arminius should be classified as hypothetical universalists. Both of these claims go against the usage that developed certainly by the time of late orthodoxy: there *universalismus hypotheticus* was used as the descriptor of the doctrines of Cameron, Amyraut, Testard, Daillé, and others, while the Arminian or Remonstrant doctrine was described as *universalismus categoricus*: see Joachim Lange, *Gloria Christi et Christianismi apocalyptico-prophetica*, 2 vols. (Amsterdam: Romberg, 1740), II, *Appendix de gratia Dei universali*, p. 148. The distinction is significant inasmuch as Arminius' definition of universal redemption was located in an "absolute" decree of God, and Amyraut's definition was located in a hypothetical or conditional decree; and, conversely, Arminius' definition of the limitation of redemption was placed in a conditional decree and Amyraut's in an absolute decree. If one must use the imprecise term "limited atonement," Amyraut can be said to have taught it while Arminius denied it.

4. On Davenant's life, see Morris Fuller, *The Life, Letters & Writings of John Davenant, D.D., 1572-1641, Lord Bishop of Salisbury* (London: Methuen, 1897); and see the memoir in John Davenant, *An exposition of the Epistle of St. Paul to the Colossians ... to the whole is added, a translation of Dissertatio de morte Christi*, 2 vols., trans., with a life of the author and notes by Josiah Allport (London: Hamilton, Adams, 1831), I, pp. ix-lii.

5. G. Michael Thomas, *The Extent of the Atonement: A Dilemma for Reformed Theology from Calvin to the Consensus (1536-1675)* (Carlisle: Paternoster Press, 1997), pp. 151-152; and note p. 180, where Thomas assimilates Davenant to Cameron.

6. W. Robert Godfrey, "Reformed Thought on the Extent of the Atonement to 1618," *Westminster Theological Journal*, 37/2 (1975), pp. 167, 170; Mark Shand, "John Davenant: A Jewel of the Reformed Churches or a Tarnished Stone," *Protestant Reformed Theological Journal*, 31/2

as the proponent of a non-Amyraldian form of hypothetical universalism.[7] Closer to Davenant's own time, Richard Baxter associated Davenant's views with those of James Ussher and identified both as somewhat distinct from Amyraut and as offering antecedents to his own views on the subject.[8] Shortly thereafter, the noted Dissenter, Edmund Calamy wrote that Davenant had "vigorously asserted and defended that middle way in the Synod of Dort, in opposition to Remonstrants and Supralapsarians, but had also been at no small pains to support it in several of his writings."[9]

A significant but little-examined index to Davenant's views on the subject and therefore to a resolution of the question of his place in the development of Reformed thought on the satisfaction of Christ is his brief but rather explicit response to a query concerning the universalizing views of John Cameron and of various delegations that had been present at the Synod of Dort.[10] The undated document, which presumes both the decisions of Dort and the beginnings of controversy over hypothetical universalism, was left in manuscript among Davanent's papers, was given by Davenant's nephew to James Ussher, and published for the first time posthumously as an appendix to his treatises on the death of Christ and predestination.[11] The title of the document, De Gallicana controversia D. Davenantii sententia, is obviously editorial, while the initial heading of the document, Contenditur inter Galliae Reformatae Theologos, may represent the beginning Davenant's own

(1998), pp. 43-69 and 32/1 (1998), pp. 20-28; and David Wenkel, "Amyraldianism: Theological Criteria for Identification and Comparative Analysis," Chafer Theological Seminary Journal, 11 (2005), pp. 89-90, 92. Wenkel's essay is based largely on a collation of secondary- and tertiary-source definitions of Amyraldianism and is therefore of negligible value.

7. Moore, English Hypothetical Universalism, pp. 187-208.

8. Richard Baxter, Certain Disputations of Right to the Sacraments, and the true nature of Visible Christianity (London: William Du Gard, 1657), fol. b2 verso.

9. Edmund Calamy, An historical account of my own life, with some reflections on the times I have lived in 1671-1731, ed. John Towill Rutt, 2nd ed. 2 vols. (London: Henry Colburn and Richard Bentley, 1830), I, p. 471.

10. A translation of the document is cited in extenso in Fuller, Life, Letters & Writings of John Davenant, pp. 193-200, but is left unanalyzed. The discussion of the document in Shand, "John Davenant," pp. 60-65, is highly biased, based only on the translation, and devoted largely to a negative reading of Davenant as proto-Amyraldian and, therefore, in Shand's view, holding to doctrines that "continue to plague the Reformed community" (pp. 27-28). Shand's approach is rendered problematic by a failure to observe the boundaries and character of Reformed orthodoxy as defined by the early modern confessional documents, including the Canons of Dort.

11. De Gallicana controversia D. Davenantii sententia, appended to John Davenant, Dissertationes duae: prima de morte Christi ... altera de praedestinatione et reprobatione (Cambridge: Roger Daniel, 1650), unpaginated; cf. ibid., fol. A3v, concerning James Ussher; also in idem, Dissertatio de morte Christi ... quibus subnectitue eiusdem D. Davenantii Sententia de Gallicana controversia: sc. De Gratiosa & Salutari Dei erga Homines peccatores voluntate (Cambridge: Roger Daniels, 1683) pp. 286-294; in translation, in Davenant, Exposition of the Epistle of St. Paul to the Colossians, II, pp. 561-569. Citations in the following essay reference the text of Davenant's sententia as found in the Dissertation de morte Christi (1683).

manuscript. Since the document presumes a knowledge both of the doctrinal determinations of the English and Bremen delegations to the Synod of Dort and of the controversy concerning Cameron's teachings, as well as Davenant's elevation to the episcopate (1621), it cannot reference the earliest worries over Cameron's doctrine, circa 1610-1614.[12] The concern over Cameron's doctrine expressed by the Gallican questioners most probably dates from the time of Cameron's first tenure at Saumur (1618-1621), when his inaugural disputation and lectures raised suspicion concerning the relationship of his doctrine of the divine will to the Canons of Dort and the condemnations of Remonstrant positions,[13] and the initial worry over Cameron's doctrine was exacerbated when Cameron's dispute over the Canons of Dort with the newly Arminian Daniel Tilenus (1620-1621) garnered the antagonism of the faculty at Leiden,[14] although neither the Synod of Alais (1620) nor the Synod of Bearne (1623) includes any reference to problems concerning either his doctrine or that of the English and Bremen delegations to the Synod of Dort. Indeed, the way in which the query of the Gallican theologians is worded—they wish that this portion of the English and Bremen delegations had been rejected by Dort or remanded to another synod—implies proximity to Dort.[15] Far less likely, given the French provenance of the query, is that its worries reference the resurfacing of the dispute with Tilenus during Cameron's brief stay at the University of Glasgow (1622-1623).[16] Cameron's brief tenure at Montauban (1624-1625) was not troubled by

---

12. See Robert Wodrow, "Collections on the Life of Mr. John Cameron, Minister at Bordeaux, Professor of Divinity at Saumur, Principall of the College of Glasgow, and Professor of Divinity at Montauban," in *Collections upon the Lives of the Reformers and most eminent Ministers of the Church of Scotland*, 2 vols. (Glasgow, 1848), II/1, pp. 92-109; and note H. M. B. Reid, *The Divinity Principals in the University of Glasgow, 1545-1654* (Glasgow, 1917), pp. 180-190.

13. Cf. Cameron, *Joannis Cameronis Scoto Britanni Theologi Eximij TAΣΩZOMENA sive Opera partim ab auctore ipso edita, partim post eius obitum vulgata, partim nusquam hactenus publicata, vel è Gallico idiomate nunc primum in Latinam linguam translata* (Geneva: Petrus Chouet, 1658), pp. 330-336 (Cameron's theses on grace and free choice), 355-363 (objections to the theses and responses); with Wodrow, "Collections on the Life of Mr. John Cameron," II/1, pp. 124-142. Armstrong, *Calvinism and the Amyraut Heresy*, pp. 42-70, follows Moltmann in exaggerating both the importance of covenant to Cameron's theology and the differences between Cameron and the Reformed orthodox writers of the era in general; for a critique of Armstrong and Moltmann, see Richard A. Muller, "Divine Covenants, Absolute and Conditional: John Cameron and the Early Orthodox Development of Reformed Covenant Theology," in *Mid-America Journal of Theology*, 17 (2006), pp. 11-56; cf. Thomas, *Extent of the Atonement*, pp. 162-186.

14. John Cameron, *Amica collatio de gratiae et voluntatis humanae concursu in vocatione & quibusdam annexis, instituta inter Cl. Danielem Tilenum et Ioannem Cameronem*, in *Opera*, pp. 606-708); and idem, *Epistola facultatis theologiae academiae Leydensis ad Cameronem* and *Cameronis ad praecendentem epistolam responsio*, in ibid., pp. 709-710; and see Wodrow, "Collections on the Life of Mr. John Cameron," II/1, pp. 142-154; cf. Gaston Bonet-Maury, "John Cameron: A Scottish Protestant Theologian in France," *Scottish Historical Review*, 7 (1910), pp. 336-337; and Reid, *Divinity Principals*, pp. 207-209.

15. Davenant, *De Gallicana controversia D. Davenantii sententia*, p. 287.

16. Bonet-Maury, "John Cameron," pp. 340-341; and Reid, *Divinity Principals*, pp. 211-214.

internecine controversy among the Reformed and is also, therefore, an unlikely date for the appeal to Davenant against Cameron's doctrine, and the acts of the Synod of Castres (1626) and Charenton (1631) indicate no doctrinal disturbances.[17] Also unlikely, given the focus on Cameron and the absence of reference to Amyraut and Testard, is the controversy that began shortly after the appearance of Amyraut's *Brief traitté de la predestination* in 1634 and continued at the Synod of Alençon in 1637, when Pierre du Moulin explicitly identified the root of Amyraut's thought in Cameron.[18] The probable time of Davenant's response, therefore, is the early years of his episcopacy—referencing the early debates over Cameron's doctrine, and written after 1621 and before Cameron's death in 1625.

The document begins with a statement of significant disagreements among the Reformed churches, indicating that some of the Reformed, while advocating the doctrine of "the particular election in Christ, of some persons, by the mere good pleasure of God," also argue, without any indication of a contradiction, that God also "by a general intention [*generali quadam intentione*]" of "universal grace [*gratiam universalem*]" grounded in the work of Christ "gives to all individual human beings [*omnibus et singulis*] that they may be saved if they so will."[19] This opinion, the query goes on to indicate, is clearly that of John Cameron and also, most probably, that of the English and Bremen delegations to the Synod of Dort. Other Reformed thinkers, however, stand firmly against Cameron and "deny that Christ died for all individual human beings with the intention of saving them, and [deny] that God wills that all individual human beings should be saved."[20] Those who deny the Cameronian view, moreover, identify it as nothing less than Arminianism, "a hydra of errors, opposed to the Synod of Dort, a subversion of the nature of the Divine law, of the gospel, [and] of the necessity of the Christian Religion" that ought to be cast out of the Reformed churches.[21] The document concludes with a plea to the theologians of the Church of England to respond with a view to resolving the controversy and assisting

---

17. Cf. John Quick, *Synodicon in Gallia Reformata: or, the Acts, Decisions, Decrees, and Canons of those famous National Councils of the Reformed Churches in France*, 2 vols. (London: T. Parkhurst and J. Robinson, 1692), II/1, pp. 157-251, 257-318; Fuller, *Life, Letters & Writings of John Davenant*, p. 192, appears to date Davenant's *Sententia* from 1627, some six years after Davenant became bishop of Salisbury, which is also the year in which Fuller places the *Dissertatio de morte Christi* (cf. p. 214), despite the indication given in the 1683 preface that the *Dissertatio* dates from the time of Davenant's career as a professor at Cambridge (1609-1620). There is no reason to associate the writing of the *Sententia* directly with the composition of the *Dissertatio*—and, clearly, neither dates from 1627.

18. See Du Moulin's letter in Quick, *Synodicon in Gallia Reformata*, II, p. 410; and cf. Armstrong, *Calvinism and the Amyraut Heresy*, pp. 60, 80-103.

19. Davenant, *De Gallicana controversia D. Davenantii sententia*, p. 286; N.B., I have rendered the standard Latin phrase "omnibus & singulis" as "to all individual human beings" throughout the following essay.

20. Davenant, *De Gallicana controversia D. Davenantii sententia*, pp. 286-287.

21. Davenant, *De Gallicana controversia D. Davenantii sententia*, p. 287.

in bringing peace to the Reformed church in France. Davenant alone appears to have written in reply to the Gallican query, and he seems also not to have made the response public.

Whatever the actual date of the document, Davenant's reaction and response were undoubtedly conditioned by his presence at the Synod of Dort, as a member of the British delegation. The way in which the Gallican query was framed left little or no distance between the views of the English and Bremen delegations and John Cameron, on the one side, and a purely particularistic reading of the divine intention underlying Christ's sacrifice, on the other. Indeed, one of the underlying characteristics of the debate over the divine intentionality underlying Christ's work, as illustrated by the neat—in fact, all too neat—dichotomizing of the options available to Reformed theologians of the era into those who denied that God in any way willed that all should be saved and those who affirmed a hypothetical universalism, was a tendency, if only for polemical purposes, to identify all proponents of hypothetical universalism as Cameronian or, later, as Amyraldian.[22]

Analysis of Davenant's response indicates a different perspective: in his view, which intentionally remained in accord with the final declaration or "suffrage" of the British delegation to Dort, there was a viable perspective on the doctrine of Christ's work between a denial of the intentional universality of its sufficiency and the Cameronian formulation. His response to the query concerning the Gallican controversies indicates both his reservations concerning Cameron's doctrine and his continued support for the doctrine expressed by the British delegation to Dort, the language of which provides some background to his analysis of the issues. In what follows, we first examine the decision of the British delegation and then analyze Davenant's response to the Gallican controversy, with the intention of clarifying the nature and character of that "middle position," as Calamy identified it, between the Remonstrants and the supralapsarians—and beyond that, as a position neither simply infralapsarian nor Cameronian. In other words, examination of Davenant's approach to the problem of the extent of the application of Christ's work evidences a broader spectrum and a variety of Reformed thought beyond the simple (or perhaps simplistic) division of opinion between supralapsarians and infralapsarians or, indeed, among supralapsarians, infralapsarians, and Cameronian or Amyraldian hypothetical universalists.

Davenant, the British delegation, and the Synod of Dort. John Davenant came to the Synod of Dort eminently well prepared to engaged the issue of the extent of Christ's satisfaction, having most probably already penned his elaborate *Dissertatio de morte Christi*—which references Grevinchovius' response (1615) to Ames'

---

22. As, arguably, was the tactic of George Gillespie in the debates at the Westminster Assembly; see Alexander F. Mitchell and John Struthers, ed., *The Minutes of the Sessions of the Westminster Assembly of Divines* (Edinburgh: William Blackwood, 1874), p. 153.

treatment of Arminius' *Declaratio sententiae*.[23] During the debates at Dort, the British delegation had a significant internal debate in which Davenant and Samuel Ward, differed with "the three other" members of the delegation, presumably, George Carleton, Thomas Goad, and Walter Balcanqual (the author of the letter) over the implication of the Thirty-Nine Articles, Article xxxi, "Christ was offered or died for the whole human race, or for the sins of the whole world"—specifically over whether the article was "to be understood of all particular men, or only of the Elect, who consist of all sorts of men."[24] The issue in debate, as clarified by a subsequent letter from Balcanqual, was that the Remonstrants had "studied to overthrow that distinction, *sufficientiae & efficaciae mortis Christi*, and go about to prove that those places of Scripture, which say, that Christ dyed *pro peccatis totius mundi*, are to be enlarged to all particular Men, not to be restrained *ad modum electorum*,"[25] namely, to be viewed as an *impetratio generalis* or accomplishment for all human beings without qualification, albeit having a limited *applicatio* to believers.[26] Samuel Ward had suggested the use of an alternative set of distinctions, describing the general or universal grace of redemption not as a full objective *redemptio, reconciliatio*, or *impetratio*, but as a *redimibilitas, reconciliabilitas*, or *impetrabilitas*—as the capability or possibility of redemption, reconciliation, or salvific accomplishment—arguably rather well encapsulating the conclusions of the delegation, albeit not in a language that they would adopt in their *Collegiate Suffrage*.[27]

Debate within the British delegation, accordingly, looked specifically to the last major Remonstrant declaration, the articles submitted in 1611 to the Hague Conference, together with the Contra-Remonstrant response, which, among other particulars, had recourse to the sufficiency-efficiency distinction. As a way past their own disagreement and, in addition, past the impasse of the Remonstrant/Contra-Remonstrant debate, the British delegation argued to omit "the receaved distinction

---

23. See Davenant, *Dissertatio de morte Christi* (1650), fol. A3 recto, where the editors recognize that the work could have been written either before or after the Synod of Dort, but was clearly to be identified with Davenant's work as Lady Margaret Professor; and cf. *Dissertatio de morte Christi* (1650), p. 3, where Davanent references Grevinchovius, *Dissertatio theologica de duabus quaestionibus hoc tempore controversis, quarum prima est de reconciliatione per mortem Christi impetrata omnibus ac singulis hominibus: altera, de electione ex fide praevisa* (Rotterdam: Matthias Sebastianus, 1615).

24. Walter Balcanqual to Dudley Carleton, 9 February 1619, in John Hales, *Golden remains of the ever memorable Mr. John Hales of Eaton-Colledge, &c. With additions from the authors own copy, viz., sermons & miscellanies, also letters and expresses concerning the Synod of Dort. From an authentick hand*, 3rd impression (London: T. B. for George Pawlet, 1688), p. 471. Note that Joseph Hall had fallen ill and was replaced by Thomas Goad as of January 1619: leaving Balcanqual himself as the third of the three delegates opposing Davenant and Ward; cf. Milton, *British Delegation*, p. 148.

25. Walter Balcanqual to Dudley Carleton, 2 March 1619, in Hales *Golden Remains*, p. 492.

26. George Carleton to Sir Dudley Carleton, 18 February 1619, in Hales, *Golden Remains*, p. 579.

27. George Carleton to Sir Dudley Carleton, 18 February 1619, in Hales, *Golden Remains*, pp. 578-579. Note the comments in Milton, *British Delegation*, pp. xliv-xlv, on the tendency of the British toward the use of scholastic distinctions.

of *sufficientia & efficacia mortis Christi*, as likewise the restruction of those places, which make Christs suffering general to the world, onely *ad mundum electorum*."[28] Omission of the received distinction was most probably recommended not only because it came from the Contra-Remonstrance but also and, arguably, more importantly, because the distinction is so general as not to resolve the issue.[29] Omission of the second point (concerning *ad mundum electorum*) was recommended, certainly on the ground that it had the effect of equating Christ's sufficiency or merit with the limited efficacy of his work and undermining the indiscriminate preaching of the gospel. Controversial language would then be removed, distinctions avoided, and the result would stand fully and clearly in agreement with the Thirty-Nine Articles. As a later letter from the whole delegation to Archbishop Abbot commented, their intention in addressing the issue of "*Christ's Death*, and the application of it" was to follow "as near a possibly may be" the language employed by the church fathers "against the *Pelagians* and *Semi-Pelagians*" rather than "any *new Phrase* of the *Modern Age*" and thereby also agree with the various Reformed confessions, with "as little distaste and umbrage to the *Lutheran* Churches as may be," setting aside all distinctions rather than adopting Ward's.[30]

We have, from the pen of Davenant, a series of specific comments on the articles of the Hague Conference, summarizing the conclusions of the British delegation on the extent of redemption and quite clearly adumbrating the full statement later presented in the *Collegiate Suffrage* to the Synod of Dort.[31] Davenant begins by

28. Sir Dudley Carleton to Archbishop Abbot, 9/19 March 1619, in Milton, ed. *British Delegation*, p. 215. Note that the Contra-Remonstrance itself does imply the sufficiency-efficiency distinction, arguing in Christ a "ransom for the sins of all mankind" that is efficacious "only in the elect": see the document in *Schriftelicke Conferentie, gehouden in 'sGravenhaghe in den iare 1611* (Den Haag: Hillebrandt Jacobsz, 1612), p. 21; also in Bakhuizen van den Brink, et al., eds., *Documenta Reformatoria: Teksten uit de geschiedenis van Kerk en theologie in de Nederlanden sedert de Hervorming* (Kampen: J. H. Kok, 1960-1962), I, pp. 293-300. The restriction of sufficiency derived, it appears, from more highly particularistic Contra-Remonstrant argumentation beyond the document and at the Synod of Dort, particularly as presented as examples by the Remonstrants; cf. Milton, *British Delegation*, p. xlvi.

29. The perceived absence of clarity in the distinction is evident in Davenant's further argumentation concerning "ordained" and "mere" or "naked" sufficiency in his *De morte Christi* (1650), iv (pp. 37-38); cf. Moore, *English Hypothetical Universalism*, p. 190; and note the comments in Stephen Strehle, "The Extent of the Atonement at the Synod of Dort," *Westminster Theological Journal*, 51/1 (1989), pp. 1-23.

30. George Carleton, John Davenant, Samuel Ward, Thomas Goad, and Walter Balcanqual to Archbishop Abbot, 21 March 1619, in Hales, *Golden Remains*, p. 584; cf. the comment in George Carleton to Sir Dudley Carleton, 18 February 1619, in Hales, *Golden Remains*, p. 578. On the term "Semi-Pelagian," see further below.

31. John Davenant, *Touching the Second Article*, discussed at the conference at the Hague of the *Extent of Redemption*, in Hales, *Golden remains*, pp. 586-591; also in Milton, *British Delegation*, pp. 218-222; see p. 218, note 110, on the issue of authorship and antecedents. Note that the British delegation, albeit representative of the intention of James I to see to the settlement of the Dutch controversy, was not broadly representative of the theological views of British churchmen. These ran

indicating assent to two articles contrary to the Remonstrant position—namely, that
"Christ died for the Elect by the special love & intention of both God the Father and
Christ himself, that they might obtain remission of sins & eternal salvation, &
infallibly conferred it" and that "By the same love & according to the merit &
intercession of Christ, gives to these same Elect faith, perseverance, and all other
things, through which the condition of the covenant is fulfilled, & its promised
benefits, i.e., eternal salvation are infallibly obtained."[32] Nonetheless, Davenant
indicates, the Church of England also agrees to two other propositions that were
opposed to the Contra-Remonstrant position—namely, "God having mercy on the
fallen human race sent his Son, who gave himself as the price of Redemption for the
whole world," and "On this merit of the death of Christ is founded the universal
Promise of the Gospel, according to which all who believe in Christ receive remission
of sins & life eternal."[33] The first of these two latter propositions, Davenant
indicates, is "equi-pollent" to Article xxxi of the Thirty-Nine Articles and, therefore,
is a matter of confessional integrity to his church. The two propositions, taken
together, moreover, yield the conclusion that "our *Blessed Saviour* by God's
Appointment did offer up himself to the *Blessed Trinity* for the *Redemption of
Mankind*, and by this Oblation once made, did found, confirm, and ratifie the *Eternal
Covenant*, which may and ought to be preached seriously to all Mankind without
exception."[34] As a corollary to this conclusion, Davenant also indicates—specifically
against the more particularistic Contra-Remonstrants—that the "whole of Christ's
merit" could not be "confined so to the Elect only" so as to deny that many who hear
the gospel and are not ultimately regenerated and justified nonetheless receive
limited, non-saving, benefits. Nonetheless, while insisting on the "Universality of the
Promise," Davenant also insists, against the Remonstrant view, on the special divine
intention to redeem the elect only and the extension of effectual grace to the elect
alone.[35]

The final *Collegiate Suffrage* of the British delegation offered a brief but lucid series
of paragraphs on the issue. Their first statement concerning the second article of the
Remonstrance references the fact that "by the special love & intention both of God
the Father and of Christ" Christ died for the elect and that remission of sins and
eternal salvation of the elect are "infallibly applied" on them.[36] Next, the *Suffrage*

the gamut from strongly sympathetic to the Remonstrant position to more fully favoring the views
of the Contra-Remonstrants; see Milton, *British Delegation*, pp. xxviii-xxxii.

32. Davenant, *Touching the Second Article*, p. 586.
33. Davenant, *Touching the Second Article*, p. 586.
34. Davenant, *Touching the Second Article*, p. 587.
35. Davenant, *Touching the Second Article*, p. 587.
36. George Carleton, John Davenant, Walter Balcanquall, Samuel Ward, and Thomas Goad,
*Suffragium collegiale theologorum magnae Britanniae de quinque controversis Remonstrantium articulis,
Synodo Dordrechtanae exhibitum, anno M.DC.XIX* (London: Robert Milbourne, 1626), ii.1 (p. 26);
in translation, *The Collegiat Suffrage of the Divines of Great Britaine, concerning the Five Articles*

makes clear that "by the same love and through the merit and intercession of Christ" the elect are given faith and perseverance. This gracious gift of faith, moreover, is that by which "the condition of the covenant is fulfilled."[37] In other words, God, by grace, fulfills the condition of faith: the conditionality of the covenant does not imply a conditional election as the Remonstrants would have it.[38] This special, effectual grace, moreover, is a grace not "by which men may be redeemed, if they will, but by which they are mercifully redeemed, because God wills it."[39]

Having affirmed quite explicitly the limited divine intention to save the elect and this specific purpose of the death of Christ, the *Suffrage* goes on to consider how Christ was given as a "ransom for the sins of the whole world [*pretium Redemptionis, pro peccatis totius mundi*]" and in his death opened an "infinite treasure of merits and spiritual blessings [*infinitus thesaurus meritorum & benedictionum spiritualium*]."[40] Without using the language, the *Suffrage* has raised the issue of the infinite sufficiency of Christ's satisfaction, to be juxtaposed with its limited efficacy or application. The issue, moreover, is resolved with a view to stating precisely how Christ can be said to have "died for all" and yet how not all are saved or, specifically, how the infinite merit of Christ's death can be considered under two modes: first, as the "universal promise of the gospel" to all who believe, and, second, as a "fruit" that is "not beneficial to all," but only to the elect.[41] This promise, moreover, is accompanied by a grace sufficient to convince the impenitent, so that those who do not accept the gospel are left without excuse.[42] It is in this distinction of persons that "the eternal and hidden decree of Election" manifests itself:

> Thus, Christ died for all so that all individual human beings might, by means of faith, obtain remission of sins and eternal life by virtue of [that] ransom. But he died for the elect, so that by the merit of his death, as uniquely appointed to them according to the eternal good pleasure of God, they might infallibly obtain faith and eternal life.[43]

The *Suffrage* also includes the qualification that the universality of the promise implies not its publication "to all in every time and place" but rather its "nature," according to which it could be published validly anywhere—the "nature of the promise" is such that it extends to all, but "knowledge of the promise" is confined to those nations where, according to God's "special providence" it had actually been

controverted in the Low Countries. Which Suffrage was delivered by them in the Synod of Dort, March 6. Anno 1619. Being their vote or voice foregoing the joint and publique judgment of that Synod (London: Robert Milbourne, 1629); also in Milton, *British Delegation*, pp. 226-293.

37. *Suffragium collegiale*, ii.2 (p. 27).

38. *Suffragium collegiale, theses heterodoxae*, i.3-4 (pp. 35-36).

39. *Suffragium collegiale*, ii.2 (p. 27).

40. *Suffragium collegiale*, ii.3 (pp. 27-28).

41. *Suffragium collegiale*, ii.3-4 (pp. 28-29).

42. *Suffragium collegiale*, ii.5 (pp. 29-30).

43. *Suffragium collegiale*, ii.3 (pp. 28-29).

preached.[44] "God is not bound," the *Suffrage* continues, "by any covenant or promise to communicate the gospel, or saving grace, to all individual human beings"—it belongs to the "divine freedom" to have the gospel brought to some nations and not others, and to impart saving grace to some individuals and not to others.[45] Nor is this limitation ground for excuse, given that the Apostle Paul points toward the condemnation of sinners under the "law of nature."[46]

By way of conclusion: it is certainly a mistake to regard the first two theses of the *Suffrage* as reflecting the basic orthodoxy of Carelton, Balcanqual, and Goad, with the last four theses offering "concessions" to the views of Davenant and Ward as they attempted to argue a middle position between the Reformed and the Remonstrants.[47] Nor, indeed, is it a sound reading of the documents to indicate that Davenant's and Ward's objections to the sufficiency-efficiency formula were part of an attempt to move toward what would be the Amyraldian notion of universal grace: their universalism remained hypothetical, and the promise of grace was assumed to be limited to the actual preaching of the gospel—just as it is a misreading of the Canons of Dort to view them as quietly repudiating hypothetical universalism. Here again, it only serves to confuse the issue if the term "limited atonement" is brought into play, identified with Dort, and set against the views of Davenant and the British Delegation.

Davenant's response to the Gallican controversy. Davenant's response to the Gallican query concerning Cameron and the views of the English and Bremen delegations proceeds as a series of footnotes to significant clauses in the query. It begins with a response to the introductory heading, which noted that "the gracious and saving will of God toward sinful human beings" is "debated among the Reformed theologians of France."[48] The gracious and saving will of God can be considered in two ways, Davenant argues, one related to the statement of the Apostle Paul that God "has mercy on whom he wills" (Rom. 9:15), the other related to the words of the Evangelist, John, "God so loved the world" (John 3:16). According to the former text, the gracious and saving will of God is applied effectively on the ground of God's "special mercy" to "some"—according to the latter text, the gracious and saving will of God appoints means of grace "sufficiently for all," on the basis of his common love for humanity. These means of grace are "applicable to all for salvation, according to

44. *Suffragium collegiale*, ii.4 (p. 29).

45. *Suffragium collegiale*, ii.6 (pp. 32-33), citing Prosper of Aquitaine, *Epistola ad Ruffinum* and idem, *De vocatione gentilium*, II.iii, on the limitation of the preaching of the gospel.

46. *Suffragium collegiale*, ii.6 (p. 33).

47. Contra Shand, *John Davenant*, pp. 54-56, who appears to rest too much on the account in Daniel Neal, *The History of the Puritans, or, Protestant Non-Conformists*, new rev. ed. 5 vols. (Bath: R. Cruttwell, 1794), II, pp. 107-108.

48. Davenant, *De Gallicana controversia D. Davenantii sententia*, p. 286, response as note "a," ibid., p. 287.

the tenor of the covenant of grace [*sub tenore pacti evangelici*]."[49] Of those who are not recipients of the special grace of God, some partake of the means of grace and some do not, but none are given the gift of life eternal.

Davenant goes on to agree with the authors of the query that Cameron did indeed hold the opinion that God intentionally, according to a universal grace, offered salvation to all those who would respond to the call to repentance, thereby leaving the entire blame for their damnation on themselves. In order to respond to Cameron's thought with precision, Davenant indicates that the opinions attributed to him needs to be parsed with great care. Davenant takes the first two points together, namely, that (1) according to "the particular election in Christ ... some persons, by the mere good pleasure of God," would be effectively and irrevocably called "to grace and glory," and, (2) that Christ nonetheless also "died for all people individually" according to a "general intention" of God.

The first "member" of the argument, Davenant indicates, "is legitimately constructed" as long as it is rightly understood—specifically, understood in such a way as to rest both calling and effectual grace on the divine will, so that the will of God is "not kept at a distance" from foreseen acts of the human will in the manner of the Semi-Pelagians.[50] Of interest here is that Davenant employs the relatively new term, Semi-Pelagian, to the problem of separating foreseen acts of human will from the course of divine willing to argue that God elects on grounds of a certain kind of foreknowledge. The origin of the term has been associated with the debates of the later sixteenth century, particularly in the controversies *De auxiliis* between the Dominicans and the Jesuits and in Reformed reactions to various synergistic theologies of the era.[51] Davenant's most probable referent, in order to clarify his

---

49. Davenant, *De Gallicana controversia D. Davenantii sententia*, p. 287.

50. Davenant, *De Gallicana controversia D. Davenantii sententia*, p. 288: "si particularem electionem, merum beneplacitum, efficacem vocationem ad gratiam & gloriam, ita pendere a Divina voluntate intelligat, ut hanc divinam voluntatem a praevisis humanae voluntatis actibus non arcessat. Nam qui hoc fecerit, in Semipelanianorum errorem labitur." Davenant's definition, it needs to be noted applies equally to Arminius and to Jesuit advocates of *scientia media*—and it also parallels the definitions found among the Dominicans: see John of St. Thomas, *Cursus theologicus in primam partem divi Thomae* (Antonius Vasquez, 1637), d. 20, a. 3, q. 13 (p. 644).

51. Note the use of "Semipelagiani" as a characterization of those who ground predestination in divine foreknowledge in *Novum D. N. Jesu Christi Testamentum, latine jam olim a vetere interprete, nunc denuo a Theodoro Beza versum* (Geneva: Stephanus, 1556), Eph. 2:3; 1 Tim. 2:4 (fol. 249v, 273r); also in Theodore Beza, *Confessio christianae fidei* (Geneva: Ioannes Bona Fides, 1560), iv.17 (p. 57); and idem, *Responsio ad defensiones & reprehensiones Sebastiani Castellionis: quibus suam Novi Testamenti interpretationem defendere adversus Bezam, & eius versione vicissim reprehendere conatus est* (Geneva: Stephanus, 1563), p. 111; and also in William Perkins, *A Golden Chaine or the Description of Theologie* (London: William Alde, 1591), fol. A2r; cf. M. Jacquin, "A quelle date apparait le terme semipélagien?," *Revue des sciences philosophiques et théologiques*, 1 (1907), pp. 506-508, who demonstrates use of the term by Dominicans in the very late sixteenth century; Beza's usage is, of course, earlier and points to an anti-Roman, Protestant origin of the term. A similar conclusion can be drawn from the Lutheran usage in *Von der semptlichen unterschreibung der Augsburgischen*

views of the errors of which Cameron had been accused, is those who advocate a doctrine of middle knowledge as the key to understanding divine predestination—namely the Jesuits and Arminius.[52] The comment, then, both
indicates that this aspect of Cameron's definition is correct and that Davenant
himself, in identifying it as doctrinally correct, is intent on distancing himself from
Arminianism.

The second member of the sentence, referring to a general intention of God to
save all people, is highly ambiguous in Davenant's view and is also so "convoluted"
around a series of major issues that it needs to be divided into subtopics and each of
the subtopics analyzed separately. It is correct to state that Christ died for all human
beings in the world in terms of the grounding of his death on the *pactum salutis*.[53]
This reference to a *pactum salutis* is explained by the language of the *Collegiate
Suffrage*, which Davenant is, by implication, defending in his exposition of the issues
presented by the Gallican query—although this doctrinal usage became generally
current only after 1635 and, then, in British circles as an answer to Arminianism,[54]
the British Delegation to the Synod of Dort had used the language of an *Evangelicum
foedus* or *pactum* and *pactum universalis de salvandis credentibus* to indicate a covenant,
established by the death of Christ, underlying the universal promise of the gospel.[55]
This *pactum*, therefore, is not defined as an eternal covenant grounding the covenant
of grace, as later theologians would define it, but as the basis of the universal
preaching of the gospel and of the promise of salvation to all who would believe, as
agreed upon by the Father and the Son.

The administration or course (*tenor*) of the new covenant (*novum pactum*) is such
that any and all individuals who fulfill it will be able to receive its benefit of

---

Confession (S.l.: s.n., 1561), fol. Aiii recto; and in the *Formula concordiae* (1580), *Epitome* II, *Negativa*
iii, in *Concordia Triglotta: Libri symbolici Ecclesiae Lutheranae* (St. Louis: Concordia, 1921), p. 788.

52. Cf. John Davenant, *Animadversions written by the Right Reverend Father in God, John, Lord
Bishop of Sarisbury, upon a treatise intituled, Gods love to mankinde* (London: Iohn Partridge, 1641), pp.
8-9, 12, 58, where he identifies Arminius' teaching as standing in relation to the Jesuit doctrine of
predestination on the basis of foreseen merits and also uses the term Semi-Pelagian both historically
and as a term for the Remonstrants. On Arminius' appropriation of the doctrine of *scientia media*, see
Eef Dekker, *Rijker dan Midas: Vrijheid, genade en predestinatie in de theologie van Jacobus Arminius,
1559-1609* (Zoetermeer: Boekencentrum, 1993), pp. 178-190, 208-209, 213, 244-245; and idem,
"Was Arminius a Molinist?" in *Sixteenth Century Journal*, 27/2 (1996), pp. 337-352. The Arminians
of the era argued against the accusation of Semipelagianism: see Ioannes Corvinus, *Petri Molinaei novi
anatomici mala encheiresis: seu censura Anatomes Arminianismi* (Frankfurt: Erasmus Kempffer, 1623),
p. 334; as did the Jesuits: see, e.g., Roderigo de Arriaga, *Disputationum theologicarum in Primum
Secumdum D. Thomae, tomus secundus: sive universi cursus theologici, tomus quartus* (Lyon: Laurentius
Anisson, 1647), pp. 416, c. 27; 562, n. 42.

53. Davenant, *De Gallicana controversia D. Davenantii sententia*, p. 288.

54. Cf. Richard A. Muller, "Toward the *Pactum Salutis*: Locating the Origins of a Concept," *Mid-
America Journal of Theology*, 18 (2007), pp. 11-65.

55. *Suffragium collegiale*, ii.5, 6 (pp. 30, 32).

salvation—whereas any who fail to fulfill the covenant cannot be recipients of its salvation even, Davenant adds, if they were elect. According to the covenant,

> If Cain or Judas had believed, and had repented, he would be saved through the benefit and merit of the death of Christ. If David or Peter had not believed, nor had repented, he would not be saved. In this sense the death of Christ may be understood to be set equally before all individual human beings.[56]

The issue of how an elect individual might fail to believe and repent is not explained by Davenant. It is clear, however, that as far as the covenant of salvation is concerned, Christ's death is appointed for the salvation of all who believe and repent.

If the conditions of salvation are clear, what remains questionable, in Davenant's view, in the Cameronian doctrinal statement is its claim that there is a general intention in God to save all people individually in Christ. This particular statement needs to be set into the context of the biblical approach to divine willing or, as Davenant adds, what the scholastics identify as the "common order of providence [*communis providentiae ordo*]," whereby God appoints and also reveals that he has appointed certain means to a particular end, without, however, having a "determinate will of producing that end by those means."[57] There can, then, be a divine intention or will to make means available and validly so, as is clear in the divine will and intention that apostate angels would be obedient and be saved should they, in and of themselves, avail themselves of saving divine gifts. The example is significant in its context inasmuch as it was a commonplace of the theology of the day to note that fallen angels do not have a mediator to pay the price for their sins. "In this sense," Davenant continues, "God with a general intention wills life to all human beings, inasmuch as he willed the death of Christ to be the source and cause of life [*fontem & causam vitae*] to all individual human beings, according to the tenor of the evangelical covenant."[58] The Cameronian doctrine of a general divine intention to save all is, then, acceptable if interpreted in this way—namely, as reflecting the general call of the gospel. It is a divine will or intention in the loose or improper sense of the terms. Scripture, however, also indicates another divine will or intention, understood in a strict or "proper" sense, a will or intention "which never fails in producing the good intended, and which the scholastics identify as belonging to the order of special Predestination."[59]

A further aspect of the argument, however, is different from Calvin's recourse to a distinction between a revealed or preceptive will of God identifiable in the

---

56. Davenant, *De Gallicana controversia D. Davenantii sententia*, p. 289.

57. Davenant, *De Gallicana controversia D. Davenantii sententia*, p. 289: "voluntatem vel intentionem divinam, aliquando denotare, solum ordinationem mediorum ad Finem, quamvis in Deo non sit determinata voluntas, illum finem per illa media producendi."

58. Davenant, *De Gallicana controversia D. Davenantii sententia*, p. 289.

59. Davenant, *De Gallicana controversia D. Davenantii sententia*, p. 289.

indiscriminate preaching of the gospel and the hidden will of the divine good pleasure to save some by means of the gospel—but Davenant has also argued that this generalized, loosely understood divine intention does imply a divine willing, albeit ineffectual, of salvation, distinct from the decree of election, to all who hear and believe. Where Calvin did not move toward a form of hypothetical universalism, Davenant made the step—even though, much like Calvin, he denied a fully universal grace. In addition, like Calvin, Davenant allowed only a single, saving intention to belong to the eternal, effective will of God. The hypothetical aspect of his doctrine was lodged in the temporal proclamation of the gospel and in a notion of a twofold willing on the part of Christ directly related to the issue of the indiscriminate preaching of the gospel.[60]

In order further to explain this issue of general but unwilled divine intention in contrast to a special effective divine willing, Davenant goes on to cite Augustine's *Enchiridion* at the point where Augustine asks what it means for the apostle to say that God will have all people to be saved, "when indeed not all, nor even very many will be saved"—concerning this special will of God, Augustine wrote, "There are some things in heaven and in earth which [God] did not will and did not do; some things which he willed and did not do, but all that he has done he has willed."[61] Davenant also cites Aquinas: "Whatever God simply wills, he does,"[62] underlining the point that, if God had indeed willed the salvation of all people, all would be saved. With reference, then, to the definition put forth as representing the Cameronian position, Davenant indicates two possible highly problematic constructions, both yielding the same theological result. First, "if ... by this general intention of God to procure the salvation of all human beings by the death of Christ, they wish to exclude the special will, and the special and effectual operation of God in effecting the salvation of the elect ... they are proposing Semi-Pelagianism."[63] Second,

> if they would infer from this that the fruit of the death of Christ, that is, the grace of God and eternal salvation of human beings (as pertains to God) is intended for all individual human beings with the same kind of will, and is applied by the same mode of operation, really and actually to be had and obtained by each individual, according as he makes good use of his own free choice: they are proposing Semi-Pelagianism.[64]

---

60. Davenant, *Dissertatio de morte Christi* (1650), III, obj. 7, solutio (pp. 27-28); cf. Moore, *English Hypothetical Universalism*, p. 193.

61. Davenant, *De Gallicana controversia D. Davenantii sententia*, p. 289, citing Augustine, *Enchiridion*, cap. 97.

62. Davenant, *De Gallicana controversia D. Davenantii sententia*, p. 289, citing Aquinas, *Summa theologiae*, 1a, qu. 10, art. 6.

63. Davenant, *De Gallicana controversia D. Davenantii sententia*, pp. 289-290.

64. Davenant, *De Gallicana controversia D. Davenantii sententia*, p. 290.

This latter construction quite clearly identifies an Arminian danger if the universalistic arguments are pressed too far, specifically if they fail to distinguish between a divine intention not related to divine willing and an actual will of God, thereby interpreting both the intention to save universally and the intention to save some as distinct wills on the part of God—the understanding of predestination enunciated in Arminius' *Declaratio sententiae* of 1608.[65]

There is, however, a construction of the definition that in Davenant's view falls within the boundaries of orthodoxy:

> If by the general intention they mean nothing more than a general aptitude and sufficiency in the death of Christ to effect the salvation of all individual human beings in the mode of a universal cause, or [in the mode of] a general appointment of God concerning the salvation of all individual human beings, who, through the grace of God, duly apply to themselves this universal cause, this formulation need not be rejected.[66]

The argument here is very much in accord with the *Collegiate Suffrage*. It is also quite similar to a point made by the supralapsarians Gomarus and Twisse on the issue of the extent of Christ's death: no one, Gomarus indicated, would deny that the value of Christ's death was of "infinite power" capable of the salvation of a thousand worlds. They insisted, however, that this power or potency was not conjoined with a divine will to that end.[67] The debate, therefore, was not merely a matter of supralapsarians against hypothetical universalists—rather, there was a fairly broad opposition to a central assumption of the Cameronian approach on the part of supralapsarians, infralapsarians, and advocates, like Davenant, of other forms of hypothetical universalism.

The second major point of Cameronian doctrine on which Davenant comments is the proposition "That God, by his universal grace founded in the death of Christ, which was sufficient in itself, and by a suitable invitation and calling to repentance, although in different ways, grants to all individual human beings, that they may be saved if they will."[68] The Cameronian point, it should be noted, runs counter to the

65. Jacob Arminius, *Declaratio sententiae*, in *Opera theologica* (Leiden: Godefridus Basson, 1629), p. 119; also in *The Works of James Arminius*, trans. James Nichols and William Nichols, 3 vols. (London, 1825, 1828, 1875), I, pp. 653-654; and see Arminius, *Articuli nonnulli*, xv.4, in *Opera*, p. 957 (*Works*, II, pp.718-719).

66. Davenant, *De Gallicana controversia D. Davenantii sententia*, p. 290; cf. the discussion n Moore, *English Hypothetical Universalism*, pp. 201-202.

67. Franciscus Gomarus, *An Christus pro omnibus et singulis hominiubs mortuus?*, in *Opera theologica omnia, maximam partem posthuma*, 2 parts (Amsterdam: Joannes Jansson, 1664), I, p. 459; cf. William Twisse, *Vindiciae gratiae, potestatis, ac providentiae Dei hoc est, ad examen libelli Perkinsiani de praedestinatione modo et ordine, institutum a J. Arminio, responsio scholastica*. Amsterdam: Joannes Jansson, 1648), I.ii.21 (pp. 230-231).

68. Davenant, *De Gallicana controversia D. Davenantii sententia*, p. 290.

language of the *Collegiate Suffrage*.[69] As an initial objection to the language of the proposition, Davenant notes that the term has Pelagian overtones. Universality, he continues, is typically associated in orthodox doctrine not with the "grace of Christ" but with the "common philanthropy of God": to claim that the grace of Christ "is given and actually communicated to all individual human beings" is utterly indefensible.[70] Taking a point from Prosper of Aquitaine that had significant echoes in both Calvin and Beza and that had been cited also in the *Collegiate Suffrage* of the British delegation to Dort—and that would also have a parallel in later Reformed thinkers, including some noted for their more particularistic view of Christ's work[71]—Davenant notes that the grace of Christ, rightly understood as communicated in and through the preaching of the gospel, cannot be universal—as Prosper indicated, "They live without grace, and are not partakers of Christian grace, to whom Christ was never preached."[72] This point, Davenant continues, was made by the apostle Paul in his Epistle to the Ephesians (2:12). Elsewhere, Davenant explains his basic point in terms very much like those we have already noted in Calvin and Beza:

> when we say that this death or this merit *is represented in the holy Scriptures as the universal cause of salvation*, we mean, That according to the will of God explained in his word, this remedy is proposed indiscriminately to every individual of the human race for salvation, but that it cannot savingly profit any one without a special application.[73]

Nonetheless, Davenant continues, the Cameronian proposition may be acceptable if it refers only to a "universal capacity for salvation in all individual pilgrim souls [*in omnibus & singulis viatoribus*] or a universal propensity in God to save every person, if he would believe in Christ," a point paralleling Ward's language of *redimibilitas, reconciliabilitas*, or *impetrabilitas*. But, Davenant adds, if this is the meaning of the

---

69. *Suffragium collegiale*, ii.2 (p. 27), as cited above; note that the same point is found in Peter Martyr Vermigli, *Most learned and fruitfull commentaries upon the Epistle to the Romans* (London: John Day, 1568), fol. 304v.

70. Davenant, *De Gallicana controversia D. Davenantii sententia*, pp. 290-291.

71. Cf. John Owen, *Salus Electorum, Sanguinis Jesu; the Death of Death in the Death of Christ. A Treatise of the Redemption and Reconciliation that is in the Blood of Christ ... and the whole Controversy about Universal Redemption fully Discussed*, in *The Works of John Owen*, ed. William H. Goold, 24 vols. (Edinburgh: Johnstone and Hunter, 1850-1853), X, pp. 381-383; with a similar argument in the hypothetical universalist, Pierre Du Moulin, *Esclaircissement des controverses Salmuriennes, ou defense de la doctrine des eglises reformées sur l'immutabilité des decrets de Dieu, l'efficace de la mort de Christ, la grace universelle, l'impuissance à de se convertir et sur d'autres matières* (Leiden: J. Maire, 1648), VIII.ii, iii (pp. 201-204, 212-213).

72. Davenant, *De Gallicana controversia D. Davenantii sententia*, p. 291; cf. Calvin, *Sermons sur le premiere Epitre a Timothée*, 2:3-5 (sermon 13), in CO 53, col. 151; Theodore Beza, *Quaestionum & responsionum christianarum libellus* (London: Henry Bynneman, 1571), pp. 122-124; idem, *Christian questions and answers* (1578), fol. 79v-80v.

73. Davenant, *Dissertatio de morte Christi* (1683), p. 25 (*Dissertation*, p. 341).

proposition, its author ought to emend his language in order not to give offense to the "orthodox."[74]

Unsupportable also is the argument that there is a sufficient universal grace that calls all people to repentance and salvation. This notion is refuted by the point already made from Prosper of Aquitaine: since there is no calling to repentance and salvation outside of the church's preaching of the gospel and since the preaching of the gospel has not gone out to all people in the world, there is no universal calling sufficient to save all people. So too is it fundamentally mistaken to claim that "God by his universal grace grants to all human beings individually [omnibus & singulis] that they may be saved if they will."[75] Infants dying "outside of the church" surely cannot be saved "if they will" inasmuch as infants lack the full use of reason and free will. Nor, indeed, does it make sense to argue that all adults can be saved "if they will" inasmuch as all human beings seek happiness, and, in that sense, no one could be unwilling to be saved.[76] The statement might be clarified, Davenant notes, to say that all can be saved if they are all willing to believe in Christ. It is not a matter of dispute that all who rightly will to believe in Christ are saved and, indeed, cannot be damned—but the existence of "universal grace" is not demonstrated by a willingness or power to obtain salvation: once again making the point found in both Calvin and Beza, Davenant comments, "the condition, If they are willing to believe in Christ, cannot be fulfilled by man, unless God wills to send them preachers of the gospel."[77] He concludes,

> there are, therefore, multitudes who cannot be saved, because they cannot believe in Christ. They cannot believe in Christ for obtaining remission of sins, because the act of believing presupposes the object having been proposed to the sinner, in which he may believe.[78]

Davenant then comes to the final Cameronian proposition: "It is through themselves alone and through the hardness of their hearts that human beings are not saved."[79] Several points can be made in favor of the proposition. In the first place, the genuine, "positive cause" of perdition is certainly the corruption and hardness of the human heart. Second, God himself will not, in fact, cannot, bring about a contempt or abuse of the means of grace in those human beings to whom he wills to grant grace by these means: "God cannot cause malice and wickedness in the human heart."[80] Nonetheless, it also needs to be said "that there is no hardness in the human will so obstinate, that God cannot soften it if he will, and which he will not

---

74. Davenant, De Gallicana controversia D. Davenantii sententia, p. 291.
75. Davenant, De Gallicana controversia D. Davenantii sententia, p. 291.
76. Davenant, De Gallicana controversia D. Davenantii sententia, p. 292.
77. Davenant, De Gallicana controversia D. Davenantii sententia, p. 292.
78. Davenant, De Gallicana controversia D. Davenantii sententia, p. 292, citing Rom. 3:25-26.
79. Davenant, De Gallicana controversia D. Davenantii sententia, pp. 292-293.
80. Davenant, De Gallicana controversia D. Davenantii sententia, p. 293.

at length soften in all of the elect, by that special mercy of which the Apostle speaks, *He hath mercy on whom he will, &c.*"[81] Davenant concludes with the comment that, at least in the statements or propositions proposed to him, the Cameronian position was poorly presented.

By way of conclusion, Davenant offers two statements that distance not only his views but those of the British delegation to the Synod of Dort from the Cameronian doctrine. First, there is nothing in the decisions of the British delegation to the synod that either argues a universal grace or indicates that sufficient means of salvation are ever granted to people who have not heard the gospel. Second, he notes,

> I think that no divine of the Reformed Church of sound judgement, will deny a general intention or appointment concerning the salvation of all people individually by the death of Christ, on this condition: If they should believe. For this intention or appointment of God is general, and is plainly revealed in the Holy Scriptures, although the absolute and infrustratable intention [*intentione Dei absoluta & infrustrabilis*] of God, concerning the gift of faith, is special, and is limited to the elect alone.[82]

This general intention, however, certainly must be interpreted in terms of Davenant's previous statement that such an intention on God's part is not connected with a divine will to bring it about. The denial of a "frustrated intention" is a point shared by Davenant with Du Moulin. Given, moreover, that the general intention of God, as posited by Davenant and the British delegation generally, embedded in the proclamation of the gospel, belongs to a revealed or preceptive rather than an effectual divine willing, it belongs—as had been argued by Davenant—to a particular line of argument within the Reformed tradition and is not to be regarded as a median or compromise position between the Arminian and the Reformed.[83]

Pierre Du Moulin on the Extent and Efficacy of Christ's Satisfaction

Du Moulin and the debate over hypothetical universalism. Pierre Du Moulin, insofar as he is known to modern scholarship by way of studies of the Amyraut controversy, has been identified as an implacable enemy of hypothetical universalism and by implication a staunch proponent of "limited atonement." Indeed, in Armstrong's reading of the controversy between Du Moulin and Amyraut, there were two fundamentally opposed options among the seventeenth-century Reformed, namely, Cameronian or Amyraldian hypothetical universalism, purportedly in accord with Calvin, and "Bezan" limited atonement, defined as the doctrine that Christ died solely for the elect. A virtually identical paradigm, painted with even broader strokes,

---

81. Davenant, *De Gallicana controversia D. Davenantii sententia*, p. 293.

82. Davenant, *De Gallicana controversia D. Davenantii sententia*, pp. 293-294.

83. Contra Shand, "John Davenant," p. 54.

was pressed by Hall and Kendall. Armstrong, moreover, pitted Du Moulin as a representative of this Bezan orthodoxy against what he took to be the more genuinely Calvinian theology of Amyraut.[84] It might therefore come as a surprise that, in his own time, as noted by no less a scholar than Gisbertus Voetius, Du Moulin was numbered among those orthodox who not only accepted the traditional distinction between the sufficiency of the merit or death of Christ and its efficiency, but who also, along with Calvin, Kimedoncius, and Pareus, held that Christ's death was sufficient for all including the reprobate, albeit effective for the elect only. Voetius also, rather pointedly, distinguished this view from the hypothetical universalism of Cameron, Amyraut, and Testard, but also distinguished it from the views of Beza and other supralapsarians.[85] Furthermore, in confirmation of his understanding of Du Moulin's place in the broader paradigm of Reformed opinions, Voetius cites the *Anatome Arminianismi* (1619), where Du Moulin writes, "the death of Christ is sufficient for the salvation of whoever believes: Indeed & abundantly sufficient to save all human beings, if all people in the entire world would believe in him."[86] Du Moulin repeats the statement in his debates with Amyraut.[87]

In the following paragraphs, I propose to examine Du Moulin's views more closely, with the intention of clarifying his relationship to the varieties of universalism found among his contemporaries. It is instructive of the nature of Du Moulin's approach to the satisfaction of Christ and its universal scope that he posed it, without

---

84. Armstrong, *Calvinism and the Amyraut Heresy*, pp. 41, 91, 137-138, assuming the validity of the old central dogma thesis; also note idem, "The Changing Face of French Protestantism: The Influence of Pierre du Moulin," in *Calviniana: Ideas and Influence of John Calvin*, ed. Robert V. Schnucker (Kirksville: Sixteenth Century Journal Publishers, 1988), pp. 145-149; cf. Basil Hall, "Calvin against the Calvinists," in *John Calvin*, ed. Gervase Duffield (Appleford: Sutton Courtnay Press, 1966), pp. 27-28; and R. T. Kendall, *Calvin and English Calvinism to 1649* (Oxford: Oxford University Press, 1979), pp. 29-32. An older study by Gédéon Gory, *Pierre du Moulin. Essai sur sa vie, sa controverse, et sa polémique* (Paris: Fischbacher, 1888), identifies Du Moulin as intolerant, does not argue the central dogma thesis, and confuses the debates over Arminian doctrine with the those of the later Amyraldian controversy; see especially p. 55. A more balanced approach that recognized the pastoral side of Du Moulin's work is L. Rimbault, *Pierre du Moulin, 1568-1658: un pasteur classique à l'age classique. Etude de théologie pastorale sur des documents inédits* (Paris: J. Vrin, 1966); also on Du Moulin's life, see *La France Protestante ou vies des protestants français qui se sont fait un nom dans l'historie*, ed. Eugène and Émile Haag, 10 vols. (Paris, Joël Cherbuliez, 1846-1859); second edition, 6 vols. (Paris: Sandoz et Fischbacher, 1877-1888), 1st ed., IV, pp. 420-429; 2nd ed., V, pp. 800-824.

85. Gisbertus Voetius, *Selectae disputationes theologicae*, 5 vols. (Utrecht: Joannes à Waesberge, 1648-1669), II, pp. 252-253.

86. Pierre Du Moulin, *Anatome Arminianismi seu, enucleatio controversiam quae in Belgio agitantur, super doctrina de providentia: de praedestinatione, de morte Christi, de natura & gratia* (Leiden: Abraham Picard, 1619), xxvii.9 (p. 202): "Christi mortem sufficientem esse ad servandos quoslibet credentes: Immo & abunde suffecturam ad servandos omnes homines, si quotquot sunt toto orbe homines in eum crederent"; cf. idem, *The Anatomy of Arminianisme: or the opening of the Controversies lately handled in the Low-Countryes, Concerning the Doctrine of Providence, of Predestination, of the Death of Christ, of the Nature of Grace* (London: T. S. for Nathaniel Newbery, 1620), pp. 227-228.

87. Du Moulin, *Esclaircissement*, VI.i (p. 130).

alteration, against two alternative approaches to universal redemption—first against the Arminians and later against the Amyraldians.

Du Moulin against the Arminians. Pierre du Moulin, alumnus of the Academy of Sedan, eminent Huguenot clergyman, recognized as a philosopher and noted as a polemicist, was one of the Gallican theologians who would have served as a delegate to the Synod of Dort had not a royal edict forbidden the attendance of the French delegation.[88] As a friend of the great Leiden theologian Franciscus Junius and a member of the faculty of philosophy at Leiden from 1592 to 1596, Du Moulin retained close connections with orthodox Reformed theologians in the Netherlands and had begun to write a treatise against Arminianism and appears to have sent a manuscript version to Synod of Dort.[89] After the synod had completed its work and published it decisions, Du Moulin was one of the French pastors and theologians most influential in seeing to the acceptance of the Canons of Dort by the synods of the French church—and, as part of his work to further the cause of Dort and to end what he took to be the Arminian threat to French Reformed theology, he published the *Anatome Arminianismi*, or *Anatomy of Arminianism*, at the time of the conclusion of the Synod of Dort and prior to the French Synod's examination and ratification of the canons.

An underlying problem with Arminius' doctrine, from Du Moulin's infralapsarian perspective, was its highly speculative division of the eternal decree into four distinct decrees, a problem that would resurface in his complaint against Cameron and controversy with Amyraut. Indeed, this was a fundamental problem that Du Moulin referenced first at the very beginning of his treatise.[90] Throughout his writings, Du Moulin advocated a clearly defined infralapsarianism and, despite his aversion to Arminianism, shared with Arminius a series of objections to supralapsarian formulations concerning the divine decrees.[91] Armstrong is, therefore, quite correct in stating that Du Moulin saw supralapsarian approaches to predestination as one of the causes of controversy in the Netherlands. Where Armstrong mistakes the issue, however, is in his claim that Du Moulin became more "scholastic" and shifted his focus when identifying the problem in Amyraldianism as involving the order of the decrees.[92] Du Moulin's early polemic against Arminianism not only indicated

88. See the report of Jean Chauvé concerning himself, Pierre du Moulin, Daniel Chamier, and André Rivet to the Synod of Alais, in Quick, *Synodicon*, II, p. 14; cf. Aymon, *Tous les synodes*, II, p. 156.

89. Cf. Rimbault, *Pierre du Moulin*, p. 89; with Armstrong, *Calvinism and the Amyraut Heresy*, pp. 133-134.

90. Du Moulin, *Anatome Arminianismi*, ii, iii.3, xii.9-10, 16-17, xiii-xv; xvi.9-12 (pp. 5, 7, 75, 77-78, 82-99, 102-104); *Anatomy*, pp. 5, 7, 83, 85-86, 91-111, 114-115.

91. Cf. Du Moulin, *Anatome Arminianismi*, xiii.4 (p. 84); *Anatomy*, pp. 93-94; with Arminius, *Examen thesium D. Francisci Gomari*, p. 64 (*Works*, III, p. 579); idem, *Disputationes privatae*, XXVII.iii.

92. Armstrong, "Changing Face of French Protestantism," pp. 147-149.

problems with supralapsarian definition; it also critiqued the Arminian order of the decrees—just as his later polemics against Amyraut embodied his own infralapsarian definitions and continued to deal with the problem of the decrees, as later surfacing in Amyraut's own writings. Both the antagonism to supralapsarian definition and the problem of the order of the decree were central to Du Moulin's debates. Indeed, his later polemics against Amyraldianism were framed by his perception of a fundamental problem first identified in Arminius' theology and later in the thought of Amyraut.

Thus, in the initial pages of his *Anatome Arminianismi*, Du Moulin argues that Arminius had invaded the secret ways of God and had "cut the decree of election in pieces," examining the decree as if a human being might penetrate its depths.[93] In dividing up the divine will, moreover, Arminius violated the fundamental doctrinal truth that the "will of God cannot be resisted" and, against Perkins, had argued an "antecedent will" that could be resisted by human beings, indeed, that the end or goal proposed by God to himself in this antecedent decree might be frustrated: *Deum posse frustrari particulari fine quem sibi proposuit.*[94] The language here is important: contrary to Armstrong's sense of a major shift in Du Moulin's focus, this problem of Arminius' theology would be brought to the fore once again in Amyraut's model of the decrees, specifically of an antecedent divine will capable of being "frustrated." In Du Moulin's view, a point shared with other infralapsarian hypothetical universalists like Davenant and readily grounded in Calvin's exegesis, both the two-will structure found in Arminius' theological disputations and the four-decree structure of Arminius' fully developed doctrine of predestination exemplified the problem. In the first of these formulations, Arminius had distinguished between a legal purpose of God to bestow life on those who are obedient and an evangelical purpose to save those who believe, not precisely between a legal and an evangelical decree of God as Du Moulin implies, but clearly enough indicating a primary conditional decree of God.[95] In his final four-decree model, Arminius had developed a structure consisting in two antecedent and absolute decrees, one establishing redemption in Christ, the other to bestow eternal life on believers; a third decree providing gracious means sufficient to belief; and a fourth consequent and conditional decree to save those foreknown as believers. The antecedent decrees were formulated as a general will of God to save in Christ all who believe, without specification of individuals— the final consequent decree was framed as a specific divine willing of the salvation of individuals.[96]

93. Du Moulin, *Anatome Arminianismi*, iii.2 (p. 6); *Anatomy*, p. 6.

94. Du Moulin, *Anatome Arminianismi*, iii.3 (p. 7); *Anatomy*, p. 7.

95. Du Moulin, *Anatome Arminianismi*, xii.16 (p. 77), citing Arminius, *Disputationes publicae*, xv.3; *Anatomy*, p. 85.

96. Arminius, *Declaratio sententiae*, in *Opera*, p. 119; also idem, *Articuli nonnulli*, [xv] *De decretis Dei*, 4, in *Opera*, p. 957; cf. Du Moulin's accurate summary of Arminius in *Anatome Arminianismi*, xii.16.

This definition of predestination embodies, Du Moulin continues, a fundamental misunderstanding of the doctrine, inasmuch as the divine decree, rightly understood, concerns what God intends to do with human beings, not what God would have human beings do. The decree of predestination, in other words, is a will of divine good pleasure, not a preceptive willing: Arminius errs by including a divine commandment in the decree. Thus, Du Moulin can, much like Calvin, argue a twofold, or "duplex," character of divine willing, drawing on the traditional distinction between the *voluntas beneplaciti* and the *voluntas praecepti*, without arguing two wills in God:

> The will of God is certainly twofold [*duplex*], one is his decree [*decretum*], the other is his injunction [*mandatum*]. The decree of God pertains to God's providence, and the injunction to his justice. By his decree, he disposes and orders occurrences; by his injunction, our actions. By the former will, he establishes what will be [*quid acturus sit*]; by the latter, what he wants us to do. By the former all creatures are governed, even devils; by the latter the faithful, albeit not perfectly.[97]

These kinds of divine willing are distinct, but they cannot, without grave error, be set against one another or identified as contraries.[98]

The problem in Arminius' doctrine carries over into his way of distinguishing between an antecedent and a consequent will in God. There is, Du Moulin notes, a legitimate way of understanding the distinction as referring to an order in the purpose or purposes of God. Thus, God wills first to create human beings and second, consequently, to provide them with nourishment and clothing. What is illegitimate, he argues, is the Arminian claim of an antecedent divine willing prior to a human act and a consequent divine willing subsequent to the act, with the former understood as resistible and the latter irresistible. This leads to the conclusion that God can be disappointed or frustrated in his intentions and can act in self-contradictory ways—such as willing from eternity something that he knows he shall never do, namely, willing to save all human beings.[99]

The error of basic definition is compounded by Arminius' correct identification of predestination as a "part of providence," inasmuch as providence, rightly understood, is distinct from the rules or ordinances of law (*regulae legis*), even as predestination, rightly understood, is distinct from rules or ordinances of the gospel (*Evangelii regulae*). Thus, Arminius' contrasting of an evangelical with a legal decree evidences the same problem as his model of four decrees, specifically the confounding of a conditional or preceptive willing with a divine decree.[100]

---

97. Du Moulin, *Anatome Arminianismi*, iv.3 (p. 19), citing John 6:39-40; Heb. 10:36; on the issue of Calvin's understanding of the twofold will in God see above, chapter 4.

98. Du Moulin, *Anatome Arminianismi*, iv.10 (p. 22).

99. Du Moulin, *Anatome Arminianismi*, v.2-3 (pp. 25-26).

100. Du Moulin, *Anatome Arminianismi*, xii.17 (pp. 77-78); cf. ,Arminius, *Disputationes publicae*, xv.1, 3.

Given that the second of these decrees is not in fact an eternal decree but rather the doctrine of the salvation presented in the gospel, Du Moulin concludes that Arminius' structure of decrees is obliterated: with the second link in the concatenation of decrees removed, the entire structure collapses.[101] What is more, Arminius' approach actually denies the doctrine of election inasmuch as it assumes the number of the elect is determined not by God but by human free choice, and if God does not determine the number of the elect, then no one is actually elected:

> when Arminius indicates that all human beings are elected by a conditional election, that is, they will to believe, & by free choice rightly use the grace that is offered them, he proposes an election that is not election, because it is equally extended to all: [God] does not elect unless some are preferred over others. Are Simon Magus & Simon Peter equally elected by this general election? & is election extended to Judas & Pharaoh?[102]

Conditionality, then, renders salvation indeterminate even from the perspective of the divine willing, and it raises the spectre of universal damnation even in the same breath that it hypothesizes universal salvation. There is a decree to make Christ the foundation of salvation and the head of the church at the same time that the conditionality of salvation makes possible that there be no church and that Christ be a head without a body![103]

Given that Arminius' structure of the decrees argued that Christ's death "accomplished and acquired remission of sins, & reconciliation & salvation for all individual human beings" and also that "that God equally intended & desired the salvation of all human beings" with human unbelief identified as the sole cause of the limited application of salvation, Du Moulin also raised at some length the question of how Christ can be said to have died for all human beings.[104] The Arminian assumption of a general divine will to save all human beings by means of the death of Christ implies that Christ's death was not ordained by a precise divine will for the salvation of particular human beings. Indeed, Du Moulin notes, citing Grevinchovius, that Arminian doctrine did not conjoin the universal accomplishment (*impetratio*) of redemption in and through Christ to any necessary application (*applicatio*) of Christ's work. Christ's work merely serves to render salvation possible.[105] This distinction made by the Arminians between accomplishment or impetration and application allows them to argue the universality of reconciliation and redemption and limitation of actual salvation, so that all

101. Du Moulin, *Anatome Arminianismi*, xii.18 (p. 78).
102. Du Moulin, *Anatome Arminianismi*, xii.20 (p. 79); cf. ibid., xii.19, 21.
103. Du Moulin, *Anatome Arminianismi*, xii.26 (p. 81).
104. Du Moulin, *Anatome Arminianismi*, xxvii.1 (p. 199).
105. Du Moulin, *Anatome Arminianismi*, xxvii.3 (p. 200).

human beings have the right (*ius*) to salvation but not to the communication of salvation.[106]

Over against this understanding of the universality of Christ's death, Du Moulin defines the Reformed view as teaching that "Christ died for all human beings [*pro omnibus*]" but also that Christ's death did not accomplish or impetrate salvation or remission of sins for all.[107] In this view, remission of sins is not accomplished for anyone whose sins are not actually forgiven, and the price of salvation is not paid for anyone who has been decreed to condemnation in eternity—such vain purchase is, Du Moulin avers, the Arminian doctrine. Therefore,

> When we say that Christ died for all human beings, we understand it as follows: That, namely, the death of Christ is sufficient to save whoever believes: Indeed, that it is abundantly sufficient to save all human beings, if all human beings in the whole world would believe in him. And the reason why all are not saved is not in the insufficiency of the death of Christ, but in the wickedness and unbelief of human beings.[108]

Reconciliation is acquired, then, only by the faithful; as Paul taught, "God has set forth Christ to be a propitiation through faith in his blood" (Rom. 3:25). And as there is no propitiation (*placamentum*) without faith, so also is there no accomplishment of reconciliation.[109]

From Arminius to Cameron to Amyraut: Du Moulin's perceptions in 1637. Du Moulin and Amyraut, both alumni and professors in major French academies at the time of their debates, Du Moulin at Sedan and Amyraut at Saumur, came to the controversies over predestination and the extent of Christ from nearly opposite directions. Prior to his appointment to Sedan in 1621, Du Moulin had not only been closely associated with André Rivet, Jean Chauvé, and Daniel Chamier in efforts to bring about a union of Protestants; he had also been delegated with them to attend the Synod of Dort, where one of the fundamental issues had been to craft a doctrinal agreement among the Reformed churches that would hold them together while at the same time rejecting Arminian or Remonstrant doctrines. In addition, both as minister of the Reformed church in Paris and as an invited visitor to the court of James I, Du Moulin had been deeply involved in defending the orthodoxy of the Reformed faith, both that of the French Reformed and of the Church of England

---

106. Du Moulin, *Anatome Arminianismi*, xxvii.5 (p. 201).

107. Du Moulin, *Anatome Arminianismi*, xxvii.8 (p. 201).

108. Du Moulin, *Anatome Arminianismi*, xxvii.9 (p. 202); note that Armstrong, *Calvinism and the Amyraut Heresy*, p. 86, entirely misses the point of Du Moulin's position and claims that "Du Moulin feels that for one to say that God sent his Son to die for all men upon condition of faith ... is to represent God more unworthily than by saying He sent Christ only for the elect," whereas Du Moulin actually affirms the hypothetical universalist argument.

109. Du Moulin, *Anatome Arminianismi*, xxviii.21 (p. 211).

against the attacks of Roman Catholic theologians such as Du Perron, Coton, De Raconis, and Arnoux.[110] He came to the debate with Amyraut with a clear sense of Arminianism as a threat to Reformed identity and of Roman polemics as a threat to the legitimacy of the Reformed faith.

Amyraut, by contrast, nearly three decades Du Moulin's junior, had not experienced the persecution of French Protestants prior to the Edict of Nantes and had been involved neither in major debates with Roman Catholic polemicists nor in controversy over Arminian doctrines. His views on predestination and the extent of Christ's death, as expressed in his *Brief traitté de la predestination* (1634), had no explicit reference to the problem of Arminian thought and were directed primarily toward Roman Catholic interlocutors in an irenic attempt to explain Reformed doctrine, in particular, to ameliorate the particularistic accents of the Reformed doctrine of predestination.[111] As a professor of Saumur who during his years as a student at the same institution had studied with John Cameron, Amyraut also bore a mark of suspicion, given the doubts that had early on been expressed concerning Arminian tendencies in his teacher's theology by the faculty at Leiden.

As Du Moulin argued in his letter on Amyraut and Testard to the Synod of Alençon, he understood the thought of John Cameron to be the foundation of Amyraut's and Testard's teachings—and he also viewed Cameron's alternative understanding of the order of the divine decrees as a "New Method" having "the same Foundation on which the *Arminians* have established their Doctrine."[112] That foundation Du Moulin identified explicitly as a an overturning of the order of divine decrees defined by the Synod of Dort, a direction that Cameron perhaps might not have taken had he "exhaustively & seriously considered the Consequences of his own Dogmas"; still, Du Moulin added, "at least one third of all of Cameron's writings were intended to "refute *Calvin, Beza*, and the rest of our most Famous Teachers."[113] Nonetheless, Du Moulin continued, for all of the problems inherent in Cameron's theology, he appeared never to have espoused the extreme conclusions that Amyraut and Testard pressed in their attempt to create a "New Religion" out of a *mélange* of "Papism and Cameronianism." Specifically, Du Moulin exonerated Cameron and at the same time accused Amyraut and Testard of teaching, as doctrines of Cameron,

> that it is not absolutely necessary to Salvation to have a clear Knowledge of *Jesus Christ* ... that Jesus Christ died equally and indifferently for all People ... that the Reprobate could be saved if they willed, or that *God* has Counsels & Decrees that will never produce their Effect ... that *God* has removed the Natural Inability of People

---

110. Gory, *Pierre du Moulin*, pp. 21-50, 54-55.

111. Moïse Amyraut, *Brief traitté de la predestination et de ses principales dependances* (Saumur: Lesnier & Desbordes, 1634).

112. *Lettre de Monsieur du Moulin, Pasteur & Professeur à Sedan, écrite au Synode National d'Alençon, l'An 1637*, in Aymon, *Tous les Synodes*, II, p. 617; cf. Quick, *Synodicon*, II, p. 410.

113. *Lettre de Monsieur du Moulin*, in Aymon, *Tous les Synodes*, II, p. 617.

to believe, & turn themselves to him ... that he renders the Efficacy of the regenerating Spirit dependent on a Counsel that might change.[114]

It needs to be added that Du Moulin was hardly alone in his views—a letter to the synod from Diodati, Tronchin, Chabray, Prevost, and Pauleint, professors of the Academy of Geneva, warned against the "New Hypotheses, Phrases, & Distinctions" arising from the theology of Amyraut and Testard.[115] Two other letters, the first from Poliander, Walaeus, Thysius, and Triglandius, professors at Leiden, and the second from Gomarus and Alting at Groningen, commended André Rivet's treatise against Amyraut.[116]

The Synod of Alençon also heard testimony from Amyraut and Testard, who answered the charges against them, offered modifications and explanations of their language and arguments, and received synodical injunctions to refrain from further use of problematic terminology. The synod specified that all parties should avoid using the contested language of "Conditional & Revocable Decrees" and should refer to the divine will, and in cases previously referenced by Amyraut and Testard as conditional and revocable, to the notion of a "Revealed Will of God [*Volonté de Dieu Revelée*]."[117] The synod, in other words, argued a usage more in accord with Calvin's understanding of the universal promise of the gospel and the general orthodox use of a distinction between the divine *voluntas arcana* and *revelata* or its parallel, the distinction between *voluntas beneplaciti* and *signi*.[118]

The efficacy of Christ's death and universal grace: Du Moulin against Amyraut. Du Moulin's main polemic against Amyraldian hypothetical universalism, as presented in his *Esclaircissement des controverses Salmuriennes*, continued to engage the issue of the order of the divine decree or decrees, much as Du Moulin had argued against Arminius, as it also raised the issues of the "efficacy" of Christ's death and the problem of universal grace. On the issue of the order of the decree or decrees, Du Moulin does appear more willing in response to Amyraut than he had been in his polemic against the Arminians to state an order, although remaining highly conscious of the problem of multiple decrees even when they cohere in intention and execution, he offers the disclaimer that the language of several decrees can be well understood as series of "degrees" in an order of God's willing that ordains both ends and means and does so in such a way that the means arise first and the end follows. The order of the decrees, then, is not a matter of temporal order or a matter of more

114. *Lettre de Monsieur du Moulin*, in Aymon, *Tous les Synodes*, II, p. 618.

115. *Lettre que les Pasteurs & Professeurs de Geneve écrivirent au Synode National d' Alençon*, in Aymon, *Tous les synodes*, II, p. 610.

116. *A notre très-honoré & très excellent Collegue, André Rivet*; and *Approbation des Professeurs de l'Université de Groningue*, in Aymon, *Tous les synodes*, II, pp. 614-615.

117. Aymon, *Tous les synodes*, II, p. 574.

118. Note the argumentation, above, chapter 4; and see Muller, *PRRD*, III, pp. 457-459, 461-463, on the use of these distinctions.

than one divine purpose. God's decrees are, after all, eternal and only represent an order in the counsels of God according to which subsequent decrees serve the execution of the prior decree—without disrupting the singleness of God's purpose. Thus, God in a first decree wills, out of pure grace, to save some human beings out of the corrupt mass of humanity and leave the rest in corruption to their deserved condemnation. In a second decree God wills to send his Son to reconcile through faith those who have been predestined to salvation. And in a third decree, God wills to bestow his Holy Spirit on the elect, bringing them to faith and repentance by means of the preached word, and sustaining them to eternal life.[119] This order, Du Moulin indicates, is both the order found in Romans 8:28-30 and in the Canons of Dort.[120]

Significantly, after positing this understanding of predestination at the beginning of his treatise against Amyraut and Testard, Du Moulin returns to the problem of the Arminian ordering, repeating arguments we have already noted from his *Anatome Arminianismi*.[121] Amyraut, he contends, has followed Arminius' order of the decrees, changing only the fourth decree. Thus, like Arminius, Amyraut posits as a first decree the love of God and the divine desire to save all human beings, calling it an "Antecedent will," "general Predestination," and the "First Mercy." In the second place, Amyraut indicates a decree of God to send his Son to save all human beings, to acquire (*acquerir*) redemption for them, and to accomplish (*impetrer*) the remission of sins for all: "and to the end that all might be saved, he has given to all a grace sufficient to believe, if they will, & to be saved if they will."[122] In Du Moulin's view, the result of this doctrine is identical to that of Arminius: it assumes that God has mutable counsels and intentions that have no hope of success, unfulfilled wills for which God has both regret and sorrow. Du Moulin also notes, reserving his full discussion of the "Semi-Pelagian" doctrine of universal grace to a later section,[123] Amyraut's contention that the offer, indeed, the grace, of salvation is universal in the specific sense that salvation is available to all who will be saved, even if they have lived in places where the gospel has not been preached, indeed, even if they do not

---

119. Du Moulin, *Esclaircissement*, I.i (pp. 1-2).

120. Du Moulin, *Esclaircissement*, I.i (pp. 2-3), citing the Canons of Dort, i.7. Note that Du Moulin's argument also reflects Dort's Rejection of Errors (ii.1), where the text indicates the accomplishment (*impetratio*) of redemption by a "certain and definite counsel" of God.

121. Du Moulin, *Esclaircissement*, I.ii (pp. 4-6).

122. Du Moulin, *Esclaircissement*, I.iii (p. 7). It is this latter decree of the Amyraldian scheme that, certainly as far as the French synods were concerned in their cautious exoneration of Amyraut and Testard, places Amyraut within the bounds of the Canons of Dort, whether of the canons of Dort, i.7 or of the Rejection of Errors, ii.1. In other words, the canons can be argued to allow Amyraut's antecedent decree—just as they in no way rule our a supralapsarian schema that also assumes a divine will to draw the elect out of the fallen mass of humanity.

123. Cf. Du Moulin, *Esclaircissement*, VIII (pp. 198-231).

know the name of Christ. Du Moulin merely identifies this doctrine as a variety of Arminianism.[124]

There is also a problem underlying Amyraut's notion of conditional decrees of God: decrees that God executes through certain means are not rightly called conditional. God does not, for example, will that someone live on condition that he breathes—God wills that someone breath so that he may live! "Respiration is not a condition, but a means of living."[125] Amyraut and his followers argue two decrees: the first conditional, by which God preordains all to salvation on condition of faith; the second absolute, by which he predestines some human beings to faith. In the first God presupposes faith as a condition; in the second he accomplishes it by faith. The problem is that faith is not a condition of a decree but a means by which the decree is executed.[126] Faith, however, is a condition in the promise of salvation: God promises salvation to those who believe—but he makes no promise to provide means conditionally. Thus, conditional promises belong to the providence of God, not to God's eternal decrees.[127] Du Moulin's declamation against the notion of *conseils de Dieu frustratoires* derives, moreover, from Amyraut himself, who had declared that "the nature of humanity was such that, if God had not set forth another counsel in ordaining to send his Son to the world than the one that proposed him as the Redeemer equally and universally to all ... the sufferings of his Son would have been utterly in vain."[128]

Again appealing to both Scripture and the Canons of Dort, Du Moulin argues that Scripture in no way indicates a divine decree to save all human beings.[129] Such a "general predestination" or "First Mercy [*Premiere Misericorde*]" proposes a powerful divine love toward those whom God rejects and who are the objects of the divine hatred in eternity; by contrast, Scripture teaches that the covenant under the Old Testament was only for Abraham and his posterity. Paul similarly taught that God allowed the nations to follow their own ways (Acts 14:16). Christ himself taught that many are called and few are chosen (Matthew 22:14). Amyraut's counter to such passages as these, Du Moulin comments, is to amass passages from the Old Testament that are not to the point. To the Synod of Dort's pronouncement against a "general and indefinite" election, Amyraut responded that it does not follow from the passages in Scripture that speak of the precise election of individuals that there can be no general decree and no universal grace.[130] Like Davenant, Du Moulin

124. Du Moulin, *Esclaircissement*, I.iii (pp. 7-8); on the latter point, see Amyraut, *Brief traitté de la predestination*, vii (pp. 80-83).

125. Du Moulin, *Esclaircissement*, II.i (p. 15).

126. Du Moulin, *Esclaircissement*, II.i (p. 16).

127. Du Moulin, *Esclaircissement*, II.ii (p. 21).

128. Amyraut, *Brief traitté de la predestination*, ix (pp. 102-103).

129. Du Moulin, *Esclaircissement*, V.i (p. 87).

130. Du Moulin, *Esclaircissement*, V.i (p. 87-89); cf. Thomas, *Extent of the Atonement*, pp.200-203 on Amyraut's doctrine of universal grace and its implications.

borrows the term "Semi-Pelagian" to describe contemporary proponents of universal grace, on the ground that their doctrine resembles not precisely that of Pelagius but rather that of the later opponents of Augustine identified by Prosper of Aquitaine—calling the Arminians pure "Semi-Pelagians in all things" and the "innovators," Amyraut and Testard, "three quarters" Semi-Pelagian.[131]

If God actually did have a general decree to save all human beings, it would nonetheless have to be accomplished through means—and the only means given by God are "knowledge of Jesus Christ through the gospel, faith and repentance engraved on the heart by the Holy Spirit."[132] Without these means there can be no salvation. Du Moulin, therefore, objects in particular to Amyraut's hypothesis that some who do not know Christ but who have an "indistinct faith" and know God by way of creation might receive salvation in some other manner. These, Du Moulin comments, are baseless conjectures fashioned in *la boutique des Arminiens*—divine truth does not arise from conjecture![133] Further, if God by some prior decree loved all human beings equally, Judas as much as Peter, Pharaoh as much as Joseph, pagans as well as faithful believers, one would expect this equal love to have equal effects. Why then give faith to some and not others? Why reveal Jesus Christ to some and not others?[134]

Similarly, Du Moulin raises the issue of the extent of Christ's death and does so using the sufficiency-efficiency distinction of the Synod of Dort. The dispute is over the issue of whether Christ died for all human beings, specifically whether he died equally for the reprobate and for the elect. It is utterly true, Du Moulin argues, "that the death of Jesus Christ was a price sufficient to save all human beings if all human beings would believe in him" and that the reason that some human beings are lost eternally "arises not from the imperfection of the price that Jesus Christ has paid, but from the blindness and evil disposition of human beings."[135] Thus, Christ's death is sufficient to save all if they would believe—but it is not sufficient to save those who persevere in their rebellion and unbelief. How dare we claim "that the death of Jesus Christ is sufficient to do something unjust, contrary to the justice of God, and to what he has ordained in his eternal counsel?"[136]

It is not, therefore, the case that Christ can be said to have died for all in the same manner, in the words of the Synod of Dort, "efficiently" for the elect. The opposite argument, as found in Amyraut's theology, proposes an alternative order of the divine decrees, much like that proposed by the Arminians. Amyraut places a decree to send Christ as the savior of all in general prior to the decree to elect

131. Du Moulin, *Esclaircissement*, VIII.i (pp. 198-201).
132. Du Moulin, *Esclaircissement*, V.ii (p. 92); see further, ibid., VII.i-ii (pp. 180-187).
133. Du Moulin, *Esclaircissement*, V.ii (p. 93), citing Amyraut, *Brief traitté de la Predestination*, chap. 7.
134. Du Moulin, *Esclaircissement*, V.ii (p. 93-94).
135. Du Moulin, *Esclaircissement*, VI.i (p. 130).
136. Du Moulin, *Esclaircissement*, VI.i (p. 131).

individuals. Testard argues that God has "acquired" or "impetrated" salvation for all but provides its "application" only for the elect. Du Moulin had already objected to the Arminian use of the formula: the equation of application with efficacy was not so much the problem as the identification of sufficiency with impetration or accomplishment. That Christ's death was sufficient for all did not imply that it had actually and intentionally accomplished salvation for all. In none of these theologies, Du Moulin notes, does this universal, general redemption involve the bestowing of faith on any individual—and yet there is no salvation apart from faith.[137] This general decree, which does not involve the gift of faith, also can be framed, Du Moulin indicates, quite absurdly, to mean that Christ has died for the reprobate according to divine "intention" but not according to "outcome [evenement]."[138] In a line of argument that cuts against Davenant's version of hypothetical universalism as well as Amyraut's, Du Moulin concludes that it is also quite unconvincing to argue that God might have a truly universal "intention" to save all human beings but also not will to save all: if God wills to save only some, it must clearly be the divine intention only to save some.[139]

Conclusions

The approaches of John Davenant, a member of the British delegation to the Synod of Dort, and Pierre Du Moulin, who would have been a French delegate to Dort had the French crown permitted Huguenot representatives to be present at the synod, were both proponents of the assumption that Christ's death paid for the sins of the whole world and was therefore sufficient to save all if all would believe—and, therefore can be identified as hypothetical universalists. Both theologians, however, Davenant on grounds set forth in the British Collegiate Suffrage at the synod and Du Moulin on grounds of conclusions drawn from canons and rejections of the synod, opposed variant forms of hypothetical universalism as found in the thought of the Saumur theologians, John Cameron and Moïse Amyraut.

Although the broader context of both Davenant and Du Moulin included the Synod of Dort, its canons, and its aftermath, their more immediate contexts were rather different. Early on in his episcopacy and in the years immediately after Dort, Davenant addressed the issue not only of Cameron's orthodoxy but, given the hypothetical universalism identifiable in the Collegiate Suffrage of the British delegation to Dort, the orthodoxy of his own theology and of the Church of England as well. The question had been posed by French churches, but Davenant also faced, on the other side of the argument, a level of English dissatisfaction with Dort. Davenant's response had to tread the fine line of distinguishing between the hypothetical universalism of the Collegiate Suffrage and that of Cameron—and he did

137. Du Moulin, Esclaircissement, VI.i, ii (pp. 131, 133-134).

138. Du Moulin, Esclaircissement, VI.ii (p. 135).

139. Du Moulin, Esclaircissement, VI.ii (pp. 135-137).

so, notably on grounds of problematic elements in Cameron's formulae and the underlying problem of Cameron's affirmation of universal grace.

Davenant's conclusion, that there is a general "intention or ordination" of God to save "all individual human beings by the death of Christ," underlines his advocacy of what he himself had called an "ordained sufficiency" of Christ's satisfaction and also indicates his distance from to the Cameronian position: this general intention is not related to any "determinate will" to produce a particular end. The point arguably draws on a distinction between the divine *voluntas beneplaciti* ultimate will of God (which Davenant has defined as a special intention to save the elect) and the *voluntas signi* or *praecepti*, a designated or preceptive will (which Davenant understands as the universal proclamation of the gospel, undergirded by the ordained sufficiency of Christ's satisfaction). His initial distinction between a preceptive intention of God not associated with positive willing would certainly not have pleased Du Moulin, although Davenant had not placed the unfulfilled intentionality in an eternal decree, as would Amyraut. Davenant's concluding statement that "the absolute and infrustratible intention of God, concerning the gift of faith and eternal life to some persons is special, & limited to the elect alone" is remarkable akin to Pierre Du Moulin's declamation against any notion of *conseils de Dieu frustratoires*. Davenant can hardly be called a forerunner of Amyraut!

Du Moulin's initial polemic against the Arminian structure of the divine decrees and the Arminian approach to universal grace was roughly contemporary with Davenant's response to his Gallican questioners, and directly reflects the situation of the Reformed churches in the immediate aftermath of Dort. His polemics against Amyraut, framed along many of the same lines presented in the *Anatome Arminiansmi*, dates from a later time, after the death of Cameron and in the midst of the Amyraldian controversy in France. And although Du Moulin's main point of confessional reference was the Canons of Dort, as ratified by the French National Synod, his more specific frame of reference was the internal debate among the Reformed churches in France and, even more pointedly, between the faculties of their major academies.

Given the confessional focus on Dort, Du Moulin drew more consistently on the sufficiency-efficiency distinction than Davenant, although his argumentation indicates a problem with the distinction similar to that expressed by the British delegation and Davenant and, indeed, earlier adumbrated by Calvin. The distinction, probably most useful in the context of a confessional document designed as much to include as to exclude various views, was ultimately capable of multiple interpretations, some of which, at least in Du Moulin's view, fell outside the pale. The language of impetration and application also contained pitfalls: it had been used by Arminius and the Remonstrants and also by Amyraut.

Once it is recognized that Du Moulin's approach to the problem of the extent of Christ's work was grounded not on a loosely defined notion of so-called limited atonement, as Armstrong and others have implied, but on a fairly nuanced form of the traditional sufficiency-efficiency formula, it also becomes clear that his polemic against Amyraut was not directed against hypothetical universalism per se. Du Moulin himself clearly advocated a form of hypothetical universalism—what he saw as problematic and dangerous in Amyraut's teaching was not its assumption that the sacrifice of Christ was sufficient to save all who would believe but that Amyraut had rested his own version of this doctrine on a speculative doctrine of the divine decrees. Just as in the case of his polemic against Arminius, so also against Amyraut, Du Moulin objected strenuously to a doctrine of multiple decrees signaled by a language of multiple divine intentions and accurately described it (contrary to Amyraut's contention) as different from the formulations he found in Calvin. His own language of a twofold will or of three divine decrees, given their coherence, rather easily resolved into a doctrine of a single ultimate decree or counsel described as a series of degrees, or *gradus*, and is therefore compatible with Calvin's argumentation. Ironically, Amyraut's speculation concerning the will of God places him more firmly than Du Moulin into Armstrong's problematic definition of Protestant scholasticism.

Taken in context, moreover, Du Moulin's declamation against Amyraut's referencing Calvin as an authoritative predecessor—on the ground that Amyraut was thereby playing into the hands of Roman Catholic polemicists—appears less a rhetorical device used in debate than a plea from one who identified the Reformed faith as genuinely catholic, who was deeply involved in attempts at Protestant union, and who viewed appeals to Calvin's authority as creating a problematic identity that could be used by Roman Catholics against the Reformed and that would stand in the way of Protestant union.[140]

Arguably, moreover, Du Moulin's and also Davenant's view of the extent of Christ's work is far closer to Calvin's than Amyraut's—Calvin, after all, had distinguished between a secret or ultimate will of the divine good pleasure and a revealed will for humanity, but did not speculate concerning an unfulfilled divine will concerning all humanity, a point on which he stood in agreement with virtually all the opponents of Cameron and Amyraut, whether supralapsarian, infralapsarian, or hypothetical universalist. In addition, both Davenant and Du Moulin follow Calvin (and Beza) in denying universal grace and in identifying historical and geographical limitations placed on the extent of salvation by the absence of the preaching of the gospel from some times and places—a point on which Amyraut differed radically with the main trajectories of Reformed thought.

Beyond these particulars, the analysis of Davenant's and Du Moulin's arguments concerning the sufficiency of Christ's satisfaction, particularly when seen in light of our examination of Amyraut's appropriation of Calvin, points toward a fundamental problem in the paradigm of Reformed orthodoxy found in the work of Armstrong,

---

140. Cf. W. Brown Patterson, "James I and the Huguenot Synod of Tonneins of 1614," *Harvard Theological Review*, 65 (1972), pp. 241-270; with Jacques Courvoisier, "Pierre du Moulin," *Ecumenical Review*, 1/1 (1948), pp. 76-82.

Kendall, Hall, Clifford, and others: that paradigm proposed a monolithic, scholastic "Bezan" orthodoxy that had departed from Calvin's views on the work of Christ and its application by deducing a theory of "limited atonement" only to pose it against the teachings of one of the only pure Calvinians left on the face of the earth, Moïse Amyraut. Examination of the thought of Davenant and Du Moulin, quite to the contrary, offers a glimpse of the varieties of formulation found among the Reformed orthodox—indeed, in both cases, an infralapsarian hypothetical universalism that specifically opposed not the particularism of Beza but the variant hypothetical universalism of Amyraut and his teacher, Cameron. Armstrong was certainly incorrect in claiming Davenant as a "near-Amyraldian." Davenant's verdict on Cameron stands firmly in the way of such a conclusion. The verdict against Cameron, moreover, like the later verdict of Francis Turretin and the Formula Consensus Helvetica, was not, pace Armstrong, that Cameron was a heretic, but as was later argued concerning Amyraut by his Reformed opponents, that he was the author of a problematic formulation that should be set aside but that was not such that it ought to be identified as a heretical violation of the Reformed confessional standards. And Du Moulin, certainly, did not represent a "Bezan" turn in Reformed theology against the purer "Calvinian" theology of Amyraut—just as his polemic was not directed, any more than was Davenants,' against hypothetical universalism per se.

This conclusion returns our attention, briefly, to the issue of the term "hypothetical universalism" or its often referenced Latin version, *universalismus hypotheticus*. Given that the term itself, if it appeared at all in the debates of the seventeenth century, was not widely used, attempting to understand the controversy over Cameron's and Amyraut's doctrine primarily with reference to their hypothetical universalism contains certain methodological and theological problems. Use of the term as a descriptor can be justified inasmuch as the debates were concerned with forms of universalism, particularly as they related to the notion of hypothetical or conditional willing in God and, specifically, as they focused on the question of divine willing or intention in relation to the hypothetical "if all would believe." In this sense, a fairly significant series of theologians of the early modern era, ranging from Bullinger to Zanchi, Arminius, Davenant, Du Moulin, and Amyraut, can be identified as hypothetical universalists. The very vagueness or inclusiveness of the term, like the vagueness or inclusiveness of the sufficiency-efficiency distinction, illustrates both continuities of conversation and debate that ran throughout the era and the diversity (within confessional boundaries) of the older Reformed tradition.

As the examination of both Davenant and Du Moulin indicates, however, the determining issues in the debate concerned both the logical ordering of the eternal decree as inferred from and related to its temporal execution and the problem of universal grace. Recognition of this focus of the debate serves to clarify the polemical association made between Cameron and Amyraut, on the one hand, and Arminius on the other, despite the general agreement of Cameron and Amyraut with the Reformed confessions, including the Canons of Dort.

6

The "Golden Chain" and the Causality of Salvation: Beginnings of the Reformed *Ordo Salutis*

The *ordo salutis*, or order of salvation, comprising the doctrines of calling, regeneration, faith, justification, sanctification, perseverance, and glorification, is a concept that contemporary Reformed theology, particularly as it is encountered in the more traditionally constructed and confessionally oriented systems, tends to take for granted. Even when it is recognized that some variety exists in Reformation and post-Reformation Reformed discussions of the *ordo*, the fact of this variety is not allowed to interfere with the assumption of a general consensus concerning the usefulness of discussing the *ordo* as well as the priority of grace in the work of salvation indicated in such basic issues as the placement of grace and faith before justification and justification before sanctification.[1] Several writers have noted the historical fact that the technical application of the term *ordo salutis* arose in the early eighteenth century and have concluded that the whole concept belongs to the waning years of the scholastic era of Protestantism and ought not to be viewed as a product of the sixteenth-century wellspring of Protestant faith[2]—with some weighing the doctrine itself and concluding on theological grounds that although it stands in need of some modification, it does indeed address a series of crucial issues in theology.[3] From a purely historical perspective, therefore, the idea of an *ordo salutis* in Reformed theology stands in need of elucidation, particularly since the major

---

1. Louis Berkhof, *Systematic Theology* (Grand Rapids: Eerdmans, 1939), pp. 415-422 (on the idea and arrangement of the *ordo*), pp. 432-549; Charles Hodge, *Systematic Theology*, 3 vols. (1871-1873; repr., Grand Rapids: Eerdmans, 1975), II, pp. 639-732; III, pp. 3-258; A. G. Honig, *Handboek van de Gereformeerde Dogmatiek* (Kampen: J. H. Kok, 1938), pp. 529-539 (on the idea and arrangement of the *ordo*), 539-609; Herman Hoeksema, *Reformed Dogmatics* (Grand Rapids: Reformed Free Publishing Association, 1966), pp. 446-451 (on the idea and arrangement of the *ordo*), pp. 452-560; Henry B. Smith, *System of Christian Theology* (New York: Armstrong, 1884), pp. 515-589.

2. Reinhold Seeberg, "Heilsordnung," in *RE*, vol. 7, pp. 598-599; G. C. Berkouwer, *Faith and Justification* (Grand Rapids: Eerdmans, 1954), p. 25.

3. Berkouwer, *Faith and Justification*, pp. 25-27.

historical studies of the concept have virtually all looked at the Lutheran development.[4]

There is also the question of the relationship of the Reformers' thought on the subject to developments in later Reformed theology. Various recent studies, several focused on the doctrine of union with Christ in Calvin's thought, have approached the issue of an order of salvation as if later "Calvinist" views on the doctrine either diminished or replaced a Calvinian emphasis on union—as if Calvin himself did not devote much thought to the causality of salvation and as if that language of causality in the later Reformed tradition led to an understanding of salvation substantially different from Calvin's.[5] One study in particular argues as if the notion of a "chain" of salvation were foreign to the thought of Calvin and his contemporaries and arose significantly later among the post-Reformation orthodox.[6] Despite this claim, there

---

4. E.g., Markus Matthias, "*Ordo salutis*: Zur Geschichte eines dogmatischen Begriffs," *Zeitschrift für Kirchengeschichte*, 115/3 (2004), pp. 318-346; Schröder, "Über die Lehre von der Heilsordnung: Ein kritisch-dogmatischer versuch," *Theologische Studien und Kritiken*, 30 (1857), pp. 689-734; Hermann Schultz, "Der *Ordo salutis* in der Dogmatik," *Theologische Studien und Kritiken*, 72 (1899), pp. 350- 445; Emil Wacker, *Die Heilsordnung* (Gütersloh: Bertelsmann, 1898); Max Koch, *Der ordo salutis in der alt-lutherischen Dogmatik* (Berlin: Duncker, 1899); Reinhold Seeberg, "Heilsordnung," in *RE*, vol. 7, pp. 593-599.

5. See, e.g., Julie Canlis, "Calvin, Osiander, and Participation in God," *International Journal of Systematic Theology*, 6/2 (2004), pp. 169-184; William B. Evans, *Imputation and Impartation: Union with Christ in American Reformed Theology* (Carlisle: Paternoster, 2008); Richard B. Gaffin, "Justification and Union with Christ," in *A Theological Guide to Calvin's Institutes: Essays and Analysis*, ed. David W. Hall and Peter A. Lillback (Phillipsburg: Presbyterian and Reformed, 2008), pp. 248-269; idem, "Calvin's Soteriology: The Structure of the Application of Redemption in Book Three of the Institutes," and "A Response to John Fesko's Review," *Ordained Servant*, 18 (2009), pp. 68-77, and 104-113; and Charles Partee, *The Theology of John Calvin* (Louisville: Westminster/John Knox, 2008), pp. 240-250. There is a potentially significant parallel (despite their radically different conclusions) between these more recent dogmatic critiques of the order of salvation in traditional Reformed theology and the nineteenth-century attack on Reformed orthodox approaches to justification and sanctification by Eduard Böhl, who protested against the development of an order of salvation, declaring it to be indicative of a "Reformed Middle Ages" on the ground that any notion of inward righteousness associated with sanctification had departed from the *sola fide* of the great Reformers; see his *Von der Rechtfertigung durch den Glauben. Ein Beitrag zur Rettung des protestantischen Cardinaldogmas* (Leipzig: K. Gustorff, 1890); in translation, Edward Boehl, *The Reformed Doctrine of Justification*, trans. C. H. Riedesel (Grand Rapids: Eerdmans, 1946), pp. 57-73, 252-261, 270, 301-303. Note that Böhl praises Beza on imputation, includes Augustine and Bucer among those in "error" on this issue, and identifies the later Reformed development as Osiandrian. Where Böhl argues strictly for imputation without impartation of righteousness or holiness, lamenting an *ordo salutis* that distinguishes but includes both, Evans argues for impartation of righteousness, lamenting an *ordo salutis* that he views as separating it from imputation and understanding salvation as primarily "extrinsic." Böhl and Evans identify Calvin's approach as sound, albeit for opposite reasons, and both identify the language of an order of salvation as a problem of developing scholasticism and as a departure from the true meaning of the Reformation—again for opposite reasons, each in pursuit of a form of "Calvin against the Calvinists" thesis.

6. Evans, *Imputation and Impartation*, pp. 52-53.

has been little or no scholarly effort to examine the backgrounds, specifically, the exegetical backgrounds and the causal language of the Reformed doctrine of the order of salvation either among the Reformers or among the Reformed writers of the era of orthodoxy. In the this and the following chapter, I propose to bring together a discussion of the exegetical roots of Reformed discussion of the ordering of salvation in the "golden chain" of Romans 8:28-30 and an analysis of causal language of Calvin and various of his contemporaries with a discussion of the continuation of these lines of argument into the era of Reformed orthodoxy. The essay will demonstrate, rather than a significant disjunction between the thought of Calvin and other Reformed thinkers, whether among his contemporaries of among the later Reformed, a trajectory of formulation and development in which Calvin's thought played a significant role but was hardly the sole or consistently the most important influence.

Ordo Salutis: The Term and Its Origins

It is a matter of historical record that the origin of the now-standard dogmatic use of the term *ordo salutis* was in the early eighteenth century and among the Lutheran orthodox and that the greatest concentration of debate over the concept occurred among the Lutheran and the Reformed orthodox over issues raised by Lutheran pietists and Reformed proponents of the *Nadere Reformatie* in the late seventeenth and early eighteenth centuries.[7] The concept of an ordering of the work of salvation—from election and calling to repentance, justification, adoption, renovation, sanctification, and glorification—had, of course, been developed earlier but had not been either thoroughly defined or given a technical designation, i.e., *ordo salutis*. Thus, Quenstedt's *Theologia didactico-polemica* (1702) and Hollazius' *Examen theologicum acroamaticum* (1718) were instrumental in moving Lutheran dogmatics from a less strictly organized order of salvation toward the point where the doctrine became so clearly defined that a term was applied to it. Quenstedt gathered together the topics found in Calovius' *Systema locorum theologicorum* (1655-1677) into a *locus de gratia spiritus sancti applicatrice*, a pattern in which he was followed by Hollazius.[8] In his now classic monograph on the subject, Koch held that the term was first used by Jacob Carpov in 1737,[9] while Seeberg was able to note the phrase "göttlicher Ordnung" in Spener's *Glaubenslehre* (1710) and to identify the actual term *ordo salutis* in Buddaeus' *Institutiones theologiae dogmaticae* of 1723.[10] The term can also be found in the work of Buddaeus' brilliant pietist pupil, J. J. Rambach, in his *Dogmatische Theologie*, written between 1727 and 1735, but published

---

7. Seeberg, "Heilsordnung," pp. 593-594, with Koch, *Der ordo salutis*, pp. 5-6.
8. Schröder, "Über die Lehre von der Heilsordnung," pp. 701-703.
9. Koch, *Der ordo salutis*, p. 5.
10. Seeberg, "Heilsordnung," p. 593-594.

posthumously in 1744.[11] Buddaeus and his contemporaries, then, gave a name to a pattern that was already in the process of becoming normative in Lutheran theology—nonetheless, the creation of a technical term does mark a recognition that the doctrinal model had become standardized.

Despite, however, its absence from the more systematic works of the Reformers and even from the theology of their seventeenth-century orthodox successors and despite its Lutheran origins, the term *ordo salutis* has become indigenous to modern discussion of confessional or orthodox Reformed theology—almost as if it had originated there—and refers to an aspect of the Reformed system that stands at the very heart of the faith in its confessional form.[12] As Seeberg remarked, the issue underlying the term is an irreducible element in the older Protestant dogmatics,[13] and there are certainly many references to various kinds of *ordo* as well as a few notable comments concerning an *ordo salutis* and *causae salutis* in writings of the Reformers.[14] Still, the term itself is not typically found in either Reformation-era formulations or in the era of orthodoxy. Perhaps by way of oversimplification, one might say that the phrase *ordo salutis* is found early on, development of discussion concerning the order of the application of Christ's work to the elect came next, and the standardized use of the phrase as a technical term describing the application of Christ's work came last—in fact, came after the seventeenth-century development of Reformed orthodoxy.

A preliminary word of caution needs to be voiced, therefore, concerning the terminology and character of early modern Reformed approaches to the language of application of salvation. Although it is certainly suitable to speak cautiously about the development toward a conception of the order of salvation, or *ordo salutis*, among the Reformers and their successors in the Reformed tradition, it would be a significant historiographical mistake to speak of Calvin's or Vermigli's or Beza's, Perkins', Ames', or indeed, Turretin's doctrine of the *ordo salutis* inasmuch as the

11. Johann Jacob Rambach, *Dogmatische Theologie oder christliche Glaubens-Lehre, vormals in einem Collatio thetico über des hochberuhmten Herrn D. Joachim Langens ... Oeconomiam salutis dogmaticam, mit Zuziehung des gewöhnlichen Compendii theologiae positivae des sel. D. Bayers ... aus desselben eigenhandigem Manuscript ... gestellt von D. Ernst Friedrich Neubauer* (Frankfurt and Leipzig: Wolfgang Ludwig Spring, 1744), II, pp. 1472-1473; cf. his earlier *Schrifftmässige Erläuterung der Grundlegung der Theologie Herrn Johann Anastasius Freylingshausens ... aus dessen eigenhandigen MScto ... herausgegeben von* Christian Hecht (Frankfurt am Main: Wolfgang Ludwig Spring, 1738), pp. 12-14, where Rambach offers an outline for his discussion of the redeemed life under the rubric of *status refectionis* and divides the topic into *Gnaden-Wohltaten*, *Gnaden-Mittel*, and *Gnaden-Ordnung* without attempting to argue a strict *ordo*. On Rambach's life and work, see Richard A. Muller, "J. J. Rambach and the Dogmatics of Scholastic Pietism," *Consensus: A Canadian Lutheran Journal of Theology*, 16/2 (1990), pp. 7-27.

12. Thus, Berkhof, *Systematic Theology*, pp. 415-422; cf. Berkouwer, *Faith and Justification*, pp. 25-27.

13. Seeberg, "Heilsordnung," p. 594.

14. As noted in John V. Fesko, *Beyond Calvin: Union with Christ and Justification in Early Modern Reformed Theology (1517-1700)* (Göttingen: Vandenhoeck & Ruprecht, forthcoming).

term had not yet come into use in its later technical or dogmatic sense. Although various nontechnical references to an *ordo salutis* can be found among the Reformers,[15] the Reformers did not apply the phrase as a term for the movement from election to calling, justification, regeneration, sanctification, and glorification. Nor did the major theological systems of the Reformed orthodox typically use the term *ordo salutis* to describe the application of salvation in calling, faith, justification, and sanctification. Furthermore, apart from the issue of the use of the phrase, the Reformed theologians of the sixteenth or seventeenth centuries did not move to develop a strict ordering of the components of an order of salvation much beyond what they found in Romans 8, namely, a complex of issues related to life *in Christo*, summarized in the language of verses 28-30, that those, namely, the elect, who are "called according to [God's] purpose" have been foreknown and predestinated, called, justified, and glorified. On both of these issues, therefore, the current scholarship falls remarkably short, particularly when it argues a sudden shifting of gears in the generations after Calvin from a foundational focus on union with Christ to a strictly arranged *ordo salutis*. Indeed, the absence of a single technical term used to describe the ordering of the application of Christ's work to believers is an indication of the fluidity of expression and gradual formulation of the doctrinal issue that remained characteristic of the Reformed throughout the early modern era.

Various high orthodox writers among the Reformed discuss the elements of what would be identified as the *ordo salutis* without, however, establishing a definitive *ordo* and without using the term *ordo salutis* as a descriptor. Marckius, for example, identifies the works (*officia*) of the covenant of grace as faith and repentance, followed by a series of benefits (*beneficia*) of the covenant, vocation, justification, sanctification, and conservation, followed ultimately by glorification.[16] These benefits Marckius in turn relates to a further set of adjunct terms, regeneration, adoption, reconciliation, and liberation or redemption, connecting regeneration with vocation, adoption and reconciliation with both vocation and justification.[17] Turretin similarly identifies primary elements of the work of salvation: calling, faith, justification, and sanctification, as well as their adjuncts, relating perseverance to faith, remission of sin and adoption to justification.[18] Even in the mid-eighteenth century, Reformed

---

15. On the origins of the term, the classic monograph of Koch, *Der ordo salutis in der alt-lutherischen Dogmatik*, remains a significant work; also see Matthias, "Ordo salutis: Zur Geschichte eines dogmatischen Begriffs." Other literature on the subject is cited below, in chapter 7. Note that in the following essay, I use "application of salvation" and "sequence" for the sake of avoiding the anachronistic connotations of either *ordo salutis* or its English equivalent, "order of salvation."

16. Johannes Marckius, *Compendium theologiae christianae didactico-elencticum* (Groningen, 1686; Amsterdam: R. & G. Wetstenius, 1722), xxii.1; xxiii.1.

17. Marckius, *Compendium theologiae christianae*, xxviii.1.

18. Francis Turretin, *Institutio theologiae elencticae, in qua status controversiae perspicue exponitur, praecipua orthodoxorum argumenta proponuntur, & vindicantur, & fontes solutionum aperiuntur*, 3 vols. (Geneva: Samuel de Tournes, 1679-1685), xv, xvi, xvii; in particular, xv.16 (perseverance); xvi.5, 6 (remission of sin, adoption).

writers like Wyttenbach, Vitringa, and de Moor avoided the term, probably because of its Lutheran origins. Nothing approaching the term appears in Wyttenbach's theology, despite his obvious interest in divine causality. Vitringa writes of the *oeconomia gratiae* and indicates that there is an *ordo*, but he does not give the impression of a strict causal model that moves ineluctably through the elements of the order. De Moor, commenting on Marckius, retains the usage *officia foederis gratiae* or even *officia aut conditiones foederis gratiae* in distinction from *beneficia foederis gratiae*.[19]

There remains, however, a question concerning the point of origin of fairly clear and well-defined understandings of an order or ordering in the Reformed discussion of the application of salvation (even when the term *ordo* itself is not used)— particularly in view of the somewhat varied expositions found in various early Reformed attempts at definition and formulation, like Calvin's *Institutes*, Musculus' *Loci communes*, the *loci* developed by Vermigli, and Bullinger's *Confession, Decades,* or *Compendium*. It has been noted that the closest that Scripture comes to enunciating an *ordo salutis* is Romans 8:28-30.[20] This essay will argue that the architectural foundations of the Reformed concept of an *ordo* or of an ordered *officia et beneficia foederis gratiae* are to be found in Reformation and post-Reformation meditations on the text of Romans 8:28-30, specifically in characterization of this text as presenting a *catena, vinculum,* or *armilla aurea*, namely, a "golden chain," and in related discussions of the causality of salvation.[21] The development of the

---

19. Cf. Daniel Wyttenbach, *Tentamen theologiae dogmaticae methodo scientifico pertractatae*, 3 vols. (Frankfurt: Andreae and Hort, 1747-1749), IX, §1007-1223; Campegius Vitringa, *Doctrina christianae religionis, per aphorismos summatim descripta*, 6 vols. (Arnhem: Joannes Möelemann, 1761-1786), II, pp. 34-35; Bernhardus de Moor, *Commentarius perpetuus in Joh. Marckii compendium theologiae christianae didactico-elencticum*, 7 vols. (Leiden: Johannes Hasebroek, 1761-1771), V, pp. 285, 289, 292, 440.

20. Berkhof, *Systematic Theology*, p. 416

21. Cf., e.g., Ulrich Zwingli, *In Catabaptistarum strophas elenchus*, in *Opera completa editio prima*, ed. Melchior Schuler and Johann Schulthess, 8 vols. in 11, plus supplement (Zürich: Schulthess and Höhr, 1828-1842), III, p. 426 (*catena*); in translation, *Refutation of the Tricks of the Catabaptists*, in *Ulrich Zwingli (1484-1531): Selected Works*, intro. Edward Peters (Philadelphia: University of Pennsylvania Press, 1972), p. 239; Peter Martyr Vermigli, *In epistolam s. Pauli apostoli ad Romanos . . . commentarii* (Zürich: s.n., 1559), p. 539; in translation, *Epistle of S. Paul to the Romanes*, Rom. 8:30, in loc. (fol. 228 verso); Hermann Rennecherus, *Armilla salutis catena, continens et explicans omnes eius causas* (Herborn, 1589); trans as *The Golden Chaine of Salvation* (London: Valentine Simmes, 1604); William Perkins, *Armilla Aurea, id est, theologiae descriptio mirandam seriem causarum & salutis & damnationis juxta verbum Dei proponens* (Cambridge: John Legat, 1590); Anthony Maxey, *The Goulden Chaine of Mans Saluation, and the fearefull point of Hardening, together with the Churches Sleepe: Preached in three severall sermons before the King*, 3rd ed. (London: T. E. for Clement Knight, 1607); Jean Diodati, *Pious and Learned Annotations upon the Holy Bible, plainly Expounding the Most Difficult Places Thereof*, 4th ed. (London: T. Roycroft for Nicholas Fussell, 1664), Rom. 8:30, in loc.; Thomas Gataker, et al., *Annotations upon all the books of the Old and Nevv Testament this third, above the first and second, edition so enlarged, as they make an entire commentary on the sacred scripture: the like never before published in English. Wherein the text is explained, doubts resolved, scriptures parallel'd, and*

language of the *catena* or *armilla aurea*, moreover, does not evidence either a simple continuity or discontinuity with the thought of Calvin or, indeed, an alternative to discussion of union with Christ—but, as ought to be expected given the diversity of Reformed voices, a rather complex and variegated process.[22] In other words, in the course of this process, aspects or elements of formulations found in the works of Calvin and various of his contemporaries reappear and undergo development, reformulation, and augmentation in the works of later Reformed writers—without particular interest on the part of the later writers in singling out one or another of their predecessors as the source of their ideas. The concept of the chain of salvation, moreover, is arguably the key to the Reformed orthodox sense of the relationship of divine causality to the means of salvation and of the order, grades, gradations, or degrees belonging to the work of salvation. The issue of the relationship of the doctrine of union with Christ to the ordering of the application of salvation will be taken up in a subsequent discussion.[23]

Reformation-Era Backgrounds and Foundations

Reformation-era exegesis of the "golden chain." Reference to Romans 8:28-30 as a "chain" or "golden chain" has a long history. In the Protestant tradition, the text is identified in this way as early as 1527 by Zwingli,[24] in the next generation by Vermigli,[25] and after that, by numerous Reformed exegetes and theologians, certainly as far as the early eighteenth century.[26] The Reformed language of the causality of salvation, then, is based not on a dogmatic proof-texting but on the exegesis of specific biblical passages and, in the case of Romans 8:28-30, following a model of rhetorical interpretation, looking for the forms and figures of speech.[27]

The basis for the larger part of the terminology associated with the chain of salvation—namely, the language of "grades" or "degrees" (*gradus*), gradations (*gradationes*), or of an order (*ordo*) belonging to the decree that establish and

---

various readings observed; by the labour of certain learned divines thereunto appointed, and therein employed, as is expressed in the preface, 2 vols. (London: Evan Tyler, 1657), Rom. 8:29, in loc.

22. Contra Evans, *Imputation and Impartation*, pp. 37, 40-42, 44, 46, 52-57.

23. I.e., chapter 7.

24. Cf. Zwingli, *In Catabaptistarum strophas elenchus*, in *Opera*, III, p. 426 (*catena*).

25. Vermigli, *In epistolam s. Pauli apostoli ad Romanos*, pp. 539, 540 (*catena*); *Epistle of S. Paul to the Romanes*, Rom. 8:30, in loc. (fol. 228 verso).

26. Thus, e.g., Moises Amyraut, *Paraphrase sur l'epistre de s Paul aux Romains* (Saumur: Jean Lesnier, 1645), p. 189; Turretin, *Inst. theol. elencticae*, XVI.i.1; John Edwards, *Veritas redux. Evangelical truths restored. ... Being the first part of the theological treatises, which are to compose a large Body of Christian divinity* (London: for Jonathan Robinson, John Lawrence, and John Wyat, 1707), pp. 68-69.

27. On the methods of exegesis followed among the Reformed orthodox, see Richard A. Muller, *Post-Reformation Reformed Dogmatics: The Rise and Development of Reformed Orthodoxy, ca. 1520 to ca. 1725*, 4 vols. (Grand Rapids: Baker, 2003), II, pp. 484-502; and note pp. 509-520 on the issue of movement from text to doctrinal formulation.

constitute the temporal order of salvation also arises from the exegesis of Romans 8:29-30, specifically with reference to the figure of speech used in the text to link the terms "foreknew," "predestined," "called," "justified," and "glorified." Discussion of this figure as a logical "gradation," "degrees," or "sorites" is found in many of the commentaries of the sixteenth and seventeenth centuries, among them those by Pellican, Calvin, Bullinger, Musculus, Hyperius, Vermigli, Beza, Olevianus, Piscator, Diodati, and Featley.[28]

For Zwingli, the *catena* of Romans 8:28-30 offered a clear causal ordering of the work of salvation, in which human merit was excluded, salvation grounded in the divine gift of faith, and believers were called to sanctification. Thus, in addition to the specific language of the *catena*, predestination, calling, justification, and glorification, Zwingli saw the text as indicating also the divine purpose (*propositum*), faith and sanctification—and, moreover, including them in a specific relation to the other terms.[29] Looking to Romans 9:11 for the place of the divine purpose in the chain, Zwingli indicated that it is prior to election itself as the utterly free cause (*causa*) of all things working for good to those who love God, who are destined to be conformed to Christ. In Romans 8:28, this ultimate purpose is identified in the divine foreknowing of those to be predestined. Calling and justification follow, with faith understood by syndedoche to be paired with justification. Faith and justification are inseparable, Zwingli declared, given that "wherever faith is, there also is justification."[30] Calling follows predestination and precedes faith, justification is grounded in faith, and calling itself implies sanctification—indeed, Zwingli commented that it is the divine purpose that those who love God be made holy so that to be called is rightly understood as "to be truly sanctified."[31] Zwingli's ordering, then, is primarily causal, with justification and sanctification standing together as following calling.

Calvin had certainly recognized that some causal ordering or arrangement of the various elements of the order was necessitated both by his view of the priority of

---

28. Cf. Conrad Pellican, *In omnes apostolicas epistolas, Pauli, Petri, Iacobi, Ioannis, et Iudae* (Zürich: Froschauer, 1539), p. 97; John Calvin, *Commentarius in epistolam Pauli ad Romanos*, in CO 49, col. 159-160; *Commentaries on the Epistle of Paul the Apostle to the Romans*, trans. John Owen (1849; repr. Grand Rapids: Baker, 1979), pp. 319, 320, hereinafter, *CTS Romans*; Heinrich Bullinger, *In sanctissimam Pauli ad Romanos epistolam ... commentarius* (Zürich: Froschauer, 1533), Rom. 8:29-30, in loc. (p. 112v); Andreas Hyperius, *In D. Pauli ad Romanos epistolam exegema* (London: Vautrollerius, 1577), Rom. 8:28ff. in loc., (fol. 76 recto); Peter Martyr Vermigli, *In epistolam s. Pauli apostoli ad Romanos*, pp. 539, 540; Wolfgang Musculus, *In epistolam D. Apostoli Pauli ad Romanos comentarii* (Basel: Sebastian Henricpetrus, 1555), pp. 143-145. Note that Evans, *Imputation and Impartation*, pp. 52-53, appears mistakenly to view interest in the golden chain or *gradus* as something new to Reformed theology in the late sixteenth or the early seventeenth century, and as an alternative to the *unio* language that is (also!) found in Calvin.

29. Zwingli, *In Catabaptistarum strophas elenchus*, in *Opera*, III, p. 425.

30. Zwingli, *In Catabaptistarum strophas elenchus*, in *Opera*, III, p. 425.

31. Zwingli, *In Catabaptistarum strophas elenchus*, in *Opera*, III, p. 425.

God's grace and by his doctrine of election. Early on in his work, he had indicated that "the seed of the Word of God" and faith only "take root" in the elect, that justification rests on the apprehension of Christ and his righteousness through faith, and that sanctification also follows through faith and its apprehension of Christ—indeed, if sanctification is not present, neither is justification.[32] He argued quite pointedly that repentance was a result and not the cause of faith, and he noted that the traditional language of mortification and vivification was, if rightly understood, suitable to the understanding of repentance.[33] Calvin also appears to have regarded regeneration as virtually identical with repentance—as the inward and outward aspects of the same reality—and, therefore, also as a result rather than a cause of faith.[34] Since this repentance is a lifelong exercise, moreover, the sanctification that follows regeneration remains incomplete and imperfect in this life.[35] The rudiments of what would later be called the *ordo salutis* are, therefore, clearly present in Calvin's *Institutes*, and they were present from the very beginnings of his theological development, including elements of the causal and temporal structuring that would be argued by later Reformed theologians.[36]

Other aspects of Calvin's understanding of the ordering of salvation become clear in his exegetical efforts, particularly in those biblical *loci* referenced in the *Institutes*. Calvin cited Romans 8:29 seven times and Romans 8:30 four times in the 1559 edition of his *Institutes*, most prominently in the course of book III, in which Calvin presented his understandings of regeneration, faith, justification, and predestination.[37] His exegesis of Romans 8:28-30, moreover, both supports his understanding of the causality of salvation under the divine decree and offers some insight into the absence of a clearer ordering of the various aspects of salvation in his doctrinal exposition. Calvin understood the divine purpose of verse 28 in some distinction from the language of foreknowing (*proginoskein*) and predestining (*proopizein*) in verses 29 and 30. In Calvin's view, the divine purpose is presented by Paul in order to show that those who are identified as loving God "had previously been chosen by him." Calvin continues,

---

32. John Calvin, *Catechismus, sive christianae religionis institutio* (Basel: n.p., 1538), xii-xvii (pp. 16-20).

33. John Calvin, *Institutio christianae religionis* (Geneva: Robert Stephanus, 1559), III.iii.1-3. I have also consulted the translation, *Institutes of the Christian Religion*, trans. John Allen, 3 vols. (Philadelphia: Philip Nicklin, 1816).

34. Calvin, *Institutio* (1559), III.iii.9.

35. Calvin, *Institutio* (1559), III.iii.10-14.

36. Contra the argumentation in Cornelis Graafland, "Hat Calvin einen *ordo salutis* gelehrt," in *Calvinus Ecclesiae Genevensis Custos*, ed. Wilhelm F. Neuser (New York: Peter Lang, 1984), pp. 221-244.

37. Thus, Romans 8:29, Calvin, *Institutio* (1559), II.xiii.2; III,i.1, 3; viii.1; xv.8; xviii.7; xxiv.1; and Romans 8:30, Calvin, *Institutio* (1559), II.v.2; III.xiv.21; xviii.4; xxiv.6.

it is certain that the order [*ordinem*] is thus pointed out, that we may know that it proceeds from the gratuitous adoption of God, as from the first cause [*a prima causa*], that all things happen to the saints for their salvation.[38]

The notion of an *ordo* is clearly present here, and it causally connects election, calling, adoption, and salvation. Calvin also indicates that the apostle

no doubt made here this express declaration, that our salvation is based on the election of God, in order that he might make a transition to that which he immediately subjoined, namely, that by the same celestial decree, the afflictions, which conform us to Christ, have been appointed; and he did this for the purpose of connecting, as by a kind of necessary chain [*quodam necessitatis vinculo connecteret*], our salvation with the bearing of the cross.[39]

The phrase "necessary chain" reflects the traditional understanding of the passage as presenting a logical linkage, specifically the logical form of a sorites in which one proposition is linked to another, leading finally to a conclusion. Calvin did understand the language of verses 29 and 30 as referencing a series of stages or degrees, a *gradatio*, but the *gradatio* has a somewhat different point of reference than the causal *ordo* of the preceding verse—and may be using the term *gradatio* in its technical rhetorical sense of a movement toward the climax of an argument.[40] Calvin could also, by extension, place both union with Christ and sanctification into the *gradus* or *gradatio*, with election prior, calling as the cause of sanctification (*causam sanctificationis*), and sanctification standing as the goal or aim (*scopus*) of calling.[41]

The divine foreknowledge (*praecognitio*) referenced by the apostle, Calvin argues, is "not a bare prescience [*non nuda est praescientia*] ... but the adoption [*adoptio*] by which [God] had always distinguished his children from the reprobate."[42] According to Calvin, the foredetermination or foreordination leading to calling "refers not to election, but to that purpose or decree of God by which he has ordained that the cross is to be borne by [those who are] his"[43]—as indicated by the context of the Apostle's remarks in the eighth chapter. There is no diminution of the causal interest in Calvin's remarks, but his exegetical observations on the theme of the church's present sufferings (vv.17-18) and their relation to God's work of conforming Christians to the "image of his Son" (v. 29), prevents him from arguing, on the basis

38. Calvin, *In epistolam Pauli ad Romanos*, in CO 49, col. 159 (*CTS Romans*, p. 315).

39. Calvin, *In epistolam Pauli ad Romanos*, in CO 49, col. 159 (*CTS Romans*, p. 316).

40. Calvin, *In epistolam Pauli ad Romanos*, in CO 49, col. 160-161 (*CTS Romans*, pp. 319, 320).

41. Cf. Calvin, *In priorem epistolam Pauli ad Corinthios*, 1:2, in CO, 49, col. 308 (*CTS 1 Corinthians*, I, pp. 52-53); with the comment in François Wendel, *Calvin: The Origins and Development of His Religious Thought*, trans. Philip Mairet (New York: Harper & Row, 1963), p. 242, note 31.

42. Calvin, *In epistolam Pauli ad Romanos*, in CO 49, col. 160 (*CTS Romans*, p. 317).

43. Calvin, *In epistolam Pauli ad Romanos*, in CO 49, col. 161 (*CTS Romans*, p. 319).

of this text, a strict and detailed ordering of the elements or aspects of salvation under a single decree.

The same sense of a structured argument, specifically a gradation, is found in the briefer comments of several of Calvin's contemporaries. Bullinger refers to the text as a *gradatio*, indicating that the apostle here explains by a gradation or series how, according to the eternal counsel (*propositum*) of God, all those eternally foreseen by God are led to their appointed end, to be conformed to the image of his Son.[44] Hyperius likewise indicates that the apostle offers a series or gradation (*gradatio*) of propositions that indicate the "order and progression" of God's providence in the election, calling, and subsequent benefits conferred on believers.[45] Musculus both identifies the passage as a division of the counsel of God (*propositum Dei*) into its logical *membra* and as sequence of steps (*scala in gradus*).[46] The first *gradus* of the decree or *propositum*, on which all remaining *gradus* depend, is God's foreknowledge.[47] This divine prescience is not, Musculus argues, as the scholastics claimed, the general foreknowledge of God by which God knows all things before they occur—rather it is an elective foreknowing, as when the apostle elsewhere teaches that God "knows those who are his."[48] The second *gradus* is, arguably, the predetermination of predestination of those foreknown.[49] The third *gradus* is calling,[50] the fourth justification,[51] the fifth and final glorification.[52] So also, in his Romans commentary, Vermigli draws two of the terms, namely, *gradatio* and *catena*, together, commenting, "And this gradation of the Apostle [is] truly a golden chain, by which those who shall be blessed are draw into heaven ... by it we will be made invincible against all adversaries."[53] Vermigli is also one of the theologians who early on wrote of the *salutis causa* and mentioned a *salutis ordo*—on the grounds that personal righteousness was not the cause of salvation but that an efficacious grace came first in order, rendering one righteous (*iustus*) and holy (*sanctus*).[54]

Reformers on the causality of salvation. From the very beginning of Reformed thought on the subject, causality was closely associated with the issue of an *ordo* or

---

44. Bullinger, *In sanctissimam Pauli ad Romanos epistolam*, Rom. 8:29-30, in loc. (p. 112v).

45. Hyperius, *In D. Pauli ad Romanos epistolam exegema*, pp. 75v-76r.

46. Musculus, *In epistolam D. Apostoli Pauli ad Romanos comentarii*, p. 145.

47. Musculus, *In epistolam ad Romanos*, p. 143.

48. Musculus, *In epistolam ad Romanos*, p. 144, citing 2 Tim. 2:19.

49. Musculus, *In epistolam ad Romanos*, p. 144, where, however, the term *secundus gradus* does not appear; cf. ibid., p. 148.

50. Musculus, *In epistolam ad Romanos*, p. 145.

51. Musculus, *In epistolam ad Romanos*, pp. 144, 146.

52. Musculus, *In epistolam ad Romanos*, p. 148.

53. Vermigli, *In epistolam ad Romanos*, 8:30, in loc. (p. 540); *Epistle of S. Paul to the Romanes*, fol. 228v; cf. fol. 226r).

54. Peter Martyr Vermigli, *In primum librum Mosis, qui vulgo Genesis dicitur* (Zürich: Christopher Froschauer, 1569), fol. 31v.

series of *gradus* in the temporal economy of salvation. The association arose rather naturally out of the exegesis of various key biblical *loci* and the assumptions of a foundation of salvation in Christ and of the priority of grace over human response. The causal language of later Reformed expositions of such topics as election, faith, regeneration or conversion, and justification was, therefore, not without significant precedent in the writings of the major Reformers, perhaps most notably Reformers of the second generation, like Calvin, Bullinger, Vermigli, and Musculus. Calvin was particularly interested in identifying the four traditional causes—first, formal, material, and final—in his examination of the Pauline doctrine of election as found in Ephesians 1. Given that his two expositions of the text—one in the commentary, the other in his sermons—and his treatments of the same issue in the *Institutes* and in other places in the commentaries, differ slightly in their deployment of the causal model, absolutely uniform conclusions cannot be drawn about Calvin's understanding of the causality of salvation.[55]

Nonetheless, the arguments are significant. They are in basic agreement and, contrary to the impression given by writers who blithely omit them from discussion,[56] necessary to the right understanding of Calvin's doctrine. In brief, "The efficient cause is the good pleasure of the will of God [*beneplacitium voluntatis Dei*]: the material cause is Christ: the final cause is the praise of [his] grace,"[57] while the formal cause, subsequently noted by Calvin, is "the preaching of the gospel, by which the goodness of God overflows upon us."[58] Faith stands, moreover, in the place of an instrumental cause, inasmuch as "it is through faith that Christ is communicated to us, by whom we come to God, and by whom we enjoy the benefit of adoption."[59] A similar, but not identical, paradigm in which faith is identified as the instrumental cause appears in Calvin commentary on Romans 3:24:

> There is, perhaps, no passage in the whole Scripture which illustrates in a more striking manner the power [*vim*] of his righteousness. It shows that the mercy of God [*Dei misericordiam*] is the efficient cause [*causam esse efficientem*]: that Christ with his blood is the material [*materiam*]: that the formal, or instrumental [*formalem, seu instrumentalem*] is faith drawn from the word: that final [*finalem*], moreover, is the glory of the divine justice and goodness.[60]

---

55. Cf. the discussion in Richard A. Muller, *Christ and the Decree: Christology and Predestination in Reformed Theology from Calvin to Perkins*, reissued, with a new preface (Grand Rapids: Baker, 2008), p. 24.

56. Cf., e.g., Wilhelm Niesel, *The Theology of Calvin*, trans. Harold Knight (London: Lutterworth, 1956), pp. 159-169; Partee, *Theology of John Calvin*, pp. 240-250.

57. Calvin, *In epistolam Pauli ad Ephesios*, 1:5, in CO 51, col. 148 (*CTS Ephesians*, p. 200).

58. Calvin, *In epistolam Pauli ad Ephesios*, 1:8, in CO 51, col. 150 (*CTS Ephesians*, p. 203).

59. Calvin, *In epistolam Pauli ad Ephesios*, 1:8, in CO 51, col. 150 (*CTS Ephesians*, p. 203).

60. Calvin, *In epistolam ad Romanos*, 3:24, in CO 49, col. 61 (*CTS Romans*, p. 141).

The differences, although clear, are not substantial. Calvin variously identified the first cause of election as the divine will, good pleasure, or counsel,[61] God's eternal gracious will to adopt the elect,[62] and the kindness or mercy of God,[63] all referencing the divine will before the foundation of the world. He typically identified Christ as the material cause;[64] and he either conjoined faith and the preached word in the formal causality,[65] or, perhaps with a view to greater precision in his language of salvation as by grace alone, distinguished between the preached word as formal cause and faith as the instrumentality receiving the word.[66] The final cause is consistently identified as the glory of God or the glory or praise of God's goodness, justice, or grace[67]—with an occasional reference to a penultimate finality as the redeemed life of holiness before God.[68]

Calvin also has more to say about the causal relation of Christ to the eternal purpose of God in his sermon on the text of Ephesians 1. There he indicates that our eternal election is an election in Christ, in the sense that Christ is the one who "registers" believers in the book of life,[69] an echo perhaps of his identification of Christ elsewhere as the author of election.[70] This active or efficient causality on Christ's part stands, certainly, in relation to Calvin's high sense of the divinity of Christ as *authotheos* as *a se*.[71] As we will note in the following chapter, the place of faith in this causal ordering also relates directly to Calvin's understanding of the centrality of union with Christ to the ordering of the application of salvation.[72]

Calvin was convinced that, without a full identification of the divine causality at work in salvation, faith could be shaken:

---

61. Calvin, In epistolam Pauli ad Ephesios, 1:5, in CO 51, col. 148 (CTS Ephesians, p. 200).

62. Calvin, In epistolam Pauli ad Ephesios, 1:11, in CO 51, col. 152 (CTS Ephesians, p. 206); idem, In epistolam ad Romanos,, 8:28, in CO 49, col. 159 (CTS Romans, p. 315).

63. Calvin, In epistolam Pauli ad Ephesios, 1:7, in CO 51, col. 150 (CTS Ephesians, p. 202); idem, In epistolam ad Romanos, 3:22, 24, in CO 49, col. 59, 61 (CTS Romans, pp. 138, 141).

64. Calvin, In epistolam Pauli ad Ephesios, 1:5-6, 7, in CO 51, col. 148-149, 150 (CTS Ephesians, pp. 200-201, 202); idem, In epistolam ad Romanos, 3:22, 24, in CO 49, col. 59, 61 (CTS Romans, p. 141).

65. Calvin, In epistolam ad Romanos, 3:22, in CO 49, col. 59 (CTS Romans, p. 138).

66. Calvin, In epistolam Pauli ad Ephesios, 1:8, in CO 51, col. 150 (CTS Ephesians, p. 203); idem, In epistolam ad Romanos, 3:22, in CO 49, col. 59 (CTS Romans, p. 138); idem, In epistolam ad Galatas, 3:6, in CO 50, col. 205 (CTS Galatians, pp. 84-85).

67. Calvin, In epistolam Pauli ad Ephesios, 1:5, 12, in CO 51, col. 148, 152 (CTS Ephesians, pp. 200, 206); cf. idem, In epistolam ad Romanos, 3:24, 7:4, in CO 49, col. 61, 121 (CTS Romans, pp. 141, 248); and idem, Sermons sur l'epitre aux Ephesiens, 1:4-6, in CO 51, col. 277.

68. Calvin, Sermons sur l'epitre aux Ephesiens, 1:4-6, in CO 51, col. 272, 274.

69. Calvin, Sermons sur l'epitre aux Ephesiens, 1:3-4, in CO 51, col. 269.

70. Cf. Calvin, Institutio (1559), III.xxii.7; with ibid., II.xiii.3; with Calvin, Commentary on John, 13:18, 17:8-10, in CO 47, col. 310-312, 379-381 (CTS John, II, pp. 63-65. 171-174).

71. See the discussion in Muller, Christ and the Decree, pp. 25, 30-31, 35-38.

72. Cf. Garcia, Life in Christ, pp. 117-119.

The goal of the apostle, therefore, in asserting the riches of divine grace toward the Ephesians, was to protect them against having their faith shaken by false apostles: as if their calling were doubtful, or salvation were to be sought in some other way. He shows, at the same time, that the full certainty of future happiness rests on the revelation of his love to us in Christ, which God makes in the gospel. But to confirm the matter more fully, he rises to the first cause as to the fountain: namely, the eternal election of God, by which, before we are born, we are adopted as sons: this makes it evident that their salvation was accomplished, not by any accidental cause, but by the eternal and immutable decree of God.[73]

Similarly,

The foundation and first cause both of our calling and of all the benefits which we receive from God, is here declared to be his eternal election. If the reason is asked, why God has called us to participate in the gospel, why he daily bestows upon us so many blessings, why he opens heaven to us: the answer will always be found in this principle, that he hath chosen us before the foundation of the world.[74]

Calvin's intention was also clearly to exclude works from the causality of salvation: "the cause, certainly, is not later than the effect. Election, therefore, does not depend on the righteousness of works, of which Paul here declares that it is the cause."[75]

Such clear statements from Calvin serve to set aside mistaken readings of his doctrine like Partee's: "predestination in Calvin deals with *our experience* of God's grace; in Westminster it deals with *God's bestowal* of grace"[76]—as if the overtly causal argumentation found in Calvin and in the thought of the Westminster divines did not indicate, and specifically so, that the experience of grace is and must be grounded in its bestowal by God. Arguably, predestination itself or eternal election, for Calvin, is precisely about God bestowing grace, and only indirectly or by way of effect about experience. It is Calvin's understanding of calling, faith, union with Christ, and assurance that deals with the experience of grace: Calvin declares as much, following pointed warnings about attempting to find one's assurance in the eternal decree, by his turn to these topics in his chapters on predestination, election,

73. Calvin, *In epistolam Pauli ad Ephesios*, 1:3, in CO 51, col. 145-146 (CTS *Ephesians*, p. 196).
74. Calvin, *In epistolam Pauli ad Ephesios*, 1:4, in CO 51, col. 147 (CTS *Ephesians*, pp. 197-198).
75. Calvin, *In epistolam Pauli ad Ephesios*, 1:4, in CO 51, col. 148 (CTS *Ephesians*, p. 199).
76. Partee, *Theology of John Calvin*, p. 244; "Westminster" here refers to the Westminster Confession of Faith. Partee's point consists in the creation of one more unsupportable dichotomy for the sake of propping up a variation of the "Calvin against the Calvinists" thesis. Partee's statement ignores the rather different genres of the documents being compared, fails to acknowledge of largely objective statement of predestination provided by Calvin as a foundation for his approach to the experience of grace, and ignores the background and context of the Westminster Confession in the so-called experimental or experiential predestinarianism of English Reformed theology. There are, as noted in the essays in this volume, differences between Calvin's formulations of the doctrine and later Reformed formulations (just as there are differences between Calvin and various of his contemporaries in the Reformed tradition), but Partee has failed to identify them.

and reprobation.[77] This return to topics belonging to what would come to be called the *ordo salutis* when raising the issues of the experience of grace and of assurance also points toward the strong similarities and connections between Calvin's thought and the thought of later Reformed writers. It points, therefore, also to their common interest in the examination of inward experience for the sake of assurance in what is commonly called the *syllogismus practicus*.[78]

The issue of the causality of salvation also figures prominently in Peter Martyr Vermigli's commentary on Romans and therefore also in the *loci* on predestination, union with Christ, and justification subsequently inserted into his posthumously complied *Loci communes*.[79] Of interest is that Vermigli does not merely line out causes; he also offers a causal argument specifying effects. There is, first and foremost, a cause of predestination itself, namely, the ultimate purpose or will of God by which God is also the "first cause" of all that exists. Given that this will is identical with the divine essence, there can be nothing prior to it—it is not caused by anything outside or beyond God.[80]

The final causes of predestination are also clearly revealed in Scripture, specifically where Paul states concerning Pharaoh that he was raised up in order that God might show his power, and concerning the elect that God wills to show forth his glory in them. As to the material causes of predestination, there are the elect themselves and the blessings decreed by God to be given to them, namely, calling, justification, and glorification; these things are the *materia* or material causes with which predestination is "occupied."[81] Vermigli notes, however, that these material causes are in a sense effects of predestination and aspects of the efficiency of salvation, so that in a proximate sense they may be regarded as efficient causes themselves—although clearly, good works cannot be viewed both as effects of predestination (which they are) and as causes of the divine predestinating will, as if God elected on grounds of foreknowledge (which they clearly are not!). Thus,

> it is possible if the effects of predestination are considered together with one another, that one may be the cause of another. But they cannot be causes of the divine purpose [*propositum*]. For calling, which is the effect of predestination, is the cause of our justification. Justification is also the cause of good works: and good works although the are not causes, are the means by which God brings us to eternal life.

---

77. Thus, note specifically, Calvin, *Institutio* (1559), III.xxiv.1-11.

78. See below, chapter 8, on the *syllogismus practicus*.

79. Peter Martyr Vermigli, *In epistolam s. Pauli apostoli ad Romanos . . . commentarii* (Zürich: s.n., 1559); note that the 1560 edition published in Basel by Perna appears to be abbreviated; in translation, *Most learned and fruitfull commentaries upon the Epistle to the Romans* (London, 1568); idem, *P. M. Vermilii loci communes*. (London: Thomas Vautrollerius, 1576; editio secunda, 1583); in translation, *The Common Places of Peter Martyr*, trans. Anthony Marten (London: Henrie Denham et al., 1583).

80. Vermigli, *In epistolam ad Romanos*, p. 698 (*Commentaries*, fol. 294r).

81. Vermigli, *In epistolam ad Romanos*, p. 698 (*Commentaries*, fol. 294r).

None of these is the cause, or the means why we are elected by God: as conversely sins are the causes why we are damned, but not why we are reprobated by God. For if they were the cause of reprobation, no one would be elected.[82]

The first effect of predestination is, in Vermigli's enumeration, Christ himself, "for the elect can have none of the gifts of God unless they are bestowed by our Savior."[83] Beyond this first and foremost or foundational effect, Paul also indicates the other effects in Romans 8:28-30: "from which it appears," Vermigli continues, "that the effects of predestination are vocation, justification, and glorification, to which can be added conformity to the image of the son of God. ... Good works can also be added, inasmuch as God is said to have prepared them that we might walk in them."[84] Vermigli is clear that justification by faith is the "head, source and support of all piety" [caput sit, fons et columen totius pietatis],"[85] but like Calvin recognizes that it was not a cause of salvation, strictly so-called. The apostle's statement that "that there is no condemnation to those who are in Christ" identifies the "efficient cause" of justification, of the beginnings of personal holiness, and of obedience to the law.[86] Specifically, Christ is the "author" and efficient cause, faith is the instrument.[87] The certainty or confirmation of salvation that follows on identification of these effects in oneself and the "declaration of the riches of God" also can be identified as effects of predestination.[88]

As to the effects of reprobation, which Vermigli also considers, they are to be identified in a rather oblique manner, so as not to identify God in any positive way as the author of sin. There is a series of things the follow on reprobation, Vermigli indicates, but God is not the cause of all of them in the same manner. Thus, God did not cause the sin of Adam but rather refrained from bestowing further grace that might have utterly prevented Adam's choice. The reprobate themselves are all to be found in the fallen seed of Adam, and their condemnation arises not out of positive divine act but of their being justly left in their sin by God. Even so, God justly condemns sin and brings final damnation on sinners. Vermigli enumerates only two actual effects of reprobation—first, the hardening and blinding of the reprobate in their sinfulness, and second, the ultimate declaration of the power and justice of God.[89]

Vermigli rejects the accusation that advocates of predestination teach a doctrine of "fatal necessity," understood as a force flowing from the stars that binds all things,

82. Vermigli, In epistolam ad Romanos, p. 699 (Commentaries, fol. 294r-v).

83. Vermigli, In epistolam ad Romanos, p. 718 (Commentaries, fol. 302r).

84. Vermigli, In epistolam ad Romanos, p. 718 (Commentaries, fol. 302r).

85. Vermigli, Loci communes (1583), III.iv.8 (p. 513).

86. Vermigli, In epistolam s. Pauli apostoli ad Romanos, 8:1 (p. 450).

87. Vermigli, In epistolam s. Pauli apostoli ad Romanos, 8:1 (p. 451); cf. idem, Loci communes (1583), III.iv.16.

88. Vermigli, In epistolam ad Romanos, p. 718 (Commentaries, fol. 302r).

89. Vermigli, In epistolam ad Romanos, pp. 718-719 (Commentaries, fol. 302v).

including God, together in an "unbreakable connection of causes," but he also argues that the right doctrine indicates "an order of causes that is governed by the will of God."[90] In expositing this issue of divine causality, Vermigli also recognizes that the issue of divine foreknowledge impinges on the issue of necessity and contingency, inasmuch as, by definition, acts of free choice are contingent—they could be otherwise—and, therefore, albeit foreknown by God, do not arise out of an utterly necessary connection of causes.[91] The order of causes and effects is, in other words, freely determined by the will of God, including the free acts of creatures, which God wills to occur freely according to the nature of the creature. God foreknows what he wills, and he therefore foreknows the entire order of things as contingent as, in other words, a necessity of the consequence or a necessity of certainty that does not coerce.[92]

Vermigli distinguishes between various understandings of necessity. There is the simple or absolute necessity of something that cannot be otherwise and that would involve a contradiction in order to be otherwise. God is absolutely necessary in this sense, as is the fact that four is an even number and that four plus three equals seven. There are also relative or natural necessities, that occur in the normal course of things, arising from an "inward principle" that cannot be otherwise, such as a fire burning. There is also a distinction to be made between necessities of certainty and necessities of compulsion. The latter occurs when something is forced to be what it is against its nature or will, the former arises when something occurs that could be otherwise but, of course, can only be what it is at that particular moment. Works that proceed from the human will are free, and things occurring in the order of nature that could be otherwise are contingent—and they are necessary as a matter of certainty, not of compulsion. Even God's predestination, which, Vermigli declares, is absolutely certain, involves the willing of God in relation to the free willing of creatures and is not a matter of compulsion.[93]

Zacharias Ursinus on the Causality of Salvation

Further development of this causal language and, therefore, of the ordering of the various aspects of the appropriation of salvation occurred after the time of Calvin and his contemporaries, but before the time of Rennecherus and Perkins, who, at the very end of the sixteenth century inherited a relatively fully formulated approach to the order of application of Christ's work. Specifically, much of this development

---

90. Vermigli, *Loci communes* (1583), III.i.5 (pp. 445-446).

91. Vermigli, *In epistolam ad Romanos*, pp. 736-737 (*Commentaries*, fol. 310v).

92. Vermigli, *In epistolam ad Romanos*, pp. 731-732, 734, 736 (*Commentaries*, fol. 307v-308r, 309r-v).

93. Vermigli, *In epistolam ad Romanos*, pp. 731-732 (*Commentaries*, fol. 308r).

occurred in the era of third-generation Reformed theologians like Ursinus, Olevianus, Zanchi, Beza, and Danaeus.

Of this group, Beza has typically been singled out as the primary formulator and developer of any theological structure related to the divine decrees, and certainly Beza did contribute to the concept and language of a causal order, if only through the publication of his famous *Tabula praedestinationis* and the accompanying aphorisms, wherein Beza offered a *"descriptio et distributio causarum salutis electorum."*[94] Still, Beza's *Tabula* lacks full use of the standard fourfold causality and does little by way of elaboration of the causal interrelationships of the various elements of what would become the *ordo salutis*. The *Tabula*, then, disappoints those looking to it for a strict, fully developed *ordo salutis*, just as it disappoints those who would try to find in it the mythical "predestinarian system" attributed to the Reformed orthodox.[95] Elements of what would develop into the *ordo salutis* are als found in Beza's *Quaestionum et responsionum christianarum libellus* of 1570, but there is little concern in the document to lay out the causal interrelationships of the terms.[96] In the same generation, Zanchi is remembered for his discussion of the doctrine of predestination,[97] although not for any detailed presentation of an order of causes of salvation and damnation, nor, indeed, for any detailed discussion of an order of the application of salvation, whether causal, logical, or temporal.[98] What is frequently overlooked, however, is the role of the other thinkers of Beza's and Zanchi's generation, notably the role of Ursinus.

Faith and its causes in the theology of Zacharias Ursinus. The theology of Zacharias Ursinus (1534-1583), as embodied preeminently in his lectures or commentary on the Heidelberg Catechism,[99] played a significant role in the

94. Theodore Beza, *Tabula praedestinationis*, in *Tractationes theologicae*, 3 vols. (Geneva, 1582), I, pp. 170-205.

95. See Muller, *Christ and the Decree*, pp. 79-83; and idem, "The Use and Abuse of a Document: Beza's *Tabula praedestinationis*, the Bolsec Controversy, and the Origins of Reformed Orthodoxy," in *Protestant Scholasticism: Essays in Reassessment*, ed. Carl Trueman and Scott Clark (Carlisle: Paternoster Press, 1999), pp. 33-61.

96. See the discussion of the document below, chapter 7.

97. See Otto Gründler, *Die Gotteslehre Girolami Zanchis und ihre Bedeutung für seine Lehre von der Prädestination* (Neukirchen-Vluyn: Neukirchner Verlag, 1965).

98. See below, chapter 7, for an analysis of Zanchi on union with Christ and the development of an *ordo salutis*; and cf. Muller, *Christ and the Decree*, pp. 110-125, for a discussion of Zanchi's teaching and a critique of Gründler.

99. Zacharias Ursinus, *Explicationes catecheseos*, in *Opera theologica*, ed. Quirinius Reuter, 3 vols. (Heidelberg: Johannes Lancellot, 1612), vol. I. Earlier sixteenth-century editions of the catechetical lectures, entitled *Doctrinae christianae compendium* (Neustadt, 1584; Leiden: Johannes Paetsius, 1584; London, 1585) and *Explicationum catecheticarum, editio altera* (Cambridge: Thomas Thomasius, 1587), were subsequently augmented by Ursinus' students Paraeus and Reuter from other writings of Ursinus and published under the titles *Corpus doctrinae christianae ecclesiarum a papatu Romano reformatarum. Ex ore quondam magni theologi D. Zachariae Ursini in explicationibus catecheticis rudi*

transition in Reformed theology from the era of second-generation codifiers like Calvin, Bullinger, Musculus, Vermigli, and Hyperius, to the era of early orthodoxy.[100] Ursinus offers an expanded examination of the catechetical question, "What is true faith?" (q. 21), that not only explains why the topic of faith is discussed immediately following the discussion of the saving work of the Mediator but also presents a series of questions within the catechetical topic covering such queries as "What are the efficient causes of justifying faith?" and "What are the effects of faith?" He engages in similar causal discussion in his explanation of the questions on justification (qq. 59-60), conversion (q. 88), and in an overarching view of the divine ordering of salvation in the added *locus* on predestination (following q. 54).[101] Taken together these explanations and discussions present, perhaps more clearly than any previous Reformed theology, the rudiments of an *ordo salutis*, albeit without the term.

In the order of the catechism and, consequently, of Ursinus' commentary, the topic of faith follows the discussion of the Mediator. Ursinus begins his exposition of the catechetical question by explaining this arrangement of the topics: the question of faith follows the questions on Christ as Mediator because faith "is the means by which we are made partakers of the Mediator" and because "without faith the preaching of the Gospel profits nothing."[102] The order of the argument (as distinct from the order of the catechism as a whole) is, therefore, synthetic, beginning with the cause, identifying the means, and pointing toward the effect—as also will be the arrangement of the later fully developed orderings of salvation among the Reformed.

Immediately, therefore, faith is placed into the causality of salvation as the means *sine qua non*—it looks back toward the work of Christ and makes it effective in the present, and it looks forward to the hearing of the Word and, similarly, receives its benefits. Ursinus qualifies and defines the relationship between Christ, faith, and preaching by noting that "the principal efficient cause" of justifying faith "is the Holy Spirit," while "Word and sacrament" are the "instrumental cause."[103] Thus, as a later

---

Minerva exceptum ed. David and Philip Pareus (Hanau: Jacob Lasche, 1602), and *Explicationes catecheseos* (Reuter, in the *Opera*). There are significant differences, largely in the form of augmentations of text, sometimes in the form of omissions, among these various editions. On the text history of the catechetical lectures, see T. D. Smid, "Bibliographische Opmerkingen over de Explicationes Catecheticae van Zacharias Ursinus," *Gereformeerd Theologisch Tijdschrift*, 41 (1940), pp. 228-243. In the present essay I have followed the *Explicationum catecheticarum* (1587) as my basic point of reference, noting augmentations found in the *Explicationes catecheseos* from the 1612 *Opera*.

100. See Derk Visser, *Zacharias Ursinus: The Reluctant Reformer, His Life and Times* (New York: United Church Press, 1983); and cf. the discussion in Muller, *Christ and the Decree*, pp. 97-110, 121-125.

101. See the discussion of Ursinus' placement of the doctrine in Muller, *Christ and the Decree*, pp. 108-109, cf. ibid., pp. 162-163; and note my subsequent reconsideration of issues of placement in "The Placement of Predestination in Reformed Theology: Issue or Non-Issue?," *Calvin Theological Journal*, 40/2 (2005), pp. 184-210.

102. Ursinus, *Explicationum catecheticarum*, p. 236.

103. Ursinus, *Explicationum catecheticarum*, p. 241.

addition indicates, the causality lies entirely outside the realm of human willing, with "the will and heart of man" being understood as the "subject" of the divine action.[104] This divine foundation being established, Ursinus indicates that faith itself has a series of effects:

> 1. Our justification before God. 2. Peace of conscience, or joy finding comfort in God, Rom. 5:1: justified by faith, we have peace with God. 3. Full conversion, which in a manner follows, and with faith existing at one and the same time. 4. The fruits of conversion and repentance, namely good works.[105]

Later editions of the catechetical lectures alter the passage, in some places, rather significantly:

> 1. Our justification before God. 2. Joy finding comfort in God, and peace of conscience: justified by faith, we have peace with God (Rom. 5:1). 3. Conversion, regeneration, and full obedience: by faith God purifies the heart (Acts 15:9). 4. Consequences also pertain to these effects: the increase of spiritual and bodily gifts, and the reception of these things.[106]

Inversion of the phrases in the second effect of faith makes little difference, but the addition of regeneration and full obedience to the third effect is significant, lessened somewhat by the pairing of conversion and repentance in the later version of the fourth effect. Quite significant, however, are the two other alterations: omission of the phrases "which in a manner follows, and with faith existing at one and the same time [*quaesidem sequitur, & cum fidei simul tempore existis*]"—the later version indicates the causal priority of faith without qualification; the earlier version, with its language of temporal simultaneity argues against a simple equation of causal and temporal orderings. Even more significant is the replacement of the positive reference to good works (*bona opera*) as the fruit of conversion and repentance with the term "full obedience [*tota obedientia*]" presented in tandem with conversion and regeneration. The pairing of conversion and regeneration before the reference to obedience—namely, of the passive act of conversion, the receiving of God's grace, and the active act of conversion or regeneration, the positive turning of the human being toward God—removes any possible implication that human acts in any way cooperate with the initial redemptive act of God. The alterations arguably reflect the pressure of polemic against Rome and perhaps an attempt to prevent any interpretation of the confession along slightly synergistic Melanchthonian lines.

The effect of faith, specifically of justifying faith, Ursinus emphasizes, is justification. The other effects of faith that he has identified follow once justification has taken place. He implies that these further gifts, namely, conversion,

---

104. Ursinus, *Explicationes catecheseos*, in *Opera*, I, col. 107.

105. Ursinus, *Explicationum catecheticarum*, p. 244.

106. Ursinus, *Explicationes catechesios*, in *Opera*, I, col. 108, scripture citations given in margin; cf. *Commentary*, p. 113.

regeneration, and obedience, can also be considered as caused by justification, inasmuch as in assigning them to faith, he notes, "that which is the cause of a cause, is also the cause of the effect" and "if therefore faith is, with respect to us, the proximate cause of our justification, it is also the cause of those things which necessarily follow upon it."[107] Both editions conclude the section with the summary comment, "The effects of faith are justification and regeneration, [the latter] incomplete in this life, to be completed in the next, Rom. 3:28 & 10:10; Acts 13:39."[108]

Ursinus on the causality of justification and conversion. Given that he has already identified faith as a cause of justification but is sensitive to the issue that faith itself, as an effect or result of grace, cannot be identified as something done or achieved by human beings—and given that the imputation of Christ's righteousness is to be understood as a divine act arising only out of mercy and grace, Ursinus moves to qualify and clarify his understanding of faith as a cause of justification when he comes to the doctrine of justification proper. Justification is the unmerited "application of the merit of Christ" to believers. The cause of this gracious application lies "in God alone," and "all gifts" of God in us are the "effect of the application of the merits of Christ."[109] Faith and justification are both utterly gracious gifts of God, bestowed according to the good pleasure of his will (*beneplacitum voluntatis suae*).[110]

The later text of Ursinus' commentary adds that, since believers are justified through faith and Christ, Christ together with the faith that receives him belong to the causality of salvation: the grace of God, the merits of Christ, and faith are all causes of justification, but not "in the same sense."[111] Ursinus first identifies four ways in which Christ relates to justification and faith. First, Christ is the "subject and matter [*subiectum & materia*]" of justification. Second, Christ is the "impelling cause [*causa impulsiva*]" of justification inasmuch as he "obtains" it for believers. Third, Christ is also to be understood as the "principal efficient [*efficiens principalis*]" cause of justification. Fourth, "because he gives us faith, by which we apprehend [justification]."[112]

Together with these causal statements made in relation to Christ, Ursinus adds a fuller argument that turns on his point that, in different senses, the grace of God,

107. Ursinus, *Explicationum catecheticarum*, p. 244.

108. Ursinus, *Explicationum catecheticarum*, p. 244: "*Breviter*: Effecta fidei sunt, *iustificatio, & regeneratio* hic inchoata, & perficienda in altera vita. Rom.3.28. & 10.10. Act. 13:39"; *Explicationes catechesios*, in *Opera*, I, col. 108: "Summa: Effectus fidei sunt iustificatio & regeneratio, incoata in hac vita, & perficienda in altera."

109. Ursinus, *Explicationum catecheticarum*, p. 572.

110. Ursinus, *Explicationum catecheticarum*, p. 572, citing Eph. 1:5; 1 Cor. 4:7; Eph. 2:8.

111. Ursinus, *Explicationes catecheseos*, in *Opera*, I, col. 234.

112. Ursinus, *Explicationum catecheticarum*, p. 572.

the merit of Christ, and our faith are all causes of justification: the impelling cause of justification is God; Christ's satisfaction is the formal cause; and faith is the instrumental cause of justification.[113] Thus, the *misericordia seu gratia Dei* is the principal impelling cause (*causa impulsiva principali*), lying in God himself, inasmuch as it is by this movement or, indeed, inspiration (*motus*) of mercy or grace that we are justified and saved. The merits of Christ serve both as the formal cause but also (as indicated in Ursinus' initial series of causal statements) as an efficient or impelling cause and as the meritorious cause (*causa impulsiva & meritoria*) of justification. As formal cause, Christ's merits are applied to believers as the foundation of their reconciliation to God: they are counted righteous because they are clothed in the merits of Christ. As the impelling and meritorious cause, Christ's merits are the reason that absolves believers of sin. Faith serves as the instrumental cause inasmuch as it is through faith that believers apprehend the righteousness of Christ imputed to them.[114]

The earliest forms of Ursinus' commentary here offer an entire section that is omitted from later printings: Christ's satisfaction, is made ours by faith alone (*sola fide*)—and this must be so on three grounds:

> 1. Faith is the sole instrument [*unicum instrumentum*] that apprehends Christ's satisfaction. 2. Because the proper act [*proprius actus*] of faith, and not of any other virtue, is the application or apprehension [*applicatio vel apprehensio*] of Christ's merit; indeed, faith is nothing other than that acceptation itself, or the apprehension of an alien righteousness [*iustitiae alienae*] ... 3. It is by faith alone: because we are justified only by the object of faith, namely, solely by the merit of Christ.[115]

Believers, therefore, are justified freely, apart from works, for Christ's sake alone. Faith is only an instrument and not a work. The "papists" are, therefore, in error when that identify faith as something by which we apply Christ to ourselves: "the merit of Christ justifies us, not faith itself: that which is apprehended justifies us, not the apprehending instrument."[116] The proposition that "we are justified by faith [*fide*

---

113. Ursinus, *Explicationum catecheticarum*, p. 572, indicating the impelling and formal causes; *Explicationes catecheseos*, in *Opera*, I, col. 234, adding the instrumental cause.

114. Ursinus, *Explicationes catecheseos*, in *Opera*, I, col. 234.

115. Ursinus, *Explicationum catecheticarum*, p. 572; cf. *Doctrinae christianae compendium* (1585), p. 529; and note the absence of this text from *Explicationes catecheseos*, in *Opera*, I, col. 234, where the text moves from the analysis of the three causes, grace, Christ's merit, and faith to a discussion of how faith justifies "correlatively" with Christ's merit. The two earlier texts give this latter discussion of faith and Christ's merit as correlative in a shorter form; the earliest texts both also include a lengthy series of objections to the doctrine of justification followed by responses that does not appear either in the *Explicationes catecheseos* of 1612: see *Doctrinae christianae compendium*, pp. 529-536; and *Explicationum catecheticarum*, pp. 573-579.

116. Ursinus, *Explicationum catecheticarum*, p. 573: "Meritum Christi nos iustificat, non ipsa fides: apprehensum nos iustificat, non ipsum apprehendens instrumentum"; cf. *Explicationes catecheseos*, in *Opera*, I, col. 235.

iustificamur]" may be stated "without correlation" when faith is rightly understood as the means (*medium*) of justification. When, however, the apostle Paul indicates that "faith was imputed to him for righteousness" the correlation with Christ's merit and righteousness is necessary to an understanding of the statement, inasmuch as faith here also is to be understood as the instrument or means and Christ's merit as the thing apprehended. Faith is merely the acceptation or apprehension of an "alien righteousness" and in no way a cause of that righteousness. Faith is, therefore, "utterly excluded from that which is received by faith."[117]

In his discussion of conversion (*conversio*), Ursinus returns to the issue of causality, distinguishing again between efficient and instrumental causes. Conversion, according to its most general definition is a change or mutation, taken in a more special sense as referring to the change, or *metanoia*, identified in the Greek New Testament as the beginning of God's saving work. Ursinus does not dispute that *poenitentia* or *paenitentia* can be used to translate the Greek; rather he points out that it is a rather obscure way of speaking of a conversion, given its association with penance—but it does well signify sorrow for sin. *Conversio* is the better theological term inasmuch as it indicates not only the sorrow and turning away from sin but also the new life of the believer. Conversion, then, signifies a series of things: deep sorrow over sin, the hatred of and flight from sin, the joy of knowing of reconciliation to God by means of the Mediator, and an earnest desire to obey God. It can be defined further in several ways, among them, "a mutation of the corrupt soul, life, and will to the good, brought forth in the elect by the Holy Spirit through the preaching of the law and the gospel, from which follow good works, namely, life according to all of God's commandments.[118]

As in the doctrine of justification, the efficient causality in this conversion belongs to God alone. Citing Lamentations 5:21, "convert us and we shall be converted," Ursinus identifies the Holy Spirit as the "principal efficient cause" of conversion. Still, as in all other aspects of salvation, there is a temporal secondary causality through which God works. Thus, the instrumental causes are the law and the gospel—with Ursinius' arguing strongly for the third use of the law, as already indicated in the structure of the catechism itself, where the law is considered initially under the introductory topic of human misery and then at length under the third major topic of human gratitude for salvation. Thus, the instrumental causes or means of conversion are the law in its preparatory or pedagogical function, the gospel, and then "teaching," understood as a the positive teaching of the law.[119] This latter instrumental function of the law clearly indicates Ursinus' broader use of

---

117. Ursinus, *Explicationum catecheticarum*, p. 573: "fides prorsus excluditur ab eo quod fide accipitur."

118. Ursinus, *Explicationum catecheticarum*, pp. 703-704, citing Acts 16:18; Isa. 1:16; 1 Cor. 6:11; Ps. 34:14.

119. Ursinus, *Explicationum catecheticarum*, p. 707: "Instrumentalis causae seu mediae sunt primo, Lex, deinde Evangelium, & post Evangelii doctrinam rursus doctrinae Legis."

conversio as indicating both the passive moment of the initial divine act of regeneration and the active continuation of conversion in sanctification.

Faith is the second or proximate instrumental cause of conversion given that, apart from faith, there can be no true love of God. It is by faith that we know God's will, specifically his will to remit our sins through and by Christ (*per & propter Christum*). Faith purifies the human heart, yielding both parts of conversion, mortification and vivification. This order is important, given that the law must come first, preparing for the gospel by instilling a knowledge of sin and yielding in the human heart a sorrow for sin. The preaching of the gospel follows, "since without the gospel, there is no faith"—and after the preaching of the gospel, the preaching of the law follows inasmuch as the law is "the norm of our actions."[120] Significantly, Ursinus identifies mortification not as caused by the law but as the first part of conversion and therefore belonging to the instrumentality of faith—even so, inasmuch as sin is not of faith, its antithesis, good works, find their source in faith. It is faith, therefore, through which we have peace with God.[121]

Conversion can also be identified according to contributing causes, its subject or material cause and object, its formal cause, and its final causes. Among the contributing causes are divine chastisements for sin and divine blessings as delivered both on the individual human subject and on others. The subject or material cause of conversion lies in the mind, the will, and the heart or, in the more technical language of the faculty psychology, the intellect, will, and affections. The *forma* or formal cause of conversion, corresponding directly with the description of the subject of material cause, Ursinus indicates, is conversion itself and its properties: the intellect must come to a right understanding of the will and works of God, the will to a prompt and sincere desire to obey God's commandments, and the affections to a new and reformed desire for God. The objects of conversion are, accordingly, sin and righteousness—the sinfulness or disobedience from which believers are converted and the righteousness or new obedience to which they are converted.[122]

The final causality of conversion is concerned both with penultimate and ultimate goals. The penultimate goals, identified as "proximate and subordinate" to the ultimate end are, principally, the goodness, blessedness, and eternal fruition of believers and also the "less principal" goal of the conversion of others, as Scripture states, "Let your light shine before men, that they may glorify your heavenly father."[123] Thus, also, the effects of conversion are good works, Christian obedience, and the desire to convert others into the right path. The ultimate goal or "principal end" of conversion is the glory of God.[124]

---

120. Ursinus, *Explicationum catecheticarum*, p. 707.
121. Ursinus, *Explicationum catecheticarum*, p. 707, citing Rom. 14:23 and Rom. 5:1.
122. Ursinus, *Explicationum catecheticarum*, pp. 707-708.
123. Ursinus, *Explicationum catecheticarum*, p. 708, citing Luke 22:32 and Matt. 5:16.
124. Ursinus, *Explicationum catecheticarum*, p. 708.

Predestination, Christ, and the order of salvation. Ursinus' discussion of predestination includes fairly detailed presentations of the issue of causality, both of the causes of predestination and of its effects. Ursinus also argues a double, albeit clearly infralapsarian doctrine of predestination. After distinguishing predestination from providence as a part or *species* of providential willing, Ursinus offers his definition:

> Predestination is, therefore, the eternal, most righteous & and immutable counsel of God, concerning the creation of human beings, the permission of their fall into sin & eternal death, the sending of his Son in the flesh, that he might be a sacrifice, followed by the conversion of some, for the sake of the Mediator, by the word and the Holy Spirit, saving them in true faith and conversion, [justifying them by and for him, raising them to glory, and giving them eternal life:] relinquishing the rest to sin and eternal death, raising them to judgment, and casting them into eternal punishment.[125]

He follows it immediately with definitions of election and reprobation:

> The parts of predestination are Election and Reprobation. Election is the eternal, immutable, gracious, and most just decree of God, by which he decreed to convert some to Christ, to conserve them in faith & repentance, and through him to give then eternal life. Reprobation is that decree of God, by which he decreed by his most just judgment to leave some in sin, punish then with blindness & condemnation, and because they are not made participants in Christ, to condemn them in eternity.[126]

Several comments are in order. Prior to his lining out the causality of predestination, Ursinus' definitions already indicate orders of salvation and damnation flowing out of the decrees of election and reprobation. Ursinus also answered the objection that the doctrine leads to spiritual laxity, given that God's elect are those in whom God works both repentance and the desire to persevere, citing Romans 8:30 as the basis of his argument.[127] What is more, particularly in the main definition, the elements or degrees of election indicate both a referencing of Romans 8:30 and expansion of the *gradus* beyond calling, faith, and justification. Ursinus also makes clear reference, albeit in the negative, to the broader scope of the text in Romans 8 and to the Reformed exegetical understanding of the chapter, identifying union with or participation in Christ as requisite to salvation and, therefore, as an anchor of the order or *gradus*.[128]

Given that the decree is eternal, its causality cannot ultimately be grounded in or caused by anything temporal. Indeed, "since there is nothing new in God, but all [in him] is eternal," Scripture states declaratively that God elects "before the foundation

---

125. Ursinus, *Explicationum catecheticarum*, p. 539; with the clauses in the bracket supplied from the later edition, *Explicationes catecheseos*, in *Opera*, I, col. 214.

126. Ursinus, *Explicationum catecheticarum*, p. 539.

127. Ursinus, *Explicationum catecheticarum*, p. 538.

128. Ursinus, *Explicationum catecheticarum*, p. 539.

of the world."[129] Ursinus' assignment of causes here closely reflects the argumentation, whether topical or exegetical, of Calvin and other Reformers. The "efficient and impelling cause [*causa efficiens & impulsiva*]," then, "is the good pleasure [*beneplacitum Dei*]" or "utterly free mercy of God [*sola Dei misericordia gratuita*]," as taught in Ephesians 1:5, "he predestined us in himself for adoption as children through Jesus Christ, according to the good pleasure of his will."[130] Ursinus indicates that there is nothing in the elect that could be identified as a foreknown basis for their election: God elects graciously, and there is nothing either in the elect or done by them that could be understood as "good" and meriting election. Indeed, whatever good there is in the elect is entirely the effect of the divine work in them: "there is nothing effected in us that he did not decree to effect from eternity."[131] "Accordingly," Ursinus comments, somewhat more fully, "the efficient and impelling cause of our Election is solely the gracious and most free good pleasure of God, or solely the freely given mercy of God."[132]

Ursinus next turns to the causality of reprobation. If sin were the cause of reprobation, he comments, all humanity would perish. Therefore, given the promise of salvation for some, the cause of reprobation cannot be in humanity, but rather "in the will of God, for the illustration of his justice"—even so, "the efficient cause of reprobation is the most free good pleasure of God."[133] The reason why some are elect and others are reprobate can have no other reason than the divine good pleasure.

There are, however, also proximate or penultimate causes of both election and reprobation to be considered, causes that, among other things, identify clearly the differences in causality, the absence of utter parallelism of the decrees, and the assumption that God is not the author of sin but only of the good. The "proximate final cause" of election, Ursinus indicates, is the justification of the elect when God freely counts them righteous in Christ. So also is there a proximate causality related to reprobation, a causality the specifically relieves God from the accusation that he is the author or sin and the direct cause of final condemnation. Whereas the cause of reprobation is in God alone, the cause of damnation is solely in human beings—namely, their sin.[134]

Beyond these proximate causes and penultimate ends, there are also the ultimate ends of the divine willing or utterly final causes. Thus, the "highest final cause [*finalis causa suprema*]" of predestination is the glory of God," while the "ultimate [*ultima*] and proper [*ac propria*]" cause of election is the "revelation of the goodness and

129. Ursinus, *Explicationum catecheticarum*, p. 539.

130. Ursinus, *Explicationum catecheticarum*, p. 539, also citing Rom. 9:11; Col. 1:12; 2 Tim. 1:9-10.

131. Ursinus, *Explicationum catecheticarum*, p. 539.

132. Ursinus, *Explicationum catecheticarum*, p. 539: "Proinde solum gratuitum, & liberrimum Dei beneplacitum, aut sola misericordia gratuita, est causa efficiens & impulsiva nostrae Electionis."

133. Ursinus, *Explicationum catecheticarum*, pp. 539-540.

134. Ursinus, *Explicationum catecheticarum*, p. 540.

mercy of God in the gracious salvation of the Elect."[135] The final causality of election, both ultimate and penultimate, moreover, is most clearly indicated by the apostle Paul in Ephesians 1:5-6. Ursinus cites the text in an abbreviated form: "Having predestined us ... to the praise of his glory and grace, by which he has made us freely accepted in his beloved." Identifying the contrary of the Pauline text, Ursinus continues, provides a sense of the final cause of reprobation, namely, "the declaration of justice, severity, and hatred against sin in the reprobate."[136]

Ursinus also notes several objections to these arguments, all of which point toward his later broader outlining of the order or degrees of the causes of election and reprobation. A first objection is probably (although not explicitly) drawn from an alternative reading of Romans 8:29: God foreknows our good works and therefore elects on the basis of good works. Certainly, Ursinus responds, God foreknows both the persons and their works—but he foreknows good works in persons as things that he wills to effect in them, not as grounds of his election. Similarly, God does not reprobate on the basis of a foreknowledge of sin, inasmuch as all of the sins he foreknows are sins that he permits.[137] Simply put, as far as Ursinus is concerned, the objection places carts before horses, effects prior to causes.

A second objection is stated briefly in the early editions of Ursinus' commentary and somewhat expanded in the final edition. In its short form, the objector indicates that "The merit of Christ applied by faith is the cause of out election: Therefore the good pleasure of God is not." The answer is equally brief: "Christ's merit is not the cause of election, but is counted among the effects."[138] Therefore, as the later edition of the commentary adds, as it is an effect of election, the merit of Christ is counted as one of the causes of salvation. Inasmuch as the elect are chosen in Christ, as he is the head of the elect, it should be clear that the head was first chosen and "ordained to the work of mediator."[139] This formulation has resonances in Calvin and stands as a clear predecessor to subsequent early orthodox formulations concerning the election and ordination of Christ as a prior fully trinitarian work in the order of the divine decree.[140] Ursinus concludes, "love [of God] therefore, namely, gratuitous election, is the cause of the sending of the Son [causa missionis filii], the sending of his Son is not the cause of his love."[141]

---

135. Ursinus, *Explicationum catecheticarum*, p. 540.

136. Ursinus, *Explicationum catecheticarum*, p. 540.

137. Ursinus, *Explicationum catecheticarum*, p. 540, objection 1; cf. *Explicationes catecheseos*, in *Opera*, I, col. 215, objection 1, virtually identical.

138. Ursinus, *Explicationum catecheticarum*, p. 540, objection 2; N.B. given as objection 3 in *Explicationes catecheseos*, in *Opera*, I, col. 215.

139. Ursinus, *Explicationes catecheseos*, in *Opera*, I, col. 215, objection 3: "meritum Christi non est inter causas sed inter effecta electionis, inter causes vero salutis nostrae numeratur. *Eligit nos in Christo*, nempe tanquam in capite. Caput igitur primo elegit & as officium mediatoris ordinavit."

140. See the discussion of such formulations in Perkins and Polanus in Muller, *Christ and the Decree*, pp. 156-167.

141. Ursinus, *Explicationes catecheseos*, in *Opera*, I, col. 215.

The formulation also points toward the issue of the identification of the *fundamentum electionis* and the reason why so many later Reformed writers denied this term or title to Christ at the same time that they identified Christ as the *fundamentum salutis electorum*. A *fundamentum*, or foundation, is not understood in the more or less colloquial sense of a basis or reason for something—rather it is understood rather strictly in early modern formulations as the ultimate source, beginning point, or *terminus a quo* of an act (or, in logic, of an argument). Christ, as the divine-human Mediator, is the proper foundation of salvation inasmuch as the entire work of salvation or reconciliation between God and human beings begins in him. But, as Mediator, Christ is not and cannot be the source or *terminus a quo* of the entire divine willing concerning the work of salvation: that is an eternal, divine work attributable to the full, triune Godhead—and God, therefore, in his willing of the work, is the *fundamentum electionis*.

A similar objection is inserted as the second of the group in the final edition of the commentary, based on the order of Paul's statements in Ephesians 1:3-4: Paul first teaches (v. 3) that God "has blessed us with all spiritual blessings in heavenly places through Christ" and then (v. 4) that God "has chosen us in [Christ] before the foundation of the world." The objector states his case syllogistically:

> Those whom God elects in Christ are those he found in Christ: the reason [*ratio*] for this being that he benefits no one in Christ who is not in Christ. God elects us in Christ. Therefore he found us in Christ: i.e., he foresaw that we would be in Christ, that rather than others would believe, & would be more worthy [*meliores*], and accordingly he elected us.[142]

The major proposition of the syllogism, Ursinus responds, is flawed, and for the same reason provided in the earlier, short form of the objection and answer: there is a confusion of causes and effects, evident in the problematically stated *ratio* of the proposition. "The *ratio* is true, not of election, but of the effects of election, and in the consummation of Christ's benefits, which are bestowed on none but those who are in Christ by faith," as Christ himself taught, unless a person abides in him, that person will have no life.[143] Even so, Ursinus continues, the objector has misread the text of Ephesians, given that Paul teaches that we are elect "before the foundations of the world" not because we were foreknown to be holy and blameless, but in order that we be made holy and blameless—not because we were known to be already in

142. Ursinus, *Explicationes catecheseos*, in *Opera*, I, col. 215, objection 2.

143. Ursinus, *Explicationes catecheseos*, in *Opera*, I, col. 215, citing John 15:4, reading *vitis*, vine, as *vita*, life. Note that Theodore Beza, *Jesu Christi Nostri Novum Testamentum, sive Novum Foedus, cuius Graeco contextui respondent interpretationes duae ... Eiusdem Theod. Bezae Annotationes* (Cambridge: Roger Daniel, 1642), in loc., comments that the vine is Christ "by similitude" both as he is God and has eternal life in himself and as he is human and human beings are united to him "spiritually and by faith ingrafted." That Christ is the "true vine," Beza continues, indicates that he has a "vivifying power" for those united in him. Similarly, at less length, cf. Calvin, *Commentary on the Gospel according to John*, 15:1 (CTS John, II, p. 107).

Christ, but in order that we might be engrafted into Christ and adopted as God's children. Foreseen faith and holiness are, then, not the causes but the effects of election. The objector, Ursinus concludes, is little better than a Pelagian, who claims, against Scripture, that God foreknew those who would, by their own free will, be holy and accordingly chose them to be his.[144]

A final objection, found only in the last edition of the commentary, argues that, inasmuch as evil works are the cause of reprobation, good works must be the cause of election. "The antecedent," Ursinus responds, "is denied."[145] The problem here is a confusion of reprobation with damnation. Evil works are the cause not of reprobation but of damnation—specifically both of damnation and of the ordination to damnation. As noted before in the initial discussion of reprobation, if evil or sin were the cause of reprobation, all human beings would be reprobate since, as Paul teaches, all human beings are the children of wrath. As to the consequent claim of the objector, given that good works do not precede justification, they can hardly be thought to precede election. Rather, good works follow upon justification as effects of the pure grace of God.[146]

Given the direction of each of the objections and of the responses, the next question identified by Ursinus for discussion reads, "What are the effects of predestination." He begins with election. "The effect of election is the entire work of salvation [totum opus salutis], and all of the degrees of our redemption [omnes gradus redemptionis nostrae]."[147] Ursinus use of the term "degrees" or "gradations" (gradus) here is significant on two counts: first, it reflects the language typically used to describe the sequence of salvation found in Romans 8:28-30, notably in the commentaries of Vermigli, Musculus, and Ursinus' close colleague Olevianus; and, second, it marks the developing doctrinal or dogmatic usage of the term among the Reformed in discussing the eternal decree and its execution.[148]

Ursinus' enumeration of the degrees, or gradus, of election also already indicate an expansion of the order of Romans 8:30 to include more elements than calling, justification, and glorification. Thus,

1. The creation and gathering of the church.
2. The sending [missio] and gift [donatio] of Christ the Mediator, and of his sacrifice.
3. Effectual calling and the knowledge of it, namely, the conversion of the Elect by the Holy Spirit and the word.
4. Faith, justification, regeneration.

---

144. Ursinus, Explicationes catecheseos, in Opera, I, col. 215.

145. Ursinus, Explicationes catecheseos, in Opera, I, col. 215, objection 4.

146. Ursinus, Explicationes catecheseos, in Opera, I, col. 215, citing Rom. 9:11.

147. Ursinus, Explicationum catecheticarum, p. 540: "Electionis effectus est totum opus salutis, & omnes gradus Redemptionis nostrae."

148. Cf., e.g., William Perkins, De praedestinationis modo et ordine (Cambridge: Iohn Legat, 1598), p. 11, for the use of gradus; and see chapter 5 for an analysis of the language of degrees or gradations with reference to Rom. 8:28-29.

5. Good works.
6. Final perseverance.
7. Resurrection to glory.
8. Glorification & life eternal.[149]

There is also, according to Ursinus, a series of the "effects of reprobation," which, unlike the *gradus* stemming from election, he leaves unnumbered: "the creation of the reprobate, the privation of divine grace, blindness and hardening, perseverance in sin, resurrection to judgment, & banishment to eternal punishment."[150]

The order and its parts given here are similar to the sequences found both in Beza's (earlier) and more elaborately in Perkins' (later) table of divine causality, although the differences are also notable. In all cases, predestination is defined as double, consisting in election and reprobation—with Ursinus' definition fully infralapsarian, Beza's as stated in the text of the *Tabula* tending toward or implying the supralapsarian, and Perkins' clearly supralapsarian. All indicate that the decree is concerned with the creation of human beings and the permission of the fall. Once the order branches into effects of election and reprobation, a primary difference between Ursinus' sequence and the others is evident: neither Beza's nor Perkins' charts indicate the "creation and gathering of the church," an element related to Ursinus' placement of predestination under the creedal topic of the church. It is also the case that Ursinus is enumerating the degrees of redemption and the entire structure of causality: unlike Beza and Perkins, his sequence of degrees simply presumes the eternal decree and, indeed, presumes creation and fall, beginning with a temporal order that is strictly associated with the redemption of fallen human beings. Accordingly, Ursinus' ordering lacks the trinitarian foundation that Perkins would add, but it carries forward the christological emphasis found in Beza's *Tabula* that would also be found in Perkins' schema, just as it lacks an ordering of the eternal decree, such as can be found in Perkins' work.

Before leaving his discussion of the causality of salvation and damnation, Ursinus confronts two objections to his views. The first of these argues that inasmuch as different or, specifically, "contrary causes" bring about "contrary effects," the contrary causalities of election and reprobation ought to be understood as producing the contrary effect of good and evil works.[151] Underlying the short syllogistic form of the objection is the problem that, if election and reprobation are precisely parallel in the order of causality, then God could be argued to be as much the author of evil as he is assumed to be the author of the good. Ursinus disputes the entire argument, indicating the less-than-equivalent nature of election and reprobation. Drawing on traditional understandings of necessary and contingent causality, Ursinius argues that the major proposition of the argument, that contrary causes bring about

---

149. Ursinus, *Explicationum catecheticarum*, p. 540.
150. Ursinus, *Explicationum catecheticarum*, p. 540.
151. Ursinus, *Explicationum catecheticarum*, p. 541.

contrary effects, is not always true—particularly in the case of voluntary or free causes (*causa voluntaria*). It was a truism that in necessary causality, an effect can be known in its causes, but in contingent causality or in its subset, voluntary or free causality, in which the effects by their very nature as contingent could be otherwise, effects cannot be known in their causes. As voluntary causes, election and reprobation have contingent effects—in other words, effects that cannot be inferred from the causes. Beyond this basic problem in the objector's argument, there is the further and more important issue that election and reprobation are not utterly parallel, and the ways in which God wills good and evil effects are "dissimilar." Whereas God actively effects the good in the elect, he only decrees to permit the evil acts of the reprobate. It is the Devil and wicked human beings who are the active causes of evil.[152]

Ursinus allows an attempt at rebuttal: God hardens and blinds human beings; blindness (in this spiritual sense) is an effect of reprobation; sin is therefore an effect of reprobation. Here Ursinus does not so much refute the premises and conclusion as accept them, albeit in scholastic fashion, with a distinction. Spiritual blindness can be considered in two ways: as sin and as punishment for sin. Blindness is a sin insofar as human beings commit it or accept it to their own demerit; as brought about by God, it is a just penalty for sin. And it needs to be added that God does also, out of his mercy, free human beings from their blindness.[153]

Ursinus' response draws on his sense of divine concurrence and the distinct levels of primary and secondary causality: the same event can be (in fact, must be) caused both by God and by the human being, although in different ways—a point that he had made in considerable detail in his earlier discussion of providence. There, Ursinus had indicated that, although God can and does work "immediately," in a manner not belonging to the established order of things, the greater part of God's providential work is "mediate," namely, in and through the established order and by means of secondary causes. There is, therefore, a twofold causality, with God working his own ends in and through the finite causality of the world order in the context of which rational creatures act, within the overarching divine causality, but according to their own natures, having their own ends.[154]

A second objection attempts to make a similar point, namely, that the doctrine of a divine decree of reprobation presents God as the author of sin, albeit indirectly. Thus, "Hardening [*induratio*] is the effect of reprobation, and hardening is sin: God is the author of reprobation: Therefore, he is the cause of hardening and thereby also of sin."[155] Ursinus agrees with the major premise, but, again, with a distinction, drawing on his previous argument: hardness or hardening is indeed an effect of reprobation, but it is not a direct effect that comes in a strict sense "from" (*ex*)

---

152. Ursinus, *Explicationum catecheticarum*, p. 541.
153. Ursinus, *Explicationum catecheticarum*, p. 541.
154. Ursinus, *Explicationum catecheticarum*, pp. 326-328.
155. Ursinus, *Explicationum catecheticarum*, p. 541.

reprobation—rather it is an indirect effect that arises "after" (*secundum*) reprobation. Further, whereas hardening and blindness follow on reprobation or on divine predestination inasmuch as they are sins, they are more strictly from reprobation or predestination (*ex reprobatione vel praedestinatione*) when understood as the punishments of sin.[156]

Early Orthodox Developments

Reformed commentators of the late sixteenth and seventeenth centuries. The basic exegetical understanding of Romans 8:28-30 as a golden chain, logical sorites, or series of causal degrees or gradations can be identified, moreover, in various Reformed commentaries on the text produced between the middle decades of the sixteenth century and the middle decades of the seventeenth. There was, in other words, a clear tradition of reading the text in this manner, specifically as a *locus classicus* for the ordering of the work of salvation under the divine decree, rooted in the writings of Reformers like Bullinger, Calvin, and Vermigli, and maintained or developed in later Reformed writers of the orthodox era.

By way of example, Beza indicates that the text is concerned with "the series of causes of our salvation" including the order of "means."[157] Olevianus' homilies on the text specifically identify the series of aspects of salvation deriving from the decree as "the causes of our salvation, and as if a golden chain [*causarum nostrae salutis & veluti catenam auream*]."[158] Piscator notes that on the basis of the decree as the "first and highest cause" Paul argues the end of believers in glory by means of a "sorites" and then lines out the text as a series of propositions representing the *ordo graduum in causis salutis*.[159]

Similarly, several decades later, Diodati's comments on the text of Romans 8:30 summarize the point: "This verse, joyned with the former, is a figure of speech called Gradation, viz., when men ascend by degrees, or step by step."[160] Daniel Featley in the *Westminster Annotations* makes a similar point, referring to the figure with a more technical, Greek term, *sorites*, namely, an interlinked syllogistic argument, and identifying the *sorites* as a "golden chaine."[161] The text of Romans 8:29-30, therefore,

---

156. Ursinus, *Explicationum catecheticarum*, p. 541.

157. Beza, *Annotationes* (1642), Rom. 8:28, in loc (p. 424).

158. Caspar Olevianus, *In epistolam D. Pauli apostoli ad Romanos notae, ex Gasparis Oleviani concionibus excerptae, & a Theodoro Bezae editae* (Geneva: Eustathius Vignon, 1579), p. 373.

159. Johannes Piscator, *Analysis logica Epistolae Pauli ad Romanos* (Herborn: Christpoh Rab, 1589), p. 146.

160. Diodati, *Pious and Learned Annotations*, Rom. 8:30, in loc.

161. Thomas Gataker, et al., *Annotations upon all the books of the Old and New Testament wherein the text is explained, doubts resolved, Scriptures parallelled and various readings observed by the joynt-labour of certain learned divines, thereunto appointed, and therein employed, as is expressed in the preface* (London: John Legatt and John Raworth, 1645), Rom. 8:29, in loc. Hereinafter cited as *English Annotations* (1645).

offers a "chaine ... no link whereof can be unclinched, because the fastening thereof is the work of Gods omnipotence."[162] Given this chain, the salvation of the elect rests utterly on "the death, the resurrection, and the Almighty power of Jesus Christ."[163] Robert Harris commented, in a different classical metaphor echoing Calvin's cautions about speculation,

> of that golden chaine, *Rom.* 8, two linkes he hath let downe to us, namely, that of vocation, and that other of sanctification, whereby to climbe up to the state of glory: the first linke of his secret will he hath reserved to himself. *Make* then *your election sure*, by becomming sure of your calling ... for otherwise, by soaring above your measure, and seeking to prie into Gods eternall purpose, you may, *Icarus*-like, leave you name for a Proverb, and yourselfe be drowned in the sea of perdition.[164]

The term was so much a standard that Jeremiah Burroughs could remark in a treatise of 1641, "to our Coronets we shall have added a crowne of life ... to our costly garments, the glorious shining robe of a Saviours righteousnes ... to our chaines of gold, the golden chaine of salvation, the linkes whereof are described, *Rom.* 8."[165] Or again, in his 1643 commentary on Hosea 2,

> There is a concatenation of second causes. ... As in our salvation there is a golden chaine which we have *Rom.* 8, so in the creatures there is a golden chaine of comely order and mutuall supplyance. ... God is at the higher end of the chaine, and nothing can be done by any link of the chaine of second causes, but by Gods being at the uppermost link.[166]

Formalizing the chain: Rennecherus, Perkins, Bucanus, and Maxey on the sequence of causes of salvation. If Calvin and his contemporaries did not argue a full *ordo* on the basis of Romans 8:28-30, the theologians of early Reformed orthodoxy moved toward a more clearly enunciated sequence (albeit not with the utter uniformity or rigidity often attributed to them), and they came close to providing Reformed theology with a technical term a full century before the Lutheran orthodox wrote of an *ordo salutis*: namely, the *armilla* or *catena salutis*, the "chain of salvation," and the "order of causes of salvation and damnation." At least four theologians, Herman Rennecherus, William Perkins, Gulielmus Bucanus, and Anthony Maxey, can be identified as instrumental in raising this terminology to some prominence in the era of early orthodoxy—not, however, as a radically new

162. *English Annotations* (1645), Rom. 8:29, in loc.

163. *English Annotations* (1645), Rom. 8:33, in loc.

164. Robert Harris, *Grace and glory knit together*, in *The Workes of Robert Harris, bachelor in divinity and Pastor of Hanwell* (London: R. Y. for J. Bartlett, 1635), p. 265.

165. Jeremiah Burroughs, *Moses His Self-Denyall. Delivered in a Treatise upon Hebrewes 11. the 24. verse* (London: T. Paine, 1641), p. 43.

166. Jeremiah Burroughs, *An Exposition of the Prophesie of Hosea. Begun in divers lectures upon the first three chapters* (London: W. E. and J. G. for W. Dawlman, 1643), I, p. 668.

point of departure in theology, but as the expression of a general theological consensus based on an exegetical tradition, adapted or confirmed to the more formal doctrinal setting of a *locus* or topic in theology.[167] As Maxey commented, "the auncient Fathers" had, "in the course of their writings" identified the text and the sequence of predestination, calling, justification, and glorification as "the Golden Chaine of our Salvation," given that the terms are "so coupled and knit together, that if you hold fast one linke, you draw unto you the whole chaine: if you let goe one, you loose all."[168]

Herman Rennecher's *Armilla salutis catena, continens et explicans omnes eius causas* (1589) and William Perkins' *Armilla aurea, id est, Miranda series causarum salutis et damnationis* (1590), very similar in title, both dealing with the subjects of predestination, calling, justification, glorification, and related topics, were published in very close temporal proximity toward the end of the sixteenth century. The connection of the term "golden chain" is far clearer in Rennecherus' treatise than in Perkins' work. Rennecherus' summary statement of the purpose of his work, preceding chapter 1, identifies the *aurea salutis catena* as derived from "the words of Paul, Rom. 8. v. 29 & 30."[169] Rennecherus indicates that the purpose of his treatise, setting forth the order of the causes of salvation, required that he find some place in Scripture where that order was clearly presented—and of all the many places in the Old and New Testaments touching on the issue, by far the most suitable was Romans 8:29-30. In this passage, the terms indicating the several aspects or elements of salvation are set forth clearly in "integral sentences," each presenting "brief and succinct" explanations—evidencing a divinely given technique of exposition (*artificium*) and a "logical way through" the topic (*Dialectica methodus*) suited to the accurate and coherent exposition of the topic.[170]

This perspicuous way through the topic begins with the divine foreknowledge as "the first and supreme cause" followed by predestination and then moves on to discuss the effects of both in the "proximate" or "intermediate and secondary causes of salvation."[171] Following traditional definitions of providence and predestination,

---

167. Herman Rennecherus, *Armilla salutis catena: continens et explicans omnes eius causas* (Herborn, 1589; Lich: Nicolaus Erbenius, 1597); in translation, *The Golden Chaine of Salvation* (London: Valentine Simmes, 1604); William Perkins, *Armilla aurea*, in translation, *A Golden Chaine, or the description of theologie, containing the order of the causes of salvation and damnation, according to Gods woord* (London: Edward Alde, 1591); and Anthony Maxey, *The Goulden Chaine of Mans Saluation, and the fearefull point of Hardening, together with the Churches Sleepe: Preached in three severall sermons before the King* (London: T. Este for Clement Knight, 1606). On the organization and significance of Perkins' *Armilla aurea* or *Golden Chaine*, see Richard A. Muller, "Perkins' A Golden Chaine: Predestinarian System or Schematized *Ordo Salutis?*," *Sixteenth Century Journal*, 9/1 (1978), pp. 69-81.

168. Maxey, *Goulden Chaine*, fol. A.ii verso-A.iii recto.

169. Rennecherus, *Armilla salutis catena*, i (p. 1).

170. Rennecherus, *Armilla salutis catena*, ii (p. 5).

171. Rennecherus, *Armilla salutis catena*, ii (pp. 5-6).

Rennecherus understands the foreknowledge of God as the general decree of providence concerning *omnia & singula*, and predestination as a part of providence concerning the ends of particular human beings, some being chosen in Christ to eternal salvation, the others being appointed to eternal punishment for sin. Once these ultimate causes have been declared, the apostle proceeds to identify the "intermediate causes" by the manner (*modus*) and degrees (*gradus*) of which the elect are brought to life eternal and the reprobate to eternal punishment.[172] We note that the exegetically grounded language of *gradus* carries over into Rennecherus' doctrinal discussion.

These causes, Rennecherus continues, relate to human temporality in a particular way. The ultimate or primary causes precede and transcend all times and are appointed form eternity. Next, there are causes, subordinate to the eternal causality, the belong to the temporal sequence, namely, vocation and justification—the former belonging to the outward proclamation of the word and the inward work of the Spirit, the latter gained and gratuitously bestowed on human beings by the "power & merit" (*virtus & meritum*) of Christ's suffering.[173] There are also causes that are "mixed," belonging in part to this life and in part to life in the future, beyond our present life, inasmuch as they are begun in this life and completed in the final glorification of believers. Thus, the regeneration that results from calling continues throughout the entire course of a human life and is completed in the full conformity of the human will to the divine and in the full restoration of the image of God that takes place in final glorification. Rennecherus continues, "These subordinate and secondary causes of salvation are, then, a kind of means and interposed degrees [*gradus*] by which human beings, sanctified to God by his eternal counsel, are drawn to possession and enjoyment of the fulness of eternal salvation and life."[174]

It is also the case that these causes "cohere" in their order and arrangement (*ordo & collocatio*) in such a way that they cannot be rearranged or diminished without the ruin of the entire series: they constitute a "golden and royal chain" (*aurea & regia catena*) that stands as a whole in all of its links and that is nothing less than an "admirable mirror of the divine goodness and mercy," forged and linked together from the greatest blessings or benefits of God. The chain cannot be broken. There are five links in the chain: foreknowledge, predestination, calling, justification, and glorification. Metaphorically, this chain is also a "golden and heavenly hook" let down from heaven by the Son of God in order to draw the elect "out of this world, as from a turbulent and storm-tossed sea, to their heavenly and eternal rest, as if to a harbor safe from every storm."[175] Significantly, Rennecherus does not add links to the chain in order to develop a model that places other aspects of salvation like adoption, regeneration, and sanctification into a rigid order: he is quite content with

172. Rennecherus, *Armilla salutis catena*, ii (p. 6).
173. Rennecherus, *Armilla salutis catena*, ii (p. 7).
174. Rennecherus, *Armilla salutis catena*, ii (pp. 7-8).
175. Rennecherus, *Armilla salutis catena*, ii (p. 8).

the Pauline model taken from Romans 8:28-30, although he clearly will identify these other aspects of the work of salvation as part of the larger divine work.

At the conclusion of his treatise, after a lengthy discussion and analysis of the doctrine of predestination and the order of causes of salvation, Rennecherus returns to the issue of the golden chain to enumerate the benefits of predestination, the assurance gained from an understanding of the nature of the chain, and the ultimate gift of life everlasting identified in the final link. The first effect of predestination, in Rennecherus view, is Christ as the *principium & caput* of the elect and as the *basis & fundamentum* of salvation, inasmuch as apart form Christ there can be no election. The second effect is the creation of the elect, the third effect being their effectual calling to conversion by the Holy Spirit through the word of the gospel. The fourth effect is justification, understood as a "firm faith and certain hope that apprehend and apply Christ and his merit, and rely on him alone."[176] The fifth and sixth effects are regeneration and the increase in faith and sanctification. Rennecherus adds that good works are necessarily present, not as a beginning or cause of election, "as the Papists dream," but as "effects and means … interposed by degrees" to bring the elect to their eternal salvation.[177] Next in order, seventh, eighth, ninth, and tenth, are patience in adversity, constancy and perseverance in faith, resurrection from the dead, and glorification to life eternal.[178]

In an argument that pointed directly toward the issue of assurance of salvation, Rennecherus indicated, next, that given the unbreakable character of the chain, possession of one link meant possession of the entire chain. Believers are, therefore, called on to consider how many links or degrees (*gradus*) of the chain they have experienced, to take comfort and assurance from what they have received, and to have hope for receipt of the rest, given that all rests on the promises of God.[179] The world and all of its benefits will perish, but divine gifts that belong to the golden chain of salvation are eternal and can never pass away.[180]

My earlier studies of Perkins and Beza examined the contents of Perkins' *Golden Chaine* and Beza's *Tabula*, in comparison with Perkins' own *Exposition of the Symbole or Creed*, and the fairly standard series of doctrinal *loci* in the theological systems of the era of orthodoxy and concluded that, contrary to much of the earlier scholarship, neither of these works serves as a theological system or, indeed, as a paradigm for a theological system.[181] The issue that was not raised with reference to either document

---

176. Rennecherus, *Armilla salutis catena*, xxxv (p. 268-269).

177. Rennecherus, *Armilla salutis catena*, xxxv (p. 269).

178. Rennecherus, *Armilla salutis catena*, xxxv (p. 270).

179. Rennecherus, *Armilla salutis catena*, xxxvi (pp. 273-274).

180. Rennecherus, *Armilla salutis catena*, xxxvii (p. 274).

181. See Muller, "Perkins' A Golden Chaine," pp. 69-81; and idem, "The Use and Abuse of a Document: Beza's *Tabula praedestinationis*, the Bolsec Controversy, and the Origins of Reformed Orthodoxy," in Trueman and Clark, *Protestant Scholasticism*, pp. 33-61; contra such works as Basil

was the fairly clear rootage, particularly in the case of Perkins' work, in a reading of Romans 8:28-30. Perkins' very title would have indicated as much had its exegetical background been brought into view.

The language of Perkins' title, describing the *armilla aurea* as a "wondrous series of causes of salvation and damnation" (*miranda seriem causarum & salutis & damnationis*) not only reflects the ascription of the term "golden chain" to Romans 8:28-30, it also parallels Beza's description of the text as the *causarum salutis nostrae serie* and Olevianus' identification of it as the *causarum nostrae salutis & veluti catenam auream*. Although Perkins does not give an initial prominence to the text of Romans 8:28-30 and, indeed, cites a multitude of biblical texts in his marginal references, when he comes to the topic of the "decree of election and its foundation Jesus Christ," his introduction of the topic of the execution of the decree and the specific statement, "For those elected to the end [*Electi ad finem*], namely, eternal life, were also elected to those subordinate means [*subordinata media*], by which they may be brought by degrees to this end [*ad finem gradatim perduci*]," Perkins does cite the text.[182] What also should be clear from Perkins argumentation is the intimate relationship between his understanding of the order of causes of salvation with union with Christ—indeed, as Perkins' diagram of the order of causes indicates, all of the links of the chain, from calling to sanctification, are grounded in the love of God to those in Christ and related directly to the work of Christ as it is applied to the believer.[183]

The exegesis of Romans 8:29-30 as a rhetorical gradation carries over into the doctrinal argumentation of Perkins' *Treatise of the Manner and Order of Predestination*. Perkins cites the text and then explains,

> *Paul* distinguisheth betweene the decree, and the execution thereof, which he maketh to be in these three, Vocation, Iustification, and Glorification. Moreover hee distinguisheth the decree into two acts, foreknowledge, whereby he doth acknowledge some men for his owne before the rest, and predestination, whereby he hath determined from eternity to make them like unto Christ.[184]

The apostle Peter had similarly indicated that "the faithful are elected according to the foreknowledge of God the father, unto sanctification of the Spirit." In neither place, Perkins insists, does this "foreknowledge" imply a "foreseeing of future faith" inasmuch as those foreknown by God are predestined to be like Christ, "that is, that they should be made just, and the sonnes of God. ... But those which are predestined

---

Hall, "Calvin Against the Calvinists," in *John Calvin: A Collection of Distinguished Essays*, ed. Gervase Duffield (Grand Rapids: Eerdmans, 1966), pp. 19-37.

182. Perkins, *Armilla aurea* (1590), vii (p. 10); cf. idem, *Golden Chaine* (1591), xv (fol. D2r).

183. See the chart in Perkins, *Golden Chaine* (1591), insert before fol. B.1r.

184. William Perkins, *A Christian and Plaine Treatise of the Manner and Order of Predestination, and of the Largenesse of Gods Grace*, in *The Whole Works of ... Mr. William Perkins*, 3 vols. (London: John Legatt, 1631), II, p. 607, col. 1.

to be just, and to be the sonnes of God, are also predestined to beleeve, because Adoption and Righteousness are received by faith."[185] In the execution of the decree, Perkins also distinguishes between the "exhibiting of the Mediator," the "application" of Christ's work, and the "accomplishment of the application," the latter two categories belonging to the chain of causes from Romans 8:29-30:

> The application is, when as Christ is given unto us of God the Father by the Spirit, in the lawfull use of the Word and Sacraments; and is received of us by the instrument of a true faith, And Christ being given, is made unto us of God wisdome, righteousnesse, sanctification and redemption. The accomplishment of the application is Glorification, whereby God shall be all in all by Christ in all the elect.[186]

As will be noted at greater length in the following chapter, such formulations clearly place union with Christ in a foundational relationship to other aspects of the ordering of salvation without, as has sometimes been alleged, implying a rigid temporal order.[187]

The full doctrinal or dogmatic impact in the early orthodox era of the use of the golden chain of Romans 8:28-30 as a basis for ordering the work of salvation is evident as early as 1602 in Gulielmus Bucanus' *Institutiones theologicae, seu locorum communium Christianae religionis* (1602).[188] After his brief introduction to the terminology of the doctrine of the divine decrees—providence, purpose, prescience, predestination, election, reprobation, "book of life," counsel, decree, good pleasure, knowledge (*notitia* or *scientia*), and determination, Bucanus notes the issue of divine simplicity and then posits that in the order of nature (*ordine naturae*) and with respect to human beings (*nostri respectu*) there is an order to be observed.[189]

The question must be dealt with very carefully, he indicates, given that the various distinctions made by the terms cannot be taken to imply divisions within the one, simple essence of God, to whom all things are always present—yet, there is an order and series (*ordo & series*) of the terms used to define the divine decree and it is proper to distinguish "degrees" (*gradus*) or "parts" (*partes*) of the decree.[190] Bucanus' language clearly reflects the Reformed exegetical tradition on Romans 8:28-30 but significantly also folds in citations of Ephesians 1, the other primary

---

185. Perkins, *Manner and Order*, p. 607, col. 2.

186. Perkins, *Manner and Order*, p. 610, col. 1.

187. Contra, e.g., Canlis, "Calvin, Osiander, and Participation in God," pp. 169-184.

188. Gulielmus Bucanus, *Institutiones theologicae, seu locorum communium Christianae religionis, ex Dei verbo, et praestantissimorum theologorum orthodoxo consensu expositorum* (Geneva: Ioannes Le Preux, 1602; Bern: Iohannes & Isaias Le Preux, 1605; Geneva: Jacob Stoer, 1625; Geneva: Samuel Chouet, 1658); in translation: *Institutions of the Christian Religion, framed out of God's Word*, trans. R. Hill (London, 1606; London: for Daniel Pakeman, 1659).

189. Bucanus, *Institutiones* (1605), xxxvi.3 (p. 419), *Institutions*, xxxvi (p. 450). Bucanus, it should be noted, appears to hold a rather Ockhamist notion of simplicity, according to which the attributes are distinguished only *ad extra* in their operation; see *PRRD*, III, pp. 289-290.

190. Bucanus, *Institutiones* (1605), xxxvi.3, 7 (pp. 419-421); *Institutions*, xxxvi (pp. 450-451).

source of causal argumentation concerning election. In the form given by Bucanus, the order proceeds as follows:

[1.] ... knowledge [*notitia*], or πρόγνωσις, the general foreknowledge of God.

2. Πρόθεσις, or the purpose [*propositum*] of God, which is also called βουλή, or his counsel and decree [*consilium & decretum*], Acts 2:23 and Eph.1:11.

3. Προορισμῶς, Predestination [*praedestinatio*], Rom. 8:28, 29.

4. Election [*electio*], the order given in Eph. 1:4, 5, *He elected us in Christ*, after which he predestined: Reprobation stands over against Election.

5. Effectual calling in time [*efficax vocatio in tempore*], which is subordinate to Election from eternity; and a casting away in time, which is subordinate to reprobation, as in Rom. 11:1, *Has God therefore cast away his people*.

6. Vocation is followed by Justification.

7. Justification by Glorification, *Rom.* 8:30, as casting off [*abiectio*] if followed by impenitence or hardening [*induratio*], hardening by condemnation [*condemnatio*].[191]

This ordering, resting largely on Romans 8:28-30, is identified quite consistently as the "golden chain" or "chain of salvation" by numerous Reformed writers, most notably Rennecherus, Perkins, and Maxey, whose works of that title are, in effect, large-scale workings out of the implications of the passage. It is, moreover, one more instance of the importance of seeking continuities and commonplaces in the exegetical tradition; the doctrinal works using the term offer, in fact, a reflection on the exegetical tradition and the considerable number of commentaries that reference the text in this manner.[192] The identification of the golden chain raises explicitly, also, the issue of the means of the execution of the decree, and of the relationship and inseparability of the ends and means:

this is the true golden chain of salvation [*salutis catena vere aurea*], and the indissoluble connection [*nexus insolubilis*], that leads from the highest cause through ordained and applied means to the final effect. Therefore, that end cannot be hoped

---

191. Bucanus, *Institutiones* (1605), xxxvi.3 (p. 419); cf. idem, *Institutions*, xxxvi (p. 450).

192. Cf. Vermigli, *In epistolam ad Romanos*, p. 539 (*Commentaries*, fol. 228v); Robert Rollock, *Analysis dialectica ... in Pauli Apostoli Epistolam ad Romanos* (Edinburgh: Robert Waldegrave, 1593), Rom. 8:29-30, in loc. (p. 138); Bucanus, *Institutions*, xxxvi (p. 462); William Cowper, *Heaven Opened* (London: Thomas Snodham, 1619), pp. 361-370; Elanthan Parr, *A Plaine Exposition upon the 8. 9. 10. 11. Chapters of the Epistle of Saint Paul to the Romans* (London: George Purstowe, 1618), Rom. 8:30, in loc. (p. 116); Thomas Wilson, *A Commentary on the Most Divine Epistle of St. Paul to the Romans* (London, 1627), Rom. 8:30, in loc. (p. 320); *English Annotations* (1645), Rom. 8:29, in loc.; Matthew Poole, *Annotations on the Holy Bible* 2 vols. (London, 1683-1685), Rom. 8:30, in loc.; David Dickson, *Truths Victory over Error. Or, an Abridgement of the Chief Controversies in Religion ... between those of the Orthodox Faith, and all Adversaries whatsoever*. (Edinburgh: John Reid, 1684), iii.4 (p. 36); Matthew Henry, *An Exposition of the Old and New Testament: wherein each chapter is summed up in its contents: the sacred text inserted at large, in distinct paragraphs; each paragraph reduced to its proper heads: the sense given, and largely illustrated; with practical remarks and observations*. 6th ed. 6 vols. (London: for J. Clark, 1725), Rom. 8:29, in loc.

for without the means to the end, nor can the end to be separated from the means, nor, omitting the means, can the one ultimate be reached from the other.[193]

Anthony Maxey's *Goulden Chaine of Mans Saluation, and the fearefull point of Hardening* (1606), is a compilation of two sermons, the first on Romans 8:30 and the second on Exodus 10:20, preached in 1604 and 1605, when Maxey was chaplain to King James.[194] It offers a significant example of the acceptance of the language of the "golden chain" as a theological commonplace as well as an element of exegetical argumentation. Maxey begins by noting that all Scripture is inspired of God and profitable for instruction, but this particular text, "of all others … is most divine, most excellent."[195] Every text of Scripture is "rich in sense, and full of divine and holy misteries," but Romans 8:30 is especially rich and full inasmuch as "it containeth the whole summe of our religion; for the manner, it consisteth of a sweet gradation; for the matter, it is full of comfortable instruction; for the depth of the understanding, it hath in it, such sweet profound, and heavenly misteries."[196]

The doctrine taught in the text concerns salvation, and especially the assurance of eternal life. Maxey notes that if a person could be certain in his heart that he had been chosen by God to eternal life, he would be "the most happie and blessed creature alive."[197] And if there is one place in Scripture that provides the basis for this assurance, it is Romans 8:30, the text identified, Maxey indicates, by the "auncient Fathers" as "the Golden Chaine of our Salvation"—specifically as a gradation in which "*Predestination, Calling, Iustification* and *Glorifying*, are so coupled and knit together, that if you hold fast one linke, you draw unto you the whole Chaine: if you let goe one, you loose all."[198]

The "high point" of the chain, predestination, Maxey warns, is a deep mystery that must be addressed with humility, "plainely, and with … moderation," lest one give "offence" to one's hearers.[199] The key to achieving this proper address to the doctrine, he implies, is to identify clearly the purpose of the apostle in raising the topic—and that is clear from the chapter as a whole, namely, to teach the Roman congregation that their misery and affliction under persecution could in no way set aside their salvation, given that salvation "stood sure and most certaine … upon the unfallible purpose of God, which here is called *Predestination*."[200]

---

193. Bucanus, *Institutiones*, xxxvi.31 (p. 431); *Institutions*, xxxvi (p. 462).

194. Anthony Maxey, *A copie of the sermon preached before the King at White-hall on Tuesday the eight of Ianuarie, 1604* (London: Humphrey Lownes, 1605); and idem, *An other sermon preached before the King at Greenwich on Tuesday before Easter, being the 26. of March. 1605* (London: George and Lionell Snowdon, 1605).

195. Maxey, *Goulden Chaine*, fol. Aii recto.

196. Maxey, *Goulden Chaine*, fol. Aii recto.

197. Maxey, *Goulden Chaine*, fol. Aii verso.

198. Maxey, *Goulden Chaine*, fol. Aii verso-Aiii recto.

199. Maxey, *Goulden Chaine*, fol. Aiii recto.

200. Maxey, *Goulden Chaine*, fol. Aiii recto-Aiii verso.

Conclusions

Examination of Reformed understandings of Romans 8:28-30 as constructed in the form of logical argument and, accordingly, as referencing a chain or series of degrees or gradations belonging to the divine plan of salvation, particularly when taken together with other explanations of the causality of salvation, several of them also exegetically derived, provides insight into the development of what is commonly called the *ordo salutis* in Reformed theology. Absence of the actual technical term *ordo salutis*, or "order of salvation," among the Reformed until long after the era of orthodoxy, coupled with the actual usage of such exegetically derived terms as *catena aurea* or *armilla aurea*, also serves to underline the source and the trajectory of Reformed thought on the ordering of the aspects or phases of salvation as primarily a matter of exegetical and interpretive conversation leading toward the formulation of a theological *locus*. What also should be clear is that the various early orthodox writers to appealed to the golden chain as the basis for their ordering of salvation retained its basic form as taken from Romans 8:28-30 and did not develop what could be called a "rigid" ordering based either on the insertion of other terms like "adoption" and "sanctification" into a strictly defined *ordo* or on the assignment of a strictly argued temporal or logical sequence to the terms. This latter point will become still clearer after examination of the relationship of the early Reformed discussion of union with Christ in relation to the other aspects of the work of salvation.

7

Union with Christ and the *Ordo Salutis*:
Reflections on Developments
in Early Modern Reformed Thought

There has been, since the rise of a body of neo-orthodox studies of Calvin's thought, an increasing interest in the Reformer's understanding of union with Christ.[1] Several recent studies have argued a major contrast between Calvin's

---

1. Edward Dowey, *The Knowledge of God in Calvin's Theology* (New York: Columbia University Press, 1952; 3rd ed. Grand Rapids: Eerdmans, 1994), pp. 197-204; Wilhelm Niesel, *The Theology of Calvin*, trans. Harold Knight (London: Lutterworth, 1956), pp. 120-126; Ronald S. Wallace, *Calvin's Doctrine of the Word and Sacrament* (Grand Rapids: Eerdmans, 1957), pp. 143-174; more recently, Charles Partee, "Calvin's Central Dogma Again," *Sixteenth Century Journal*, 18/2 (1987), pp. 191-200; idem, *The Theology of John Calvin* (Louisville: Westminster/John Knox, 2008); Dennis E. Tamburello, *Union with Christ: John Calvin and the Mysticism of St. Bernard* (Louisville: Westminster John Knox, 1994); Jae Sung Kim, "*Unio cum Christi*: The Work of the Holy Spirit in Calvin's Theology" (Ph.D. diss., Westminster Theological Seminary, 1998); Craig B. Carpenter, "A Question of Union with Christ? Calvin and Trent on Justification," *Westminster Theological Journal*, 64 (2002), pp. 363-386; Julie Canlis, "Calvin, Osiander, and Participation in God," *International Journal of Systematic Theology*, 6/2 (2004), pp. 169-184; Mark A. Garcia, "Imputation and Union with Christ: Calvin, Osiander, and the Contemporary Quest for a Reformed Model," *Westminster Theological Journal*, 68 (2006), pp. 219-251; idem, *Life in Christ: Union with Christ and Twofold Grace in Calvin's Theology* (Milton Keynes: Paternoster, 2008); idem, "Imputation as Attribution: Union with Christ, Reification and Justification as Declarative Word," *International Journal of Systematic Theology*, 11/4 (2009), pp. 412-427; Thomas L. Wenger, "The New Perspective on Calvin: Responding to Recent Calvin Interpretations," *Journal of the Evangelical Theological Society*, 50/2 (2007), pp. 311-328; idem, "Theological Spectacles and a Paradigm of Centrality: A Reply to Marcus Johnson," *Journal of the Evangelical Theological Society*, 51/3 (2008), pp. 559-572; J. Todd Billings, *Calvin, Participation, and the Gift: The Activity of Believers in Union with Christ* (Oxford: Oxford University Press, 2007); idem, "United to God through Christ: Assessing Calvin on the Question of Deification," *Harvard Theological Review*, 98/3 (2005), pp. 315-334; idem, "John Calvin's Soteriology: On the Multifaceted 'Sum' of the Gospel," *International Journal of Systematic Theology*, 11/4 (2009), pp. 428-447; W. Duncan Rankin, "Calvin's Correspondence on Our Threefold Union with Christ," in *The Hope Fulfilled: Essays in Honor of O. Palmer Robertson*, ed. Robert J. Penny (Phillipsburg: Presbyterian and

approach to union with Christ and later Reformed theological formulations of an *ordo salutis*.[2] Specifically, it has been claimed that Calvin emphasized union with Christ and (without referencing any documents of the era) that later Reformed writers did not, indeed, that they "traded union for a chronological *ordo salutis*, making union dependent upon prior 'steps' in the soteriological process."[3]

The underlying problem of much of the literature on the subject (one might even call it a cottage industry) is the rather massive, highly theologistic, and ahistorical attention given to Calvin's understanding of the *unio* in isolation from the thought

---

Reformed, 2008), pp. 232-250; Randall Zachman, "Communio cum Christo," in *The Calvin Handbook*, ed. Herman Selderhuis (Grand Rapids: Eerdmans, 2008), pp. 365-371; Christian Adjemian, "L'union en Christ chez Calvin," in *L'actualité de Jean Calvin* (Lausanne: L'Age d'Homme, 2008), pp. 177-200; Richard B. Gaffin, "Justification and Union with Christ," in *A Theological Guide to Calvin's Institutes: Essays and Analysis*, ed. David W. Hall and Peter A. Lillback (Phillipsburg: Presbyterian and Reformed Publications, 2008), pp. 248-269; idem, "Calvin's Soteriology: The Structure of the Application of Redemption in Book Three of the *Institutes*," and idem, "A Response to John Fesko's Review," *Ordained Servant*, 18 (2009), pp. 68-77, and 104-113; Marcus Johnson, "New or Nuanced Perspective on Calvin? A Reply to Thomas Wenger," *Journal of the Evangelical Theological Society*, 51/3 (2008), pp. 543-558; John V. Fesko, "A Tale of Two Calvins: A Review Article," *Ordained Servant*, 18 (2009), pp. 98-104; Cornelis P. Venema, "Union with Christ, the 'Twofold Grace of God,' and the 'Order of Salvation' in Calvin's Theology," in *Calvin for Today*, ed. Joel R. Beeke (Grand Rapids: Reformation Heritage, 2009), pp. 91-113; and Paul Wells, "Calvin and Union with Christ: The Heart of Christian Doctrine," in *Calvin: Theologian and Reformer*, ed. Joel R. Beeke and Garry J. Wells (Grand Rapids: Reformation Heritage, 2010), pp. 65-88.

2. Cf. Gaffin, "Response to John Fesko's Review," pp. 105, 106.

3. Canlis, "Calvin, Osiander, and Participation," pp. 172-173; and Partee, *Theology of John Calvin*, pp. 3, 4, 25, 27; in neither of these works is there any significant examination of the later Reformed tradition despite statements about its doctrinal tendencies. William B. Evans, *Imputation and Impartation: Union with Christ in American Reformed Theology* (Carlisle: Paternoster, 2008); and idem, "Déja vu All Over Again? The Contemporary Reformed Soteriological Controversy in Historical Perspective," *Westminster Theological Journal*, 72 (2010), pp. 135-151, offer some examination of developments in seventeenth- and early eighteenth-century Reformed theology, notably, attempts to relate justification and sanctification more clearly to union with Christ in terms of legal and spiritual relationships (Evans, *Imputation and Impartation*, pp. 68-69). Nonetheless, he makes too neat a distinction between early Reformed views on union with Christ and what he takes to be the concerns of later thinkers over an *ordo salutis*, he assumes too quickly that distinction in modes of union was new to the seventeenth century and implied a separation of modes, and his analysis of Reformed orthodoxy is sketchy and excessively dependent on secondary sources. Evans' conclusions concerning the primary emphasis on a legal union with Christ found in a few late seventeenth- and some eighteenth-century Scottish theologians should not, moreover, be seen as a necessary or inevitable outgrowth of the main lines of Reformed orthodox development, nor should it be read through the dogmatic lens of Scottish Barthianism and detached from its background in the standard Reformed distinction between the results of union with Christ in justification and sanctification, a distinction also present in the thought of Calvin and his contemporaries. Note the critique of Evans' arguments in John V. Fesko, "Methodology, Myth, and Misperception: A Response to William B. Evans," in *Westminster Theological Journal*, 72 (210), pp. 391-402; and Evans' response, "Of Trajectories, Repristinations, and the Meaningful Engagement of Texts: A Reply to J. V. Fesko," in ibid., pp. 403-414.

of other Reformers and of later Reformed theologians—in contrast to the near absence of attention paid to the doctrine as it was taught by other Reformed thinkers in the late sixteenth and seventeenth centuries. The few current studies that do exist of later Reformed thought on union with Christ arguably indicate, contrary to the assertions found in studies of Calvin by Canlis and Partee, an increased rather than a decreased interest in the subject, particularly in relation to Reformed piety or spirituality,[4] as well as in connection with Reformed, eucharistic thought. Two studies have argued the importance of the *unio* in the thought of Zanchius,[5] and a series of essays by John Fesko has begun to broach the issue of the relationship of union with Christ to justification and to the development of a Reformed *ordo salutis*, contesting the claim that the doctrine of union with Christ and the concept of a order of salvation were opposed to each other.[6]

This essay will argue, along lines similar to those outlined by Farthing and Fesko and contrary to the implications and claims of other recent studies, that Calvin was hardly an isolated figure in the early development of Reformed thought on union with Christ and that the Reformation-era connection of the doctrine of union with Christ with the earliest forms of what has come to be called the *ordo salutis* was an exegetical conclusion that did not disappear from Reformed approaches to the application of salvation in the era of orthodoxy, only to be replaced by a rigid chronological ordering of the stages of redemption, but was in fact incorporated carefully into Reformed orthodox language of the application of salvation. The equally prominent use among the Reformed orthodox of the language of *unio* in connection with the doctrine and piety of the Lord's Supper will be left to another essay.[7] As Heinrich Heppe commented more than a century ago, "the entire doctrine

---

4. See R. Tudur Jones, "Union With Christ: The Existential Nerve of Puritan Piety," *Tyndale Bulletin*, 41/2 (1990), pp. 186-208; Kelly M. Kapic, *Communion with God: The Divine and Human in the Theology of John Owen* (Grand Rapids: Baker, 2007); Stephen J. Yuille, *The Inner Sanctum of Puritan Piety: John Flavels' Doctrine of Mystical Union with Christ* (Grand Rapids: Reformation Heritage, 2007).

5. John L. Farthing, "*De coniugio spirituali*: Jerome Zanchi on Ephesians 5:22-23," *Sixteenth Century Journal*, 24/3, (1993), pp. 621-652; cf. the similar conclusions in John V. Fesko, "Jerome Zanchi on Union with Christ and Justification," *Puritan and Reformed Theological Journal*, 2/2 (2010), pp. 55-78.

6. John V. Fesko, "Heinrich Bullinger on Union with Christ and Justification," *Confessional Presbyterian*, 6 (2010), pp. 3-10; idem, "Peter Martyr Vermigli on Union with Christ and Justification," *Reformed Theological Review*, 70 (2011), pp. 37-57; idem, "William Perkins on Union with Christ and Justification," *Mid-America Journal of Theology*, 21 (2010), pp. 21-34.

7. But note, e.g., the arguments in Zacharias Ursinus, *Explicationum catecheticarum* (Cambridge: Thomas Thomas, 1587), pp. 588-589, 619-620, 650; Amandus Polanus von Polansdorf, *Syntagma theologiae christianae* (Hanau: Wechel, 1615), VI.lvi (pp. 500, 502); Sibrandus Lubbertus, *Commentarius in catechesin Palatino-Belgicam* (Franecker: Ioannes Lamrink, 1618), pp. 558-561; Heinrich Alting, *Theologia elenctica nova: sive systema elencticum* (Amsterdam: Joannes Jansson, 1654), p. 613; Franz Burman, *Synopsis theologiae*, VII.xii (II, pp. 383-390); Francis Turretin, *Institutio theologiae elencticae, in qua status controversiae perspicue exponitur, praecipua orthodoxorum argumenta*

of the appropriation of salvation rests upon the *insitio* or *insertio in Christum*," and therefore, the older Reformed dogmaticians "discuss it with special emphasis."[8]

Foundational Formulations of the *Unio cum Christo*

Calvin on union with Christ and the application of salvation. Calvin's understanding of union with Christ, as accomplished by the work of the Spirit through faith, was foundational to his soteriological expression from the time of the second edition of his *Institutes* and the initial publication of his Romans commentary.[9] Given, moreover, the significant interconnection between Calvin's work on the Romans commentary and the 1539 revisions of the *Institutes*,[10] the appearance of the doctrine in both places and, indeed, the role of the *unio* in the argumentative structure of Romans 8 and of the revised *Institutes*, identify both an initial exegetical background to Calvin's doctrine and illustrate the way in which Calvin's process of theological formulation (like that of his contemporaries) moved from the study of a biblical *locus* or *topos* to doctrinal discourse in the form of *loci communes* or *disputationes*.[11] There is also, it needs to be observed, a distinct interest in the ordering of salvation in terms of the relationship of election to faith, faith to justification and sanctification, repentance and regeneration, in Calvin's earliest writings, notably in his catechisms of 1537-1538.[12]

The doctrine of union with Christ continued to play a key role in Calvin's thought, as seen in the argumentative structure of book III of the 1559 *Institutes*,

---

proponuntur, & vindicantur, & fontes solutionum aperiuntur, 3 vols. (Geneva: Samuel de Tournes, 1679-1685), XIX.i.15; iv.4, 11. Note also that this aspect of the Reformed understanding of *unio cum Christo* has a significant medieval background; e.g., Thomas Aquinas, *Summa theologiae*, IIIa, q. 73, a. 3, ad obj. 3; Thomas à Kempis, *Of the Imitation of Christ*, with an introductory essay on the authorship of the work (London: Suttary, 1883), IV.ii.6; iv.2.

8. Heinrich Heppe, *Die Dogmatik der evangelisch-reformierten Kirche*, neu durchgesehen und herausgegeben von Ernst Bizer (Neukirchen: Moers, 1935), p. 412; in translation, *Reformed Dogmatics Set Out and Illustrated from the Sources*, foreword by Karl Barth; revised and ed. by Ernst Bizer; trans. G. T. Thomson (London: George Allen & Unwin, 1950; repr., Grand Rapids: Baker Book House, 1978), p. 511; cf. idem, *Die Dogmatik des deutschen Protestantismus im sechzehnten Jahrhundert*, 3 vols. (Gotha: Perthes, 1857), II, pp. 312-315.

9. As noted by Garcia, there is a hint of the doctrine in the 1536 *Institutes* as well, referencing 1 Cor. 1:30 and various texts from Romans: cf. John Calvin *Christianae religionis institutio, totam fere pietatis summam, et quicquid est in doctrina salutis cognitu necessarium, complectens: omnibus pietatis studiosis lectu dignissimum opus, ac recens editum* (Basel: Platter & Lasius, 1536), i (pp. 86-87); with Garcia, "Imputation and Union," p. 231.

10. See Richard A. Muller, *The Unaccommodated Calvin: Studies in the Formation of a Theological Tradition* (New York: Oxford University Press, 2000), pp. 28-30, 128-130, 135-136.

11. Cf. the discussion of the Romans commentary and the *Institutes* in Garcia, *Life in Christ*, pp. 89-114.

12. Cf. John Calvin, *Le Catéchisme français de Calvin, publiée en 1537, reimprimé pour la première fois*, avec deux notices par Albert Rilliet & Théophile Dufour (Geneva: H. Georg, 1878), pp. 32-44; with idem, *Catechismus, sive christianae religionis institutio* (Basel: n.p., 1538), xiii-xviii (pp. 15-22).

developed in light of his christological debate with Osiander,[13] although the debate involved editorial additions to the original 1539 doctrinal statement and little in the way of new doctrinal content. Union with Christ also figures in Calvin's discussions of the work of salvation throughout his commentaries and sermons. To claim that the doctrine is the central motif or "viewpoint" accounting for the structure of the entire 1559 *Institutes* and serving as a "comprehensive way of introducing and surveying Calvin's theology" would be, of course, absurd and a serious distortion of Calvin's patterns of exposition and argumentation[14]—to place it, however, not in isolation, but together with the work of the Holy Spirit, as foundational to Calvin's understanding of "the manner of receiving the grace of Christ,"[15] is crucial to a reading of Calvin's approach to the ordering of the several aspects or elements of the work of salvation.

The framework for Calvin's understanding of this complex of issues is clearly attested both in the Romans commentary, where Calvin (like various of his Reformed contemporaries) understands Romans 8:1ff. as an important *locus* for the doctrine of union and communion with Christ,[16] and in all of the editions of his *Institutes* from 1539 onward. In his commentary on Romans 8, at verse 4, Calvin commented in the 1540 edition that we receive Christ's benefits "when we have been received into participation in Christ [*in Christi consortium*]." The additional Pauline phrase "not according to the flesh" indicates both that this is a "perpetual association" and that "when we are conjoined to Christ" the effect is a "spiritual

13. Cf. François Wendel, *Calvin: The Origins and Development of His Religious Thought*, trans. Philip Mairet (New York: Harper & Row, 1963), pp. 234-240.

14. Contra Partee, *Theology of John Calvin*, pp. 40-43; and idem, "Calvin's Central Dogma Again," pp. 192, 194, especially note 11, 196-199.

15. John Calvin, *Institutio christianae religionis, in libros quatuor nunc primum digesta, certisque distincta capitibus, ad aptissimam methodum: aucta etiam tam magna accessione ut propemodum opus novum haberi possit* (Geneva: Robertus Stephanus, 1559), the title to book III. English citations follow John Calvin, *Institutes of the Christian Religion*, trans. John Allen, 3 vols. (Philadelphia: Philip Nicklin, 1816), emending the translation as necessary from the Latin; on the issue of the centrality of the theme of union, see Billings, *Calvin, Participation and the Gift*, pp. 18-19; Gaffin, "Calvin's Soteriology," pp. 70-71; and Wendel, *Calvin*, pp. 235, 238-239.

16. Romans 8 is, of course, not the only biblical text associated with the doctrine of union with Christ and is emphasized here and in the following discussion simply as one of several important *loci* for the doctrine, of particular importance to the relationship of union with Christ to the ordering of aspects of the work of salvation (cf. Billings, *Calvin, Participation and the Gift*, p. 51), given the linkage established by the chapter itself between faith, union, and the work of the Spirit, on the one hand, and the sequence of predestination, calling, justification, and glorification, on the other; note also Calvin's argument in John Calvin, *Commentarii in priorem epistolam Pauli ad Corinthios* (Strasbourg: Wendelin Rihel, 1546), 1 Cor. 30; also in *Opera quae supersunt omnia*, ed. Baum, Cunitz and Reuss, 59 vols. (Brunswick: Schwetschke, 1863-1900), 49, col. 330-332; hereinafter, *CO*; following, with emendation, John Calvin, *Commentary on the Epistles of Paul the Apostle to the Corinthians*, trans. John Pringle, 2 vols. (1848; repr., Grand Rapids: Baker, 1979), hereinafter *CTS Corinthians*; cf. the analysis in Garcia, "Imputation and Union," pp. 233-234.

life."[17] In the final edition of 1556, the altered text reads, "Christ communicates his righteousness to none but to those whom he joins to himself by the bond of his Spirit, regeneration [*regeneratio*] is again mentioned, so that Christ should not be understood as the minister of sin."[18] The theme continues in the comment on verse 5, "the grace of Christ belongs to none but to those who, having been regenerated by the Spirit [*spiritu regenerati*], strive after purity [*innocentiae*]."[19] Here again, union with Christ has priority over justification and regeneration, and the striving after purity follows on regeneration. Calvin concludes his point at verse 6, returning to the utter graciousness of salvation: "Those who attribute salvation to works are deceived. Since although God begins our salvation, and at length completes it by renewing us after his own image, the only cause is his good pleasure, by which he makes us partakers of Christ."[20]

With the *unio cum Christo* in mind, Calvin considers the Pauline sequence of predestination, calling, justification, and glorification at the close of the same chapter, identifying the series but without elaboration beyond the actual language of verses 28-30, although he does not here draw out connections between the sequence of terms following predestination and his earlier comments about the *unio*, regeneration, and striving after purity.[21] Calvin does not, therefore, take opportunity in his commentary to develop the relationship between union with Christ and what he identifies as the sequence or gradation (*gradatio*) of salvation in Romans 8:28-30. What remains clear, however, is that both of these aspects of the later Reformed approach to the administration or application of salvation are present in Calvin.[22]

This development does, however, occur in the *Institutes*, where Calvin had, from 1539 onward, integrated elements of the argumentative ordering of the Epistle to the Romans into the original catechetical structure of the *Institutes*.[23] The path or *methodus* of book III of the *Institutes* moves from the themes of union with Christ as accomplished in the work of the Spirit, by way of reference to faith, regeneration, and justification, to a meditation on the Christian life emphasizing self-denial and the future life, and after that to election—all key elements of the Pauline line of argument in Romans 8. And if Calvin's argument has moved not from predestination

---

17. John Calvin, *Commentarii in epistolam Pauli ad Romanos* (Strasbourg: Wendelin Rihel, 1540), Rom. 8:4 (p. 201).

18. Calvin, *In epistolam Pauli ad Romanos* (1556), in CO 49, col. 140, 141; following, with emendation, *Commentaries on the Epistle of Paul the Apostle to the Romans*, trans. John Owen (1849; repr., Grand Rapids: Baker, 1979), p. 283, hereinafter, CTS *Romans*.

19. Calvin, *In epistolam Pauli ad Romanos* (1540), Rom. 8:5 (p. 202).

20. Calvin, *In epistolam ad Romanos* (1556), in CO 49, col. 142 (CTS *Romans*, p. 286); cf. the briefer statement in *In Epistolam Pauli ad Romanos* (1540), Rom. 8:6 (p. 203).

21. Calvin, *In epistolam ad Romanos* (1556), in CO 49, col. 158-161 (CTS *Romans*, pp. 314-320).

22. Calvin, *In epistolam Pauli ad Romanos* (1556), in CO 49, col. 160 (CTS *Romans*, pp. 319, 320); missed by Evans, *Imputation and Impartation*, pp. 7-41, who nonetheless notes the incompleteness or ambiguity of aspects of Calvin's formulation.

23. Cf. Muller, *Unaccommodated Calvin*, pp. 119-130.

to calling and justification, but from justification to predestination, partially reversing the order of Romans 8:30, it has followed the broader outline of the chapter and, in addition, affirmed the generally *a posteriori* or analytical approach of the epistle as a whole.[24] It is utterly unwarranted, moreover, to conclude from the pedagogical arrangement of the *Institutes* that Calvin "deliberately subverts any chronological" or other ordering of salvation "by not only putting sanctification first, followed by justification, but by placing predestination last" on the ground that these "are all graces that flow from union with Christ."[25] There are numerous places, including his argumentation in the *Institutes*, in which Calvin clearly identifies a sequence and, in addition, related union with Christ to that sequence.

At the outset of book III of the 1559 *Institutes*, Calvin indicates that "as long as there is a separation between Christ and us, all that he performed for the salvation of humanity is useless ... he must therefore become ours, and dwell within us ... the Holy Spirit is the bond by which Christ efficaciously unites himself to us."[26] This is a theme that had been clearly present in the *Institutes* since the 1539 edition; there, at the outset of chapter 6, on justification, faith, and good works, Calvin begins by referencing the gracious gift of Christ, argues a twofold work of grace first in justification and then regeneration, and indicates the priority (albeit not necessarily in a temporal sense) of faith to justification and of justification to sanctification:

> Christ, being given to us by the kindness of God [*Dei benignitate*], to be apprehended and possessed by us by faith, we especially receive a twofold grace [*duplicem gratiam*] by participation in him; certainly [*nempe*], being by his innocence reconciled to God [*Deo reconciliati*], we have in heaven a propitious Father instead of a judge; and then [*deinde*], being sanctified by his Spirit [*Spiritu sanctificati*], we devote ourselves to innocence and purity of life. I have already said what I thought was sufficient concerning regeneration [*regeneratione*], which is the second grace [*secunda est gratia*]. The method of justification [*iustificaitonis ratio*] has been only briefly examined, because it was necessary, first to understand that the faith, by which alone we obtain a gratuitous righteousness through divine mercy [*qua sola gratuitam iustitiam, Dei misericordia obtinemus*], is not unattended with good works. ... That [i.e., justification], therefore, must now be fully discussed, and discussed with the recollection that it is the principle hinge by which religion is supported.[27]

---

24. Cf. Muller, *Unaccommodated Calvin*, pp. 135-136.

25. Canlis, "Calvin, Osiander and Participation," p. 173.

26. Calvin, *Institutio* (1559), III.i.1; cf. the argumentation in Hans Boersma, "Calvin and the Extent of the Atonement," *Evangelical Quarterly*, 64 (1992), pp. 339-343.

27. John Calvin, *Institutio christianae religionis, nunc demum suo titulo respondens* (Strasbourg: Wendelin Rihel, 1539), vi (p. 186); paragraph taken over virtually unchanged in *Institutio christianae religionis* (1559), III.xi.1. There has been a lengthy debate in the secondary scholarship on the question of the relationship of justification and regeneration in Calvin's thought, with specific reference to the imputation of Christ's righteousness and the question of whether justification is entirely forensic or represents also a renewal of the person. Evans, *Imputation and Impartation*, pp. 8-14, offers a good survey and analysis of the scholarship. Although this particular debate is beyond the

Faith stands first in the order of Calvin's argument, inasmuch as Christ is apprehended by faith and it is union with Christ that is the basis of the twofold grace.[28] There is, perhaps, a certain lack of clarity in the passage, given that Calvin does not specifically identify the first grace: after writing of a *duplex gratia*, he makes no reference to a *prima gratia* and only later specifically states that regeneration is the *secunda gratia*. Nonetheless, the syntax of the rather long first sentence in the passage indicates that the twofold grace is to be identified in the two structurally parallel independent clauses, the first beginning with *nempe* and the second, with *deinde*. Thus, "certainly" (*nempe*), by the first grace, believers are reconciled to God; "and then" or perhaps even "thereafter" (*deinde*) by the second grace, believers are "sanctified by his Spirit."[29] When Calvin then goes on to indicate that he has already written of regeneration, now defining it as the second grace, a question may be raised concerning the identification of sanctification as that second grace—probably to be resolved in Calvin's frequent use of the terms "regeneration" and "sanctification" as virtual synonyms.[30]

Regeneration, which Calvin here identifies as liberation from "the servitude of sin," is so closely linked to repentance that the two terms can be taken to indicate two sides of the same divine work—much as later writers would distinguish but also relate *conversio passiva* and *conversio activa*.[31] Repentance, consisting in mortification

---

scope of the present essay, it needs to be remarked that Calvin wrote at a stage of the development of the doctrine at which the later rather firm distinction between justification and sanctification was only beginning to be established. Thus, Calvin held a forensic understanding of justification, but there also was a forensic aspect in his understanding of regeneration and sanctification, particularly as it related to the issue of good works. Some of the scholarship persists in calling this a "tension" and in viewing the doctrines of union with Christ and justification as somewhat at odds with each other rather than recognizing that forensic justification is conceivable for Calvin only on grounds of communion with Christ by grace through faith, that both justification and sanctification flow from the union, that they are in Calvin's view distinct but never separate, that there remained a fluidity in the development of these doctrines throughout the early modern era, and that much of what has been called a "tension" is actually the result of placing a grid based on modern concerns of system over the thought of Calvin and, for that matter, of other Reformed thinkers of the early modern era. See the discussion in Cornel Venema, *Accepted and Renewed in Christ: The "Twofold Grace of God" and the Interpretation of Calvin's Theology* (Gottingen: Vandenhoeck Ruprecht, 2007), pp. 137-145, 148-149, 268-271; and note Garcia, "Imputation and Union," p. 238.

28. On Calvin's doctrine of the *duplex gratia Dei*, see Venema, *Accepted and Renewed*; cf. Gaffin, "Calvin's Soteriology," p. 71-72; and note Jonathan Rainbow, "Double Grace: John Calvin's View of the Relationship of Justification and Sanctification," *Ex Auditu*, 5 (1989), pp. 99-105; cf. Tamburello, *Union with Christ*, pp. 85-86.

29. Cf. Billings, *Calvin, Participation and the Gift*, pp. 106-107.

30. Cf. Calvin, *In priorem epistolam Pauli ad Corinthios*, 1:2, in *CO*, 49, col. 308 (*CTS 1 Corinthians*, I, p. 52); with the comment in Wendel, *Calvin*, p. 242, note 31.

31. This connection was established very clearly by Calvin already in his early catechism; cf. Calvin, *Catechismus* (1538), xviii (pp. 21-22).

and vivification, is an effect of "participation in Christ."[32] It would appear then, that the second grace, regeneration, follows logically (not temporally) upon the first grace just as participation follows union, much as the grace of justification is identified as a prior *gradus* to the grace that brings forth good works and "after a certain manner [*quodammodo*]" as its cause.[33] Calvin clearly did not view the issue of order as "indifferent theologically."[34]

What Calvin does not indicate is whether this priority of union and justification over regeneration-repentance-sanctification is entirely causal, or also a matter of reason or logic, or a matter of temporal ordering—his use of *deinde* leaves the issue undecided. As noted, however, the grace of justification can be understood, "after a certain manner," as the cause of the grace that yields good works, placing justification prior causally, albeit not necessarily temporally, to sanctification. Calvin's use of *gradus* here is reminiscent of the exegesis of Romans 8:30, with its sequence of calling, justification, and glorification.

Indeed, the issue of temporal ordering only arises when the issues of the priority of faith and the continuance of repentance and sanctification are considered. That there is a priority of some sort, however, and perhaps involving both temporal and logical as well as causal orderings, is clear: faith, bestowed by the Spirit, is the instrument of union and of the first grace, justification; regeneration-sanctification is the second grace; and repentance is effected by the union.[35] Later, when Calvin turns to sanctification as a topic, it clearly belongs to the progress of justification but also follows regeneration, at least in the order of the discussion—and like justification and regeneration is grounded in faith and union with Christ.[36] And although Calvin does later include mortification and vivification as aspects of repentance and Christian life,[37] he does not attempt a formal integration of these or the other terms he has used with the sequence of calling, justification, glorification

---

32. Calvin, *Institutio* (1539), v (p. 160); sentence unchanged in *Institutio* (1559), III.iii.9.

33. Calvin, *Institutio* (1539), vi (p. 205); sentence unchanged in *Institutio* (1559), III.xiv.21, adding the citation of Rom. 8:30 in the margin; contra the reading in Richard B. Gaffin, "Biblical Theology and the Westminster Standards," *Westminster Theological Journal*, 65 (2003), p. 177; Johnson, "New or Nuanced Perspective on Calvin," pp. 551-557; and Garcia, *Life in Christ*, pp. 96-97, where there appears to be no acknowledgment of logical and/or causal priority; cf. idem, "Imputation and Union," pp. 233-234.

34. Thus, Gaffin, "Biblical Theology," p. 177.

35. Cf. Tamburello, *Union with Christ*, p. 86; Fesko, "Tale of Two Calvins," pp. 101-102; Gaffin, "Calvin's Soteriology," p. 73-75; idem, "Response to John Fesko," pp. 107-109; and Garcia, *Life in Christ*, pp. 18, 76, 282-283.

36. Calvin, *Institutio* (1559), III.xiv.1-6, 9; cf. Calvin, *Acts of the Council of Trent with the Antidote*, in *Selected Works*, ed. Henry Beveridge, 7 vols. (Grand Rapids: Baker, 1983), III, p. 128.

37. Calvin, *Institutio* (1559), III.iii.8-9; vii.7; xiv.9.

found in Romans 8:30. Nor does he typically indicate that justification is a cause of sanctification.[38]

There is also the question of the ordering of topics in the argumentative flow of the *Institutes* itself. Specifically, Calvin first discusses union with Christ (*Institutes*, III.i), then faith (III.ii), then regeneration and repentance by or through faith (III.iii), then aspects of the Christian life as repentance and self-denial (III.iv-x), and only then does he come to justification by faith and reconciliation to God (III.xi) and the issue of the twofold grace. In other words, after having moved from faith to regeneration and then to justification, he turns his argument around and identifies justification and reconciliation as the first grace and regeneration-sanctification as the second. A few authors have attempted to argue that Calvin's order either places regeneration and/or sanctification prior to justification in the actual order of salvation or that Calvin simply does not indicate a sequence (thereby indicating a rather marked difference between Calvin and other Reformed writers of the era, who are assumed to argue a strict temporal sequencing of the application of salvation).[39]

Several points can be made at this juncture. First, as will be indicated in subsequent sections of this study, the ordering of the application of the work of Christ in early modern Reformed theologies was neither uniform nor strictly temporal—so that the differences between Calvin's thought and the thought of other Reformed writers will need to be weighed more carefully than has been typical of the scholarship. Second, Calvin's language of the *duplex gratia* does quite clearly indicate a sequencing, albeit not an exclusively temporal one: faith and union with Christ ground the entire sequence and with justification and regeneration-sanctification following not temporally but causally. Justification, moreover, is imputed and forensic; regeneration and sanctification reference the transformation of the believer—with both the imputation and the transformation being grounded in the union.[40] And if Calvin's ordering of the *Institutes*, book III, formally placed his comments concerning union with Christ prior to his discussion of faith, his careful delineation of the *duplex gratia* clearly identified faith as the way in which Christ is apprehended and possessed in union.[41] Third, and more importantly, the apparent conflict between Calvin's identification of an order in which the reconciliation grounded in faith, union, and justification is first and regeneration is second, and the order of argumentation in the *Institutes* probably ought to be interpreted not as a

---

38. Cf. Wendel, *Calvin*, pp. 256-257; Niesel, *Theology of Calvin*, pp. 137-138; but note the statement in Calvin, *Acts of the Council of Trent*, in *Selected Works*, III, p. 128, and Fesko's comment in "Tale of Two Calvins," p. 102.

39. Thus, e.g., Gaffin, "Response to John Fesko," pp. 105, 106; Johnson, "New or Nuanced Perspective on Calvin," pp. 551-557; Canlis, "Calvin, Osiander and Participation," pp. 172-173, 176-177.

40. Note Garcia, "Imputation and Union," pp. 231-236, on the importance of union to Calvin's understanding of imputation.

41. Calvin, *Institutio* (1559), III.xi.1, as cited above.

conflict of understandings of the application of salvation but as a distinction between Calvin's sense of the order of salvation and his assumptions concerning the *ordo recte docendi*, the proper or right order of teaching. The *Institutes*, in other words, does not, whether in its discussion of the application of Christ's work or elsewhere, typically follow the ordering patterns related to causal, logical, or temporal issues often raised in the commentaries; its structuring is largely pedagogical, whether following a catechetical model, or a model grounded in the Epistle to the Romans, or reflecting aspects of Melanchthon's *loci communes*.[42] Thus, the placement of discussion of repentance prior to the discussion of justification is, most likely, a pedagogical choice—as various writers have suggested, made for the sake of deflating Roman arguments concerning the antinomian implications of justification by faith.[43]

This reading of the ordering of the text is supported by Calvin's inclusion of a polemic against confession, satisfactions, indulgences, and purgatory and of a discussion of the Christian life as mortification, vivification, and self-denial with his discussion of regeneration, prior to discussing justification. It is also supported, perhaps even more strongly, by Calvin's insistence that both regeneration and justification are grounded in faith, yielding a structure of argument that begins with union with Christ and faith, indicates that regeneration springs from faith, and then, when it turns to justification also begins justification in faith. Faith and union with Christ come first, yielding both regeneration and reconciliation through justification. This reading of the order of argument is also confirmed by Calvin's comment at the beginning of *Institutes* III.xi.1, "The method of justification has been only briefly examined, because it was necessary, first to understand that the faith, by which alone we obtain a gratuitous righteousness through divine mercy, is not unattended with good works." In other words, Calvin offers parallel strands of argument, having noted justification briefly, moving on to regeneration, and then returning to justification, for a pedagogical purpose—but when the question of which of these graces is prior, justification-reconciliation comes first, regeneration-sanctification comes second, with both being grounded in faith and union with Christ.[44]

Other influences on the early orthodox Reformed development: Viret, Vermigli, and Musculus. Contrary to the impression given by much of the current literature, Calvin was hardly alone among his contemporaries in discussing union with Christ as a significant element of soteriology—and hardly alone as an early formulator of Reformed doctrine on the issue. What we have identified in Calvin,

---

42. On Calvin's interest in establishing the order of teaching, see Muller, *Unaccommodated Calvin*, pp. 92-96, 118-139; and cf. idem, "*Ordo docendi*: Melanchthon and the Organization of Calvin's *Institutes*, 1536-1543," in *Melanchthon in Europe: His Work and Influence beyond Wittenberg*, ed. Karin Maag (Grand Rapids: Baker, 1999), pp. 123-140.

43. Cf. Niesel, *Theology of Calvin*, pp. 130-131.

44. Cf. Wendel, *Calvin*, pp. 255-256; Niesel, *Theology of Calvin*, pp. 130-131; Venema, *Accepted and Renewed in Christ*, pp. 132-145.

moreover, namely, the interconnection of exegesis and doctrinal formulation and specifically of the exegesis of passages relating to union with Christ toward the beginning of Romans 8 with the language of a series or sequence of salvation presented by the apostle toward the end of the chapter, has significant parallels in the work of contemporaries of Calvin like Viret, Vermigli, and Musculus.[45]

Pierre Viret, Calvin's much-neglected colleague,[46] was the author of a significant catechism of the Reformed faith in which he outlined the doctrine of Christ's work and the subsequent order or economy of salvation. After identifying Christ's work as the sole sufficient satisfaction made to the divine judgment against sin, Viret first attacks the "Papist" doctrine of satisfactions made through human works and then indicates that Christ's saving work cannot be sufficient for the individual unless it is presented to the believer and becomes the basis of a "true communication" or communion with Christ in which the believer becomes a "participant" in Christ.[47] Citing a series of texts, including Romans 8, Viret indicates that this communion is attained only through faith in Christ, which is itself a "pure gift" of God through the work of the Holy Spirit in the human heart—proper to God's elect.[48] Viret goes on to define justification and discuss briefly the preached word as the means by which faith arises, regeneration is accomplished by the work of the Spirit, and true service to God is inculcated.[49] Chapters on the law and on good works as the fruit of faith follow.[50] The exposition is quite brief, but it does quite clearly indicate a basic view of the order of salvation as anchored in the work of Christ and union with him.

Peter Martyr Vermigli, for one, discussed the doctrine at some length in his commentary on Romans 8:1ff., beginning at the marginal heading *Quae sit coniunctio quam habemus cum Christo*, and in letters on the subject written to Calvin and Beza.[51] From the perspective of the commentary, the doctrine of union with Christ is far more prominent in Vermigli's analysis than in Calvin's comments on the same text.

---

45. Examination of Bullinger's doctrine of union with Christ yields similar conclusions; see Fesko, "Heinrich Bullinger on Union with Christ and Justification," pp. 3-10.

46. See Michael Bruening, "Pierre Viret and Geneva," *Archiv für Reformationsgeschichte*, 99 (2008), pp. 175-197; also Jean Barnaud, *Pierre Viret: Sa vie et son oeuvre* (Saint-Amans: Carayol, 1911).

47. Pierre Viret, *Instruction chrestienne en la doctrine de la loy et de l'evangile: & et en la vraie philosophie & theologie tant naturelle que supernaturelle des Chrestiens* (Geneva: Jean Rivery, 1563), following the critical edition, ed. Arthur-Louis Hofer (Lausanne: L'Age d'Homme, 2004), c. 20 (p. 119); in translation, *A Christian Instruction, conteyning the law and the Gospell* (London Abraham Veale, 1573), pp. 18-19; cf. idem, *Exposition familiere des principaux poincts du catechisme* (Geneva: Jean Rivery, 1561), pp. 47-48, 59.

48. Viret, *Instruction chrestienne*, c. 21 (p. 120); *Christian Instruction*, p. 19; citing Rom. 3:6; 4:5; Gal. 2; Rom. 8; 1 Cor. 12; Acts 15; and Eph. 2.

49. Viret, *Instruction chrestienne*, c. 22-23 (pp. 120-121); *Christian Instruction*, pp. 20-21.

50. Viret, *Instruction chrestienne*, c. 24-30 (pp. 121-125); *Christian Instruction*, pp. 22-28.

51. See Marvin W. Anderson, "Peter Martyr, Reformed Theologian (1542-1562): His Letters to Heinrich Bullinger and John Calvin," *Sixteenth Century Journal*, 4/1 (1973), p. 58; cf. Fesko, "Peter Martyr Vermigli on Union with Christ and Justification," pp. 38-39, 42-46.

This heading and a portion of the following text, understood as a *locus*, were subsequently excerpted and incorporated into Vermigli's posthumous *Loci communes*—pointing toward a significant influence of Vermigli's thought on the development of the Reformed language of union with Christ.[52]

In his preliminary comments on the chapter prior to approaching the *locus*, Vermigli, quite in accord with Calvin and also with Bullinger, indicates that the Spirit of Christ is the *author* of our delivery from sin and faith is the *instrumentum* by which the Spirit works.[53] This connection between Christ and the Spirit in the work of salvation is evident from the outset of the chapter: "There is therefore now no condemnation to those who are in Christ Jesus, who do not walk according to the flesh, but according to the spirit" (Rom. 8:1). The question arises as to the meaning of being "in Christ." In Vermigli's reading of the passage and in similar argumentation in his letter to Beza on the subject, the phrase has both a general or universal significance and a highly particularized soteriological significance, while the soteriological significance itself can be distinguished into a penultimate and an ultimate sense of union. In the first place, being "in Christ" indicates something universal—inasmuch as Christ, in assuming human nature assumed what is common to all human beings, he is therefore, in a sense, joined to all. This union, however, identifies only the common or universal *materia* of humanity to which Christ is united incarnation, without specifying the vast difference between the human nature of Christ and the nature of human beings. Christ's humanity is immortal, "exempt from sin," and pure; ours is impure, corrupt, and tainted with sin.[54] Calvin, it should be noted, expressed his agreement with Vermigli on this point as well as his general approval of Vermigli's argumentation on the union.[55]

Borrowing on the language often used by Reformed commentators on Romans 8:28-30 and pointing toward later Reformed development of the relationship of

52. Peter Martyr Vermigli, *In epistolam s. Pauli apostoli ad Romanos . . . commentarii* (Zürich: s.n., 1559), pp. 454-477; in translation, *Most learned and fruitfull commentaries upon the Epistle to the Romans* (London, 1568), 8:1-11, in loc. (pp. 193r-202v); the text of the commentary is extracted as a *locus* in *P. M. Vermilii loci communes* (1576; editio secunda, London: Thomas Vautrollerius, 1583), III.iii.36-38 (pp. 501-502); in translation, *The Common Places of Peter Martyr*, trans. Anthony Marten (London: Henrie Denham et al., 1583), III.iii.35-37 (pp. 77-79). Note that the 1560 Basel edition of Vermigli's commentary is much abridged.

53. Vermigli, *In epistolam s. Pauli apostoli ad Romanos*, 8:1 (p. 451); cf. Calvin to Vermigli, 8 August 1555, in CO 15, col. 722-724; Heinrich Bullinger, *In sabctissimam Pavli ad Romanos Epistolam commentarius* (Zürich: Christoph Froschauer, 1533), fol. 101v, where Bullinger indicates, regarding the union that the "Vis Christi agens in nobis"—or at greater length, "Est sutem vivificans illa fidei vis, imo ipse De spiritus, quo donati, scimus quae per Christum nobis donata sint, vita redemptio & sanctificatio." Also see the discussion of Calvin and Vermigli's correspondence on the union in Garcia, *Life in Christ*, pp. 274-283.

54. Vermigli, *In epistolam s. Pauli apostoli ad Romanos*, 8:1 (p. 454); cf. Vermigli to Beza (undated) in *Loci communes* (1583), p. 1108. Note that Evans, *Imputation and Impartation*, pp. 68-69, misses this Reformation-era anticipation of Rutherford's formulation.

55. Calvin to Vermigli, 8 August 1555, in CO 15, col. 722-723.

union with Christ to the golden chain of causes, Vermigli identifies two more understandings of *unio cum Christo*, indicating three *gradus*, or "degrees," in sequence. There is a second and particularized sense of being in Christ, namely, being conjoined with and ingrafted or "inserted" into Christ in redemption; whereas the first *conjunctio* is only that of the natures, this latter is a union (*unio*) and a deep mystery in which believers are joined to Christ as members to the head.[56] This union with Christ, whereby believers are made flesh of his flesh and bone of his bone, is bestowed by the Spirit of Christ, who, as Vermigli has already indicated, works through the instrumentality of faith—by implication, placing justification and the beginning of renovation (*instauratio*), the incomplete sanctification of the present life, in the second *gradus* of union.[57] Here again, Calvin agrees, commenting that this union does not imply (as Osiander had argued) a "mixture" of substances.[58]

There is also a third union, introduced or brought on by the renovation (*instauratio*) of the believer, namely, a final communion in which believers take on the "likeness" (*similitudo*) of Christ—a topic not taken up in Vermigli's *locus* in the Romans commentary, but developed in correspondence with Calvin and Beza, perhaps begun as an expansion of their discussions of the sacraments.[59] Vermigli indicates, therefore, what might be called an ascending series of stages or degrees of union, beginning with the union of Christ with our nature and concluding with the final fullness of union of the redeemed with Christ. Intervening between these is an intermediate (*medius*) "secret" union or "mystery," secret inasmuch as it represents a genuine but not yet visible union of believers with the flesh of Christ that belongs to the imperfect state of those who await the final resurrection and eternal life.[60] Again, Calvin registered his agreement with this point, acknowledging a third stage in the union consisting in the enrichment of life in Christ and the gifts of the Spirit.[61]

Vermigli also, rather obliquely, raises the issue of the order of the various aspects of salvation belonging to the secret or mystical union of believers with Christ: there

---

56. Vermigli, *Loci communes* (1583), p. 1109; note that Vermigli, *In epistolam s. Pauli apostoli ad Romanos*, 8:30 (p. 539), uses *catena* or "chain" to describe the logic of the text; Vermigli's English translator reads *catena* as "gradation"; and cf. the similar emphasis on union with Christ in Vermigli's comment on Rom. 5:16, in ibid., p. 268.

57. Vermigli, *In epistolam s. Pauli apostoli ad Romanos*, 8:1 (pp. 454-455; cf. p. 451); contra Garcia, *Life in Christ*, p. 282, who places justification and sanctification into the third *gradus* of the union; but also disagreeing with Rankin, "Calvin's Correspondence on Our Threefold Union with Christ," p. 246; and Fesko, "Peter Martyr Vermigli on Union with Christ," p. 46, who place justification in the *medius*, or second, *gradus*, and sanctification into the third.

58. Calvin to Vermigli, 8 August 1555, in CO 15, col. 723.

59. See Calvin to Vermigli, 18 January 1555, in CO 15, col. 387, where Calvin in passing notes that in baptism we are "inserted" into Christ's body; Vermigli's response develops the theme of *unio*: see Vermigli to Calvin, 8 March 1555, in Vermilgi, *Loci communes*, pp. 1094-1096 (also in CO 15, col. 492-497.

60. Vermigli, *Loci communes* (1583), p. 1109 (letter to Beza, undated); cf. ibid., p. 1095 (letter to Calvin, 8 March 1555).

61. Calvin to Vermigli, 8 August 1555, in CO 15, col. 723.

is the fundamental or foundational union with Christ accomplished by the work of the Spirit through the instrumentality of faith, and there is also the regeneration of believers as they look toward the perfect renovation of the final spiritual *unio*. Vermigli comments, "this, our communion with the head, at least is prior in nature [*natura*], although perhaps not in time [*tempore*], to that latter communion, which is arises by renewal [*instaurationem inducitur*]."[62] Vermigli's language here reflects the standard scholastic distinction between priority in nature or causality, in reason or logic, and in time—and like Calvin, Vermigli does not establish a clearly temporal *ordo*, but he does assume a priority of faith and the *unio* over regeneration and renovation.[63] The renewal and renovation or sanctification of believers is, of course, a temporal process between faith, regeneration, and justification, on the one hand, and final full renovation or glorification, on the other.

Thus, as his exegesis of Romans 8:1ff. indicates, union with Christ occupied a prior or fundamental place in Vermigli's exposition of the doctrinal topics concerning salvation. Given, moreover, that the union of Christ with believers is accomplished by the Spirit of Christ with the instrumentality of faith, Vermigli by implication identifies the place of the union in the *catena* of Romans 8:30: the church, he comments, is gathered by the foreknowledge, predestination, and calling of God, and justification follows immediately (*statim*) on calling. There is, therefore, nothing that can intervene between calling and justification other than faith—and faith intervenes not as the cause of justification but as the instrument by which we apprehend our calling.[64] This sequence, as in Calvin, is primarily causal, and implications of temporality only arise in terms of the distinctions between Christ's union with our nature, the remaining imperfection of the redeemed in the *unio mystica*, and the perfection of the final *unio*. Calvin's stated agreement with Vermigli on the meaning of union with Christ and its stages also serves to provide a word of caution to those who try to describe the union between Christ and the believer as "ontological" or as evidence of a "relational ontology."[65] The ontological or, in a strict philosophical sense, substantial union, is hypostatic, namely, the union of natures in the person in which Christ, as Mediator, is substantially united with humanity and is, as divine and human, a single subsistent individual. The union with believers is genuine, true, spiritual, and perhaps even "substantial" in Calvin's nonontological eucharistic senses of the term as indicating something fully bestowed

62. Vermigli, *Loci communes* (1583), p. 1095 (letter to Calvin, 8 March 1555).

63. Cf. Anderson, "Peter Martyr," p. 58, noting the agreement between Vermigli and Calvin on this issue.

64. Vermigli, *In epistolam s. Pauli apostoli ad Romanos*, 8:30 (p. 539).

65. Contra Evans, *Imputation and Impartation*, pp. 27-28, 81-83, where Evans appears to assume that ontological union is the only alternative to a purely extrinsic union; also contra E. David Willis, "Calvin's Use of *Substantia*," in *Calvinus Ecclesiae Genevensis Custos*, ed. Wilhelm F. Neuser (New York: Peter Lang, 1984), pp. 289-301; idem, "The Unio Mystica and Assurance of Faith according to Calvin," in *Calvin: Erbe und Auftrag: Festschrift für Wilhelm Heinrich Neuser zum 65. Geburtstag*, ed. Willem van 't Spijker (Kampen: Kok Pharos, 1991), pp. 77-84.

and "nourishing."[66] The basic issue, for both Calvin and Vermigli, is that the personal union of divinity and humanity in Christ provides the foundation for the further, spiritual or mystical union that is best explained in the metaphor of Christ as the head and believers as members of his body. Vermigli's argumentation and Calvin's agreement also undermine the claim that distinctions between different modes of union began with the later orthodox writers. Indeed, the later understanding of the union as federal drew directly on the standard metaphor.[67]

The ground of distinction among the *gradus* of the sequence in Romans 8:30 is also primarily causal, with temporal issues arising between eternal predestination and temporal calling and between justification and final glorification, but not between calling, faith, and justification.[68] The two sequences interrelate or interconnect, moreover, inasmuch as the union with Christ identified in 8:1ff., and described by Vermigli as occurring in two stages, the present secret or mystical, the future spiritual and final, is the foundation of the conformity of believers to Christ—indeed, in Vermigli's understanding of Romans 8:29, the divine foreknowledge of those predestined to be conformed to the image of the Son is a foreknowledge of the divine "favor" and "approbation" of the elect in Christ.[69] What Vermigli does not do, however, is directly correlate his interpretations of union with Christ with his reading of the chain or *gradus* in Romans 8:28-30—a point of argument that will be taken up later in the early orthodox development of the language of the order of the application of Christ's work.

Wolfgang Musculus' soteriological *loci* present a similar view of the *unio*, albeit with far less elaboration. Inasmuch as his primary focus on the language of union, communion, and participation in Christ is focused on the Lord's Supper,[70] Musculus' *Loci communes* do not offer any lengthy comments on union with Christ in relation to the application of salvation. Nevertheless, the doctrine is present and occupies a foundational place in relation to the economy of salvation. As Musculus writes in his *locus de iustificatione*, "According to this faith, by which we are conjoined to Christ, we are absolved of our sins and freed from their stain or justified, and that gratuitously by grace."[71] The argument parallels Calvin and Vermigli: faith, as the gift of God's grace, is the source of repentance and the basis of our apprehension both

66. See the careful analysis of Calvin's usage in Jill Raitt, "Calvin's Use of *Persona*," in Neuser, *Calvinus Ecclesiae Genevensis Custos*, pp. 273-275; and cf. Venema, *Accepted and Renewed in Christ*, pp. 159-161.

67. Contra Evans, *Imputation and Impartation*, pp. 68-69, 82. Evans' remark (p. 71), posed against later Reformed federal language, that Calvin "waged bitter battle" against "the nominalist *pactum*" has no basis in the Reformer's thought—nor does "the nominalist *pactum*" find an easy analogy in the federal theology of the seventeenth century.

68. Vermigli, *In epistolam s. Pauli apostoli ad Romanos*, 8:30 (pp. 539-540).

69. Vermigli, *In epistolam s. Pauli apostoli ad Romanos*, 8:29 (p. 536).

70. Wolfgang Musculus, *Loci communes sacrae theologiae* (Basel: Johannes Hervagius, 1567), pp. 807, 816-817, 820, 824, 834.

71. Musculus, *Loci communes sacrae theologiae*, p. 582.

of reconciliation and of justification.[72] Justification is grounded in the apprehension of Christ by faith, as he dwells in the heart. Even so, good works arise in the justified because Christ dwells in their hearts by his Spirit.[73]

The order and argumentation of Musculus' *loci* on the application of salvation clearly identify the priority of faith: he moves from faith to election and then to repentance, justification, and good works. Musculus does employ other terms associated with a developed sequence of the application of salvation—namely, adoption, reconciliation, forgiveness, perseverance—but evidences little interest in moving beyond the basic issue that faith is the gift of God's grace and serves as the beginning of salvation. Faith, specifically, has a threefold efficacy: the first efficacy concerns what faith "brings about" or "causes"; the second, what it "apprehends"; and the third, what it "works" or "produces."[74] Faith brings about or causes (*gignit*) repentance. It apprehends (*apprehendit*) six things: the grace of reconciliation and justification, adoption in Christ as children of God, the Spirit of God understood as the spirit of adoption, true knowledge of God and Christ, everlasting life, and the gifts of God.[75] And it works or produces (*operatur*) eight results: contentment of conscience, love of God and Christ, hope of the glory to come, confidence of salvation in Christ, acknowledgment of God's truth, obedience to God, perseverance (*perseverantia*) of the believer in Christ, and a final commendation of the soul to God in death.[76] Apart from the issues raised by Musculus' references to perseverance and to the work of faith in the moment of death, his ordering of the topic offers little indication of temporal order, nor is Musculus' order a matter of purely rational distinction; rather he assumes that it is a natural or causal ordering.

A similar approach is evident in Musculus' commentary on Romans, where he indicates that the focus of the eighth chapter is the application of the merits of Christ and the presence of the work of the Spirit in those who are *in Christo*.[77] Being in Christ or in union with Christ means quite specifically for Musculus being "engrafted" (*insitus*) in Christ "by faith and baptism."[78] This engrafting is entirely of grace, just as it is grace of God apprehended by faith in Christ that sets aside the condemnation for sin: there is no quality in believers that places them beyond divine condemnation, but only the gracious work of the Spirit in them, enabling them to walk not of the flesh but in Christ, according to the Spirit. As with Calvin and

72. Musculus, *Loci communes sacrae theologiae*, pp. 526-527.

73. Musculus, *Loci communes sacrae theologiae*, pp. 583, 591.

74. Musculus, *Loci communes sacrae theologiae*, p. 526.

75. Musculus, *Loci communes sacrae theologiae*, p. 526-528.

76. Musculus, *Loci communes sacrae theologiae*, p. 529-530.

77. Wolfgang Musculus, *In epistolam d. Apostoli Pauli ad Romanos commentarii* (Basel: Sebastian Henricpetrus, 1555), p. 122.

78. Musculus, *In epistolam ad Romanos*, p. 122.

Vermigli, faith has a certain priority over the union, inasmuch as it is faith that apprehends and receives Christ—what Musculus adds is an accent on baptism.[79]

The theme of union with Christ, evident throughout the chapter, concludes in Musculus' comments on the catena in Romans 8:28-30 and the verses following. The consummation of the work of salvation is the conforming of believers to the image of Christ, Musculus writes, as the chapter has indicated, first in suffering and ultimately in glory. Thus, "in Christ is the true justification and sanctification."[80] Even so, when the apostle teaches that nothing can separate the elect from the love of God, it is because they are in Christ and God loves the elect "in his Son."[81]

Unio cum Christo in Developments Leading to Early Reformed Orthodoxy

After the establishment of several basic patterns of argument concerning union with Christ and its relation to the application of Christ's work in the sequencing of such aspects of salvation as calling, faith, regeneration, and justification on the part of Calvin, Vermigli, Musculus, and others of their generation, there was a further development of this language of salvation in the thought of a group of thinkers whose work was instrumental in the rise and eventual development of what can be called early Reformed orthodoxy. Among these thinkers, Jerome Zanchi, Theodore Beza, and Caspar Olevianus were significant formulators.

Zanchi on union with Christ. As studies of the thought of Jerome Zanchi by John Farthing and, more recently, J. V. Fesko have shown, the emphasis on union with Christ found in Calvin and various of his contemporaries did not disappear as the Reformation passed into the era of early orthodoxy. Not only his profound emphasis on union with Christ in relation to the whole application of salvation, but also his impact on the next generation of Reformed theologians can be seen from Zanchi's Brief discourse on perseverance and assurance of election, translated and appended to William Perkins' Case of Conscience (1592). Zanchi's approach to the execution of the decree of predestination identified its "first effect" as "Christ himself; as he is Mediator and a Saviour, dwelling in out hearts by his holie Spirit."[82] This definition rests on the premise that all who are saved are elected in Christ and cleansed by his blood. More specifically, Christ, as Mediator is understood to be the "first effect" of predestination

---

79. Musculus, In epistolam ad Romanos, p. 123.

80. Musculus, In epistolam ad Romanos, p. 144.

81. Musculus, In epistolam ad Romanos, p. 158.

82. Jerome Zanchi, A Briefe discourse, taken out of the writings of Her. Zanchius. Wherein the aforesaid case of Conscience is disputed and resolved (London: Iohn Porter and Tho. Man, 1592), p. 59.

because we can enjoy none of the gifts of God, either of the election, vocation, or justification, except in Christ, and by Christ.... In that therefore, everie elect faithfull man feeleth Christ to dwel in him, and to quicken him.[83]

In accord, moreover, with the exegetical tradition of identifying Romans 8 as a *locus* for the doctrine of *unio cum Christo* in its foundational relation to the sequence of salvation, Zanchi indicates that, as testified by the apostle Paul, the three principal effects that follow from our union with Christ are "our calling, (to wit, effectual) our Iustification & glorification."[84]

This understanding of the priority of union with Christ over the various aspects of the application of salvation carries over into Zanchi's confession of faith, the *De religione Christiana fides*.[85] After his chapter on the doctrine of Christ the Redeemer, Zanchi offers an entire chapter on the dispensation of redemption focused on union with Christ, followed by chapters on the gospel, the sacraments, faith (together with hope and love), repentance, justification, free choice in the regenerate, and good works—not a strict *ordo salutis*.[86] Zanchi's confession makes a point similar to the argument in his *Brief treatise*: those eternally predestined to salvation in Christ are "in their time called by the gospel, given faith by the holy Spirit, engrafted into Christ, and made one with him."[87] Inasmuch as there is no salvation outside of Christ, salvation can be received only by being ingrafted into Christ and "conjoined" to him "in a true and real union."[88] Nor can this union occur apart from the work of Christ and of the Holy Spirit, Christ first uniting himself to us: "we approach him by our spirit, because he first came to us by his: and therefore we embrace him by faith, because first, by the power of his spirit he grasps us [and] kindles faith in us: we therefore cannot cling and unite to him, unless he first conjoins and unites himself to us."[89]

Much like Vermigli, Zanchi identifies the union as threefold, grounding all aspects of the economy or application of salvation. There is the initial and fundamental union "made in our nature." There is the ongoing union made each day in the persons of the elect, even in their imperfection, as they journey toward God—Vermigli's "secret union." And there is the final union when the redeemed are present with the Lord, and God is all in all; as Zanchi explains, "nature is ordained

83. Zanchi, *Briefe discourse*, pp. 59-60.

84. Zanchi, *Briefe discourse*, p. 61, citing Rom. 8:30.

85. Jerome Zanchi, *De religione christiana fides* (Neustadt: Matthaeus Harnisch, 1588; also London: Iacobus Rimeus, 1605); in translation, H. *Zanchius, his Confession of Christian Religion* (Cambridge: John Legat, 1599).

86. Zanchi, *De religione christiana fides*, cap. xi-xxi; note the table in Fesko, "Zanchi on Union with Christ," p. 62, comparing Zanchi's ordering with the Second Helvetic Confession.

87. Zanchi, *De religione christiana fides*, xii.2 (p. 60); *Confession*, p. 76.

88. Zanchi, *De religione christiana fides*, xii.3 (pp. 60-61); *Confession*, p. 77, citing John 15:1-7.

89. Zanchi, *De religione christiana fides*, xii.4 (p. 61); *Confession*, p. 77, citing 1 John 4:10.

to grace, and grace to glory."[90] Thus, as with Vermigli, Zanchi not only moves to link the language of union with the language of application of salvation; he also conceives of the *unio cum Christo* as a implying, in itself, a *gradus* or *ordo* paralleling the language of application found in Romans 8:30.

Thus, in subsequent chapters, Zanchi returns to the theme of union with Christ. The gospel is the instrument by which we are engrafted into Christ and the sacraments are conjoined to the Word in order to make communion with Christ complete.[91] The Lord's Supper is "not only a testimony of our communion with Christ ... but also an implement [*organum*] of the holy Spirit to confirm and promote [our communion]."[92] Inasmuch as it is by the faith instilled by the Spirit that we "embrace Christ," faith is "necessary" to "union with Christ [and] participation in his benefits."[93]

In coming to his chapters on repentance and justification, Zanchi for the first time indicates an order of application or appropriation. Faith, hope, love, repentance, justification, good works, and the godly life are utterly inseparable and are mutually interdependent. Still, they can be distinguished from one another: faith is fundamental or "necessary" to union and communion with Christ, while repentance is its "perpetual and inseparable companion," a necessary, albeit not in itself sufficient, condition or adjunct of faith for justification.[94] According to Zanchi as well as Calvin (at least as implied by the argumentation in the *Institutes*), initial repentance not only stands in relation to faith but also has an intimate relationship with justification: "no one is justified without repentance."[95] Repentance, brought about by God through the preaching of the law and the gospel, revealing both our sins and our salvation, comprehends both sorrow for sin and an alteration in mind and heart, will and intention—and, beyond this, the mortification of the "old man" and the vivification of the new. This latter progress in repentance continues in the justified.[96] Those who, through the work of the Holy Spirit, are genuinely repentant are also, by the work of the Spirit, given a living faith in Christ, joined to him as members to their head, forgiven their sins, and filled with his righteousness.[97] Language of ingrafting into Christ and union with Christ pervades Zanchi's chapter on justification.[98]

---

90. Zanchi, *De religione christiana fides*, xii.5 (p. 62); *Confession*, p. 78.
91. Zanchi, *De religione christiana fides*, xiii.8; xiv.1 (p. 78); *Confession*, pp. 98-99.
92. Zanchi, *De religione christiana fides*, xvi.1 (p. 96); *Confession*, p. 122.
93. Zanchi, *De religione christiana fides*, xvii.1 (p. 107); *Confession*, p. 136.
94. Zanchi, *De religione christiana fides*, xviii.1 (p. 112); *Confession*, p. 142.
95. Zanchi, *De religione christiana fides*, xviii (p. 112); *Confession*, p. 142.
96. Zanchi, *De religione christiana fides*, xviii.2, 3, 6 (pp. 112-114); *Confession*, pp. 143-145.
97. Zanchi, *De religione christiana fides*, xix.1 (pp. 115-116); *Confession*, p. 147.
98. Thus, Zanchi, *De religione christiana fides*, xix.1, 2, 4, 5, 6, 12 (pp. 115-119, 123); *Confession*, pp. 147-152, 156.

The implication of Zanchi's argumentation is that faith and repentance, both wrought by grace, mark also the beginning of union with Christ—while justification and the new life in Christ are products of the union, although, again, the sequencing appears to be more causal than temporal, and the temporal element, when it arises, has to do with progress in the new life and the distinction between the incompleteness and progress of salvation in this life and the fullness of salvation in glorification and in the consummation of union with Christ. The causal aspect, moreover, affirms the priority of the gracious work of the Spirit, the instrumentality of the gospel and of faith, and the adjunctive character of repentance. Faith and repentance, in other words, are not efficient causes; faith does not cause repentance, and neither faith nor repentance causes justification.

Theodore Beza and the *unio*. Perhaps even more than Calvin and Vermigli, Theodore Beza stresses union with Christ in his discussion of salvation from sin. He introduces the topic of union in his *Quaestionum et responsionum christianarum libellus* (1570) at the point of moving from his christological exposition into the remainder of the work, by asking the question, "What therefore is the way to life eternal?" and responding, "Christ himself."[99] Beza then notes that not all are saved, but only those who "by belief conjoined to Christ" and "in a manner incorporated into him" (*quoddammodo sese illi incorporare*).[100] These comments lead Beza to a brief definition of faith and then to a lengthy discussion of the sinful corruption of humanity.[101] He returns to the issue of union with Christ and faith, commenting, "the remedy of this evil is to be one with Christ by faith, which is the gift of God."[102]

Union with Christ, in Beza's view, should be understood as an apprehending (*apprehensio*), ingrafting (*insitio*), and incorporation (*incorporatio*)—but neither as a conjoining of spiritual and corporeal substances or in the sense of a physical conjunction of bodies such as would result in a single person, nor is the union merely a reception of the power and efficacy of Christ's work. Rather, as Scripture teaches, Christ is given and communicated to believers so that they are "flesh of his flesh and bone of his bone" in an entirely "spiritual and mystical" manner.[103]

The union is spiritual even though it is a communication of the whole Christ, soul and body. Beza makes clear, then, that "spiritual" union does not mean merely a communion with the spirit of Christ or a communion that takes place only in the mind, in a purely rational way, or that is a matter of consent as in the case of believers being of one heart and mind. Spiritual union with Christ, Beza argues,

99. Theodore Beza, *Quaestionum et responsionum christianarum libellus, in quo praecipua Christianae religionis capita kat' epitome proponuntur* (Geneva: Eustathius Vignon, 1577), pp. 33-34; in translation *A Booke of Christian Questions and Answers* (London: William How, 1578), fol. 23v.

100. Beza, *Quaestionum et responsionum*, p. 34; *Questions and Answers*, fol. 23v.

101. Beza, *Quaestionum et responsionum*, pp. 34-49; *Questions and Answers*, fol. 23r-33r.

102. Beza, *Quaestionum et responsionum*, p. 49; *Questions and Answers*, fol. 33v.

103. Beza, *Quaestionum et responsionum*, pp. 49, 51; *Questions and Answers*, fol. 33v-34v.

reflecting his and Calvin's language of Christ's presence in the Lord's Supper, is a full "apprehension" in the soul, by faith, with the power of the Spirit conjoining things disparate in place—just as there is a spiritual union of Christ as head with the church as his body.[104] That this union is more than merely a communication of Christ's "power" (*energia*) and "efficacy" (*efficacia*) is evident from the way in which the Apostle Paul describes the union of Christ with the church in Ephesians 5: the union is not only Christ working in us; rather the union is the foundation (*fundamentum*) of both the effectual working of Christ in believers and of the imputation of his righteousness to them.[105]

Beza engages the issue of union with Christ and the ordering of salvation by noting the possible question that arises when, on the one hand, we understand that believers take hold of Christ by the gift of faith while, on the other, all of the gifts of Christ flow into believers who have taken hold of him by faith. In other words, is faith a human act that precedes one's being in Christ and is the basis of being in Christ? Beza's answer makes a distinction between the beginning of salvation "before the foundation of the world," when the elect are chosen in Christ prior to being given to and engrafted into Christ in this life.[106] If one asks concerning the "temporal moment" of salvation, Christians believe and at the same time "apprehend" Christ, cause and effect concurring. If, however, one considers the "order of causes" (*causarum ordo*), "true faith" is prior to the apprehension of Christ: faith is given, not to those already ingrafted into Christ, but to those who are about to be ingrafted. Nonetheless, faith is given *in Christo* inasmuch as God has chosen and known Christians in Christ before the foundation of the world: it is as if Christ himself has first taken hold of us in order that we might subsequently take hold of him. Thus, "according to the order of causes" grace first operates so that we might be ingrafted into Christ and continues, once Christ is apprehended by faith, to increase and confirm the believer.[107] The primary issue in the sequencing, therefore, for Beza, just as for Calvin and Vermigli, is causal, not temporal, although there is an element of temporality implied, certainly as Beza moves to discuss the benefits or fruits of union with Christ.

The benefits of union with Christ, Beza continues, are clearly and briefly encapsulated in Paul's words in 1 Corinthians 1:30, where Christ is said to have been made our "wisdom, justification, sanctification, redemption."[108] By these terms, Beza understands the knowledge of salvation in Christ, the forensically imputed

---

104. Beza, *Quaestionum et responsionum*, pp. 51-52; *Questions and Answers*, fol. 35r.

105. Beza, *Quaestionum et responsionum*, pp. 53, 56-57; *Questions and Answers*, fol. 36r-v, 38v; cf. the similar formulation in Theodore Beza, *Confessio christianae fidei* (London: Thomas Vautrollerius, 1575), pp. 26-27; in translation, *A Briefe and Pithie Summe of the Christian Faith, made in the Forme of a Confession* (London: Robert Waldegrave, 1585), iv.9 (pp. 35-36).

106. Beza, *Quaestionum et responsionum*, pp. 57-58; *Questions and Answers*, fol. 39r.

107. Beza, *Quaestionum et responsionum*, p. 58; *Questions and Answers*, fol. 39v.

108. Beza, *Quaestionum et responsionum*, p. 59; *Questions and Answers*, fol. 40r.

righteousness of Christ, the holiness that results from spiritual rebirth in Christ by grace, and the ultimate end of Christ's work and its application.[109] There is an implied ordering here, although Beza invokes neither temporal nor causal language at this point: both justification and sanctification follow on union with Christ, and the sanctification is a process or progress in Christian life. Redemption, as the end or goal (finis) toward which justification and sanctification lead, is "the participation of eternal life in him" by whom "we have been redeemed from sin and death," namely, "in Christ."[110] Remission of sin, freedom from death, and possession of eternal life are all, therefore, "in Christ" as apprehended by faith—in short, Beza concludes, all that is necessary for salvation is to be found in Christ.[111]

Union with Christ, then, is both the beginning and the end of the work of redemption. He has indicated a priority of election over the temporal beginning of salvation and a priority of grace and faith in relation to union with Christ. The priority of grace and faith over union, moreover, is according to Beza primarily causal and not temporal. What Beza has not done, however, is continue to line out a strict sequence, whether causal, or temporal, or logical—he has not, in other words, argued a strict sequencing of justification, sanctification, or other potential elements of an ordo, such as repentance, regeneration, redemption, mortification, and vivification. Rather, he has indicated that both justification and sanctification arise from union with Christ, without giving priority to either, except insofar as sanctification implies a temporal progress toward final redemption. There is a similar approach to order and causality found in the theses disputed under Beza and Faius in the Academy of Geneva: the theses on "the causes and effects of faith" identify God, Father, Son, and Spirit, as the efficient cause of faith, brought about by the means of "preaching God's Word."[112] The "effects of faith," whether "extrinsic" or inward (intra nos ingenerant), arise not as faith itself causing the effects but rather as results of the union with Christ brought about through faith—the extrinsic effect being the remission of sins, imputed righteousness, and the restoration of human nature "in the flesh of Christ"; and the inward effect being the sanctifying work of the Spirit.[113]

109. Beza, Quaestionum et responsionum, pp. 59-60, 64-65, 84-85; Questions and Answers, fol. 40r-v, 43v-44r, 57r-v.
110. Beza, Quaestionum et responsionum, pp. 84-85; Questions and Answers, fol. 57r-v.
111. Beza, Quaestionum et responsionum, p. 86; Questions and Answers, fol. 59v.
112. Theodore Beza and Antonius Faius, Theses theologicae in schola Genevensi ab aliquot sacrarum literarum studiosus sub DD. Theod. Beza & Antonio Fayo ss. theologiae professoribus propositae & disputatae. Geneva, 1586), xxiii.1-2 (p. 41); in translation, Propositions and Principles of Divinitie Propounded and Disputed in the University of Geneva.under M. Theod. Beza and M. Anthonie Faius (Edinburgh: Robert Waldegrave, 1595), p. 49.
113. Beza and Faius, Theses theologicae, xxiii.11-13; cf. xxv.1-3 (p. 42); Propositions and Principles, pp. 51, 54.

Caspar Olevianus—exegesis and the *unio cum Christo*. Reminiscent of Calvin's argument at the beginning of book III of the *Institutes*, Olevianus' initial presentation of the work of the Spirit in his *Exposition of the Creed* focuses on the various "effects" of the work of the Spirit—witnessing to the love of God the Father in the human heart and enlightening the mind with a knowledge of Christ to the end that "by faith" Christians may be "implanted" (*inserat*) into Christ and made "partakers of his benefits."[114] Citing Romans 8, Olevianus indicates that the work or office of the Spirit is to conjoin (*coniungere*) believers to Christ by faith and then to continue to work in them to bring about new life and finally glory. The clearest sign that we are truly ingrafted into Christ and walk after the Spirit, not after the flesh, is a deep dissatisfaction with self (*displicentia sui*), a hatred of sin (*odium peccati*), and an ongoing battle against sin (*pugna adversus peccatum*): "for the flesh does not fight against itself."[115] This ingrafting is also the fulfillment of God's covenant with Abraham and his seed—as Paul teaches in Galatians, "and if you are Christ's, then you are Abraham's seed, and heirs according to the promise."[116]

As might be concluded from his foundational referencing of Romans 8 in his exposition of the creed, Olevianus' homiletical commentary on Romans is of particular significance for the early Reformed development of language of union with Christ and the ordering of salvation. Like most exegetes of the era, Olevianus focuses his attention at the beginning of his comments on Romans 8, on the theme of union with Christ. The first section of the chapter, Olevianus indicates, presents two fundamental "propositions" concerning the barriers standing in the way of human freedom from sin and its afflictions. The first is the consolation that "the remnants of sin will not be counted as condemnation for those who are in Christ, who walk not according to the flesh, but according to the Spirit"; and the second is the warning that "those who walk according to the flesh are not in Christ, or who have not true faith, such are not exempt from condemnation, but are left in death."[117] Those who do not walk according to the flesh are delivered from divine condemnation, not because they have achieved perfection, but solely because they are "ingrafted by true faith into Christ."[118]

What follows next in the chapter is the proof of Paul's first proposition. Whereas God condemns sinners who labor under the law, incapable of fulfilling its demands,

---

114. Caspar Olevianus, *Expositio symboli apostolici, sive articulorum fidei: in qua summa gratiuti foederis aeterni inter Deum et fideles breviter & perspicué tractatur* (Frankfurt: Andreas Wechel, 1580), pp. 173-174; in translation, *An Exposition of the Symbole of the Apostles* (London: H. Middleton 1581), p. 232.

115. Olevianus, *Expositio symboli apostolici*, pp. 174, 176, citing Romans 8; *Exposition of the Symbole*, pp. 232, 235.

116. Olevianus, *Expositio symboli apostolici*, p. 175, citing Gal. 3:29; *Exposition of the Symbole*, pp. 233-234.

117. Caspar Olevianus, *In epistolam D. Pauli apostoli ad Romanos notae, ex Gasparis Oleviani concionibus excerptae, & a Theodoro Bezae editae* (Geneva: Eustathius Vignon, 1579), pp. 315-316.

118. Olevianus, *In epistolam ad Romanos*, p. 316.

Christ, by "becoming sin for us," has made it possible that the Father, in eternity, might condemn all of our sins in him—and we might be freed from the law and death.[119] Paul next provides the reason why there is no condemnation for those in Christ: the law of the Spirit of life has freed them from the law of sin and death. This law, Olevianus adds, is "vivifying faith, or the Spirit of faith" which frees the believer from sin and death because, by it, the hearts of those who are in Christ are enlivened and purified. To say that "there is no condemnation in those who are in Christ" is identical to saying that they are justified by faith.[120] In short order, Olevianus has connected ingrafting into Christ and the concomitant deliverance from condemnation not only with faith but, by way of faith, with the vivification, purification, and justification of believers.

What is of significance to the development of the Reformed approach to union with Christ and the order of salvation is that Olevianus maintains this fundamental theme in his exposition of the entire chapter, bringing the language of consolation and deliverance in Christ to bear on his interpretation of the ordering of salvation in what he identifies as the *catena aurea* of Romans 8:28-30. All things work for good for those who are called according to God's purpose (v. 28) because, Olevianus comments, they are conformed to Christ and, in Christ, earthly afflictions are no longer impediments but have become "the way to glory."[121] Paul's reference to those "who are called" leads Olevianus back to the theme of union with Christ in a comment on the nature of inward, effectual calling and outward, general calling: inasmuch as many are called and few are chosen, effectual calling should be recognized as "the gift of faith by which we are ingrafted into Christ."[122] This faith is a sign of election inasmuch as faith is not a matter of free choice but is implanted in believers by a heavenly election—effectual calling is the ingrafting into Christ and is, therefore, a ground for assurance of one's election.[123]

Reformed Orthodoxy and *Unio cum Christo*: From Exegesis to Doctrinal Formulation

Union with Christ in early orthodox exegesis of Romans 8. Exegetical interest in Romans 8:1ff. as a *locus* for the understanding of union with Christ and its relation to other aspects of the application of Christ's work was not unique to Olevianus' commentary in the development of early Reformed orthodoxy but continued to be developed in the work of Reformed commentators on the text. Thus, Benedictus

---

119. Olevianus, *In epistolam ad Romanos*, pp. 317, 318, citing 2 Cor. 5:21.

120. Olevianus, *In epistolam ad Romanos*, pp. 318, 321.

121. Olevianus, *In epistolam ad Romanos*, p. 372.

122. Olevianus, *In epistolam ad Romanos*, p. 373: "Haec est donatio fidei quam inserimur in Christo."

123. Olevianus, *In epistolam ad Romanos*, pp. 373-374: "fides non ex libero arbitrio venit (quemadmodum gramen e terra crescit) sed e coelo in nos plantatur ex electione. ... Ergo vocatio efficax, sive insitio in Christum, est annullus ille alius under cognoscitur electio."

Aretius identified the *argumentum* of chapter 8 as an explanation of how the godly are liberated in Christ from the curse of the law and drawn to their end in God by the "spirit of regeneration"—yielding in his view, two parts of the chapter, the first concerning liberation from condemnation and the second dealing with life according to the spirit and patience in adversity—plus, presumably, a concluding section.[124] Robert Rollock, writing a few years later, divided the chapter into three parts, the first (vv. 1-18) dealing with liberation in Christ, the second (vv. 19-30) lining out the glory of the children of God, and a third part (vv. 31-39) glorifying God.[125] The initial theme of the chapter, the ingrafting of believers in Christ, reappears when Rollock lines out the sequence of causes and means of salvation following his *loci* on predestination at the close of the chapter.[126]

A similar structure of the chapter is argued by David Pareus and, after him, Andrew Willet, who identify three parts unified around the theme of union with Christ or participation in Christ. The first (vv. 1-16) concerns the removal of impediments to justification through union with Christ. The second (vv. 17-30), exhorts to patience in affliction to those who participate in Christ, inasmuch as all things work for their good, in the end conforming them to Christ, as confirmed by its "first cause ... flowing from the eternal counsel of God." The third (vv. 31-39) celebrates the end of "the faithful in the immutable counsel of God."[127] Union with Christ and ultimate conformity with Christ, therefore, are the theme of the chapter and the sequence of the application of salvation rests on it: the language of being "with" or "in Christ" is found throughout the argument of the chapter.

Willet also identified the *unio* as the first major "question" to be discussed in the interpretation of chapter 8. Citing Vermigli first, Willet notes the point that none who are in Christ are condemned and takes Vermigli's point about Christ's union with the common nature of humanity, concluding that therefore "the privilege of grace is common to all that are sanctified."[128] This grace assumes both a twofold "conjunction" and a twofold effect. The conjunction, in Willet's terms, is both "materiall" and "formall"—material in the sense that we are truly made one with

124. Benedictus Aretius, *Commentarii in omnes epistolas d. Pauli et canonicas, itemque in Apocalypsin d. Joannis*, editio altera (Geneva: Ioannes le Preux, 1589), p. 79.

125. Robert Rollock, *Analysis dialectica in Pauli Apostoli Epistolam ad Romanos. Respersa est analysis, doctrinae theologicae quorundam capitum, quae in ea Epistola sparsim reperiuntur, explicatione quadam brevi ac dilucida* (Edinburgh: Robert Walde-graue, 1593), p. 114.

126. Rollock, *Analysis dialectica in Pauli Apostoli Epistolam ad Romanos*, pp. 194, 200.

127. David Pareus, *In divinam ad Romanos s. Pauli apostoli epistolam commentarius* (1609; Geneva: Paulus Margellus, 1617), pp. 503-505; cf. Andrew Willet, *Hexapla: that is, a Six-Fold Commentarie upon the most Diuine Epistle ... to the Romans* (Cambridge: Cantrell Legge, 1611), p. 349; Willet appears to borrow heavily from Pareus.

128. Willet, *Commentarie upon the Epistle to the Romans*, p. 350; cf. the similar use of this understanding of Christ's union with the "common nature" of humanity in Nathaniel Homes, *Christ offering himself to all Sinners*, in *The Works of Dr. Nathanael Homes* (London: for the Author, 1652), p. 7.

Christ, both in flesh and in spirit, so that as he partakes of our nature we, in union with him, partake of his spirit; formal in the sense that the means or instrument of the union is faith. The twofold effect is that, by faith we are "graft into Christ" and made one with him and that, as the fruit of faith, we no longer "walke after the flesh."[129] When he turns to the text of Romans 8:28-30, Willet indicates that predestination is not only to the end but also to the means of redemption, namely, to calling, justification, and adoption in Christ.[130]

Daniel Featley, the commentator for the Pauline epistles in the annotations commissioned by Parliament at the time of the Westminster Assembly,[131] understood the structure of Romans as a set of disputations, the first of which reached its conclusion at chapter 8, as indicated by its initial sentence, "There is therefore no condemnation to those who are in Christ Jesus"—"seeing that we being justified by faith in Christ," Featley wrote in summary of the argument and its conclusion, "do obtain remission of sinnes, and imputation of righteousnesse, and are also sanctified by the Spirit: it followeth from hence that they that are engraffed into Christ by faith are out of all danger of condemnation."[132] Ingrafting into Christ, then, sums up the entire initial argument of the epistle and appears as the foundation of the order or application of salvation. Indeed, Featley indicates that "the fruits of the Spirit or effects of sanctification, which is begun in us, do not engraffe us into Christ, but declare that we are engrafted into him."[133] Predestination, therefore, is God's ordination "to conformitie, both in grace and glory, with his Sonne," not only in suffering but also in sanctification and glorification.[134]

The exegetical work of various Reformed writers of the early orthodox era continued the line of argument that we have identified in the commentaries of the Reformers and in the works of several significant successors, namely, Zanchi, Beza, and Olevianus. Romans 8 remained a significant *locus* for the discussion of union with Christ, also described actively in relation to calling as engrafting into Christ. The engrafting or union was consistently understood by the commentators as the basis for the application of Christi's work, whether in the sense of eternal election in Christ or in the sense of the foundation of the remaining elements of the application of salvation following calling, namely, faith, justification, regeneration, sanctification,

129. Willet, *Commentarie upon the Epistle to the Romans*, p. 350.

130. Willet, *Commentarie upon the Epistle to the Romans*, p. 382.

131. *Annotations upon all the books of the Old and New Testament wherein the text is explained, doubts resolved, Scriptures parallelled and various readings observed by the joynt-labour of certain learned divines, thereunto appointed, and therein employed, as is expressed in the preface* (London: John Legatt and John Raworth, 1645), hereafter referenced as the *English Annotations*; and see the discussion of the annotations and of Featley's role in Richard A. Muller and Rowland S. Ward, *Scripture and Worship: Biblical Interpretation and the Directory for Public Worship* (Phillipsburg: Presbyterian and Reformed, 2007), pp. 11-22.

132. *English Annotations*, Rom. 8:1, in loc.

133. *English Annotations*, Rom. 8:1, in loc.

134. *English Annotations*, Rom. 8:29, in loc.

and glorification. As in the case of the more lengthy doctrinal expositions of the union and its effects, the exegetes typically do not argue a temporal sequencing of justification, regeneration, and sanctification, but indicate that these are all brought about in and through union with Christ.

Perkins, Polanus, and Ames—the application of salvation and union with Christ in early orthodoxy. The works of theologians like William Perkins, Amandus Polanus, and William Ames in the era of early orthodoxy evidence a continuing emphasis on the doctrine of union with Christ and on an understanding of the union as foundational to the work of salvation in believers. Among these writers, Perkins' work is the earliest and, given his explicit use of various works of Zanchi, most overtly rooted in the thought of his immediate predecessors. In his *Golden Chaine*, Perkins moves from his reflections on the divine decree and its execution in time to a series of chapters concerning the "degrees" or stages "of the declaration of Gods love," the first degree consisting in election, union with Christ, effectual calling, and faith.[135] After very briefly identifying election negatively as "a separation of the sinner from the cursed estate of mankind," Perkins enters into an extended discussion of union with Christ, presenting it as the positive analogue to the separation of the elect from the fallen mass of humanity and as a foundational consideration prior to discussion of calling and faith.

Perkins' approach to the application of salvation draws on the language used in the exegesis of Romans 8:28-30—a text typically identified in the sixteenth and seventeenth centuries as the "golden chain" and arguably the source of the title of his treatise—referring to the series of causes and means of salvation as degrees, or *gradus*. There are four degrees of this "declaration of Gods love" to the elect, namely, calling, justification, sanctification, and glorification.[136] The first of these degrees, effectual calling, can be distinguished into the temporal moment of election or the "separation of the sinner from the cursed estate of al mankind" and the "free gift of God the Father" according to which the sinner is given to Christ and Christ to the sinner, much as in wedlock, resulting in "that admirable union or conjunction, which is the ingraffing of such as are to be saved, into Christ, and their growing together with him" to the end that "every repentant sinner [is] a member of his mysticall bodie."[137]

135. William Perkins, A Golden Chaine, or the description of theologie, containing the order of the causes of salvation and damnation, according to Gods word, cap. xxxvi, in The Whole Works of ... Mr. William Perkins, 3 vols. (London: John Legatt, 1631), vol. I, p. 77.

136. Perkins, Golden Chaine, xxxvi, xxxvii, xxxviii, xlviii (pp. 77, 81, 83, 92); on Perkins' doctrine see also Fesko, "William Perkins on Union with Christ and Justification," pp. 21-34; note that my earlier study, "Perkins' A Golden Chaine: Predestinarian System or Schematized Ordo Salutis?," Sixteenth Century Journal, 9/1 (1978), pp. 69-81, rather loosely referred to Perkins' ordering of the causes as an ordo salutis, a usage from which I now refrain on historical grounds.

137. Perkins, Golden Chaine, xxxvi (p. 77).

This union is to be considered in terms of "the things united," "the manner of their union," and "the bond of union." As to the first, Perkins makes clear that it is not merely the human soul that is united to Christ, not merely our flesh to his flesh; rather "the whole person of every faithful man, is verily conjoined which the whole person of our Saviour Christ God and man."[138] Perkins is also clear that the union of believers with Christ is of a different status than the hypostatic union of Christ's person. Believers are not directly conjoined to Christ's divinity—indeed it is the incarnation that provides the connection between believers and God in Christ:

> A faithfull man first of all and immediately is united to the flesh, or humane nature of Christ, and afterward by reason of the humanitie, to the Word it selfe, or divine nature. For salvation & life dependeth on that fulnesse of the godhead which is in Christ, yet it is not communicated unto us, but in the flesh, and by the flesh of Christ.[139]

The bond itself is called a "spiritual union" because it is "made by the Spirit of God applying Christ unto us: and on our parts by faith receiving Christ Jesus offered unto us."[140]

The argument here is much like that of the Reformers—the salvific action in the union belongs to both Christ and the Spirit, with the Spirit creating the union itself and Christ effecting its blessings in the believer. Perkins, however, returns to his discussion of effectual calling immediately after his discussion of the union, given that there is a distinction to be made between those who are decreed eternally to be members of Christ and those who "actually are so." Actualization of the union, then, occurs through effectual calling in the preaching of law and gospel, the "mollifying of the heart" for the reception of grace, and the bestowal of faith to the end that Christ be apprehended and applied by the Spirit.[141] Indeed, the first "benefit" of union with Christ is the regeneration brought about by the "conveyance of grace" to the end that the believer "hath his beginning and being in Christ."[142] The second benefit of union, distinguished not temporally but presumably by an order of being or nature, is unity with God through Christ, resulting in the "eternall fellowship" of the believer with the Father, Son, and Holy Spirit.[143]

---

138. Perkins, Golden Chaine, xxxvi (p. 78).

139. Perkins, Golden Chaine, xxxvi (p. 78), citing John 6:53; similarly, Perkins, An Exposition of the Symbole or Creed of the Apostles, in Works, I, pp. 299-300, on the nature of the mystical union. Note that Perkins' argument reflects the typical Reformed assumption of the eternity of the incarnation, contrary to the rather odd readings of this issue found in the works of Johannes Quistorp and Jürgen Moltmann: see Richard A. Muller, "Christ in the Eschaton—Calvin and Moltmann on the Duration of the Munus Regium," Harvard Theological Review, 74, (1981), pp. 31-59.

140. Perkins, Golden Chaine, xxxvi (p. 78).

141. Perkins, Golden Chaine, xxxvi (pp. 78-79).

142. Perkins, Exposition, p. 300, col. 1.

143. Perkins, Exposition, p. 300, col. 1.

The second degree, or *gradus*, in the chain and the third "benefit" of the union, justification, consists both in "remission of sins, and imputation of Christs righteousness."[144] This righteousness or justice belongs both to Christ and to believers because of their union with him:

> This iustice is both anothers and ours also. Anothers, because it is in Christ as in a subject: ours, because by meanes of the fore named union, Christ, with all his benefits, is made ours.[145]

Given this relation of the union to justification, the adoption of believers as children of God in Christ is "annexed" to justification.[146] In his *Exposition of the Symbol*, where he speaks of justification as the third benefit of union, Perkins nuances his forensic understanding of justification, indicating that the imputation of Christ's righteousness to believers is, in God's sight, truly the righteousness of the believer, given that this perfect righteousness is in Christ "as in a subject" but is in the believer because of the union with Christ.[147]

A significant departure from the earlier models we have examined occurs in Perkins' identification of the third degree, or *gradus*, and fourth benefit, as sanctification, adding a fourth term to the Pauline ordering of Romans 8:30. This ordering is also more a logical or argumentative order than a temporal one inasmuch as Perkins identifies sanctification as flowing from union with Christ, not from regeneration or justification: "from this fountaine springs our sanctification, whereby we dye to sinne, and are reneued in righteousness and holinesse."[148] No distinction is made here between regeneration and sanctification—a characteristic of Perkins' argument that also stands in the way of arguing a temporal sequence or even a strict prioritization of the degrees of salvation resulting from union with Christ.

Not only does this definition add to the language of the Pauline sequence; it also is the place where Perkins places mortification and vivification.[149] The difference between Perkins' argument and that of Calvin and Zanchi is subtle: whereas they had placed repentance and justification as coordinates, with repentance arguably having some precedence, Perkins pairs repentance and virtually equates it with sanctification, indicating its subordination to regeneration, faith, and justification.

---

144. Perkins, *Golden Chaine*, xxxvii (p. 81); cf. Perkins, *Exposition*, p. 300, col. 1.

145. Perkins, *Golden Chaine*, xxxvii (p. 82).

146. Perkins, *Golden Chaine*, xxxvii (p. 82).

147. Perkins, *Exposition*, p. 300, col. 2.

148. Perkins, *Exposition*, p. 300, col. 2; cf. Fesko, "William Perkins on Union with Christ," p. 26; Fesko argues a "priority" of justification over sanctification, but it is difficult to argue priority here except in the pairings of the Ramistic structure of the argument: both justification and sanctification flow from union with Christ; cf. also, similarly, Perkins, *A Godly and Learned Exposition upon the whole Epistle of Jude*, in *Works*, III, p. 594, col. 2, noting the communication of Christ to believers by "imputation" and infusion or "propagation" deriving "grace from his grace" and indicating not a temporal order or priority so much as an order in argument by bifurcation.

149. Perkins, *Golden Chaine*, xxxviii (p. 83).

Perkins has, in other words, made a clearer distinction between regeneration and sanctification. Nonetheless, his identifying of sanctification as consisting in mortification and vivification still reflects something like the formulations of Calvin and Zanchi, given that this identification belonged to their definitions of repentance and that repentance, as Perkins says, albeit "derived" from sanctification, is nonetheless the beginning of the "amendment of life." In order for a person to deny himself, express hatred of sin, and desire to "imbrace righteousness," Perkins comments, he would have to be regenerate, justified, and possessed of true faith—"therefore albeit in such as are converted, repentance doth first manifest it selfe, yet regarding the order of nature, it followeth both faith and sanctification."[150] There is, then, according to Perkins a natural or causal order in which repentance follows faith and sanctification, but there is also a temporal order in which repentance appears first. The fourth degree, or *gradus*—returning to the language of Romans 8:30—is glorification, the final and full conformity of the elect to Christ.[151]

Polanus' less elaborate approach to the application of the work of salvation, both in his earlier *Partitiones* and in the *Syntagma*, moves from external calling to internal calling as the work of the Spirit by which human beings are "are called to Christ by supernatural grace" and "come to Christ through faith."[152] Calling, therefore, precedes faith causally, and union is achieved in and through faith, much as in the arguments we have seen in earlier writers, notably Calvin and Vermigli. Polanus then begins his discussion of the economy of salvation proper with a section devoted to union or communion with Christ:

> Communion with Christ [*communio cum Christo*], is the benefit of God, in which he gives Christ himself and his merits to believers, that he might effectively work eternal life in them. John 3:16; Rom 8:32. This is also called joining together [*conjunctio*], union [*unio*], becoming one in Christ [*coalitio cum Christo*], engrafting into Christ [*insitio in Christum*], eating of the flesh of Christ, drinking the blood of Christ, *anakephaliosis*, namely, being drawn under one head, conjoined in one body under the one head of Christ. Eph. 1:10.[153]

This union or communion is twofold: either with Christ himself or with his blessings or benefits. The former, defined at greater length, is his union with those who belong to him, "by which he truly and really [*vere & realiter*] conjoins with us, and by which he in us and we in him remain in eternity."[154] Much in the manner of Vermigli and

---

150. Perkins, *Golden Chaine*, xxxviii (p. 85).

151. Perkins, *Golden Chaine*, xlviii (p. 92).

152. Amandus Polanus, *Syntagma theologiae christianae* (Hanau: Wechel, 1615), VI.xxxii (p. 448).

153. Amandus Polanus, *Partitiones theologiae iuxta naturalis methodi leges conformatae duobus libris, quorum primus est de fide: alter de bonis operibus* (London: Edmund Bollifant, 1591), xxxv (p. 56); in translation, *The Substance of Christian Religion, soundly set forth in two bookes, by definitions and partitions, framed according to the rules of a naturall method* (London: R. F. for Iohn Oxenbridge, 1595), xxxv (p. 100).

154. Polanus, *Syntagma theologiae christianae*, VI.xxxv (p. 453).

Zanchi, Polanus identifies this former member of the division, union with Christ himself, as threefold—first, in nature by reason of the incarnation; second, in grace with the individual elect or sojourners on their way to the Lord (*perigrinantibus a Domino*); and third, in glory after the final resurrection when God is all in all.[155]

Union with Christ is both individual and corporate: the union of believers with Christ is one and the same as the communion of saints. Polanus goes on to indicate that "the parts of our communion with Christ are: Justification & Regeneration: Adoption and the freedom of the sons of God."[156] Like the other thinkers we are examining, Polanus understands justification and regeneration as inseparable, albeit capable of being distinguished, given that the former is forensic and the latter transformative. In addition, regeneration here understood as synonymous with sanctification, indicates a process incomplete in this life, perfected or consummated in the next. And as with other formulations of the doctrine of union with Christ, Polanus' formulation provides both the basis of the application of salvation and its final goal.[157]

Ames turns to the theme of union with Christ in his *Medulla theologiae* and his *De conscientia*, both of which follow the method of thetical statement characteristic of the academic disputations of the era.[158] In the latter work he references union with Christ in his chapter on the sinner's preparation for conversion. *Unio cum Christo*, which "consists in faith, generated by effectual calling," stands following an "apprehension" of the gospel such that one recognizes the genuine possibility of forgiveness, an "earnest desire to obtain that mercy," and prior to "true repentance" in Ames' presentation of what is required to "put a man in the state of grace."[159] It needs to be noted here that Ames' preparationistic approach, asking "how the sinner ought to prepare himself for conversion," explores the subjective side of salvation without, however, radically altering the order of the application of salvation: although union with Christ and repentance are identified as the degrees or stages (*gradus*) of humiliation belonging to preparation, Ames' definitions place effectual calling prior to faith and identify the *unio* as consisting in faith—in other words, the preparation itself is grounded in God's grace, and faith is intrinsic to it. The

---

155. Polanus, *Syntagma theologiae christianae*, VI.xxxv (p. 453).

156. Polanus, *Partitiones*, xxxv (p. 57); *Substance*, xxxv (p. 102).

157. Polanus, *Syntagma theologiae christianae*, VI.xxxvii (p. 467); cf. ibid., VI.xxxv (p. 453).

158. Cf. William Ames, *Medulla ss. theologiae, ex sacris literis, earumque interpretibus, extracta, & methodicè disposita* (London: Robert Allott, 1630), I.iv.1; with the prefatory remarks to I.xi, xii, xiii, identifying the form of his chapters as the *disputatio*; in translation, *The Marrow of Sacred Divinity, drawne out of the holy Scriptures, and the Interpreters thereof, and brought into Method* (London: Edward Griffin, 1642); with idem, *De conscientia et eius iure, vel casibus. Libri quinque* (Amsterdam: Ioannes Ianssonus, 1643), fol. A5r, pp. 41-46; also, in translation, *Conscience with the power and cases thereof. Devided into V. bookes* (S.l.: s.n., 1639), fol. A4v, pp. 49-55.

159. Ames, *De conscientia* (1643), II.iv.7 (p. 55).

preparation, then, is not, as Kendall claimed, prerequisite to faith.[160] Ames also establishes no temporal order of union, faith, and repentance; rather he places faith and the *unio* together with repentance and argues (similarly to Calvin) that faith, which constitutes the union, precedes justification and adoption.[161]

The *Medulla theologiae* contains the more complete exposition of Ames' view of the *unio*. Much like Perkins, Ames understands union with Christ as the proximate ground or cause of the work of salvation. Ames begins his discussion of the application of salvation after working through his christological *loci* and, unlike the subjectively ordered *De conscientia*, does not include a discussion of preparation. His first topic is the application of Christ's satisfaction, broadly considered, where he adumbrates the doctrine of the *pactum salutis*. He next discusses predestination in a separate *locus* and then comes to his chapter on calling, understood as the "parts" of the application of Christ's work. Rather than immediately defining calling, he begins the chapter with the statement, "There are two parts of the application: *union* with Christ, & the *communion* of benefits that flow from that union (Phil. 3:9)."[162] Basing his definition on 1 John 5:12, "He that has the Son has life," and 1 John 3:34, "He dwells in him, and he in him," Ames identifies union with Christ as "that spiritual relation [*spiritualis illa relatio*] of human beings to Christ by which they obtain right to all the blessings that are prepared in him."[163]

The union is brought about by calling (*vocatio*), which consists both in the objective offering or presenting (*oblatio*), of Christ and its personal or subjective reception.[164] The objective side of the offer is the preaching or propounding Christ, the wisdom and power of God, as the necessary and sufficient means of salvation.[165] On the subjective side, "the reception of Christ [*Christi receptio*] is that by which the offered Christ is conjoined to the individual and the individual to Christ," as revealed in John 6:56, "He abides in me and I in him" and in a host of other places in the New Testament.[166] Given that this reception of Christ marks the beginning of new life in Christ, it is also called "conversion"—understood as a divine act in which the human being is a passive recipient of the grace the both converts the will and enlightens the mind, engendering faith and repentance.[167] Ames notes that faith and repentance have the same "causes and foundations" (*causae & principiae*) inasmuch as both proceed from the free gift of God—and that repentance is often

160. R. T. Kendall, *Calvin and English Calvinism to 1649* (Oxford: Oxford University Press, 1979), p. 159.

161. Ames, *De conscientia* (1643), II.ix.1 (p. 69).

162. Ames, *Medulla*, I.xxvi.1.

163. Ames, *Medulla*, I.xxvi.2.

164. Ames, *Medulla*, I.xxvi.3, 7.

165. Ames, *Medulla*, I.xxvi.8.

166. Ames, *Medulla*, I.xxvi.17-18, citing also 2 Cor. 5:17; Gal. 3:27; Eph. 3:17; Heb. 3:6; 2 Cor. 6:16; Eph. 5:23; John 15:5; 1 Cor. 12:12.

167. Ames, *Medulla*, I.xxvi.19, 21-24, 27, 30.

"perceived" prior to faith because a believer may have difficulty understanding himself as fully reconciled to God in Christ before he has forsaken the sinful life.[168]

The implication of the passage, indeed, of Ames entire chapter, is that the order of the various aspects of union with Christ is not primarily chronological but causal, given the priority of the divine over the human act. In addition, Ames has identified union with Christ as consisting in calling, offer and reception, conversion, faith, and repentance, namely, as a unified work of God, without establishing a strict temporal order. The union, however, precedes and stands as the foundation of the other aspects or parts of the application of Christ. Indeed, all that follows—in Ames' series, justification, adoption, sanctification, and glorification—are understood as "blessings flowing from union with Christ," as indicated from verses in Romans 8 as well as other texts.[169] Ames also departs from the model found in Perkins and reverts to the precedence of repentance, conjoined with faith, found in Calvin and Zanchi.

Kendall misrepresents Ames' point, as if repentance were prior and prerequisite to faith "in the *ordo salutis*"—indeed, as if Ames had actually spoken of *ordo salutis*![170] In favor of this claim, Kendall cites Ames to the effect that "Repentance in respect of that carefulness, and anxiety, & terror arising from the Law which it hath joyned to it, doth goe before Faith, by order of nature, as a preparing and disposing cause."[171] Kendall simply omits the second part of the same sentence (presumably because it is so inconvenient to his argument): "but in respect of that effectuall and kindly turning away from sin, as God is offended by it, so it followes Faith, and depends upon it as the effect upon the cause, and herein is proper to the faithfull."[172] Repentance and faith, as aspects of the union, work together and, given their grounding in grace, conform to the language of predestination previously argued by Ames.[173] The argument parallels that of Perkins, allowing, however, for the difference brought about by Ames' priority of initial repentance.

Ames also argues union with Christ in his chapter on the "church mystically considered," immediately following his discussion of the sequence of application of salvation. Inasmuch as Christ gave himself for his church, election, redemption, calling, justification, adoption, sanctification, and glorification pertain to the church as they do to its individual members. As in the case of individual believers, the church is not only a "subject" of this sequence of application; it is also an effect, "for it is not first a church in actuality, and afterward a participant in union and

168. Ames, *Medulla*, I.xxvi.30, 34.

169. Ames, *Medulla*, I.xxvii.1; cf. citations of Rom. 8:30 at I.xxvi.6 (union and calling);Rom. 8: 1, 3, 33, 34 at I.xxvii.7, 20, 26 (justification); Rom. 8:15, 16, 17, 22, 23, 28, 29 at I.xxviii.4, 11, 19, 22, 25 (adoption); Rom. 8:5, 6, 30 at I.xxiv.17, 20.

170. Kendall, *Calvin and English Calvinism*, pp. 159-160.

171. Ames, *Marrow*, Ixxvi.31; cf. Kendall, *Calvin and English Calvinism*, p. 160.

172. Ames, *Marrow*, Ixxvi.31.

173. Contra Kendall, *Calvin and English Calvinism*, p. 159-161.

communion with Christ; rather, because it is united to Christ, it is on that account the church of Christ."[174]

After Perkins, Polanus, and Ames—union with Christ in later Reformed orthodoxy. Although it must remain beyond the scope of an essay like the present one to line out the full trajectory of seventeenth-century Reformed approaches to the language of union with Christ in its relation to the developing notion of a sequence of application of salvation, it should be noted that Perkins' and Ames' approach to union with Christ as the primary category for understanding the application of salvation did not disappear but carried over into various theological works of the Reformed orthodox, sometimes in detail, sometimes in brief statement. Of course, as noted by Venema, this development was neither universal nor uniform.[175]

Of the full series of theological *loci* written in the seventeenth century, several follow out the argument found in Ames' *Medulla* in grounding the entire sequence of salvation in union with Christ. Downame, for example, writes of the predestination referenced in Romans 8:29 as "Predestination to bee adopted in Christ" and characterizes God's elect as those "effectually called to the knowledge and participation of Christ."[176] Downame then identifies regeneration as the beginning of the work of salvation and as the "ground-worke of the rest"of the series, defining it as "our spirituall incorporating into Christ."[177] Ainsworth's posthumous *Orthodox Foundation of Religion* indicates that "the imputation of Christs merit & satisfaction" is the most proximate cause of justification inasmuch as the application of Christ's merits to believers is a "union with Christ" such that it is "as if wee our selves had died, and satisfied for our sinnes."[178] Notable also is Edward Leigh's *System or Body of Divinity*, where the entire sequence of the application of salvation is taken up in book VII, entitled "Of our Union and Communion with Christ, and our Spiritual Benefits by him, and some special Graces."[179]

174. Ames, *Medulla*, I.xxxi.2
175. Venema, *Accepted and Renewed in Christ*, pp. 198-199.
176. John Downame, *The Summe of Sacred Divinitie Briefly and Methodically Propounded: And then More Largely & cleerly handled and explaned* (London: W. Stansby, 1625), II.i; II.vii (pp. 288, 400). Downame, it should be noted, was the publisher of this work, traditionally associated with his name. It is now recognized that the brief sum of theology at the beginning of the work was penned by Sir Henry Finch and that Finch may well be the author of the latter "more largely and cleerly handled" section as well.
177. Downame, *Summe of Sacred Divinitie*, II.viii (p. 427).
178. Henry Ainsworth, *The Orthodox Foundation of Religion, long since collected by that judicious and elegant man Mr. Henry Ainsworth, for the benefit of his private company: And now divulged for the publike good of all that desire to know that Cornerstone Christ Jesus Crucified*, ed. by Samuel White (London: R. C. for M. Sparke, 1641), p. 62.
179. Edward Leigh, *A Systeme or Body of Divinity: Consisting in Ten Books. Wherein the fundamentals of religion are opened; the contrary errours refuted; most of the controversies between us, the Papists, Arminians, and Socinians discussed and handled; several Scriptures explained, and vindicated from corrupt glosses* (London: A. M. for William Lee, 1654; 2nd ed., corrected and enlarged, 1662), VII (pp.

Edward Polhill's *Speculum theologiae in Christo* is a synopsis of Christian doctrines founded on the assumption that Christ "did not only reveal the Gospel, but he himself is the substance and marrow of it" and "the very Mirror of Divine Truths and Perfections"—and that, therefore, "in our *Emanuel* we have a body of Theology, an excellent Summary of Divine Truths, in a very lively manner set forth to us."[180] Polhill takes up the issue that Vermigli broached, arguing a "double" union or "Conjunction between *Christ* and us," namely, the common or general conjunction between Christ and all humanity given his assumption of human nature in the office of Mediator, and the "special conjunction, which is between Christ and Believers."[181] Polhill adds that the "consequence" of this special conjunction or union is the "communication of Divine Blessings from him to us" and, citing Zanchi, notes that "All our good things depend on this most necessary Union."[182] Therefore, when Christ's righteousness is imputed to believers, there are three grounds or foundations of the imputation: "the first Foundation of it, is the Divine constitution made touching Christ: the intermediate Foundation is this, that Christ was out Sponsor and satisfied for us: the immediate Foundation is this, that Christ is a communicating Head to his believing Members, and they as Members participate in his satisfaction."[183] Polhill indicates a priority of Christ's meriting justification over the union of believers with Christ, in order that Christ's righteousness might be imparted in and through the union.[184] Polhill also argues the relationship of the good works of believers to salvation and therefore the ordering of faith and sanctification on the ground that

> Faith unites us to Christ. And so it is a Divine *Medium* to have his Righteousness made ours; but Good Works follow after Union; we are by faith married to Christ, that we might bring forth fruit to God, *Rom.* 7:4. Before Faith, which is our Espousal to Christ; we bring forth no genuine Obedience; Good Works are the progeny of a man in Christ; one who by Union with him is rightly spirited to do the Will of God.[185]

As in the theologies of most of the earlier Reformed writers, Polhill clearly sets faith together with the union, not as a cause, but as that which apprehends Christ. He also echoes Calvin's language of a *duplex gratia*, identifying justification and sanctification as "Twins of Grace" that "can never be parted," always operating in "conjunction" in those united to Christ and both inseparably flowing from Christ's

---

671-833); and note the similar conclusion concerning the theology of John Owen in J. V. Fesko, "John Owen on Union with Christ and Justification," *Themelios*, 37/1 (2012), pp. 7-19.

180. Edward Polhill, *Speculum theologiae in Christo: or, A view of some divine truths, which are either practically exemplified in Jesus Christ, set forth in the gospel: Or may be reasonably deduced from thence* (London: A.M. and R.R. for Tho. Cockerill, 1678), "To the Christian Reader" (unpaginated).

181. Polhill, *Speculum*, pp. 331, 334.

182. Polhill, *Speculum*, p. 335.

183. Polhill, *Speculum*, p. 337.

184. Polhill, *Speculum*, p. 345.

185. Polhill, *Speculum*, pp. 383-384.

righteousness.[186] Once again, the order is not a primarily temporal one, the only clearly temporal aspect being the progress of sanctification—nor is justification a cause of sanctification; rather it is a concomitant arising out of faith and union with Christ.

Contemporaneously with Leigh and Polhill, Thomas Goodwin firmly grounded his understanding of the application of salvation in union with Christ:

> union with Christ is the first fundamental thing of justification, sanctification, and all. Christ first takes us, and then sends his Spirit. He apprehends us first. It is not my being regenerate that puts me into a right of all those privileges, but it is Christ takes me, and then gives me his Spirit, faith, holiness, &c. It is through our union with Christ, and the perfect holiness of his nature, to whom we are united, that we partake of the privileges of the covenant of grace.[187]

This assumption also specifically grounds Goodwin's understanding of justification, namely, that "all acts of God's justifying us depend upon union with Christ," and that "the aim of the soul casting itself on Christ is to have justification from him, so to have union with him also."[188]

Conclusions

The portion of the current literature that has dealt nearly exclusively with Calvin's formulation of the doctrine has observed, rightly, that his views, as found in the 1559 *Institutes*, can be set against the background of his broader christological polemic against Andreas Osiander. But it must also be observed that Calvin's teaching was not formulated merely as a response to Osiander: it had deeper positive roots in the older tradition, and the basis of Calvin's own approach had been formulated, whether in commentaries or in earlier editions of the *Institutes*, prior to his encounter with Osiander's thought—beginning, in fact, in the 1539 *Institutes* and the 1540 Romans commentary. More importantly, much of this literature has failed to examine other Reformed thinkers of the era and has, accordingly, failed to note how fully Calvin's teaching reflects the standard, traditional assumptions of the era. In other words, Calvin did not pose a new and highly original notion of the *unio cum Christo* against Osiander—rather he opposed Osiander with a view of the *unio* that, granting some variations in formulation, he shared with other Reformed writers of his generation and elaborated somewhat for the sake of the debate. What is more, this literature, perhaps most egregiously the studies of Partee and Canlis, has so neglected consideration of Calvin's intellectual context that it has failed to see how Calvin's own position was developed in conversation with other Reformed writers,

---

186. Polhill, *Speculum*, p. 390; cf. ibid, p. 419.

187. Thomas Goodwin, *A Discourse of Christ the Mediator*, in *The Works of Thomas Goodwin*, 12 vols. (Edinburgh: James Nichol, 1861-1866), V, p. 350.

188. Thomas Goodwin, *Of the Object and Acts of Justifying Faith*, in *Works*, VIII, p. 406.

notably Vermigli, and indeed how much Calvin's formulations owed to this conversation and, therefore, also belong to a larger discussion and pattern of formulation in the Reformed tradition.

These shared assumptions concerning union with Christ and the sequence of the application of salvation rest, arguably, on a shared identification of the exegetical foundations of the doctrine as well as a series of shared assumptions concerning the movement from exegesis to doctrinal formulation. We have seen, in other words, similar exegesis of Romans 8:1ff. in a series of Reformed commentaries, a clear connection drawn in those same commentaries between the understanding of union with Christ in the argument of the chapter and the sequence of aspects of salvation found in verses 28 through 30, followed by reflection on these exegetically-grounded understandings in more-formalized discussions of the sequence of the application of salvation both in the more systematic works of the Reformers and of the Reformed orthodox.

All of the formulations that we have examined identify union with Christ as the basis of the work of salvation. All identify it as accomplished by the work of the Spirit of Christ through the instrumentality of faith, following out a commonly held and argued exegesis of Romans 8:1ff. In addition, all place justification in immediate relation to faith and the *unio* and regard regeneration, increase in holiness or sanctification, and the attendant good works as a subsequent stage, without making clear whether the series of stages is a temporal, logical, or natural sequence. (Scholarship on the question of an order of salvation has, typically, identified only issues of temporal and logical sequencing and has failed to recognize the third possibility, namely, a natural order that is neither temporal not logical.) In the passages examined, Vermigli in particular questioned the need for identifying the sequence as temporal, while at the same time identifying it as natural.

There are also differences among the various writers over the relationship of the terms. Musculus, rather uniquely, deployed nearly all of the terms associated with the application of salvation under the working of faith. Calvin identified the source of repentance as participation in Christ, while Zanchi held that repentance was effected conjointly by the preaching of law and gospel and indicated its necessity to genuine communion with Christ. Zanchi's language, therefore, embodies some differences—he does not use the term *vocatio*, or "calling," but speaks of the effective preaching of law and gospel, and he does not use the term "sanctification," but rather includes mortification and vivification (identified by Calvin with sanctification) under repentance. His sense of repentance being required to a fullness of communion with Christ perhaps echoes Vermigli's sense of the *unio* as secret in the imperfect state of believers in this life—although Vermigli's language of a secret union prior to the final full spiritual union appears to be unique among the Reformers despite its formulation in the context of an accord with Calvin and Beza.

What ought also to be obvious from the materials examined is that, contra Canlis and Partee, and in accord with the arguments presented by Farthing and Fesko, a significant number of later Reformed theologians, particularly among the English Reformed, paid rather close attention to the doctrine of union with Christ, and that, contra Canlis in particular, union with Christ was not understood as a final product of the *ordo salutis* dependent on completion of all steps in the series—rather it was understood and typically explicitly identified as the very basis of the sequence of the application of salvation. Nor do the various sixteenth- and seventeenth-century thinkers examined offer evidence of the development of a rigid chronological notion of the order of salvation. Apart from the necessarily temporal precedence of initial regeneration over progress in sanctification and final glorification, the issue of temporal ordering does not appear to have been prominent in the thought either of various Reformers or of the later Reformed orthodox writers. Their orderings, moreover, vary both in the terms used and in the arrangements of the terms—albeit consistently obliging the basic Pauline sequence of predestination or election, calling, justification, and glorification, but varying in their integration of other terms— repentance, regeneration, mortification, vivification, renovation, sanctification—into the series.

It is also, therefore, somewhat misleading to comment that "lacking in Calvin is the notion of an *ordo salutis* … as … articulated and developed in later Reformed theology" just as it is problematic to conclude that there is a "fundamental incompatibility" between "Calvin's view of union with Christ" and "the later *ordo salutis*,"[189] inasmuch as the terminology of *ordo salutis* did not figure in the development of Reformed orthodox formulations of the application of Christ's work, and more importantly, the various sequencings of that application found among the Reformed orthodox reflected most, if not all, of the same concerns as appear in the writings of Calvin and his contemporaries—namely, grounding the sequence in calling and union with Christ and identifying the subsequent elements of the sequence as brought about in and through the union, without indicating a temporal sequencing of justification and sanctification except insofar as sanctification is a process.[190] It also is clear that Calvin's interest in the doctrinal issues of union with Christ and the ordering of the application of salvation began early on in his thought and continued throughout his career.

The importance of distinctions between natural or causal, logical, and temporal ordering needs also to be noted, given that (whether in the language of the

---

189. Gaffin, "Response to John Fesko," p. 105; Evans, *Imputation and Impartation*, p. 81; cf. the more nuanced statement of issues, contra Evans, in Venema, *Accepted and Renewed in Christ*, pp. 198-199.

190. Evans' conclusion that in Calvin's thought "salvation is an organic unity communicated *in toto* through spiritual union with Christ" while in "the *ordo salutis* model … salvation is bestowed through a series of successive and discrete acts" (*Imputation and Impartation*, p. 81; cf. ibid., pp. 54-55) fails to consider the distinct elements in Calvin's ordering of the application of salvation and the connection between these various elements and union with Christ in later Reformed theology. The phrase "organic unity" is both misleading and anachronistic.

Reformers or in the discussions of issues found among the later writers) there was clear recognition that these different kinds of order functioned in very different ways. Indication of a temporal or logical sequence did not necessarily indicate a cause-and-effect relationship: acts and events occur after other acts and events without being caused by them. Thus, the sequence in which faith precedes justification does not identify faith as the efficient cause of justification. Similarly, temporal and causal or natural sequences are not logical. The point is particularly important in the case of causal sequences that arise from free choices of either the divine or the human will; inasmuch as such acts, by definition, could be otherwise, they are not deducible. Thus, the entire sequence of predestination, calling, faith, union with Christ, justification, regeneration, sanctification, and glorification (however one wishes to arrange the intervening degrees between predestination and glorification), given that it rests on the free divine willing, cannot as a whole ultimately be a logical sequence.

There are, as we have noted, differences of nuance among the Reformers and the Reformed orthodoxy, but they are far more subtle than can be accounted for by claims of the absence or presence of an *ordo salutis* or simple matters of sequence. One of the more significant of these nuancings concerns the attempt of early orthodox Reformed writers—notably Perkins and Ames—to distinguish and then integrate more fully the various terms used by the Reformers into a structure or series of the aspects of the application of salvation. Specifically, these later writers tend to distinguish regeneration from sanctification, identifying the former as the change wrought by grace and the latter as the process of increase in holiness as faith bears fruit in good works. They also identify mortification and vivification more clearly as aspects of the process of sanctification and, in Ames case, add the category of adoption. The addition of categories, moreover, belonged primarily to the needs of piety and of dealing with the fullness of the biblical language. What is retained in these writers, however, is the intimate connection between calling, faith, and union with Christ, as well as the grounding of both justification and sanctification in grace, faith, and union. Much like the Reformers, the later Reformed writers examined assumed the necessary connection between union with Christ and justification understood as the imputation of Christ's righteousness. Also retained is the recognition that the order of salvation is primarily causal, with logical elements, and only temporal in the progress of regeneration-sanctification toward glorification—with, however, elaborations of that progress to include the other terms, in effect, inserting these terms into the chain or *gradus* already found in the sequence of Romans 8:28-30. The background for this elaboration, moreover, was both the presence of this language in Scripture and the Reformers' use of the language often without clear indication of the relationships of the terms of the sequence in Romans 8:28-30 as they related to union with Christ.

Beyond the basic reversal of the claims of writers like Canlis and Evans concerning the incompatibility of union with Christ and language concerning the ordering of salvation, a further conclusion can be drawn, namely, that the doctrine of union with Christ and participation in Christ, like other doctrinal concepts at issue in the development of Reformed theology in the early modern era, cannot properly be analyzed into a simple pattern of likeness or unlikeness to Calvin's formulations—if only because Calvin did not provide the Reformed tradition with its only foundational presentation of the doctrine. Canlis' failure to examine the thought of Calvin's contemporaries or of the later Reformed, and Evans' comparison of Calvin, taken in isolation, with a very limited sampling of later Reformed writers create a false picture, indeed, a caricature, both of Calvin's thought and of the theologies of the later Reformed. Arguably, the clearer analysis of the modes or degrees of union found among the Reformers comes from Vermigli, whether in his Romans commentary or in his epistolary dialogue with Calvin and Beza. Whether we follow Anderson to the point of declaring that Calvin might well be called the follower of Vermigli will depend on further comparative analysis of Calvin's and Vermigli's readings of other passages in Scripture and their approaches to union with Christ in the context of the sacraments.[191]

In any case, Calvin's stated agreement with Vermigli provides a basis for a more contextualized reading of Calvin's own doctrine. It may also very well be the case that Beza's well-developed understanding of union with Christ in relation to the whole application of Christ's work received impetus from Vermigli. There are also indications that, beyond the influence of Vermigli's thought, Zanchi's rich and detailed discussions of the *unio* and Olevianus' lengthy theological exegesis of Romans 8 had as much or perhaps a greater impact on later Reformed thought than Calvin's formulations, if only because their formulations were further along the historical line of argument. Among the early orthodox writers, Perkins offered a more detailed sequence of the application of salvation than we have seen from his predecessors, but the sequence, like the sequence noted in Ames, neither removed union with Christ from its foundational position nor argued a strictly temporal ordering. Variants of these approaches to union with Christ and the application of salvation are attested in the further development of Reformed orthodoxy.[192]

Beyond this, examination of the materials of the sixteenth and seventeenth centuries indicates that development of a doctrine of union with Christ and development of the language of the application of salvation toward what would become the *ordo salutis* were neither utterly distinct nor mutually exclusive projects. Given the common source of the topics, namely, Romans 8, the Reformed development ought to be understood as a complex examination of the terms supplied by the text, incorporating language of union with language of calling, faith, justification, and glorification and, further, raising the issue of the relationship of other biblical language of salvation—regeneration, sanctification, mortification,

---

191. Anderson, "Peter Martyr," p. 64.

192. Cf., e.g., Turretin, *Institutio theologiae elencticae*, XVII.i.1-3; Brakel, *ΛΟΓΙΚΗ ΛΑΤΡΕΙΑ, dat is Redelijke Godsdienst in welken de goddelijke Waarheden van het Genade-Verbond worden verklaard* (Dordrecht: Banier, 1700), cap. xxx-xxxv.

vivification, adoption—to the basic series of terms supplied by Romans 8. In a large number of the later writers, union with Christ remained foundational to the entire sequence of the application of Christ's work.

Perhaps the clearest conclusion that can be drawn from an examination of various formulations of union with Christ in the works of Reformation-era and early orthodox Reformed writers is that study of Calvin in isolation from the broader Reformed tradition, on the part of writers like Canlis and Partee and to a certain extent Evans as well, produces a rather misleading picture not only of Reformed theology in general but also of Calvin's thought in particular. What needs to be observed is that there were initially, and there remained subsequently, varieties of formulation among the Reformed; that the terminology remained somewhat fluid, often lacking a strict distinction between repentance and sanctification, and frequently incorporating logical and natural or causal as well as temporal orderings; that these varieties of formulation did not lead to extended controversy; and that the later formulations continued to recognize the priority of grace and the foundational significance of union with Christ to the language of the application of salvation.

8

Calvin, Beza, and the Later Reformed on Assurance of Salvation and the "Practical Syllogism"

The Problem of the Practical Syllogism

The practical syllogism and the early modern quest for certainty. The relationship of Calvin's teaching concerning the assurance of salvation to the so-called practical syllogism remains, if not an absolutely pressing concern, certainly a problem to be examined in Calvin studies. It is, moreover, one of several problems in Calvin scholarship that raises the issue of the relationship of Calvin's thought to later Reformed theology. Many later Reformed theologians did specifically argue a *syllogismus practicus* in their doctrine of assurance, and some, like Beza, did formulate an argument for assurance that included reference to good works, albeit not to the exclusion of the more spiritual or internalized evidences of calling, faith, and sanctification. If such a teaching were utterly absent from Calvin's thought but present in the teaching of later writers, it would stand, potentially, as one significantly discontinuous element in the development of Reformed theology. On the assumption, moreover, that Calvin stood against the practical syllogism or at least against its misuse, various modern writers have attempted to contrast his christocentric theology with either a causal metaphysics or an anthropocentric tendency in later Reformed theology.[1]

Of course, it must be open to question whether the rather restrictive dogmatic *locus* of this modern discussion and debate does justice to the sixteenth- and seventeenth-century problem of assurance—and whether the identification of the

---

1. As argued in John S. Bray, *Theodore Beza's Doctrine of Predestination* (Nieuwkoop: De Graaf, 1975); idem, "The Value of Works in the Theology of Calvin and Beza," *Sixteenth Century Journal*, 4/2 (1973), pp. 77-86; and R. T. Kendall, *Calvin and English Calvinism to 1649* (Oxford: Oxford University Press, 1979); and disputed in Richard A. Muller, *Christ and the Decree: Christology and Predestination in Reformed Theology from Calvin to Perkins* (Durham, N.C.: Labyrinth Press, 1986; reissued, with a new preface Grand Rapids: Baker, 2008); and Joel Beeke, *Assurance of Faith: Calvin, English Puritanism, and the Dutch Second Reformation* (New York: Peter Lang, 1991).

problem of the *syllogismus practicus* as a facet of the larger dogmatic debate over central dogmas and predestinarian metaphysic does not in fact obscure rather than reveal the nature of the problem. From its very beginnings, the Reformation can be said to have focused on problems of authority and assurance—whether Luther's *anfechtungen* or the more universal debate over Scripture and tradition. Nor should we forget, as E. A. Burtt has noted, that the examination of antiquity had revealed ancient alternatives to the Ptolemaic, geocentric view of the universe, at the same time that astronomers were beginning to argue the same point. So also, at the same time that the antipodes, those previously disputed human inhabitants of the nether side of the globe, were being evidenced in the concrete, the voyages of discovery proved, not that the world was round (which was well understood), but that Europe was not its genuine center.[2] In making these remarks, Burtt's intention was to establish the intellectual and spiritual context in which Copernicus' new cosmology arose, specifically, the context in which a new theory might gain acceptance, even though that theory was no more and, indeed, perhaps less empirically verifiable by sixteenth-century standards than the Ptolemaic theory. That context was one of increasing uncertainty concerning cherished views of the place and position of human beings in their world.

By extension, the question raised by the *syllogismus practicus*, albeit a dogmatic one, may find a broader *locus* of meaning and explanation in the context of the more general and generally more pressing problem of certainty that beset the sixteenth century, as a whole series of perspectives on world and humanity were subjected to significant alteration.[3] The use of a practical syllogism, namely, of various aspects of the doctrine of salvation that could be framed syllogistically for the sake of personal assurance, arose in a context in which a Protestant language of the order and pattern of salvation challenged churchly authority and removed the security once afforded by the more externalized aspects of late medieval understandings of penance, good works, and merits. Arguably, the beginnings and the development of the *syllogismus practicus* in Reformed theology should be placed into the context not only of the Protestant stress on the ultimate authority of Scripture but also of the Reformation-era development of theologies and pieties grounded in the immediacy of the work of Christ as accessed by grace through faith and, quite specifically, as defined by assumptions concerning the order or chain of salvation and its manner of explaining the believer's union with Christ.

The structure of the problem of assurance represented by the syllogism is not unlike the structure of the problem of the authority of Scripture. Musculus explained the order and arrangement of his theology, particularly the placement of a lengthy discussion of Scripture into the context of his doctrine of salvation, as a result of the

---

2. E. A. Burtt, *The Metaphysical Origins of Modern Science* (Atlantic Highlands: Humanities Press, 1952), pp. 40-41.

3. See Susan E. Schreiner, *Are You Alone Wise? The Search for Certainty in the Early Modern Era* (New York: Oxford University Press, 2011), pp. 66-72, on Calvin.

fact that "the certainty of the Christian faith" rests on the Old Testament as well as the New, since the gospel of Christ begins in the ancient word of promise.[4] Calvin, too, had spoken of faith as "une certaine et ferme cognoissance" or, in the more familiar form given in the 1559 Institutio, "divinae erga nos benevolentiae firmam certamque cognitionem."[5] Indeed, it has been argued that the concept of "certainty" is central to Calvin's teaching on faith, although the qualifier must be added from the Institutes, "as for its certainty, so long as your mind is at war with itself, the Word will be of doubtful and weak authority, or rather of none."[6] If certainty is central to Calvin's thought, then also uncertainty hovered not far from the center.

This emphasis on the "certainty" of the faith thus parallels and reflects the discussion of auctoritas, specifically of the auctoritas sacrae scripturae, granting particularly the issue of the internal self-consistency and self-evidencing character of the text raised already by the Reformers in their debates with the Roman Catholics, with the Radical or Spiritual Reformers, and with the rationalists and early Deists thinkers of the sixteenth century.[7] Underlying the question of authority, particularly in view of the magisterial Reformation's emphasis on sola scriptura, lay the question of how this authority is known—if not through the churchly tradition and magisterium or the wisdom of the individual exegete or, indeed, the revelation of new truths by the Spirit. This desire for certainty is surely reflected also in the Reformers' recourse to a discussion of evidences of the divine hand in Scripture despite their declarations of the primacy of the testimonium internum spiritus Sancti.

Thus, Calvin's often-cited comments on certainty point out the difficulty, not the resolution, of the question: he affirms, strongly, against Roman Catholic approaches to the problem of authority and certainty that "the testimony of the Spirit is more excellent than all reason" and that "the highest proof of Scripture derives ... from the fact that God in person speaks in it," and that, therefore, Scripture is "self-authenticating," but he then devotes an entire chapter of the 1559 Institutes—longer and more detailed than his discussion of the self-authenticating character of the text—to his discussion of rational evidences of the divinity and "credibility" of

4. Wolfgang Musculus, Commonplaces of the Christian Religion (London: Henry Bynneman, 1578), xxv, (p. 349, col. 2).

5. John Calvin, Catechisme (1541), in CR, vol. 34, col. 43; Calvin, Institutio christianae religionis (Geneva: Robert Stephanus,1559), III.ii.7.

6. Heribert Schützeichel, Die Glaubenstheologie Calvins (Munich: Max Hueber, 1972), pp. 133-144; cf. Calvin, Institutio (1559), III.ii.6.

7. Cf. the discussions of the problem of skepticism and unbelief in the sixteenth century in Lucien Febvre, The Problem of Unbelief in the Sixteenth Century: The Religion of Rabelais, trans. Beatrice Gottlieb (Cambridge: Harvard University Press, 1982); Richard H. Popkin, The History of Scepticism from Erasmus to Spinoza, 2nd ed. (Berkeley: University of California Press, 1979); idem, "Theories of Knowledge," in The Cambridge History of Renaissance Philosophy, pp. 668-684; and C. Constantin, "Rationalisme," in Dictionnaire de théologie catholique, ed. A. Vacant et al., 23 vols. (Paris: Librairie Letouzey et Ane, 1923-1950), XIII/2, cols. 1688-1788.

Scripture.[8] The problem here, moreover, is not unlike that of the *syllogismus practicus*, where Calvin stresses the grounding of assurance in Christ through faith but still feels constrained to deal with "latter signs" of election and, indeed, the work of the Spirit applying Christ and his work to believers.[9]

Calvin and the *syllogismus practicus* in contemporary scholarship. Much contemporary discussion takes its point of departure from a debate over the issue between Wilhelm Niesel and Karl Barth. Niesel had argued that Calvin never taught anything like the *syllogismus practicus* and, indeed, that Calvin's views on assurance of election militated against the idea of any human calculus of salvation. His views were seconded by Heinz Otten's monograph on Calvin's doctrine of predestination, only to be disputed by Barth.[10] In particular, Niesel argued against any significant consideration by Calvin of signs of election apart from Christ, on the ground that this would represent a departure from the principle of *sola gratia* that characterized early Reformed theology, whereas Barth in a more nuanced reading of the materials, pointed toward the presence of the idea as a necessary but necessarily subsidiary line of argument in Calvin's thought.

Barth's view of the later development, however, coincided with Niesel's. "Beza, Gomarus, the men of Dort, and Wolleb," Barth argued, developed a predestinarian model in which the practical syllogism became a part of a system of assurance distinct and potentially at variance from the christocentric model proposed by Calvin—indeed, that the syllogism tended toward the identification of good works as a ground of assurance that might become a ground of assurance independent of Christ.[11] Almost paradoxically, for both Barth and Niesel, a pattern of argument like the practical syllogism, by drawing attention away from Christ, proposed a theology that was both anthropocentric and predestinarian.[12] In the course of analyzing both Calvin's and Beza's approaches to assurance, we will need to question these approaches on the ground that the early modern sources do not operate on the basis of the dogmatic assumptions on which Niesel's and Barth's critiques are grounded.

In the more recent literature, Fred Klooster follows Niesel in denying the presence of the *syllogismus practicus* in Calvin but acknowledges that Calvin also includes a place for works in the question of assurance: "Calvin did not urge people to look at

---

8. Calvin, *Institutio* (1559), I.vii.4-5; viii.13.

9. Cf. Calvin, *Institutio* (1559), III.xiv.16, 18.; xxiv.1-6; and cf. the discussion in Muller, *Christ and the Decree*, pp. 25-27.

10. Cf. Wilhelm Niesel, "Syllogismus practicus?" in *Aus Theologie und Geschichte: Festgabe für E. F. K. Müller* (1933), pp. 158-179; idem, *The Theology of Calvin*, trans. Harold Knight (London: Lutterworth, 1956), pp. 178-181, pp. 169-181; Heinz Otten, *Calvins theologische Anschauung von der Prädestination* (Munich: Chr. Kaiser, 1938), pp. 54ff; and Karl Barth, *Church Dogmatics*, ed. G. W. Bromiley and T. F. Torrance, 4 vols. in 13 (Edinburgh: T. & T. Clark, 1936-1975), II/2, pp. 333-340.

11. Niesel, *Theology of Calvin*, pp. 178-179; cf. Barth, *Church Dogmatics*, II/2, pp. 335-336.

12. Niesel, *Theology of Calvin*, pp. 180-181; cf. Barth, *Church Dogmatics*, II/2, p. 339.

their own good works ... his clear emphasis is upon the work of Christ performed in believers."[13] John Bray's comparative analysis of Calvin and Beza on the point follows Barth in its interpretation of Calvin and also, more cautiously than either Niesel or Barth, echoes their conclusions about the relationship of the syllogism to a more systematic predestinarian model than Calvin's, namely, as often claimed to be in Beza's theology. Bray argues that a "lessened Christocentrism" in Beza correlated with a "more rationalistic theological methodology."[14] R. T. Kendall follows Bray almost point for point, arguing a vast difference between Calvin and Beza, much to the detriment of the christocentric direction given to Reformed theology by Calvin.[15] Kendall's assessment of the problem has distinct affinities with the discredited central dogma model that is echoed throughout Niesel's argumentation. M. Charles Bell's essay on the problem of assurance draws heavily on Niesel's argument to claim that Calvin's understanding of faith as a gift of God "necessarily precludes the use of the practical syllogism."[16] A study of covenant theology by David Poole engages in a brief digression on the *syllogismus practicus*, simply asserting the views of Niesel and Bell and referring to the attempt to find an adumbration of the doctrine in Calvin's thought as "ill-founded," without ever asking precisely what is meant by the *syllogismus practicus*.[17] One of the more recent efforts to deal with this problem is Kwang-Woong Yu's address "Syllogismus Practicus bei Calvin," delivered at the Fifth International Congress on Calvin Research. Here again, we find the arguments of Niesel confirmed along similar theological lines.[18]

François Wendel briefly argued the presence of the basic elements of the *syllogismus practicus* in Calvin's thought, in relative continuity with later Reformed theology.[19] A partial reassessment of the relationship of the *syllogismus practicus* to Calvin's thought and of its implications in the older Reformed tradition was undertaken in my early *Christ and the Decree*, where my analyses of the sixteenth-century materials were still influenced to some extent by the then pervasive neo-orthodox readings of Calvin. In dissenting from Niesel's refusal to allow any elements of a practical syllogism in Calvin, I nonetheless failed to see that his conclusions were grounded in a confused contrasting of hypothetical centers in Reformed theology and

13. Fred Klooster, *Calvin's Doctrine of Predestination*, 2nd ed. (Grand Rapids: Baker, 1977), p. 51.

14. Bray, *Theodore Beza's Doctrine of Predestination*, pp. 107-111; cf. Bray, "Value of Works," pp. 80-81.

15. Kendall, *Calvin and English Calvinism*, pp. 24-28, 33-38.

16. M. Charles Bell, *Calvin and Scottish Theology: The Doctrine of Assurance* (Edinburgh: Handsel Press, 1985), p. 31.

17. David N. J. Poole, *The History of the Covenant Concept from the Bible to Johannes Cloppenburg "De Foedere Dei"* (San Francisco: Mellen Research University Press, 1992), pp. 125, 172.

18. Kwang-Woong Yu, "Syllogismus Practicus bei Calvin," delivered at the Fifth International Congress on Calvin Research, Calvin Theological Seminary, Grand Rapids, Michigan, August 20-23, 1990.

19. Cf. Wendel, *Calvin*, p. 275-277.

that he had compounded the confusion by associating the *syllogismus practicus* with a speculative predestinarianism—a problem that carried over into my early assessment of Beza.[20] Fuller reassessment of the early modern sources is presented in Joel Beeke's examination of Reformed understandings of assurance and in Keith Stanglin's study of Arminius' approach to the problem.[21] Beeke sets the elements of *a posteriori* assurance of salvation found in Calvin's works into the context of Calvin's understandings of election, the work of Christ, and the work of the Spirit and concludes that Calvin taught a form of the practical syllogism that in no way removed his primary emphasis on the works of Christ and the Spirit.[22] Stanglin adds to this a broad reading of the practical syllogism in the older Reformed context, noting, contrary to much of the older literature, that it is not a "necessarily external or empirical" usage, nor, indeed, the declared foundation of assurance.[23]

Of course, the simple answer to the basic question posed in the Niesel-Barth debate and subsequent discussions is that Calvin never used the term *syllogismus practicus*, and that he did not reduce the problem of personal assurance of salvation to a syllogistic formula. In this sense, Calvin never taught the *syllogismus practicus*. Of course, since the phrase and the syllogistic formulae themselves arose after Calvin's death, in the theology of later Reformed theologians, Calvin did not argue against the concept. The issue, however, is complicated by the fact that Calvin did assume that some degree of personal assurance of salvation does arise from observation of the effects of grace in the believer—and by the fact that later Reformed writers, like Theodore Beza, who are identified as introducing the *syllogismus practicus*, also typically stated the point that some assurance of salvation could arise from the observation of one's own good works but often not in a strictly syllogistic form.[24] If then, the term is taken strictly as indicating only those formulations of assurance made in the form of a syllogism, it is rather rarely found before the seventeenth century, and Calvin did not employ it; if, however, the term is taken loosely, as it often appears to be used in the scholarship, as referring to resolutions to the question of assurance grounded on evidences of salvation in the human subject, it is a rather frequent occurrence in early modern Reformed thought, and as the following essay will argue, Calvin did appeal to it. His appeal, moreover,

---

20. Cf. Muller, *Christ and the Decree*, pp. 25-27, 85.

21. Beeke, *Assurance of Faith*, pp. 49-51, 72-86, 151-173; and Keith Stanglin, *Arminius on the Assurance of Salvation: The Context, Roots, and Shape of the Leiden Debate, 1603-1609* (Leiden: E. J. Brill, 2007), pp. 205-208.

22. Beeke, *Assurance of Faith*, pp. 72-78.

23. Stanglin, *Arminius on the Assurance of Salvation*, pp. 206-207.

24. Calvin, *Institutio* (1559), III.xxiv.1-6; cf. Theodore Beza, *Catechismus compendarius*, in *Tractationes theologicae*, 3 vols. (Geneva: Eustathius Vignon, 1570-1582), I, pp. 690, 691-692; cf. the discussion in John Bray *Theodore Beza's Doctrine of Predestination* (Nieuwkoop: de Graaf, 1975), pp. 108-110; and idem, "The Value of Works in the Theology of Calvin and Beza," *Sixteenth Century Journal*, 4/2 (1973), pp. 77-86, 108-110.

places him into a tradition of discussion of the issue that continued, with variation, but little change in ultimate emphasis, into the theologies of later writers like Theodore Beza.

This essay intends to demonstrate, then, not only that Calvin did use elements of what can be loosely called the *syllogismus practicus* and that his usage ought not to be taken as a sign of extreme discontinuity with later Reformed writers, including Beza, but also that the context of the various formulations, notably Beza's pastoral and catechetical context, must be taken into consideration when assessing the doctrinal issue. The theological framework for understanding the practical syllogism is not the macro-theological conflicts of christocentrism versus predestinarianism or of a myopic focus on the "Christ-event" versus an equally myopic anthropocentrism —conflicts largely invented by the nineteenth- and twentieth-century theologians whose scholarship imposed them on the early modern materials. Rather, the context is the early modern problem of certainty, specifically as focused on the relationship of good works and the inward experience of salvation to the problem of assurance, and the framework for understanding the Reformed resolutions of the problem is the developing language of union with Christ and what came to be called the *ordo salutis*.

Some definition: what is a "practical syllogism"? The practical syllogism, or *syllogismus practicus*, was hardly the invention of seventeenth-century Reformed theologians. The notion of a practical, as differentiated from a theoretical syllogism, has its roots in Aristotle, and there is a significant medieval history of reference to practical syllogisms, evident in such authors as Albertus Magnus, Duns Scotus, and Johannes Capreolus.[25] Medieval understandings of practical syllogisms and their use carried over into the Reformation; as Melanchthon indicated, "conscience is a practical syllogism in the intellect."[26] The major proposition of the syllogism is to the law of God or to God's Word for the sake of providing a precept for the believer. The minor proposition and, therefore, also the conclusion are an application of the precept, either approving or condemning something willed or desired by the rational creature and also manifesting the justice of God.[27] The connection between the notion of a practical syllogism and matters of conscience found in the later Reformed writers was, in other words, no accident—nor, if Melanchthon's definition is to be taken at face value, is the practical syllogism necessarily a matter of formal logic. The

---

25. Albertus Magnus, *Opera omnia* (Paris: Vives, 1891), VII, p. 452; Duns Scotus, *Quaestiones in secundum librum sententiarum*, d. 6, q. 1, in *Opera omnia*, ed. Wadding (Paris: Vives, 1893), XII, p. 335; Johannes Capreolus, *Defensiones theologiae divi Thomae Aquinatis*, ed. Ceslas Paban and Thomas Pègues, 7 vols. (Tours: Alfred Cattier, 1900-1908), III, d. 36, art. 1, concl. 2-3 (V, p. 424).

26. Philip Melanchthon, *Examen eorum, qui auduntur ante ritum publicae ordinationis* (Wittenberg: Johannes Crato, 1562), fol. Y6v: "Conscientia est Syllogismus practicus in intellectu." Also in Melanchthon, *Opera quae supersunt omnia* (CR), 21, col. 1083.

27. Melanchthon, *Examen*, fol. Y6v-Y7r.

law or Word of God occupies the place of the major proposition not necessarily formulated in a manner prescribed by formal logic, and both the minor proposition and the conclusion are folded into an application of the precept worked out in the conscience.

John Donne follows virtually the same definition when he notes that "*Conscientia est syllogismus practicus*, Conscience is a syllogism that comes to a conclusion; then only hath a man true knowledge, when he can conclude in his own conscience, that his practice, and conversation hath expressed it."[28] Donne continues,

> Who will believe that we know there is a ditch, and know the danger of falling into it, and drowning in it, if he sees us run headlong towards it, and fall into it, and continue in it? Who can believe, that he that separates himself from Christ, by continuing in his sin, hath any knowledge, or sense, or evidence, or testimony of Christ's being in him?[29]

Donne's point, like Melanchthon's, is that the basic notion of the practical syllogism, as applied to issues of salvation and assurance, is a logical description of the operation of conscience—an operation that, in practice, does not require formalization but that can, when analyzed, be put into syllogistic form.

Calvin and the problem of assurance. The theology of grace advocated by the Reformers, with its typically Augustinian recourse to an eternal decree of election, offered both a resolution and a further complication for the problem of the assurance of salvation. On the one hand, it resolved the great problem of attempting to work out one's own salvation by finite and fallible means through the limited structures of contrition and penance available in late medieval piety. If grace was freely given to those who did what was in them, how could a person know whether he had fully availed himself of his own powers in relation to the sacramental means? If, however, grace was freely given, not on the basis of a finite, unpredictable, and not easily quantifiable human act, but on the basis of an infinite, determinate, and unwavering divine act, the foundation of assurance was itself assured. On the other hand, the language of predestination presented the difficulty of grounding salvation ultimately in a hidden and unknowable decree. The problem of the decree and its execution in time, therefore, permeates the problem of assurance as addressed by Calvin.

This issue is implicit in Calvin's thought as early as his commentary on Romans (1539). There, Calvin could declare, in the totally objective manner of the Pauline text, that "we were enemies" with God "when Christ interposed [himself] for the purpose of propitiating the Father" and reconciling us to him. Calvin concludes, "we

28. John Donne, *Sermon XXVII*, in *The Works of John Donne*, ed. Henry Alford, 6 vols. (London: John W. Parker, 1839), I, p. 569; cf. idem, VI, p. 178.

29. Donne, *Sermon XXVII*, in *Works*, VI, p. 178.

have therefore ample arguments that confirm our hearts with confidence of salvation."[30] Christ offers, in fact, "two foundations" for the assurance of salvation,

> when we understand that life has been obtained for us, and death has been conquered: he teaches us that faith through the word of the gospel is sustained by both of these. For Christ, by dying, destroyed death: and by rising again he obtained life in his own power. The benefit of Christ's death and resurrection is now communicated to us by the gospel: there is no reason for us to seek anything farther.[31]

Here, the two foundations are identified as Christ's obtaining life and his conquering of death. In the context of the early Reformation polemic against "other mediators," Mary and the saints, and against the sacrament of penance and indulgences, Calvin's argument directs our attention toward Christ alone as the sure and certain promise of salvation: since Christ has suffered and died and come into the possession of his eternal inheritance, we who suffer in faith can look to what "is manifest in Christ" and know that "his possession of it takes away all uncertainty."[32]

The access to Christ by which this assurance can be gained cannot, for Calvin, be the mere hearing of the word preached, anymore than it could be a mere historical faith, namely, a knowledge that Christ's death has truly paid the price for sin, a mistaken reading to which Kendall comes remarkably close. Assurance does not, according to Calvin, arise because Christ (to borrow some phrases from Kendall) is "held forth to all" as its "immediate ground" or that "Christ's death is a sufficient pledge and merely seeing him is assuring"[33]—for Calvin, the issue is knowing not merely the objective datum of Christ's sufficient satisfaction but also knowing that we have been "received by Christ into his care and protection," that we truly "hear his voice," and as members of his "flock" are enclosed "within his fold."[34] There is, in other words, and must be a subjective apprehension of Christ's benefits in order for the objective work of satisfaction to be a basis for assurance. Even so, Kendall's parallel argument that a person's "persuasion" of the truth of Christ's utterly sufficient sacrifice arises from a "direct act of faith" is an anachronistic borrowing and misapplication of later Reformed language. Calvin, much like other Reformed thinkers, insisted on the volitional, third component of faith, the faithful apprehension of Christ's work in and for the believer: assurance arises not from

---

30. Calvin, *Commentarius in epistolam Pauli ad Romanos*, 5:10 in CO 49, col. 94 (*CTS Romans*, pp. 197-198).

31. Calvin, *Commentarius in epistolam Pauli ad Romanos*, 10:6-7, in CO 49, col. 199 (*CTS Romans*, pp. 389-390).

32. Cf. Calvin, *Commentarius in epistolam Pauli ad Romanos*, 8:17, with 8:28-30, in CO 49, col. 150, 158-161 (*CTS Romans*, pp. 301, 314-317).

33. Kendall, *Calvin and English Calvinism*, pp. 38, 25.

34. Calvin, *Institutio* (1559), III.xiv.6.

simply knowing that Christ's death is sufficient but from the communication of Christ's benefits, arguably, from discerning one's union with Christ.[35]

The issue is elucidated by Calvin's understanding of effectual calling. Whereas both the preaching of the gospel and salvation have their source in the election of God,[36] preaching is an outward call that is presented to the elect and reprobate alike.[37] It is, however, impossible to penetrate the eternal decree—as Calvin variously states the point, the eternal ordination of God is a labyrinth from which there is no extrication, an abyss that threatens to swallow those who look too closely into it.[38] In the background of his resolution of the problem, Calvin makes a distinction between the eternal decree and its execution or temporal outworking: whereas it is foolhardy and dangerously destructive to attempt to find assurance of election in the eternal decree, "this does not prevent believers from feeling that the benefits they receive daily from God's hand are derived from that secret adoption."[39]

This appeal to benefits of grace as signs of assurance does not, in Calvin's view, include an examination of outward works: "we must thus become wretched and lost, if we are sent back to works to find out the cause or the certainty of salvation [*salutis causa vel certitudo*]."[40] This and like comments of Calvin are, of course, the basis for the claim of Niesel and of those who follow his argumentation to deny that Calvin ever taught the practical syllogism and to argue that he had in fact warned against it.[41] Calvin's reason, however, for this exclusion of outward works from the grounds of assurance has little to do with warnings against the practical syllogism—rather it is because works are not part of the causality of salvation:

> those who would attribute salvation to works are deceived. For though God begins our salvation, and at length completes it by renewing us after his own image: yet the only cause is his good pleasure, by which he makes us partakers of Christ.[42]

Similarly, Calvin notes, reflecting his language of a twofold knowledge of God, "For if in him we are elected, it shall not be in ourselves that we find certitude of our

---

35. On which, see above, chapter 7; for a critique of Kendall's approach to Calvin's views on faith, see Richard A. Muller, "*Fides* and *Cognitio* in Relation to the Problem of Intellect and Will in the Theology of John Calvin," *The Unaccommodated Calvin: Studies in the Formation of a Theological Tradition*. New York: Oxford University Press, 2000), pp. 159-173.

36. Cf. Calvin, *Institutio* (1559), III.xxiv.1, "Evangelii praedicatio ex fonte electionis scaturit"; with ibid., III.xxi.1.

37. Calvin, *Institutio* (1559), III.xxiv.1.

38. Calvin, *Institutio* (1559), III.xxi.q; xxiv.3, 4; cf. Calvin, *De aeterna Dei praedestnatione*, in CO 8, col. 307, (*Eternal Predestination*, p. 111).

39. Calvin, *Institutio* (1559), III.xxiv.4.

40. Calvin, *Commentarius in epistolam Pauli ad Romanos*, 4:14, in CO 49, col. 78 (*CTS Romans*, p. 171).

41. Cf. Niesel, *Theology of Calvin*, pp. 175, 178.

42. Calvin, *Commentarius in epistolam Pauli ad Romanos*, 8:6, in CO 49, col. 142 (*CTS Romans*, p. 286).

election; and not even in God the Father, if we conceive him nakedly apart from the Son."[43] Just as certitude cannot be found by meditating on God the Father, so also is it impossible—even perilous—in Calvin's view to seek out one's election in the eternal decree.[44] For precisely the same reason, he elsewhere argued an *a posteriori* approach to election: "Election is prior to faith, but it is discerned by faith."[45]

It was not, however, Calvin's intention by these statements to exclude aspects of the actual causality of salvation from any consideration as grounds of assurance.[46] Nor, indeed, was it Calvin's intention, as Niesel seems to have thought, to predict a problem in later Calvinism! Rather, it was Calvin's intention, rooted in his context of polemics against various forms of synergism and emphases on the performance of meritorious acts for the sake of earning salvation, to remove outward works from the grounds of assurance, as also to remove the mere hearing of Christian preaching—at the same time that he warned against misunderstanding and misuse of his own teaching in *a priori* speculation into the eternal decree.

The connection, then, was made by Calvin not between outward acts and election, but between election, calling, and faith. Having specifically warned about finding one's election in speculations about the eternal decree, Calvin states that election ought to be considered as it is revealed in Scripture and inquiry about assurance ought "to begin with God's call and end with it"[47]—"If indeed we ask whom he calls, and according to what reason: he answers, those whom he has elected."[48] "Still," Calvin continues, "this does not prevent believers from feeling that the benefits they receive daily from God's hand are derived from that secret adoption."[49] Rather, it is one's sense of calling that identifies the connection between those daily benefits of the work of salvation, one's union with Christ, and one's secret

---

43. Calvin, *Institutio* (1559), III.xxiv.5: "Quod si in eo sumus electi, non in nobis ipsis reperiemus electionis nostrae certitudinem: ac ne in Deo quidem Patre, si nudum illum absque Filio imaginamur."

44. Calvin, *Institutio* (1559), III.xxiv.4.

45. Calvin, *De aeterna praedestinatione dei*, in CO, 8, col. 318-319; cf. *Institutio* (1559), III.xxiv.3; IV.i.2.

46. Contra Bell, *Calvin and Scottish Theology*, p. 31; Poole, *History of the Covenant Concept*, p. 125. Poole (pp. 124-125) draws on Kendall's mistaken understanding of later Reformed "voluntarism" to argue that, since faith is not a "volitional act" but a gift of God, it serves as the basis of assurance, to the exclusion of other indicators—as if Calvin did not also view other elements of the order of salvation also as gifts of God. On the issue of voluntarism and Kendall's misunderstanding of the issues, see Muller, *Unaccommodated Calvin*, pp. 159-173; and idem, "The Priority of the Intellect in the Soteriology of Jacob Arminius," *Westminster Theological Journal*, 55 (1993), pp. 55-72.

47. Calvin, *Institutio* (1559), III.xxiv.4.

48. Calvin, *Institutio* (1559), III.xxiv.1: "Si enim quaerimus quos vocet, et qua ratione: respondet, quos elegerat."

49. Calvin, *Institutio* (1559), III.xxiv.4: "Quanquam hoc non obstat quin fideles quae percipiunt quotidie beneficia ex Dei manu, sentiant ex recondita illa adoptione descendere...." Cf. the commentary on 2 Peter 1:1-12 in CO 55, col. 449-450 and Klooster, *Calvin's Doctrine of Predestination*, p. 34.

adoption and election. Clearly, a genuine inward calling and its effects within the
believer did function for Calvin as grounds of assurance:

> Therefore, they err who suspend the power of election on faith in the gospel, by
> which we feel it pertains to us: so we shall follow the best order if, in seeking the
> certitude of our election, we attend to those latter signs [iis signis posterioribus] that
> are sure testimony to it.[50]

Niesel, predictably and highly unconvincingly, identified these "latter signs" as
"God's 'objective Word'" and as calling, with calling reduced to Christ "whom we
encounter in the Word in virtue of the Holy Spirit."[51] Arguably, Calvin's version of
the practical syllogism looks to those parts of the gradation or chain of Romans 8:28-
30 that can be known to believers—not to election, which is secret, or to
justification, which is forensic and therefore has no clear relation to personal
righteousness and, specifically *not* to faith in the gospel, but to calling and to the
benefits of adoption and union with Christ, namely, regeneration and sanctification:
the issue is neither an "objective Word" nor an existential Christ-event—the former
being part of the problem to be resolved and the latter a passing quasi-
Kierkegaardian phenomenon not likely to have been dreamt of in the sixteenth
century.

Beyond this, and even in the context of his caution to exclude works and to
ground salvation itself on God's "gratuitous mercy [gratuita misericordia] toward us"
when dealing with the doctrine of justification,[52] Calvin was so certain that good
works would follow on grace, faith, and justification that in virtually the same breath
he could declare, "this confidence of works [operum fiducia] has no place unless you
have previously cast all the confidence of your soul [animi fiduciam] on the mercy of
God, it ought not to be seen as contrary to that upon which it depends."[53]

Calvin, thus, does not intend to leave works out of the doctrine of salvation and
assurance; he only seeks to place works into their proper context: he rules out
language of merit in order that the good works of Christians are not "contrary" to the
grace on which they depend. But once the believer casts his confidence entirely on
God's mercy, "conscience" has its proper foundation and "is also confirmed by the
consideration of works ... as far as they are evidences of God dwelling and reigning
in us."[54] (It is worth remembering here that Melanchthon defined conscience as a

---

50. Calvin, *Institutio* (1559), III.xxiv.4: "Ergo ut perperam faciunt qui electionis vim suspendunt
a fide Evangelii, qua illam ad nos sentimus pertinere: ita optimum tenebimus ordinem si in quaerenda
electionis nostrae certitudine, in iis signis posterioribus, quae sunt certae eius testificationes,
haereamus."

51. Niesel, *Theology of Calvin*, pp. 171-172.

52. Calvin, *Institutio* (1559), III.xiv.17.

53. Calvin, *Institutio* (1559), III.xiv.18.

54. Calvin, *Institutio* (1559), III.xiv.18: "Sic fundata, erecta, stabilita conscientia operum quoque
consideratione stabilitur; quatenus scilicet testimonia sunt Dei in nobis habitantis et regnantia."

practical syllogism.) Good works return, therefore, at the level of result and gift, with considerable significance to the life of salvation:

> Wherefore when we exclude the confidence of works, we mean only that the mind of a Christian should not be directed to any merit of works as an aid to salvation, but should entirely rely on the gratuitous promise of righteousness. We do not forbid him to support and confirm this faith by signs of divine benevolence to him. For if, when all we call to remembrance the various gifts which God has conferred on us, they are all as so many rays from the divine countenance, by which we are illuminated to contemplate the full light of that goodness, much more will the grace of good works, which demonstrate that we have received the Spirit of adoption.[55]

Similarly, Calvin notes that it would be valueless to use one's fear of God and righteous acts as a primary basis for ease of conscience or inward assurance:

> Therefore, when Solomon declares, in the fear of the Lord is strong confidence (Prov. 14:26), and when the saints beg a favorable audience form the Lord, because they have walked before him in truth and with a perfect heart (Gen. 24:40; 2 Kings 20:3), these things have no concern in laying the foundation for establishing the conscience, nor are they of any value unless they are taken a posteriori: for there nowhere exists such fear of God as can establish a full assurance, and the saints are conscious that their integrity is still intermingled with many relics of corruption.[56]

Nonetheless, "as the fruits of regeneration evidence that the Holy Spirit dwells in them, this affords them no little encouragement to expect the assistance of God in all their necessities."[57] In an a posteriori sense, godly fear and personal righteousness do indeed aid the conscience—just as good works can be "latter" or "posterior signs" of election. Thus, the objective truths of election and adoption do have an effect upon human life—this Calvin affirms, and to this extent, without any legalistic or empirical formulae, affirms the substance of the syllogismus practicus.

There is, therefore, ground to question whether Calvin's emphasis on seeking election in Christ is actually an approach to the problem of assurance that is separate and distinct from the elements of the practical syllogism also found in his writings. In the sermons on Ephesians, where he identified Christ as the "register" (registre)

---

55. Calvin, Institutio (1559), III.xiv.18: "Quare, dum operum fiduciam excludimus, hoc volumus duntaxat, ne mens christiana ad operum meritum, velut ad salutis subsidium, reflectatur, sed penitus resideat in gratuita justitia promissione. Non vetamus autem ne divinia erga se benevolentiae signis hanc fidem fulciat confirmet. Nam si, dum memoria repetuntur quaecunque in nos dona Deus contulit, sunt nobis quodammodo instar radiorum divini vultus, quibus illuminemur ad summam illam bonitatis lucem contemplandam; multo magis bonorum operum gratia, quae spiritum adoptionis nobis datum commonstrat."

56. Calvin, Institutio (1559), III.xiv.19.

57. Calvin, Institutio (1559), III.xiv.19: "Sed quoniam ex regenerationis fructibus habitantis in se spiritus sancti argumentum capiunt, inde se non mediocriter ad exspectandum in omnibus necessitatibus Dei auxilium confirmant."

of election as if he were the very book of life in which the names of believers were written, Calvin also identifies Christ as the pattern or "mirror" (*miroir*) and "pledge" (*gage*) of election, as it were, from the divine side of the elective willing. God has had compassion on sinners

> because he had already loved us in our Lord Jesus Christ. It is thus necessary, that before God could choose and call us, he had before him his pattern and mirror in which to see us: that is to say, our Lord Jesus Christ. ... It follows then, *That is in order that we should be pure and blameless before God, indeed, in love.* This word, love [*charité*] should be referred to God, since it should be said that we can find no other reason than the free love of God [*amour de Dieu gratuite*], for his acceptance of us as children.[58]

Even so, from the perspective of believers, Christ is the mirror of election and the ground of assurance because they are mirrored in him—mirrored because they are in union with Christ, and accordingly, called, justified, and sanctified. It is precisely in one of the places cited to show that Calvin could not have argued a *syllogismus practicus* that Calvin specifically makes this point: Poole cites Calvin as stating, "If you contemplate yourself, that is sure damnation," and concludes that "Calvin instructs his readers not to look to themselves."[59] Taken out of context and, in addition, identifying contemplation of oneself as one's own work apart from Christ, the text proves Poole's point—but read in context, Calvin's statement argues precisely the opposite. He argues specifically against a radical contrast between consideration of Christ and consideration of the self, noting that various opponents seem to claim, "If you consider Christ, salvation is certain; if you turn back to yourself, condemnation is certain." (Calvin's opponents here, *semipapistae* as he calls them, sound remarkably like Niesel.)[60] Taken in full the passage reads,

> Accordingly, I counter their argument in kind. If you consider yourself, condemnation [*damnatio*] is certain; but since Christ with all his benefits is communicated to you, so that all that he has becomes yours, and you become a member of him, and one with him, his righteousness covers your sins, his salvation removes your condemnation, he intercedes with his worthiness, that your unworthiness may not appear in the sight of God. This is true: that we ought by no means to separate Christ from us, or ourselves from him: but with all our might firmly retain that fellowship by which he has united us to himself.[61]

Consideration of oneself apart from Christ yields condemnation—consideration of oneself in Christ is part and parcel of the assurance of salvation. The opponent's

---

58. Calvin, *Sermons sur l'epitre aux Ephesiens*, 1:3-4, in CO 51, col. 269.
59. Calvin, *Institutio* (1559), III.ii.24, as cited by Poole, *History of the Covenant Concept*, p. 125 (following the Battles translation).
60. Cf. Niesel, *Theology of Calvin*, p. 181.
61. Calvin, *Institutio* (1559), III.ii.24.

separation of issues is, in Calvin's view, illegitimate. This point is something that Barth recognized in Calvin's argument and that led Barth, accordingly, to indicate that Calvin had, indeed, albeit with due caution, taught a form of the *syllogismus practicus*.[62] Looking to calling and sanctification, the latter signs, is hardly looking away from Christ as the neo-orthodox commentators on Calvin would have it; rather, it is looking to the way in which the believer is mirrored in Christ, to the way in which he is in Christ and Christ in him.[63] Indeed, for Calvin, sanctification was inextricably conjoined with union with Christ and, as such, was part of the *gradus* or series of *incrementa* flowing from election and, secondarily, from calling, belonging to the application of salvation as an indicator of genuine membership in the church.[64]

Assurance and the Practical Syllogism after Calvin

Theodore Beza and the *syllogismus practicus*. Beza's role in the development of later Reformed theology is no longer seen as a dominant force behind a transformation from a christocentric Calvinian theology to predestinarian metaphysic—in large part because the grandiose conflict of centrisms once argued in the secondary literature on the early modern Reformed has been shown to be mythological. Nonetheless, Beza's thought did not simply duplicate that of Calvin. As recognized by Beeke and others, one of the places in which there are somewhat different accents in Beza's thought is his doctrine of assurance, notably in his use of the *syllogismus practicus*. Still, contrary to the reading of Barth, Kendall, and to a lesser extent, Bray,[65] Beza neither moves the discussion very far from where Calvin had left it nor does he identify works as the primary ground of assurance and remove the focus of assurance from the work of Christ.

What is perhaps Beza's clearest approach to works as the outcome of faith occurs in his *Petit catéchisme* or *Catechismus compendarius* of 1575. There Beza prefaces his questions on divine commandments with the question and answer,

> Qu. But how does a person know if he has faith, or not?
> A. By good works.[66]

The commandments, in other words, are to be taught in recognition of the truth that faith, without works, is dead. Beza returns to the issue after a basic instruction on

---

62. Barth, *Church Dogmatics*, II/2, pp. 334-335.

63. See above, chapter 7, on Calvin's understanding of union with Christ.

64. Cf. Calvin, *In priorem epistolam Pauli ad Corinthios*, 1:2, in CO, 49, col. 308 (*CTS 1 Corinthians*, I, p. 52).

65. Cf. Barth, *Church Dogmatics*, II/2, pp. 335-336; with Kendall, *Calvin and English Calvinism*, pp. 32-33; and Bray, "Value of Works," pp. 79, 81-82.

66. Theodore Beza, *Petit catéchisme*, in *Recueil des principaux catechismes des eglises reformées* (Geneva: Pierre Chouet, 1673), v (pp. 6-7).

proper address to God, the Sabbath, the dedication of all life to God, and the text of the two tables of the law:

> Qu. Is it true that good life is the way to salvation?
> A. It is true that repentance and amendment are conjoined with the remission of our sins: but it does not follow from this that we acquire salvation by our works.[67]

There are several reasons, however, to refrain from drawing conclusions from this text such as those drawn generally by Niesel or more specifically by Barth and Bray. What we do not have here is a practical syllogism that detracts from the salvific focus on Christ and his work inasmuch as Beza's statement is clearly placed into a context of denying that salvation is grounded on works. More importantly, the text taken by itself is not a focal point for arguing the full content of Beza's doctrine of assurance, certainly not for the identification of an externalized and empirical basis for assurance in Beza's theology.[68]

A similar point is made, however, in the text of Beza's *Confession de la foy*, under the topic of the Holy Spirit and his work: "just as good works are testimonies of our faith, it follows that they also offer us testimony of our eternal election, since election is necessarily followed by the faith that apprehends Christ, through which, being justified and sanctified, we will enjoy the glory for which we have been destined before the foundation of the world."[69] As the larger context of Beza's *Confession* indicates, there were two reasons for this particular emphasis, one a matter of positive doctrinal and pastoral concern, the other arising out of the polemics of the era.

On the one hand, doctrinally and pastorally, Beza recognizes that it is not enough simply to know that Christ had fully, indeed, infinitely, satisfied for sin. Rather, the salvation of individuals depends on the grace of the Holy Spirit, working through faith, both to offer and to confer Christ—Christ must be applied and appropriated to the end that the believer knows that he is "in Jesus Christ by faith."[70] This understanding of salvation through faith, Beza adds, might itself be a source of anxiety or temptation: inasmuch as not all human beings will be saved, there is a sense in which, despite the infinite value of his death, Christ did not die for all—only believers receive the "fruit" of Christ's "passion and satisfaction."[71] (It is worth noting here, contra Kendall's reading of Beza, that this issue, as stated, is not driven by a supralapsarian assumption nor by any sense of the limitation of the value or worth of Christ's satisfaction. It arises, instead, out of the simple point that not all those

---

67. Beza, *Petit catéchisme*, vi (p. 8).

68. Revising my earlier reading of the *Petit catéchisme* in *Christ and the Decree*, p. 85.

69. Theodore Beza,*Confessio christianae fidei* (Geneva: Iohannis Bonae Fidei, 1560), p. 67; and idem, *Confession de la foy chrestienne, contenant la confirmation d'icelle, et la refutation des superstitions contraires* (Geneva: Jean Durant, 1561), iv.19.

70. Beza, *Confession de la foy*, iii.20, 24; iv.3, 13.

71. Beza, *Confession de la foy*, iv.13 (p. 43).

who hear the gospel will ultimately be saved.)[72] If a person is in Christ by faith, that person "cannot perish" and will, therefore, have assurance of salvation.[73]

The problem, then, becomes a test of faith: to overcome the anxiety and the temptation, a believer must examine himself in order to ascertain whether he has this genuine faith that has apprehended Christ. Beza notes that assurance begins with recognition of the effects of the work of Christ in a believer and then rises up to the cause. There are, he continues, two kinds of effect. The first is the entirely inward testimony of the Spirit that one is a child of God, as Paul indicates in Romans 8, when we inwardly cry, with assurance, "Abba, Father."[74] Second, the union with Christ that occurs through faith is a genuine spiritual conjoining that has effects, not a matter of "fantasy & imagination"—just as the soul in its union with the body operates on and affects the body. Even so, when Christ dwells in believers, his power brings about their regeneration and sanctification, freeing them from their "natural corruption," cleansing the will and leading it to desire righteousness.[75] When, therefore, believers discern these spiritual effects in themselves, "the conclusion is infallible, that [they] have faith," and that they are united to Christ to life eternal.[76] Beza returns to the issue that faith without works is dead and that a living faith issues in good works, not by the independent willing of the individual but "by the power of Jesus Christ dwelling in him," manifest by the "continual recognition of this precious testimony of the Spirit of God in the heart" and by the "continual exercise of all good works, according to one's vocation" and "the gift of regeneration."[77] Beza's argument is very close to Calvin's.[78]

This conclusion brings Beza to his more polemical reason for dealing with the issue of assurance and, specifically, for raising the issue of works. Opponents of the Reformed claim that good works are despised and excluded on the ground that justification rests entirely on the apprehension of Christ by faith alone. This, Beza insists, is false—a calumny against the Reformed. It is quite true that the Reformed give glory to God alone, but they in no way discourage Christians from doing good works: anyone who rightly calls himself a Christian will shun the vices that God has condemned and embrace true virtue. The doctrine of justification by faith alone, in other words, is not a form of antinomianism. But its advocacy does serve to manifest several differences between the Reform and Rome over the character of good works. In the first place, over against Rome, good works are to be understood as only those

---

72. Cf. Kendall, *Calvin and English Calvinism*, pp. 30-32, where the argument is predicated on the old "central dogma" theory as adapted by Hall and other exponents of the "Calvin against the Calvinists" argument.

73. Beza, *Confession*, iv.13 (p. 44).

74. Beza, *Confession*, iv.13 (p. 44), citing Rom. 8:16; 1 Cor. 2:10-12; Gal. 4:6.

75. Beza, *Confession*, iv.13 (pp. 44, 48).

76. Beza, *Confession*, iv.13 (p. 48).

77. Beza, *Confession*, iv.13 (p. 48).

78. Cf. Calvin, *Institutio* (1559), III.xiv.18, as cited above.

acts commanded by God in the law as good and acceptable to him.[79] There are, moreover, two kinds of good works, namely, the "more excellent" concerning "service to God" and those concerning one's neighbor, corresponding with the two tables of the law. The chief patterns of exercise of good works, then, Beza continues, are prayer to God and love of neighbor, the former resting on the work of the sole mediator and intercessor between God and human beings, Jesus Christ, and the latter proceeding from the love of God and the believer's reconciliation in Christ Jesus. Here Beza's argument probably reflects Viret's thought more than Calvin's.[80]

This approach to assurance, focusing it on love of God and neighbor, with both understood as service to God, not only evidences rather profound resonance with traditional Augustinian and Bernardine patterns of spirituality;[81] it also reflects in a very concrete manner the approach to spiritual oversight of the community found in the records of the Genevan Consistory.[82] The immediate, contextual background of Beza's argumentation is not, as has often been implied in modern dogmatic judgments on the practical syllogism, a conflict of predestinarianism, christocentrism, and anthropocentrism, but the ongoing, daily issue of the progress of piety in Christian life, as quite specifically identifiable in the efforts of Calvin, Beza, and their ministerial colleagues.[83]

The second difference with Rome concerns the source of good works. Both faith and works are acts of the human intellect and will, as "preceded, changed, assisted, and accompanied by the grace of God."[84] Contrary to the views of the "Papists who are demi-Pelagians," there is no "natural disposition" in human beings to receive initial grace. The source of all genuine good in human beings must be the pure grace of God, which makes "totally new creatures" of those whom it renews, changing an

---

79. Beza, Confession, iv.14-15 (pp. 49-51); cf. Calvin, Institutio (1559), II.viii.5.

80. Beza, Confession, iv.16 (pp. 52-54, 63); cf. Pierre Viret, Instruction chrestienne en la doctrine de la loy et de l'evangile: & et en la vraie philosophie & theologie tant naturelle que supernaturelle des Chrestiens (Geneva: Jean Rivery, 1563), following the critical edition, ed. Arthur-Louis Hofer (Lausanne: L'Age d'Homme, 2004), p. 156; in translation, A Christian Instruction, conteyning the law and the Gospell (London: Abraham Veale, 1573), p. 72.

81. Cf. Bernard of Clairvaux, On Loving God, with an analytical commentary by Emero Stiegman (Kalamazoo: Cistercian Publications, 1995).

82. See, e.g., Robert M. Kingdon, "The Control of Morals in Calvin's Geneva," in The Social History of the Reformation, ed. Lawrence P. Buck and Jonathan Zophy (Columbus: Ohio State University Press, 1972), pp. 3-16; Thomas Lambert, "Preaching, Praying, and Policing the Reform in Sixteenth-Century Geneva" (Ph.D. diss., University of Wisconsin, 1998); Scott M. Manetsch, "Pastoral Care East of Eden: The Consistory of Geneva, 1568-82," Church History, 75/2 (2006), pp. 274-313.

83. On Beza's piety and spirituality, see Jill Raitt, "Beza, Guide for the Faithful Life," in Scottish Journal of Theology, 39/1 (1986), pp. 83-107; and Shawn Dean Wright, "The Pastoral Use of the Doctrine of God's Sovereignty in the Theology of Theodore Beza" (Ph.D. diss., Southern Baptist Seminary, 2001).

84. Beza, Confession, iv.17 (p. 65).

evil will into a good will.[85] Beza closely parallels Calvin on the point that in this divine work there is no "concurrence of our free choice," and the resultant good works derive solely from the "second grace of God," with absolutely no merit accruing to the believer.[86]

This latter point accounts for the third difference with Rome: the Reformed do not abhor good works—rather they recoil in "horror" from the word "merits" and the notion of human beings meriting anything before God: such notions nullify the benefits of Christ. Faith precedes works, it is by faith alone that Christ is apprehended, and "good works flow from Christ dwelling in us, by the power and efficacy" of God's grace.[87] Good works, then, do offer assurance of salvation, but not as if they were causes of salvation. Rather, good works are the result of salvation, effects of faith, and therefore "testimonies" to the faith that apprehends Christ.[88] Beza's point is, again, similar to Calvin—"that the grace offered by the Lord is not merely one that every individual has full liberty of choosing to receive or reject, but a grace that produces in the heart both choice and will: so that all the good works that follow after are its fruit and effect; the only will that yields obedience being the will that grace itself has made."[89]

Still, even here Beza's emphasis is not exclusively nor even primarily on works, once the remainder of his argument is brought into view. Works, rightly understood as the results of union with Christ and the inward operation of the Spirit, are "certain testimonies to our faith," which also return the issue to the question of assurance of election: faith is what embraces Christ; by it believers are justified, sanctified, and directed toward the glory for which they were destined before the foundation of the world.[90] He continues,

> It is, moreover, of great import that the world takes little notice of this, as if the doctrine of individual election were curious or incomprehensible: on the contrary, this faith is nothing other than that by which we become more certain that life eternal is truly ours, for it is through this [faith] that we know God destined us, before the foundation of the world, to possess through Christ a salvation so great and a glory so excellent. Wherefore, everything that we have previously said concerning faith and its effects will be useless, unless we recognize this doctrine of eternal election as the sole foundation and support of Christian assurance.[91]

---

85. Beza, *Confession*, iv.17 (p. 66).

86. Beza, *Confession*, iv.17 (pp. 67-68); in the Latin, *altera Dei gratia*; cf. Calvin, *Institutio* (1559), III.xi.1, on *duplex gratia*; and also note ibid., II.iii.6: "we merit nothing, because we are created in Christ Jesus unto good works, which God has prepared. ... all the fruits of good works are originally and immediately from God"; cf. ibid., II.ii.6; v.14.

87. Beza, *Confession*, iv.18 (p. 69); cf. Calvin, *Institutio*, III.xi.1.

88. Beza, *Confession*, iv.19 (p. 74).

89. Calvin, *Institutio* (1559), II.iii.13; cf. ibid., II.v.14.

90. Beza, *Confession*, iv.19 (p. 77).

91. Beza, *Confession*, iv.19 (pp. 77-78).

Contrary to the assumptions of Niesel's critique of the practical syllogism, the association made here with the eternal decree or election does not pose a "predestination system ... concerning the relation of God and man" against a "theology of revelation ... wholly centered on Christ."[92] Beza's intention appears to have been to argue the link between true faith and the good works that proceed from it and then to place faith, sanctification, and works into the order of salvation in such a way as to draw assurance of election not apart from but because of Christ and his work.

Identifying the decree or election as the foundation or *fundamentum*, moreover, does not detract from the position of Christ in the order of salvation—rather it merely identifies the starting-point, or *terminus a quo*, of the divine willing of the salvation to be accomplished in Christ. As Beza also indicates, identification of "fruits of faith" such as sanctification and good works as grounds of assurance is not a reason to look only or primarily to "second and proximate causes" like calling or faith, but, instead points the believer "to Christ himself, in whom, as our Head, we are indeed elected and adopted; and then mounts up even to the eternal purpose."[93]

Various of Beza's other statements concerning assurance of election confirm the point, given their attention to the sanctification from which good works proceed and, beyond that, to issues of union with Christ and the order of salvation that place sanctification, both inward and outward, as an effect of God's gracious willing. Beza's point reflects Calvin's reading of James 2:20-22, namely, "the question here is not respecting the cause of our salvation, but whether works necessarily accompany faith,"[94] or, as Beza himself comments, "If faith is necessary to salvation, & true faith is necessarily followed by works, inasmuch as faith cannot be idle: surely it must follow, that good works are necessary to salvation, not however as the cause of salvation (we are justified and therefore live by faith in Christ alone) but as something that necessarily coheres with faith."[95]

The path to assurance, Beza indicates, is not to seek "resolution in the eternal counsel of God"; rather one must begin with faith, sanctification, and their fruits, and then ascend higher to assurance.[96] The pattern of argument mirrors Beza's more

---

92. Niesel, *Theology of Calvin*, pp. 180-181.

93. Theodore Beza, *Summa totius christianismi, sive descriptio & distributio causarum salutis electorum & exitii reproborum, ex sacris literis collecta*, ii.4, in idem, *Tractationes theologicae*, 3 vols. (Geneva: Eustathius Vignon, 1570-1582), I, p. 175.

94. Calvin, *Commentarius in Iacobi epistola*, 2:21-22 in CO 55, col. 406 (CTS *James*, p. 315).

95. Theodore Beza, *Quaestionum et responsionum christianarum libellus, in quo praecipua Christianae religionis capita kat' epitome proponuntur* (London: Henry Bynneman, 1571), p. 83: "Si fides ad salutem necessaria est, & veram fidem opera necessaria consequantur, ut quae otiosa esse non possit: certe & illud efficitur, necessaria esse ad salutem bona opera, non tamen ut salutis causam (Iustificamur enim, ac proinde vivimus ex sola fidei in Christo,) sed ut quiddam cum vera fide necessario cohaerens."

96. Beza, *Confession*, iv.19 (p. 78).

general advice to those wanting to teach the doctrine of predestination to others, namely, to follow an *a posteriori* path.[97] It is significant, however, contrary to Bray's, Niesel's, Barth's, and Kendall's interpretation, that this argumentation does not at all remove the focus from Christ, nor, arguably, does it emphasize the function of good works much more than Calvin had done. As Beza continues, the "sanctification from which good inward movements [*boni motus*] and good works proceed ... is a certain effect of faith or, rather, of Jesus Christ dwelling in us by faith." Those who are united to Christ, moreover, are "necessarily" those who have been "effectually called and thus destined to salvation." Given this interrelationship of election, calling, faith, union with Christ, and sanctification, it is clear, Beza indicates, that sanctification and its fruits are "the first degree by which we begin to ascend to a declaration of the first cause of our salvation, which is to say to our eternal and gratuitous election."[98] Beza warns that those whose lives have not been guided by God's Spirit cannot claim truly to have faith, and he does indicate that good works are a "certain" testimony to the conscience that Christ dwells within, but the entire thrust of the passage is to look to sanctification as the beginning of assurance.[99]

Selective citation of the passage by Kendall omits Beza's insistence on the necessary linkage between union with Christ and effectual calling, leading Kendall to the rather mistaken neo-orthodox conclusion that "Beza directs us not to Christ but to ourselves,"[100] when Beza's full text actually presses the point that looking to the effects of salvation in ourselves confirms the grounding of sanctification and good works in union with Christ. Beza's argumentation, particularly in his *Quaestionum et responsionum*, obliges the standard distinction between the decree and its execution, with the result that the practical sense of assurance is an *a posteriori* approach that moves from sanctification to union with Christ and infers election from being in Christ. This implies no penetration into the decree, no metaphysical interest—no predestinarian system as assumed by Niesel. When Beza indicates in his *Confession* that sanctification and its fruits are the first step or "degree by which we begin to

---

97. Cf. Beza, *Summa totius christianismis*, viii, in *Tractationes theologicae*, I, pp. 199-205; with Richard A. Muller, "The Use and Abuse of a Document: Beza's *Tabula praedestinationis*, the Bolsec Controversy, and the Origins of Reformed Orthodoxy," in *Protestant Scholasticism: Essays in Reappraisal*, ed. Carl Trueman and Scott Clark (Carlisle: Paternoster Press, 1999), pp. 50-54.

98. Beza, *Confession de la foy*, iv.19 (pp. 78-79).

99. Beza, *Confession de la foy*, iv.19 (pp. 78-79).

100. Cf. Kendall, *Calvin and English Calvinism*, p. 33; not only does the full passage, even as cited by Kendall, undermine his argument, but the 1565 translation that he used leaves out the phrase, found in Beza's Latin text and in the revised 1561 French as well, "boni motus" or "bonnes mouvemens," in which *motus* or *mouvemens* indicate a mental activity or movement in apposition to the outward works. Cf. Theodore Beza, *A Briefe and Pithie Summe of the Christian Faith, made in the Forme of a Confession* (London: Richard Serll, 1565?), fol. 36v-37r; with idem, *Confessio christianae fidei* (Geneva: Iohannis Bonae Fidei, 1560), p. 67; and idem, *Confession de la foy* (1561), p. 78. And note Barth, *Church Dogmatics*, II/2, p. 336.

ascend ... to the first cause of our salvation," namely, election,[101] he is affirming much of what Calvin indicated in his reference to "a posteriori" comforts or "latter signs" (*signa posteriora*) of salvation: the assurance or persuasion of the heart is that "we are constituted children of God in Christ as graciously apprehended through faith," nor is it the case, Beza comments, that acts of love produce faith—rather they are produced by faith and serve to confirm it.[102] The point is that salvation is known not in the eternal decree but in its effects—not, moreover, to the removal of the work of Christ and its application as the foundation of salvation, but as an indicator of it.[103] Neither in Beza's approach nor (contra the implication of Kendall's argumentation) in Calvin's or Vermigli's does the identification of Christ as the ground of assurance or of election as mirrored in Christ mean finding Christ *extra nos!*[104]

This pattern of argumentation was already quite clearly presented in Beza's *Summa totius Christianismi*, the famous *tabula praedestinationis*. There, in the definition of faith, where Beza concentrates on the issue of the apprehension of justification and sanctification by believers, he indicates that certainty of election arises from the faith through which Christ is applied to or apprehended by the believer. This application or apprehension of Christ is clearly the foundation of assurance—but it is known by the believer on several grounds, "partly in an inward testimony of conscience, conjoined by the Holy Spirit to external preaching and partly by the power and efficacy of that same Spirit, who delivers individual elect from sin to liberty, and leads them to begin to will and to do the things of God."[105] Given the typical placement of the practical syllogism in the conscience, the passage can be understood as implying the focus of the syllogism on apprehension of Christ.

Beza's approach in his *Quaestionum et responsionum* is similar. The questioner concludes from a previous discussion, "Therefore the vessels of mercy should praise the Lord, and the vessels of wrath condemn themselves," and asks, "Where may I flee in the midst of deepest worry over particular election" and the respondent comments,

> To the effects, though which spiritual life is certainly discerned and our election is perceived even as a body senses its life. While we toil about in the filth of this world, we are not able to raise ourselves to that highest light except by those degrees [*iis*

---

101. Beza, *Confession de la foy*, iv.19 (p. 79).

102. Cf. Calvin, *Institutio* (1559), III.xiv.19; xxiv.4.

103. Cf. Beza, *Jesu Christi Domini Nostri Novum Testamentum, sive Novum Foedus, cuius Graeco contextui respondent interpretationes duae ... Eiusdem Theod. Bezae Annotationes* (Cambridge: Roger Daniel, 1642), 1 John 3:19 (p. 372); with Calvin, *Commentarius in Iohannis apostoli epistola*, 3:19, in CO 55, col. 341-342 (CTS 1 John, p. 222). Calvin adds that the passage ought not to be read as if works provide certainty of assurance, a point absent from Beza's exegesis. But Beza does not argue the contrary.

104. Kendall, *Calvin and English Calvinism*, pp. 32-33; and see above, chapter 7.

105. Beza, *Summa totius christianismi*, iv.10, in *Tractationes theologicae*, I, p. 186.

gradibus] by which God has drawn his elect to himself according to his eternal decree, inasmuch as he has determined them to glory. That I am elected I therefore understand first from the sanctification that has begun in me, i.e., from a hatred of sin and a love of righteousness. To this I add the witness of the Holy Spirit comforting my conscience.[106]

The answer is no more formally syllogistic than are Calvin's various comments about calling or the latter signs of assurance, nor does it point at all toward outward works. The language in fact appears to reflect the concern common to Beza and Calvin that believers not attempt to search out their election in the labyrinth of the decree.

The reference to degrees (*gradus*) in Beza's argumentation, moreover, points us back to the importance of Romans 8, particularly verse 30, to Reformed discussions of assurance. As I have indicated elsewhere, the language of a *gradus*, *gradatio*, *catena*, or *armilla* as used in connection with this text identifies the Pauline argument as a logical sequence or sorites: those who are predestined are also called; those who are called are also justified; those who are justified are also to be glorified. The entire chapter, moreover, is grounded in the apostle's discussion of union with Christ as the basis for Christian life. When sanctification is added to the sequence, it provides a penultimate goal of the saving work begun in the decree and, specifically, a goal in which the work of Christ can be evidenced in this life. This is, arguably, Beza's point.

Since, moreover, this is the statement of Beza on which Barth drew his conclusion that Beza had "abandoned the caution of Calvin" and had placed an "empirical self-examination and self-evaluation ... alongside the testimony of Jesus Christ,"[107] it is important to recognize that Barth's analysis of Beza is here based on a partial quotation taken from Alexander Schweizer's *Glaubenslehre*, which Schweizer had paired with a quotation from Calvin to the effect that "good works follow on justification, they do not precede it,"[108] understanding Beza to have meant much the

106. Theodore Beza, *Quaestionum et responsionum christianarum libellus, in quo praecipua Christianae religionis capita kat' epitome proponuntur* (London: Henry Bynneman, 1571), p. 133: "Ergo Dominum laudent oportet misericordiae vasa, & se ipsos condemnent irae vasa. Sed in illa perniciosissima particularis electionis tentatione quo tandem confugiam? Ad effecta, ex quibus spiritualis vita certo dignoscitur et nostra electio sicut corporis vita sensu percipitur. Nec enim qui in huius mundi coeno adhuc volutamur, attollere nos ad illam summam lucem possumus nisi iis gradibus subvecti quibus ad se Deus electos ex aeterno illo suo decreto pertrahit, ut pote quos ad gloriam suam condidit. Electum igitur me esse primum ex sanctificatione mea inchoata, id est, odio peccati & amore justitiae intelligam. Huic adjiciam testimonium Spiritus meam conscientiam erigentis."

107. Barth, *Church Dogmatics*, II/2, p. 336.

108. Alexander Schweizer, *Die Glaubenslehre der evangelisch-reformirten Kirche dargestellt und aus den Quellen belegt*, 2 vols. (Zürich, 1844-1847), II, p. 529, citing Calvin *Institutio* (1559), III.xvii.4 and Beza, *Quaestionum et responsionum*, I, p. 124: thus, "In illa perniciosissima particularis electionis tentatione quo tandem confugiam? Ad effecta, ex quibus spiritualis vita certo dignoscitur et nostra electio sicut corporis vita sensu percipitur. Electum igitur me esse primum ex sanctificatione mea inchoata i. e. odio peccati et amore justitiae intelligam; huic adjiciam testimonium spiritus meam conscientiam vigentis." Schweizer offers no indication of the first statement of the questioner or of

same thing. Barth's conclusion ran against Schweizer's intention. What Barth presumably did not read, moreover, is the rest of Beza's answer, which continued with the observation, "We gather faith from this sanctification and consolation of the Spirit. By it we rise up to Christ, to whom whoever is given, is necessarily chosen in him from eternity and shall never be cast out"[109]—nor did he note the categorically stated question and answer elsewhere in the document, "Do you therefore conclude that all things necessary to salvation are found in Christ alone, to whom we cleave by faith, for there is no condemnation for those who are in Christ? I do conclude, and this alone is the knowledge of salvation."[110]

This development is not, as Barth, Niesel, Kendall, and others have claimed, an utter reversal of Calvin's view: Calvin clearly understood that true faith necessarily issued in good works and that these works belonged to the sanctification of the believer. Calvin also very clearly identified sanctification as among the "latter signs" of election from which believer might gain assurance, and he also very clearly insisted that, in their place, as gifts of God, examination of good works belonged to the work of conscience as it sought assurance. Beza did not, as Kendall claimed, "make good works the ground of assurance," nor did he, as Kendall indicated, equate good works with sanctification.[111] Beyond this, Beza's two primary examples of a Christian's good works—prayer to God and love of neighbor—point more toward a model of inward renewal and holy life than to a legalistic approach to conduct. Beza's approach was far more nuanced and complex than the various modern critics have assumed.

Moreover, Beza, very much like Calvin, did anchor assurance in Christ and, specifically, in union with Christ. Arguably, the basic point made by Calvin and shared by Beza was that the basis for personal assurance is not Christ standing *extra nos* in the sufficiency of his saving work, but rather personal or subjective recognition of the effects of Christ and his work in the believer as the basis of assurance. Beza's emphasis on sanctification and his referencing of good works, therefore, were not a turning away from God and Christ, as has been alleged, but a practical focusing on where and how, in Beza's view, the work of Christ was to be subjectively apprehended.

Where Beza's chief shift in argument occurred, and again, not without precedents in the thought of Calvin and other predecessors, was in the establishment of a clearer and more formal relationship between the question of assurance and early forms of

---

his omission of text after "percipitur" and no indication of Beza's further reflection on the relation of these "effects" to Christ.

109. Beza, *Quaestionum et responsionum*, p. 134: "Ex sanctificatione ista & consolatione spiritus colligimus Fidem. Inde ad Christum assurgimus, cui quisquis datus est, necessario est ab aeterno in eodem electum, nec unquam eijcietur foras."

110. Beza, *Quaestionum et responsionum*, p. 91: "Qu. Concludis igitur in uno Christo cui per fidem adhaerescimus, inveniri omnia nobis ad salutem necessaria, ut in iis qui in Christo sunt, nulla prorsus condemnatio. Re. Concludo, & hanc unam esse salutis scientiam."

111. Kendall, *Calvin and English Calvinism*, p. 36; cf. ibid., p. 33.

a Reformed ordering of salvation using the language of Romans 8, which was a primary *locus* both for establishing an order of salvation and also for anchoring salvation in union with Christ and assurance in the work of the Spirit. As in his *Tabula praedestinationis*, moreover, Beza here also emphasized the *a posteriori* approach, arguing neither a deductive predestinarianism nor a logical, rationalistic approach to the understanding of salvation. Like Calvin, he emphasized both the impossibility and the inherent danger to piety of attempts to focus on predestination as a ground of assurance. And, arguably, like Calvin as well, Beza recognized that one could not rest assurance on the datum of doctrine that Christ's death was sufficient payment for the price of all sin. There is, in other words, a notable difference in emphasis but also a significant and rather broad commonality between Calvin and Beza.

After Beza: the syllogism in some later Reformed writers. Formulation of the practical syllogism in Reformed theology after Calvin and Beza was varied, sometimes placing a greater emphasis on good works than Calvin had done but also perhaps more frequently looking to calling and sanctification. In nearly all formulations, moreover, the discussions of calling and sanctification follow out the line of argument we have noted in Beza, more clearly connecting the issue of assurance with the order of salvation as grounded objectively in Christ's work and subjectively in union with Christ, grace, and faith.

William Perkins and Johannes Wollebius are among the later Reformed writers who used one or another forms of the *syllogismus practicus* in their discussions of assurance of salvation. In Perkins' case, the syllogism is both named and presented in short syllogistic form. As is clear, however, from the initial argumentation of his *Treatise of Conscience*, the syllogisms are all designed to direct the attention of the believer to aspects or elements of the model of Romans 8:30, where the focus of assurance as previously presented by the apostle was union with Christ and Christ's work as the mediator of God's eternally willed salvation. In other words, as Beeke has noted, Perkins draws on the links—calling, justification, and sanctification—in what he had elsewhere referenced as the "golden chaine" of salvation.[112] Thus, Perkins writes, "to beleeve in Christ, is not confusedly to beleeve that he is a Redeemer of mankind, but withall to beleeve that he is my Saviour, and that I am elected, justified, sanctified, & shall be glorified by him."[113] Perkins' syllogisms will be variants on this theme.

In addition, Perkins does not so much advocate the repetition of syllogisms as argue the impact of the gospel on the mind of the believer, as wrought by the Holy Spirit. Speaking of the certainty that one is pardoned of sin, Perkins writes,

---

112. Beeke, *Assurance of Faith*, p. 113.
113. William Perkins, *A Treatise of Conscience*, in *The Whole Works of ... Mr. William Perkins*, 3 vols. (London: John Legatt, 1631), I, p. 523.

The principall agent and beginner thereof, is the holy Ghost, inlightning the mind and conscience with spirituall and divine light: and the instrument in this action, is the ministrie of the Gospell, whereby the word of life is applied in the name of God to the person of every hearer. And this certaintie is by little and little conceived in a forme of reasoning or practicall syllogisme framed in the minde by the holy Ghost, on this manner:

> Every one that beleeves is the childe of God:
> But I doe beleeve:
> Therefore I am a childe of God.[114]

What is more, Perkins identifies faith as a bond, "knitting Christ and his members together," commenting that "this apprehending of Christ [is done] ... spiritually by *assurance*, which is, when the elect are persuaded in their hearts by the holy Ghost, of the forgiveness of their owne sinnes, and of Gods infinite mercy towards them in Iesus Christ."[115]

Where Perkins differs from Calvin and, indeed, from Beza as well is in the length and detail of his discussion of assurance, specifically in his massive instruction in those "latter signs" of election and certainly in his specific naming of the practical syllogism as well as in his explicitly syllogistic formulations. The length and detail reflect a context of experiential piety that arose in the late sixteenth century, particularly in England and the Low Countries and that is associated with Puritanism and the Nadere Reformatie. Both of these movements emphasized carrying the Reformation of doctrine forward into the life and spirituality of the people

Wollebius' mention of the *syllogismus practicus*, which is one of the formulations singled out by Barth as problematically anthropocentric, does not actually move far from the patterns of argumentation we have noted in Calvin and Beza. As distinct from Calvin's and Beza's formulations, Wollebius actually does pose a syllogism and does move from sanctification directly to assurance of election in very short order. Nonetheless, his argument ought not to be severed from its context, namely, a very short-form compendium of theology that was designed to present basic definitions and not full expositions of issues. In addition, in a previous definition that bears directly on his formulation of the syllogism, Wollebius had indicated that, in relation to the eternal decree, Christ was to be understood in two ways: either as God or as the *theanthropos* and Mediator. In the first of these ways, he is, with the Father and the Spirit, the "efficient cause of our Election," in the second he is "the means of the execution of Election."[116] We are "elect in Christ," because it is "by him that we are drawn toward salvation."[117] Christ the Mediator, therefore, is not the "cause of

---

114. Perkins, *Treatise of Conscience*, in *Works*, I, p. 547.

115. William Perkins, *The Estate of a Christian Man in this Life*," in *Works*, I, p. 363.

116. Johannes Wollebius, *Christianae theologiae compendium* (Basel: Johann Jacob Genath, 1633), I.iv.9 (p. 39).

117. Wollebius, *Compendium*, I.iv.9 (p. 39).

election" but of salvation.[118] Having provided this background to his brief comment on assurance, Wollebius comments, "in searching out our election by an analytical method we ought to proceed from the means of execution to the decree, beginning with our sanctification."[119] He then poses the syllogism,

> Whoever feels in himself the gift of sanctification, by which we die to sin and live to righteousness, is justified, called or endowed with true faith, and is elected. But by the grace of God I feel this. Therefore I am justified, called & elected.[120]

The syllogism begins with sanctification, links it to election by moving up the chain of Romans 8:30, from justification to calling, to election, and then applies the sequence to the individual who, by God's grace, experiences sanctification. In the immediate context of the argument, Wollebius evidences the pastoral problem hovering always in the background, the relationship of good works to salvation. It amounts to a "diabolical argument," he comments, to exclude good works from Christian life on the grounds that the elect have no need of them and the reprobate cannot profit from them.[121]

The framework of Wollebius' argument, then, is very much like that of Calvin and Beza, albeit given his focus on sanctification he stands closer to Beza: he assumes the full chain of the causality of salvation from predestination to sanctification, identifies Christ as the cause of salvation, and then, in the syllogism, links the effect, sanctification, to its cause, election. Inasmuch as Christ is, as God, the cause of election itself and, as Mediator, the cause of the salvation of the elect, the syllogism ought not to be viewed as drawing attention away from Christ. What is more, when Wollebius defines sanctification, he calls it "a free action of God, by which the faithful by faith are engrafted into Christ & justified; by the Spirit, more and more liberated from their innate corruption, and renewed in his image, that, they may fittingly render good works to his glory."[122] Focus on Christ as Redeemer remains central to Wollebius' argumentation.

Nathanael Culverwel's formulation of the most basic practical syllogism is much like that of Perkins: "The whole work of assurance is summ'd up in this Practical Syllogism, *Whosoever beleeves shall be saved; but I beleeve: and so shall certainly be*

---

118. Wollebius, *Compendium*, I.iv.12 (p. 40).

119. Wollebius, *Compendium*, I.iv.15 (p. 41).

120. Wollebius, *Compendium*, I.iv.15 (p. 41): "Quicunque in se sentit donum Sanctificationis, qua peccato morimur & vivimus justitiae, is justificatus, vocatus seu vera fidei donatus & electus est. Ergo justificatus, vocatus & electus sum."

121. Wollebius, *Compendium*, I.iv.16 (p. 41).

122. Wollebius, *Compendium*, I.xxxi (p. 257): "gratuita Dei actio, qua fideles per fidem in Christo insitos & iustificatos, per Spiritum S. magis magisque a nativa vitiositate liberat, & ad imaginem suam instaurat, ut, ad eum bonis operibus glorificandum, idonei reddantur."

saved."[123] Culverwel also raises the question of certainty and associates it with the work of conscience. The graces of God, he indicates, are the stamp of the Spirit, marking the soul as belonging to God. Since the very beginning of grace, its "first-fruits ... if true and sincere, is sufficient to salvation," a sense of this "least grace" ought to be "sufficient to Assurance."[124] Conscience, in Culverwel's estimate, ought to provide "certain and infallible" testimony—and yet, not all Christians have assurance. Some do not inquire carefully into themselves, some are daunted by the weightiness of the question and by its grounding ultimately in God's eternity, and others have difficulty reading the evidences because of personal disquietude and new guilt.[125] A second witness, therefore, is needed, namely, not merely "the gifts and graces of the Spirit, but the Spirit itself," as indicated by the Apostle Paul, "the Spirit himself, witnessing with our Spirits that we are Sons of God."[126] There are, therefore, two distinct but interrelated testimonies: the testimony of conscience or of the human spirit and the testimony of the Holy Spirit, again resting on Romans 8.

Robert Harris, president of Trinity College, Oxford and member of the Westminster Assembly, even more clearly enunciated the issue underlying the practical syllogism in relation to the "golden chain of salvation,"[127] indicating precisely how the notion of the practical syllogism fit into understandings of an order of salvation founded in election and rooted in union with Christ:

> whomsoever God brings to heaven, he brings him in his own way. Of that Golden chain, *Rom.* 8, two linkes he hath let down to us, namely, that of vocation, and that other of sanctification, whereby to climbe up to the state of glory: the first link of his secret will he hath reserved to himself. *Make* then *your election sure*, by becoming sure of your calling: and, as our Saviour here bids, be poor in spirit, that you may be enriched with God's Kindgome; mourn, that you may be comforted: otherwise, by soaring *Icarus*-like, leave your name for a Proverb, and yourself be drowned in the sea of perdition.[128]

As Harris indicated elsewhere, the basis of Christian comfort is the knowledge that one is in Christ and, has become, in Paul's words, a "new creature," evidencing the

---

123. Nathanael Culverwel, *White Stone*, as appended to *An elegant discourse of the light of nature* (1652), p. 109.

124. Culverwel, *White Stone*, p. 109.

125. Culverwel, *White Stone*, pp. 111-112.

126. Culverwel, *White Stone*, p. 112, citing Rom. 8:16.

127. Robert Harris, *Grace and glory knit together*, in *The Workes of Robert Harris, bachelor in divinity and Pastor of Hanwell* (London: R. Y. for J Bartlett, 1635), p. 265.

128. Harris, *Works* (1635), p. 265; cf. Hermann Rennecherus, *Armilla salutis catena, continens et explicans omnes eius causas* (Lich: Nicolaus Erbenius, 1597), xxxv-xxxvii (pp. 268-274) and the discussion of Rennecherus above, chapter 6.

work of the Spirit, who "formes whole Christ in us, the minde of Christ, the heart of Christ, the tongue of Christ … we are led by the Spirit, and walk in the Spirit."[129]

The connection made here between a form of the *syllogismus practicus* and the golden chain of Romans 8:28-30 is fairly explicit—and the point is much like that made somewhat earlier by Anthony Maxey, that the links in the chain "are so coupled and knit together, that if you hold fast one lincke, you draw unto you the whole Chaine: if you let goe one, you loose all."[130] Given that it is "dangerous" to attempt to find one's salvation in the eternal decree, believers ought to look to the "spirituall blessing of the Soul" for which God has appointed both "meanes, and an order": "God by his Sonne Christ, Christ by his Word; his Word worketh by his Spirit; his Spirit doth certifie our hearts; our hearts stand fast by faith; faith catcheth hold upon Christ; and so back againe, Christ presenteth us unto God."[131] Even so, the apostle teaches that predestination is followed by calling and justification, the calling of the Word through the work of the Spirit and the justifying faith that "lifts us up unto God."[132] Since, moreover, in "every action" the means and the ends are inseparable, believers, therefore, ought to "lay hold upon *Calling* and *Justifying*, as the meanes ordained to come unto this end" of eternal salvation and final glory.[133] One cannot enter the secret counsel of God, but one can discern one's calling.

Conclusions

Inasmuch as neither Calvin nor other Reformed theologians of the early modern era posed the question of assurance in the form of an anthropological principle to the exclusion of consideration of Christ and his work, the claim found both in Niesel and in Barth that he warned against this kind of *syllogismus practicus* is a curious anachronism. In the debate over Calvin's relationship to the notion of a practical syllogism, careful examination of texts indicates that Barth's reading of Calvin prevails over Niesel's: the practical syllogism is present in a less-formal way throughout Calvin's discussions of assurance. Nor can it be argued that the sometimes subtle differences in formulation that can be identified in a comparison of Calvin's and Beza's thought on the issue indicate a vast shift in the focus of Reformed soteriology—and on this point we must part company with Barth. Both Calvin and Beza identify Christ as the primary foundation of assurance, and both identify calling and sanctification as indications that one is in Christ. Indeed, Calvin's language of Christ as *speculum electionis* appears to point not only to the

129. Harris, *A brief discourse of the threefold state of man*, in *The Workes of Robert Harris … with the addition of sundry sermons* (London: James Flesher, 1654), p. 39 (first pagination).

130. Anthony Maxey, *The Goulden Chaine of Mans Saluation, and the fearefull point of Hardening, together with the Churches Sleepe: Preached in three severall sermons before the King* (London: T. Este for Clement Knight, 1606), fol. A3r.

131. Maxey, *Goulden Chaine*, fol. C2r.

132. Maxey, *Goulden Chaine*, fol. C2v.

133. Maxey, *Goulden Chaine*, fol. C2v.

individual believer looking to Christ as a ground of assurance but also to God looking to Christ and his righteousness as the fundamental divine consideration of those in union with him. In other words, looking to calling and sanctification as grounds of assurance is not looking elsewhere than to Christ.

Niesel's insistence that "nowhere does Calvin teach the *Syllogismus practicus*," was simply mistaken. It was also a rather ahistorical dogmatic judgment based less on Calvin's own text than on a neo-orthodox sensibility concerning precisely how a metaphysically grounded predestinarian system would handle the question of assurance in contrast to the way in which a fully "christocentric" theology such as Calvin's *Institutes* was presumed to have argued the point. Niesel's argument is also, therefore, inapplicable to later Reformed uses of the *syllogismus*; in Niesel's words,

> The position which Calvin thus takes up makes it clear that his theology is something very different from a predestination system of thought concerning the relation of God and man, in which the *Syllogismus practicus* is assigned an important place. It becomes clear that Calvin is strictly concerned with the theology of revelation and that his teaching is wholly centered on Jesus Christ.[134]

The problem here is that neither Calvin nor any other early modern Reformed writer that we can identify followed out either one of these patterns—neither a predestinarian system nor a christocentric system; neither a system that derived all doctrine from the divine decree nor a system that was "wholly centered on Jesus Christ," at least not in the sense of deriving all doctrine from a Christ-principle.[135]

Indeed, Niesel's equation of a "theology of revelation" with a doctrinal system "wholly centered on Jesus Christ" is itself quite anachronistic. In the older theological tradition, including both the Reformers of the early sixteenth century and the Reformed orthodox of the following one hundred and fifty years, the doctrine of Christ certainly served as the central element of the soteriological sections of the theology, but other doctrines, such as the doctrines of the divine essence and attributes, the Trinity, predestination, creation, and providence, were developed as independent *loci*, with the full doctrine of God, namely, essence, attributes, and Trinity, occupying the principial place in the theology. What is more, Calvin's focus of his soteriology on Christ as well as his emphasis on understanding one's election as being in Christ were hardly a turning away from the believer (or from an anthropocentric emphasis) toward Christ and a "christocentric" emphasis, as implied in Niesel's and also in Kendall's argumentation. There is no such polarity implied by Calvin's formulations—and no such polarity found in later Reformed thought.

---

134. Niesel, *Theology of Calvin*, pp. 180-181.
135. See the arguments in Richard A. Muller, "A Note on 'Christocentrism' and the Imprudent Use of Such Terminology," *Westminster Theological Journal*, 68 (2006), pp. 253-260.

The framework, then, within which both Niesel and Barth analyzed the problem of the *syllogismus practicus* was faulty.[136] Niesel in particular saw the need to deal with the old "central dogma" theory and to argue that an empirical *syllogismus practicus* would, in the context of such a system, actually draw the believer's attention away from God, "who is to be found in Christ alone" and "turned towards man."[137] In effect, Niesel opposed one central dogma with another, arguing against a predestinarian system on the basis of a christomonism, failing to see that neither Calvin nor the older Reformed tradition as a whole could be wedged into either of these dogmatic models. Barth examined pieces of text taken both out of their documentary and their historical context and assessed the early modern language of largely inward self-examination through the filter of his christomonism without directly referencing the alternative (and more traditionally orthodox) approach to the work of Christ undergirding the older Reformed approach to assurance.

The extent to which subsequent scholarship has pressed these christomonistic criteria over the documents of the sixteenth century is, therefore, a measure of the misunderstanding of the documents. Calvin and Beza, with the older theological tradition generally, here noted in the work of Perkins and Wollebius, distinguished between finding the basis of one's salvation in Christ alone and finding truths concerning God and God's work in Christ alone: they affirmed the former, not the latter. What is more, when the specific issue of assurance of salvation was raised, Calvin, Beza, and other Reformed writers of the early modern era assumed that identification of the unshakable character of election and the immediate foundation of salvation in Christ and in union with him hardly removed the question of how a believer might discern his union with Christ. Such discernment, as Calvin himself put it, began and ended with one's calling and the various latter signs of calling. This interconnection of the issues of Christ's work, assurance, and the order of salvation persisted beyond the work of Calvin and Beza into the thought of such later Reformed writers as Perkins, Wollebius, Maxey, Harris, and Culverwel. Indeed, it was part and parcel of the older Reformed tradition, whatever differences in formulation can be identified in various writers.

As intimated in our introductory remarks, the point must be made that the dogmatic problem of predestinarian metaphysics and central dogmas—whether predestination or Christology—does not provide the primary perspective from which to analyze the language of assurance and the *syllogismus practicus*. After all, it is now generally recognized that the ideas of predestinarian metaphysics and central dogmas are not easily applied to Calvin—just as it is arguable that these concepts do not apply to the broader Reformed tradition in the sixteenth and seventeenth centuries. The problem posed by both Niesel and Barth, despite the differences in their analysis

---

136. Taking exception to my earlier allowance for the cogency of Niesel's assessment of the problematic impact of the *syllogismus practicus* in *Christ and the Decree*, pp. 26-27.

137. Niesel, *Theology of Calvin*, p. 181.

of the early modern texts and despite their disagreement over Calvin, assumes the central dogma problem as background. Specifically, both Niesel and Barth assume that sound Reformed theology, as formulated by Calvin, is christocentric and therefore excludes a fundamental self-examination such as provided by the *syllogismus practicus*. Niesel indicates, further, that the *syllogismus* is particularly problematic in the context of a predestinarian system that allows for a non-christocentric assurance of salvation. If, however, one removes the modern dichotomy of predestinarian versus christocentric theologies and recognizes that the older theologies did not oblige either of these more recently invented models for theological system, a rather different understanding of the place and import of the *syllogismus practicus* emerges.

Although it is certainly true that Beza's approach to assurance gave more place to sanctification and good works than Calvin's, it is also the case that this emphasis did not arise as a result of Beza's movement toward a supralapsarian definition of the divine decree, at least not for the reasons claimed by Niesel. On the one hand, it has been shown elsewhere that Beza did not produce the so-called predestinarian metaphysic once alleged to be the foundation of later Reformed theology—while on the other hand, the causal structure of decree and execution that he shared with Calvin required that assurance be found not in the decree but in its temporal effects. Beza echoed Calvin in warning Christians against speculation into the "labyrinth" of the decree. Where Beza and the other later Reformed writers we have examined differ from Calvin is in their clearer working out of an order of salvation and in their more specific identification of precisely how the believer identifies himself in relation to the *ordo* or *gradus*, thereby placing a greater emphasis on salvation and works than found in Calvin, without, of course, separating the issue of assurance from the work of Christ. This is not, as Bray put it, an "almost brutal demand for good works,"[138] but rather the development of an argument against an antinomian reading of salvation by grace alone.

If anything, Beza's and Perkins' more clearly enunciated supralapsarianism stood in the way of speculation into the decree—their somewhat stronger emphasis on the manifestation of salvation in believers was, from the perspective of their theological formulations, the result of an anti-speculative, even practical, approach on their part, a focus not on the decree, but on its execution in time. And if one inquires contextually into the intention behind their theological formulations or, indeed, of the formulations of the other Reformed thinkers just examined, surely it will have nothing to do with an invented dogmatic warfare of predestinarianism with christocentrism and much to do with their own pastoral concerns whether in dealing with issues of morality and Christian discipline or in responding to ongoing criticism of Reformed doctrine as conducing to moral sloth and having antinomian tendencies. The development after Calvin and Beza, in such thinkers as Perkins,

---

138. Bray, *Theodore Beza's Doctrine of Predestination*, p. 108.

Wollebius, Harris, Maxey, and Culverwel, consistently framed the issue of the practical syllogism with reference to an order of salvation that was grounded in union with Christ and that, accordingly, referenced sanctification and works as evidences of that union and, specifically, of the work of Christ and the Spirit in the believer.

9

Conclusions

The development of theology in the Reformed tradition, indeed, the rise and development of a Reformed tradition, was a highly complex phenomenon. That in itself is a datum that counts strongly against one of the lines of scholarship identified in the preceding chapters. The methodological considerations indicated in the first chapter and the nature of Calvin's relationship to so-called Calvinism discussed in the second both point toward the need to broaden the scope of the investigation even of Calvin's thought to include comparative analysis of the thought of his predecessors and contemporaries in the Reformed tradition.

The fundamentally problematic character of the older "Calvin against the Calvinists" and "Calvin for the Calvinists" approaches is perhaps nowhere clearer than in the topics examined here. Those approaches have begun by insisting on anachronistically identifying as "Calvinists" a host of early modern writers who, when asked, consistently refused the name of Calvinist, who quite clearly stated that Calvin's theology, however excellent it might have been, was not the sole antecedent of their thought, and who consciously measured their own theologies and the theologies of their contemporaries against the standards of a series of Reformed confessional documents, none of which were written by Calvin. In addition, their theologies were formulated in the context of debates that were not Calvin's debates and of institutional and political circumstances far removed from the early sixteenth-century setting of Calvin's Geneva.

Having identified as Calvinist these unwilling recipients of the title, the older approach has then proceeded to make point-for-point comparisons, taken out of context and without regard to historical development, between Calvin and these so-called Calvinists, usually in order to measure the quality and even the validity of their theology—as if Calvin, often the limited Calvin of the *Institutes*, could legitimately be used as the sole normative thinker for a whole tradition, and specifically one that did not think of him as its norm or even as its sole founder. The Calvin with whom these later Reformed theologians have been compared, moreover, has not been the historical Calvin, situated in the debates of the early to mid-sixteenth century. The "Calvin" used for the comparison has often been a curious twentieth-century product defined by "isms"—notably christocentrism and humanism set against predestinarianism, determinism, and scholasticism. Both in the case of Calvin himself and in the case of later Reformed theologians subjected to these comparisons, the "isms" have been reified and identified as causes: for example, supralapsarian predestinarianism is identified as a cause both of soteriological particularism, of antinomianism, and of legalism! And to complicate their anachronistic and dogmatistic argumentation even further and heap confusion on confusion, these approaches have also made their comparisons between Calvin and the unwilling Calvinists on the basis of terms and phrases such as "atonement," "universal" or "limited atonement," and "ordo salutis," that either were never used by the early modern writers in question or that, like the phrase "for whom Christ died," were declared by them to be vague and indeterminate, as distinct from the more precise terms and phrases that these early Reformed writers were actually using in their debates.

Simply put, we need to set aside the older master narratives, whether of "Calvin for the Calvinists" or "Calvin against the Calvinists." Typically, the older master narratives have not paid attention to historical detail or changing contexts and have analyzed the changing patterns of Reformed thought from an almost entirely dogmatic perspective. The complex early modern Reformed trajectories of discussion and debate on the issues of Christ's work and the order of salvation do not point either to a simple transition from Calvin's thought to Beza's and beyond that leaves purported dissidents such as Moïse Amyraut out of the main trajectory of Reformed theology, or to a transition from Calvinian theology in Calvin's own writings to a Bezan orthodoxy in which those same dissidents now register as the true Calvinians. The theological arguments and formulations of all of these writers, whether those of Calvin, his predecessors and contemporaries, or of later Reformed theologians, belong to trajectories of thought in a developing Reformed tradition and were governed in their details by often highly specified historical, geographical, and polemical contexts. What is more, while particular details of Calvin's thought do have impact on later Reformed doctrine, the impact of those details will often be registered in tandem with the impact of details in the thought of a predecessor or contemporary of Calvin, with both of these impacts belonging to a larger complex of ideas generated by long traditions of exegetical interpretation, by later debates over issues not addressed directly by Calvin and his contemporaries, and by the immediate circumstances of a particular author or debate.

The three chapters dealing with Christ's satisfaction have documented the complexity of the development. Contrary to one particular line of scholarship, these chapters have shown that there is no straight line from Calvin to Amyraut at the same time that they have indicated that there is no precise duplication of Calvin's teaching in other Reformed orthodox approaches to the work of Christ and its limited application. Over against Amyraut, Calvin categorically denied two wills in

God and categorically denied the universal grace that fueled Amyraut's version of hypothetical universalism. On these issues, Calvin stood in agreement with various later opponents of Amyraut, including two hypothetical universalists, Davenant and Du Moulin. These chapters have also shown, contra Armstrong and Clifford, that anti-Amyraldian argumentation was not uniformly Bezan (neither Davenant nor Du Moulin followed Beza!) and that there was no simple opposition between proponents of "limited atonement" and proponents of a hypothetically "universal atonement." Calvin's own position, moreover, has been shown to be rather different from that of Amyraut, given that Calvin did not teach universal grace, denied two wills in God, and did not conceive of any conditionality in the ultimate divine willing, having placed the conditions solely in the revealed will of promise of God. Calvin, nonetheless, assumed that Christ's death paid the price for all sin and that all who believe the gospel will be saved. Indeed, once the confusing terminology of limited and unlimited atonement is set aside and the theologians of the era permitted to speak in their own language, a rather complex picture emerges of different approaches to the issue of the value, merit, or sufficiency of Christ's satisfaction and its relationship to a limited application, including several rather different kinds of hypothetical universalism, all within the bounds established by the Reformed confessions.

Furthermore, it has been shown by a substantial trajectory of scholarship that Armstrong's neat dichotomy between a scholastic mode characteristic of Beza's thought and a humanistic mode characteristic of Amyraut's is quite mistaken. In the specific case of Beza and Amyraut, both thinkers exhibit humanistic and scholastic characteristics in their methods and approaches—as was also the case with Calvin and various of his contemporaries. And from a broader perspective on the intellectual development of Protestantism in the sixteenth and seventeenth centuries, it should be quite apparent that the angry humanist-scholastic interchanges of the late fifteenth and very early sixteenth centuries hardly offer a paradigm for the examination of developments in theology (or for that matter in philosophy) that took place later in the sixteenth century or in the seventeenth.

A full sense of Calvin's relationship to the later Reformed tradition on these issues will, moreover, only be clarified when further study is made of the exegesis of all the biblical passages in question in the exegetical works of Calvin's contemporaries and of writers in the later Reformed tradition. The essays presented here have only examined a sampling of these works. As we have seen from comparisons of exegetical results made throughout the present volume, there was considerable variety in the reading of individual texts at the same time that there was general agreement on the broader issues and boundaries of doctrinal formulation that were identified and defined in the Reformed confessions.

A significant lesson that can be learned from these studies, therefore, concerns the need to understand the early modern sources in terms not only of their context but also of their actual language. Quite a bit of modern scholarship has run aground on the question of "limited atonement" without recognizing that the debated doctrinal point cannot be adequately referenced by the term or, indeed, by the definitions of the term that have been proposed. Even more problematic readings of the material have been caused by recourse to the acronym TULIP. The actual terms used by the various writers from the time of Calvin through the era of orthodoxy evidence both considerable nuance in usage and considerable variety in actual expression, demonstrating the complexity of the Reformed tradition on the very questions that the "Calvin against the Calvinists" approach identified as symptomatic of the development of a monolithic orthodoxy in discontinuity with Calvin's thought.

A close reading of texts, then, demonstrates not only that differences between Calvin and various other Reformed formulations of the doctrine of Christ's work are not as great as has been sometimes claimed, but also that Calvin's argumentation is not to be regarded as the precise forebear either of Amyraldian hypothetical universalism or of the thought of Amyraut's more particularistic opponents. Opposition to Amyraut, moreover, cannot be reduced to a so-called Bezan supralapsarianism: one of Amyraut's chief opponents, Pierre Du Moulin, was an infralapsarian who himself held a less-speculative form of hypothetical universalism than Amyraut.

Rather, then, than argue a series of stark contrasts it should be recognized that various elements belonging to Calvin's thought on the work of Christ and its application, often shared by Calvin with predecessors and contemporaries in the early Reformed tradition, reappear in the work of later Reformed theologians, whether hypothetical universalist or particularist and, indeed, are sometimes argued by both the particularistic and the hypothetically universalistic writers. A particular element of Calvin's thought that carried over into the later Reformed tradition was the combination of positive reception and hesitance over the sufficiency-efficiency formula concerning Christ's satisfaction: the probable reason for his rejection of its applicability to 1 John 2:1-2 (and perhaps Bullinger's reason for omitting reference to it at this point), namely, its vagueness or flexibility with regard to the universality of Christ's objective payment, was reflected both in the broad and inclusive use of the formula by the Synod of Dort and in the protracted discussion and debate over various forms of hypothetical universalism in which the formula was adapted, nuanced with other terms, or replaced with alternative distinctions like that between impetration and application.

A similar variety of expression, grounded in a long-standing exegetical tradition and in patterns of argument set in motion by the Reformers, also characterized the Reformed approach to the issues of the economy and causality of salvation, notably as these issues were framed in relation to an understanding of union with Christ as fundamental to salvation and to an understanding of assurance as rooted in the work of Christ and the Spirit. Although far from monolithic, the early Reformed tradition was quite united in its assumption that union with Christ (notably as presented in the first part of Romans 8) and the golden chain of Romans 8:28-30 ought to provide the basis for understanding the ordering of the work of salvation in the present life and that, understood correctly, provided a way of understanding the relationship of the individual believer to that ordering.

Over against the approach of Canlis, Evans, and to a certain extent of Gaffin, the absence of a neat chronological sequence in Calvin's approach to election, grace, union with Christ, and the application of salvation ought not to be viewed as a point of radical contrast with various sixteenth- and seventeenth-century Reformed thinkers, and there was clearly no shift from a union with Christ model to an *ordo salutis* model of the economy of salvation among the early modern Reformed. Given that early modern argumentation, with its scholastic background, recognized patterns of order and indicators of priority other than time, the absence of a strict temporal sequence comprehending all of the elements of the application of salvation does not indicate an absence of order in Calvin's, much less in Vermigli's thought. In addition, these distinctions between a temporal, logical, and natural or causal ordering can be identified not only among the Reformers but also in later Protestant writers. Nor is it legitimate, particularly as Evans has done, to separate the development of early modern Reformed discussion of union with Christ from the rise of causal language concerning the *gradus* or chain of salvation, given the intimate relationship assumed by virtually all of the thinkers examined between union with Christ and the various elements of the application of salvation from calling to sanctification. It is quite clear that, for a large number of Reformed theologians, union with Christ remained the foundation of the economy or application of salvation throughout the era of orthodoxy. This last observation leads to a cautionary note over against the rather careless scholarship of those who evidence a penchant for reading Calvin out of context and passing judgment on the later Reformed tradition without having examined it fully and, in some cases, without having examined it at all.

There were certainly alterations and developments of argumentation on the subjects of union with Christ and what came to be called the *ordo salutis* that occurred within the Reformed tradition, particularly as it extended into the late seventeenth and the eighteenth centuries. It should also be clear that Calvin himself, like various of his contemporaries, argued along both of these doctrinal lines. In addition, a line of development running from the era of the Reformation into early orthodoxy maintained the close association of these two doctrinal issues and maintained it in much the way that it had been identified in the era of the Reformation. The claim, moreover, found in the writings of Partee and others that Calvin emphasized union with Christ and that later Reformed writers either ignored that emphasis or replaced it with a rigid, chronological *ordo salutis* appears to be a new variation on the old and discredited theme of a christocentric Calvin against predestinarian Calvinists.

Along much the same lines of argument, the older scholarship has also created a distorted portrait of the *syllogismus practicus* by treating it as a form of anthropocentrism and predestinarianism opposed to a purportedly christocentric theology of the Reformers, particularly of Calvin, rather than recognizing its function in connection with the application of salvation in and through Christ. This problematic approach stands in relation to what Billings has identified as a strongly "Anti-Legal School" of Calvin studies that has consistently underestimated the implications of forensic aspects of Calvin's understanding of justification even as it has devalued Calvin's approach to evidences of salvation in calling, regeneration, sanctification —largely in the interest of disconnecting Calvin's thought from the later Reformed tradition and attaching it to versions of neo-orthodoxy.[1]

What we have seen here is that the notion of a practical syllogism is, basically, an argument framed in the conscience for the sake of applying a precept or a doctrine to a particular effect. In other words, as distinct from a theoretical syllogism, the practical syllogism is directed to a concrete human result. As is the case with other forms of nominally scholastic argumentation, the form itself does not dictate either the precise content or the conclusion. A practical syllogism need not, in other words, be concerned with assurance of salvation nor, when applied to the problem of assurance, must it be, *ipso facto*, a form of legalism—nor, given its inward character, need it be formulated strictly. It may simply take the form of a thought process yielding a practical conclusion. Indeed, as we have seen, the basic pattern of inward examination that has come to be associated with the practical syllogism in matters of assurance of salvation is present in Calvin and in a series of later Reformed writers, in none of whom does it indicate the dominance of a legalistic, externalizing approach to salvation or a declension from a focus on Christ as the foundation of salvation. In addition, the formulations found among the later writers are rather varied. Some of the formulations do include good works, albeit always understood as God's work in the believer, and consistently on the assumption that faith without works is dead. The formulations also vary in their emphasis on aspects of the order of salvation in assurance, some emphasizing calling, others looking more to sanctification, some returning explicitly to the issue of the golden chain, others not referencing it directly but nonetheless looking to the series of causes belonging to the chain.

It is also worth returning briefly to the methodological issues identified in chapter 1. Study of discussion and debate concerning Christ's work, its extent and

---

1. Cf. J. Todd Billings, *Calvin, Participation, and the Gift: The Activity of Believers in Union with Christ* (Oxford: Oxford University Press, 2007), pp. 22, 105, citing as examples, Julie Canlis, "Calvin, Osiander, and Participation in God," *International Journal of Systematic Theology*, 6/2 (2004), pp. 169-184; James B. Torrance, "The Concept of Federal Theology—Was Calvin a Federal Theologian?" in *Calvinus Sacrae Scripturae Professor*, ed. Wilhelm H. Neuser (Grand Rapids: Eerdmans, 1994), pp. 15-40; idem, "Covenant or Contract? A Study of the Theological Background of Worship in Seventeenth-Century Scotland," *Scottish Journal of Theology*, 23 (1970), pp. 51-76.

application, in the eras of the Reformation and orthodoxy demonstrates the complexity of the intellectual development of Reformed Protestantism. It shows quite clearly that the Reformed theology of the sixteenth and early seventeenth centuries drew on multiple sources, was understood by its proponents as reflecting the Reformation-era theologies of a group of major early formulators, and framed its doctrinal conclusions in the light of exegetical traditions or trajectories, topical collations of exegetical results, and contextual issues and pressures such as the problem of certainty and the issue of Christian obedience in relation to a theological emphasis on salvation by grace alone.

The identification of scholasticism as primarily referencing method distinct although not entirely separable from content—rather than as a specific theology or philosophy productive of determinism, supralapsarianism, and so-called limited atonement—has also been confirmed from the diversity of theological positions examined in works following much the same method and employing many of the same distinctions, as well as from the continuities of doctrinal content and identifiable trajectories of development that have been observed in works belonging to different genres and characterized by different methods. Indeed, debate over the use and application of the scholastic distinction between the sufficiency and efficiency of Christ's satisfaction has been shown to be characteristic of Reformed theological development from the time of Calvin into the era of orthodoxy. Similarly, scholastic distinctions in the divine will are intrinsic to the theological efforts of diverse Reformed writers from Calvin to Davenant, Du Moulin, and Amyraut. So also, given among other things, the *locus* method that influences formulation in virtually all of the thinkers of the era, including Calvin, do themes and arguments carry over from the commentaries and homiletical literature, which do not typically follow scholastic method, into the more dogmatic or systematic works that followed fully scholastic models.

Finally, it should be clear from the essays in the present volume that Reformed orthodoxy, as it developed within the boundaries set by a series of confessional documents written in the mid-sixteenth century and augmented by the Canons of Dort in 1619, was a highly diverse phenomenon. This assumption has been a consistent aspect of the recent reassessments of the early modern Reformed tradition, and it is clearly borne out by the variety of argumentation on the issue of the work of Christ and its extent as well as by the differing approaches to the practical syllogism, the various nuancings of the economy and/or causality of salvation, and the differing patterns of reception of the thought of earlier Reformers found among the early modern Reformed. The Canons of Dort, as illustrated in this reappraisal, remain a document designed to exclude the Arminian or Remonstrant theologies but also now appear as a broadly formulated set of theological formulae designed intentionally to be inclusive of a wide variety of Reformed views, ranging from supra- to infralapsarian and allowing both for more particularistic as well as hypothetical universalist understandings of the work of Christ. The diversity of

Reformed orthodox approaches is also seen in the inclusion of various forms of hypothetical universalism, together with more particularistic understandings of the extent of Christ's work within the boundaries of confessional orthodoxy. Further study on a host of other issues, including detailed examination of the more particularistic approaches to the work of Christ, needs to be done in order to provide a more complete sense of this diversity, but the basic sense of diversity over against the monolithic view of orthodoxy characteristic of earlier scholarship has clearly been sustained as has the place of Calvin as one of several major second-generation formulators and codifiers of the Reformed tradition. In any case, the suitable paradigm for a historical analysis of the intellectual history of the Reformed churches in the early modern era is one not of discontinuity or continuity with the formulations of any particular thinker (whether Calvin or some other) but rather of a tradition that had multiple backgrounds and sources at its inception, that developed in relation to a series of confessionally-defined boundaries, and that, within those boundaries, became increasingly diverse as it moved into the seventeenth century.

Index

accomplishment-application distinction, 94, 102
Adam-Christ parallel, 83
adoption, 241
Ainsworth, Henry, 236
à Lasco, Johannes, 41, 56, 68
Alting, Heinrich, 152
Ames, William, 164, 229, 233–35, 241
Amyraldian controversy, 27, 78
Amyraut, Moïse, 33, 45–47, 55, 61, 70, 73n11, 77, 92, 105, 150–56, 278, 283
  on decree, 153–55
  as humanist, 269
  hypothetical universalism of, 105, 124–25, 126–27, 131, 156–57, 159
  as scholastic, 123, 158
  as true follower of Calvin, 108–9, 121–25
  on two wills of God, 106, 114–19
Anderson, Marvin W., 242
Anselm, 90
anthropocentrism, vs. christocentrism, 272–73
"Anti-Legal School" of Calvin studies, 282
antinomianism, 212, 260
a priorism vs. a posteriorism, 26, 31
Aretius, Benedictus, 226–27
Aristotelianism, 18, 24, 25, 29
Arminianism, 33, 141, 146–50, 153
Arminius, Jacob, 29, 61, 73, 127, 138, 146–49, 159, 249
Armstrong, Brian G., 27, 33, 48, 70, 73n11, 117, 118, 121, 123, 124, 144–45, 146, 157–58, 279
assurance of salvation, 50, 244–76, 282
  Beza on, 258–68
  Calvin on, 247–58
atonement, as English word, 60, 74–75
Augustine, 119n54, 140, 155, 162n5
Augustinian exegetical tradition, on "whole world," 78–85, 86, 101
Augustinianism, 21, 64, 261

Bacon, Francis, 19
Balcanqual, Walter, 132
baptism, 218–19

Barrett, William, 55
Barth, Karl, 52, 247–49, 258, 259, 264, 266–67, 272–75
Bastingius, 77n22
Baxter, Richard, 73, 128
Beeke, Joel, 249, 258
Belgic Confession, 38, 58, 68
Bell, M. Charles, 70, 89, 97–98, 248
Benedict, Philip, 57
Bernard of Clairvaux, 21
Beza, Theodore, 15, 47, 70, 83n48, 85, 105, 162n5, 248
  on application of salvation, 164
  on assurance, 275
  as "Calvinist," 56
  on causality of salvation, 168, 178, 190, 192
  as "deviation" from Calvin, 15, 43, 62
  on faith and reason, 40
  on golden chain, 196
  on good works, 258–62, 267, 274
  as humanist, 28
  on limited atonement, 60
  on practical syllogism, 249, 258–68, 272
  as scholastic, 279
  supralapsarianism of, 280
  and union with Christ, 222–24, 242
biblical theology, as humanistic, 26
Biel, Gabriel, 21, 29
Billings, J. Todd, 38, 282
Bizer, Ernst, 39
Boersma, Hans, 86n59
Böhl, Eduard, 162n5
Bouwsma, William J., 65
Bray, John, 248, 258, 259, 264
Bucanus, Gulielmus, 49, 193, 198–99
Bucer, Martin, 22, 41, 46, 52, 53, 56, 68, 162n5
Buddaeus, 163–64
Bullinger, Heinrich, 15, 47, 49, 84, 87n62, 91–92, 104, 159
  on application of salvation, 166
  as contemporary of Calvin, 56, 68
  on covenant of grace, 67
  on order of salvation, 168, 171, 172
  on predestination, 53
Burckhardt, Jacob, 19–20
Burman, Franz, 66

Burroughs, Jeremiah, 193
Burtt, E. A., 245

Calamy, Edmund, 128, 131
calling, and sanctification, 170
Calvin, John
  on application of salvation, 164, 166
  on assurance of salvation, 251–58, 272
  on causality of salvation, 169, 172–75
  as "Christocentric," 52, 58, 62–63, 281
  commentary of Romans, 172, 206–7, 238, 251
  continuities and discontinuities with later Reformed, 51, 57, 67–68
  correspondence of, 22
  on covenant of grace, 66–67
  differences with Beza, 15, 248
  differences with Bullinger, 15
  as founder and norm of Reformed tradition, 17, 34, 41, 50, 68, 277
  on good works, 208, 210, 255–56, 267, 274
  humanism of, 28–29, 64
  and limited atonement, 59, 60, 70–73, 107–8
  on Lord's Supper, 52, 53, 54, 96–98
  on order of salvation, 168–70, 240
  and practical syllogism, 244, 247–50, 255, 272
  predecessors and contemporaries of, 52–53, 56, 68–69
  on predestination, 57, 62–63
  on satisfaction of Christ, 145
  scholasticism of, 21–22, 28–29
  among second-generation codifiers of Reformed tradition, 36–38, 41, 68, 284
  studied in isolation from broader Reformed tradition, 14, 203–4, 242, 243
  on union with Christ, 205–12, 238–39
  on "whole world," 78–85
  on will of God, 101, 106, 114–19, 278–79
"Calvin against the Calvinists," 24–25, 40–43, 50, 162n5, 174n76, 277–78, 280
"Calvin for the Calvinists," 41, 277–78

285